CHOICE
AND
CHANGE

Drawings by HEIDI KLIER

VINCENT O'CONNELL, University of Florida

APRIL O'CONNELL, Santa Fe Community College

CHOICE AND CHANGE

Prentice-Hall, Inc.
Englewood Cliffs, New Jersey

AN INTRODUCTION TO THE PSYCHOLOGY OF GROWTH

Library of Congress Cataloging in Publication Data

O'CONNELL, VINCENT
    Choice and change.

    Includes bibliographies.
    1. Personality.   2. Maturation (Psychology)
I. O'CONNELL, APRIL, joint author.   II. Title.
[DNLM: 1. Growth.   2. Personality development.
BF698 018c 1974]
BF698.027   155.2'5   73-22296
ISBN 0-13-133165-5

CHOICE AND CHANGE:
An Introduction to the Psychology of Growth
by Vincent O'Connell and April O'Connell

Printed in the United States of America.

10   9   8   7   6   5

Prentice-Hall International, Inc., *London*
Prentice-Hall of Australia, Pty. Ltd., *Sydney*
Prentice-Hall of Canada, Ltd., *Toronto*
Prentice-Hall of India Private Limited, *New Delhi*
Prentice-Hall of Japan, Inc., *Tokyo*

To Margaret O'Connell
and Rose Checkaway
who were both called Pearl

CONTENTS

PREFACE

There is a great shift in consciousness taking place in our time and in our culture. This shift in consciousness has its roots in our history as a nation. Our nation was conceived and born on a continent with vast and unexplored lands to be conquered and settled. It then grew up in the Industrial Age, an age characterized by the pragmatic will to do and will to achieve. As a people we were bent on making use of our external physical environment, learning how to exploit the land to further our national ideals. In a sense, we were the descendants of those extraordinary and exciting persons of the Renaissance who were determined to investigate and survey every dimension of their geographical and sensory world: to cross the great Eastern mountains and deserts in order to get to Cathay; to sail the wild Atlantic to find India; to discover how a man is put together anatomically beneath his skin, and to portray him also with all his skin, sex, and sensuality on canvas; to come closer to the distant world of the stars telescopically and to see into the Lilliputian world of bacteria microscopically.

We inherited also the nineteenth-century desire (determination, really) to cure the physical ills of man through technology. We were no longer willing to coexist with Nature. We decided to improve on it.

And we did a fine job. We invented machines that can calculate more efficiently than man, traverse the land faster than horses, fly higher than birds; and that are stronger than elephants. We have dug tunnels that rival the great canyons, built structures as large as mountains, and we have learned how to harness energies with more potential destructive force than all the tornadoes, hurricanes, and earthquakes known to recorded history.

But we have discovered also that our technical achievements can ultimately produce our own demise. In short, we have come to realize that we can now actually obliterate ourselves from the face of the earth.

We have been brought up short by this realization. In our desire to exploit our external environment we discovered that we have actually endangered the natural resources of our planet. It seems that we have poured garbage into the waters we need to drink, that we have smogged the air we need to breathe, and that we are poisoning the earth we need to farm. This realization is a prominent factor in the present shift in consciousness.

The shift in consciousness that we speak of is a kind of total phenomenon which is seen in art, manners, the sciences, literature, sociology, and theology. In the narrower fcous in which we personally are now concerned, the discipline of psychology, the present shift in consciousness began formally when a certain German professor, Wilhelm Wundt, decided to study the mind of man: how man senses the world about him to form perceptions, and how his perceptions are put together to make thoughts and define experiences. The scientific study of the mind was given further depth and penetration by Sigmund Freud when he investigated the unconscious elements of human nature—the dark, unexplored strata of the mind which lie below our conscious awareness and which are reflected in our dreams.

Psychologists and other personality theorists are now interested in every aspect of the human personality. Furthermore, they are not just interested in learning how we function, but in *how we can function better, more fully, more creatively, more humanely!* They are less interested now in what makes a man an emotional cripple than in discovering ways to release the creative vitality in each and every human person.

The present shift in consciousness, as we see it, can be put very simply: It is a turning from the investigation solely of the external world to the investigation also of the inner psychological world of *mind.* It appears as if the next evolutionary step in the progress of mankind is for man to come to know himself at least as well as he knows his external environment. In other words, we are ready at last to become aware and conscious of ourselves—to seek what in the East has long been called self-realization and enlightenment.

We are beginning to make that crossover now! We are taking interest in things other than material possessions, status, and competition. We are searching for other kinds of values and goals, and we are using words and phrases like *self-growth, harmony, self-understanding,* and *self-actualization.* We are beginning to understand that if we would like a less violent world, then we had better (as Krishnamurti says *) eradicate the violence in ourselves. A change in the world starts with a change in ourselves. And that means becoming conscious of those aspects in ourselves that have until now remained hidden in the dark recesses of our awareness. Rather than devoting all our energy to breaking through the barriers of space, we are beginning to devote some of our energy to breaking through the barriers of our defending mechanisms—those psychological defenses that separate man from man, and man from himself.

We are becoming *psychonauts,* persons less interested in traveling outwardly to Mars and Jupiter than in traveling inwardly—and in learning the laws and geography of inner-space travel. That is what the next step in the evolution of consciousness has to do with, and it is that factor we refer to here when we speak of a shift in consciousness.

The purpose of this book is to provide you with some of the means of undertaking that journey—what Carl Rogers has called the "journey into self." † Our first objective has been to provide you with some maps (landmarks, really) so that you can determine where you are now in that endeavor; that is the focus of Part I of this book. Our second objective has been to supply you with some of the means of transportation to your "interior" self, and that is the focus of Part II of the book.

From the very beginning of this book, we are interested primarily in communicating to you, the beginning psychonaut, those factors and considerations that influence personality and that permit you to make choices and changes in your life. We want to provide you with paths and vehicles by which you can facilitate your own discoveries of the marvel which is your self in the world with other persons. Our intent, always, is to make this an exciting, fast-flowing adventure for you. Accordingly, we have chosen not to make this book a compendium of research but rather to incorporate into our discussion that research which we believe you can make use of immediately. We have tried at the same time, however, to

* J. Krishnamurti, *Life Ahead* (Wheaton, Ill.: Theosophical Publishing House, 1963).

† We take this phrase from the title of a movie made of an encounter group of which Rogers was the group facilitator, and which is now under the auspices of the Behavioral Sciences Institute.

give you some insights into the journeys that the great psychonauts have made. We have chosen, for example, to discuss at some length Freud's discoveries regarding personality. And to his discoveries in dream interpretation we have added those of Jung and Perls and the recent discoveries of the many sleep researchers. Dream interpretation is no longer the domain of the intellectual neurotic who can afford the fees of the psychoanalyst—it is now at your disposal if you have but the grit and determination to travel this road to your "interior" self.

Freud called dream interpretation the "royal road" to the unconscious, but there are other approaches as well. There are the physical approaches, for example, such as sensory stimulation, sensory relaxation, and the desensitization procedures. All of these approaches are designed to facilitate conscious awareness and alertness through concentration on your existing physical body. We discuss these methods of physical exercises and yoga insofar as they apply to your present search.

There are also the psychotherapy approaches, developed so skillfully in the West, where we learn about ourselves through dialogue with others; and the meditative, introspective approaches where we grow through dialogue with one's self. All these pathways have application to learning the geography of your own inner space-time.

One final thing. We would like to hear from you. Writing a book is a far different experience from teaching in a classroom. In the classroom, we get feedback. We know what the students understand or don't understand, what interests them, what has been particularly valuable to them. Writing a book is rather like talking to a great void. We get all the chance in the world to speak to our heart's content, but we don't get any chance at all to get to listen to you. So we really would like to hear from you. For example: How can we improve the book? What was really useful to you and what was time-wasting as far as you were concerned? What didn't we go into in detail that you would like to hear more about? Write us care of Prentice-Hall who, by the way, have abided with us over the three years in which the book was first planned. Your letters can make for a more useful book, and we shall reply to all your letters, if not at once, then certainly in time.

Vincent O'Connell
April O'Connell

Gainesville, Florida

CHOICE
AND
CHANGE

DISCOVERING OUR PRESENT PERSONALITY TYPE

PART I

1

PERSONALITY INTEGRATION: THE EVER-NEW, THE NEVER-ENDING PROCESS

A NEW DIRECTION IN PSYCHOLOGY

If you were reading this book on personality forty, thirty, or even twenty years ago, you would come upon such terms as *mental health* and *mental illness, normal* and *abnormal behavior;* and the authors would very likely discuss such concepts as the "average" person and "adjusting to one's society." [1] They might even have attempted to supply some guidelines for "mental health," perhaps describe goals for the "mature" person, and explain what distinguishes a "normal" person. (He must have a circle of friends; he must be a well-rounded person with many interests; he must be outgoing, friendly, able to get along with others; etc., etc.)

These were some of the ideas and goals that prevailed in psychology for several decades, and many persons did their best to understand themselves according to these concepts of personality. During those years, psychology was being influenced by psychiatry (which judged personality on the basis of evidence of neurosis or mental illness), adjustment psychology (which compared individuals to some ideal model), and the statistical-norm approach (which compared the individual with some mythical "average" person). That approach to personality has at last begun to fall out of fashion, and psychology is beginning to understand personality in a different way, one that emphasizes those factors of personality which make us distinctly individual as compared with those factors which we all, so to say, share in common.

At first this new approach to personality had only a few advocates,[2] but eventually other personality theorists began to listen to what these humanistic psychologists and educators had to say, and to voice their own objections to the older "adjustment" approach to personality. Today this new approach is becoming accepted, and it seems likely to endure until some other crisis in personality integration in our society demands still another look at what personality *is* and what it can *become*.

This new turning, or new approach, has many names: existential psychology, growth psychology, humanistic psychology, and "third force" psychology. For convenience we shall call it growth psychology since it emphasizes the continuing and purposeful growth of the human person toward the full potential of what he and she can become—a project, by the way, that no one can see the end of, least of all oneself. The approach thus highlights and works toward freeing those untapped resources and abilities "within" each person which lead to fuller, more creative, more satisfying ways of living, once he has gotten in touch with them. This approach chooses also not to predetermine what a particular person's directions and goals shall be; nor does it presume to predict how far in a given direction the person will be able to go in the venture of integrating personality. In like manner, this approach has rejected the "trait" method of understanding personality; compiling lists of "positive traits" and "negative traits" and juggling them so as to come up with a "mental health" quotient. It insists, finally, that "adjusting" the person to society is no longer the ultimate goal—for either the person or society in our time.

Although the differences in program and philosophy between the *adjustment* and *growth* approaches to personality may seem at first mere semantic quibbling (arguing about the meaning of words), at the root of this argument lies an essential difference in orientation to psychology between these two groups. We believe it necessary for the reader to understand what this real argument in psychology today is all about. For that reason both sides of the argument deserve a hearing.

THE ADJUSTMENT APPROACH TO PERSONALITY

We make a mistake if we think we have nothing to learn from the adjustment approach to personality. But first we must examine the historical circumstances in which the adjustment model was formed. The adjustment approach attained popularity at a time when our society was intent on developing a national character. After World War I had ended and the United States had emerged as a world power, we Americans were somewhat disenchanted with the politics and quarrels of the Old World and were determined to find out what makes us specifically American. We were desirous of "Americanizing" our hodge-podge nation of immigrants. We dreamed that out of the great "melting pot" of many ethnic groups would emerge a distinct American type. We were a society turning inward, seeking to find and test out specifically American forms of child rearing, family organization, and education so as to foster those values, beliefs, and institutions that were considered to underlie the "American Dream."

Thus psychologists, seeking to discover the kind of personality and life style that was best suited to our maturing nation, made various relevant observations. For example, it was found that families with one or two children seemed to have significantly fewer economic and personal problems than families with, say, seven or eight children. So psychologists, social workers, and eventually even some government officials began advocating planned parenthood and smaller families. School psychologists began administering IQ (intelligence quotient) tests to students and found that those who attained higher scores were more likely to complete higher education. So educators began shunting students with lower scores away from college courses and into "vocational" schools. If executives

We wanted our immigrants to become American, our black citizens to act like whites, and our "lower" classes to model themselves after the "middle" class.

began to show strain under the pressure of high-powered jobs, they were counseled to undergo therapy so they could better cope with that pressure.

A society can tolerate, at any one time, only so much deviance from a "standard" personality type called "good" if it is to continue in its present form. If there is too much deviance from the "norm" the society may end up in conflict with itself. But what we failed to realize in our determination to produce a model of American adjustment was that when a society insists on too rigid a standard of behavior, there can be adverse reactions. First, too little deviance from the society standard may produce a society which becomes static and dies. Second, we can begin to repress or discourage those variations and differences that make each person distinctly individual. Third, too much insistence on conformity (and especially if it is to too narrow a personality standard) results in psychological "straitjacketing," and citizens in that kind of society begin to show reactions against such straitjacketing. We wanted our immigrants to become American, our black citizens to act like whites, and our "lower" class to model themselves after the "middle" class. There was bound to be a reaction against this adjustment philosophy once it no longer had survival value. That reaction began to surface in the late fifties and spread like wildfire through the sixties. It began with the civil rights and black power movements and the revolt of the student generation, spreading across the nation and then the world. And psychologists began to understand finally some of the limitations of the "adjustment" model.

LIMITATIONS OF THE ADJUSTMENT THEORY OF PERSONALITY

Let's begin with the notions of "normality" and "abnormality," and attempt to understand the kind of thinking in which these concepts are based. Some scientists have suggested that we use the statistical extremes of a given trait to determine what is "normal" and "abnormal." That method may be "scientific" in the sense that it attempts to make objective the study of personality, but deeper examination of that approach to personality reveals certain logical absurdities when we pursue it to extremes.

For example, since we measure intellectual ability on an "intelligence" scale, we can accept the idea of a "mentally retarded" person as intellectually "abnormal" in the sense of falling far, far below the average level of intelligence in society. But many of us would have difficulty in accepting the notion that the "genius" is necessarily "abnormal" simply because he represents the other extreme of the scale. Many of us could accept the idea that Hitler or Nero are extreme forms of behavioral deviation, but we would be unwilling, by the same token, to place a Saint Francis, or a Ghandi, or a Martin Luther King on the "abnormal" list—just because they were men of peace instead of tyrants.

Further than that, however, the concept of "normality" has been undermined by the work of cultural anthropologists and sociologists. Some South Sea Island societies have evolved joyful, gentle, and peaceful ways of living together, while neighboring societies have evolved aggressive, suspicious, and competitive cultures.[3] If we were to suddenly take a native and remove him from one of the peaceful cultures and then somehow set him down in one of the warlike cultures, that peace-loving native would have to be considered "abnormal" in his new culture. There is a saying: In the kingdom of the blind, the one-eyed man is king. But if we follow the statistical approach to personality, we would have to consider the one-eyed man as deviant—just because he is the only one who can see in this world of blind persons. The statistical approach to personality has had severe criticisms.

> Such observations while descriptively sound can lead readily to two troublesome influences. One is that the storm trooper must be considered as the prototype of integrative adjustment in Nazi culture, the members of the Politboro [the ruling council of the USSR] as best representing human normality, Soviet style, and the cruelist adolescent in a delinquent gang as its most positively developed member. The other is that relative judgment of cultures and societies must be regarded as inappropriate. Since normality is conceived only in terms of conformity to group standards, the group itself must be beyond appraisal. Thus, the suspicion and mistrust of Dobu, . . . (the sense of resigned futility that permeates Alor) . . . and the regimentation that characterizes totalitarian nations can only be taken as norms in terms of which the individual behavior may be interpreted, not as indications of abnormal tendencies in the cultures themselves.[4]

Research studies of persons who have been identified as creative human beings, remarkable for their ability to integrate the higher functions of love and service to others, have found those individuals to be somewhat out of step with their culture, even "deviant." This is not to say they make loud protests or commit acts of destructive rebellion, but they all seem to hold beliefs that are independent of prevailing opinions. These persons are able to think and act autonomously—that is, for themselves. They resist being molded and shaped by their present circumstances. They see themselves being *of* their culture but also *apart from* it. Abraham Maslow, who studied what he called the "healthy" personality, saw them as

> not well adjusted (in the naive sense of approval and identification with the culture). They get along with the culture in various ways, but of all of them it may be said that in a certain profound and meaningful sense, they resist enculturation and maintain a certain inner detachment from the culture in which they are immersed. . . . They very frequently seem to be able to stand off from our culture as if they did not belong to it. The mixture of varying proportions of affection or approval and hostility or criticism indicated that they select from American culture what is good in it by their lights and reject what they think bad in it. . . .

. . . If we compare them with the oversocialized, the robotized, or the ethnocentric, we are irresistibly tempted to hypothesize that this group is not simply another subculture group, but rather less enculturated, less flattened out, less molded.[5]

SOCIETY UNDER INDICTMENT

For many years, we Americans have been emphasizing what seems to be (at least to the authors) a kind of patriotic chauvinism. Namely, we seem to have been wearing blinders which prevent us from seeing our faults and weaknesses—just as horses who are forced to wear blinders are prevented from seeing anywhere except straight ahead. We have come to perceive anything American to be the best and anything that contradicts that view as "un-American"—that is, treasonous, and thus bad. During the heyday of that view, not only was the "American way of life" preached from the pulpits of our own churches, but we insisted on spreading the gospel to other countries —oftentimes to their amusement and/or indignation. An instance of that nearsightedness is the "American tourist," whose attitudes have been satirized by Sinclair Lewis in *Main Street*. That individual became a source of embarrassment to our American embassies sim-

There is much to value in our culture . . .

ply because of his tendency to insist on the "self-evident" superiority of our technological culture, our way of life, and so on.

This is not to say, by any means, that there are not values in our culture and the American way of life which are good, or even excellent. No one in the world can raise a hog so lean and big on an acre of corn as can the Iowa farmer. The Imperial Valley, in California, once a desert, now produces fruits and vegetables unequalled in taste and size—thanks to American engineering and imagination regarding the facts of irrigation, farming, and harvesting. And American products are still, even now, sometimes among the best and least expensive of manufactured goods. Moreover, American education is still attempting to achieve more good for the most people—more than any other country in the world. We have produced, namely, an abundantly rich society, and we are still trying.

Yet as the saying goes, "We ain't perfect." American society still has its critics. Visitors to our country during the past century have found, for instance, much that is engaging and good; yet they have found also much that is aggressive, contradictory, overconforming, and hypocritical.[6]

These critics have been kind to us—seeing both our failings and our assets as a society. Other critics have been on occasion less kind. Charles Dickens, the famous English novelist of the nineteenth century, found us "vulgar, common, loud-mouthed, obscene, ignorant, and chuzzle-witted," and some of his most biting caricatures have been the ones that portrayed Americans.[7] But by and large, we have chosen, until recently, to ignore our critics—after all, they happened to be "foreigners."

The twentieth century has brought criticism, however, even from our own native American thinkers and writers. One voice angry enough to be heard all over the country was Philip Wylie in his portrayal of us as a *Generation of Vipers*.[8] In this book, Wylie (himself a psychologist) castigated the American mother, until then a sacred and untouchable symbol, as a domineering and possessive "smotherer" of children whose "love" produced mediocrity in children who then could never grow to become psychologically mature men and women. A decade or so later, Erich Fromm viewed us as having a "marketing" orientation of life, which is to say that we tend to perceive human friendships and relationships as so much merchandise and goods—worthwhile only from the advantages and profits that we accrue from their possession.[9] David Riesman saw us as a *A Lonely Crowd*, lacking the kind of autonomy which makes living an adventure.[10] For Riesman we seem to have lost the "strength of character" that defined the early American pioneer.

Sociology has also advanced evidence which indicates that our American ideals and the inflated concepts we have of ourselves are simply not supported by the real facts of our day-to-day lives together. In a country where all men are said to be "created equal" we have, for example, clearly documented pockets of class and caste discrimination.[11] In a land of abundance such as the world has never known, we have ignored the existence of the really poor in their ghettos—blacks, Puerto Ricans, Cubans, etc.[12] For example, while we are only now coming to understand the necessity for dialogue between our black and white societies, our treatment of the American Indian continues even now to reduce many of these once-proud peoples to apathy, disease, and in some cases virtual extinction.[13]

These continuing criticisms have been more openly expressed by America's youth, whether in demonstrations against war or pollution or in evolving new forms of dress and manners. Indeed, at the present time, this rebellion (it is not yet a revolution) against a society viewed as materialistic and dehumanizing has gone far enough so that there is clearly developing a "counterculture." [14]

Small wonder, then, that psychologists have become increasingly embarrassed by the word *adjustment*, especially when some are saying that it is our society which is sick and needs to be treated as the patient.[15] They argue, moreover, that such terms as *adjustment*, *mental health*, *mental illness*, etc. are not only meaningless, arbitrary, and mythical, but downright dangerous.[16] Such concepts, and that kind of thinking, some say, could result in a society which *is* sick—a society, namely, in which there are two classes: psychotherapists and patients! Harry Stack Sullivan, a prominent psychiatrist, suggested several decades ago that we replace the concept of "mental illness" with other kinds of concepts, such as "problems of interpersonal relationships." [17] Recently Thomas S. Szasz, another psychiatrist, has observed that we accomplish the same thing by saying that people are simply having "problems in living"! [18]

ON NOT WANTING TO ADJUST, SHAPE, FOLD, BEND, OR OTHERWISE MUTILATE YOU

Where has all the preceding discussion led us? Well, to these points: First, that we believe that such terms as *mentally ill* and *mentally healthy* belong to an earlier time and are no longer useful concepts today. Indeed, the terms are now so compromised in their meaning that we need to find other words to describe the problems people are experiencing in our world today.

Second, we no longer necessarily want you to adjust to a society which may be itself in need of healthy and constructive revision. All free societies have always had courageous reformers who keep on pointing out what they believe to be basic problems within those societies, and who do not intend to become "adjusted" to standards they do not accept as viable and good.

Finally, we believe that what is needed today are people who are not adjusted to some externally imposed standard but who are capable of changing as the society we live in is revised. One of the best-known psychologists in the world, Carl Rogers, writes:

> If the human species is to survive at all on this globe, the human being must become more readily adaptive to new problems and situations, must be able to select that which is valuable for development and survival out of new and complex situations, must be accurate in his appreciation of reality if he is to make such selections. The psychologically mature person as I have described him has, I believe, the qualities which would cause him to value those experiences which would make for the survival of the human race. He would be a worthy participant of human evolution.[19]

THE GROWTH MODEL

In contrast to the adjustment model, the *growth model* views the person as striving toward further personality integration in *his* or *her* own way, toward goals that are uniquely appropriate for *him* or *her*. The growth model does not assume that when a person has reached a certain level or achieved a certain goal that he has succeeded in becoming a "mature" person (whatever that is). On the contrary, the growth model recognizes that every person is doing his best to work out his destiny in a society which is growing ever more complex. This approach avoids the implication that one need always be "happy" or fully "independent" or "mentally healthy"—whatever those terms are taken to mean.

According to the growth model of personality, the individual who is growing also experiences pain, sorrow, moments of maladjustment, failure, etc. In fact, the growing person may be more open to his or her own suffering than the person who is closed off to other people's feelings. Yet, paradoxically, because he is open to his negative emotions (recognizing them as his own), he is less likely to be controlled by them, and so he is less likely to take out his negative feelings on others or to project these feelings onto others. To be aware of one's inner feelings and thoughts is to be more in control of one's actions. The growing person also experiences depression, and he too suffers the "slings and arrows of outrageous fortune." If he is cut, he still bleeds, and if we tickle him, he still laughs. He has not achieved any magic formula for life that makes him invulnerable to misfortunes or mistakes. The difference is simply that the growing person picks himself up, learns by what has happened to him, and keeps on growing!

But (you may ask) are there not some persons who are so crippled by their life style, so split off from inner controls and feelings that they are unable to cope without hospitalization or constant reinforcement of their feelings of insecurity? Isn't the growth model of personality just avoiding the issue that some people *are* "mentally retarded" or "insane" or "criminally delinquent"? To these questions, we can only answer "yes"—there are indeed such persons. But what we are trying to emphasize is that the very terms just used impose distinctions that stereotype our perceptions. To insist on applying these terms (and the outlook that goes with that kind of thinking) to someone who at some time suffered a suicidal depression, or who currently lacks the capability to perform school tasks, or who has been involved in a delinquent act *is to categorize him (perhaps forever) according to his limitations and weaknesses and to overlook his strengths.* As one psychiatrist has pointed out, the difference between persons who have been hospitalized or imprisoned and those persons who have not is sometimes merely a matter of money and class.[20] We send the person who holds up the corner gas station to jail, but we continue to ignore the "white-collar" thief who pads his expense account, or the one who cheats on his income tax, or manipulates the stock market for his own gain. In like manner, we label a person "mentally retarded" because he cannot perform in school; yet he could become a productive worker contributing to society if he were taught to operate a department store elevator—a job another (more gifted) person would automatically reject because "it isn't challenging"!

Most people are unaware that many business executives have broken down under the pressures of their jobs and yet, through the concerted efforts of themselves and others in their environment (no one labeled them psychotic), have been able to return to society and achieve more viable living patterns. To label a person "psychotic," "schizophrenic," "abnormal," "deviant," etc. (and this is the single point we wish to make) is to misperceive him in such a way that his growth can be hindered—precisely because of our prejudices (prejudgments). Prejudices die hard—the labels for our prejudices are the only things that change.

ON THE APPROPRIATENESS OF BEING SOMETIMES UNADJUSTED

Throughout this book we shall emphasize that any person can experience feelings of depression, contemplate suicide, suffer from anxiety, use "defense mechanisms," engage in behaviors that can be labeled "neurotic" from time to time, just as most of us also can be "unadjusted" in new situations or can experience "transient states of unreality." But we would prefer not to label you, on that account, "emotionally sick" just because these very human experiences happen to you now and then. And we would prefer you do not label yourself as such. Sometimes, indeed, the appropriate response to a situation is to be anxious, depressed, etc.—even "maladjusted." The point is not that you are *this* or *that,* but what does *this* say about your present living situation, and what can you do for yourself to get you through *that* stressful situation and its crisis?

THE CONCEPT OF PERSONALITY INTEGRATION

Webster's defines *integrate* as "to form into a whole; to unite or become united so as to form a complete or perfect whole. . . ." It is exactly that sense of the word we intend when we use the term *personality integration:* each of us, so long as there is life still in us, is constantly attempting to integrate the millions of "pieces" of information that are making up our world for us. The better able we are to integrate, make a whole of, this information which our world transmits to us, the more we are in touch with ourselves and our world. Growth of the personality involves increasingly complex information systems as we go from infancy to adulthood, and the "goal" of personality integration is to become ever more flexible and sure in our responses and interchanges with our world; to be more *there*, more *aware*, more *conscious* of what is happening here-and-now. "Integration of personality" is a kind of ideal state. It implies a level of being where we are so perfectly in tune with ourselves and our world that living becomes more and more a joyful experience, a life filled with hope, compassion, and love. As we shall be saying later on, that level of personality integration—where simply being alive is a constantly rewarding experience—is one of the marks of certain memorable men and women. It is possible, we believe, to reach this level of integration by dint of hard work, adequate genetic inheritance, an "earnest" motivation, and the kind of education that provides the information we need to study the growth process. But

Personality integration is an ongoing process from birth to death . . .

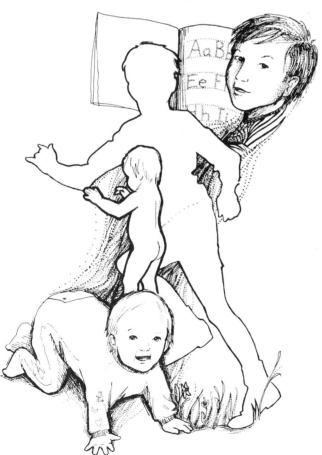

for any one of us, as long as we are alive, there will be always some variation among the levels of integration at which we can perform and be aware. The process of personality integration is a constant process of adapting to change in ourselves and in the "objects out there" which we make into a world for us. It never stops so long as we are alive.

We hope you will understand, therefore, that one cannot properly speak of someone having "achieved" personality integration. Personality integration is a lifelong process not too unlike the other biological life processes of eating, breathing, digesting, and defecating. It makes our survival possible, it is a "universal" force, and it never ends. As soon as the baby has learned to sit up, he must then learn how to crawl, and when that is accomplished he begins the task of learning how to walk. *Personality integration, then, is the ongoing process in which the person attempts to coordinate his biological, emotional, social, and intellectual experiences toward purposeful action and further growth throughout his lifetime.* It is the process (processes) involved when the person comes upon the obstacles, challenges, and crises of everyday living and attempts to cope with them. It is the person's responses to the glandular and other biological changes that occur at various times within him. It is the integration of the organic drives which urge him out toward the world, as well as the learned social prohibitions that inhibit him. It is the interaction of his intellect and his feelings. It is his present understanding of himself as he anticipates the future but remembers also his past experiences.

Some persons are, however, more evolved in their present personality patterning than are the rest of us. We shall speak of this personality patterning as the hallmark of the 'highly integrated" personality type. We hope that you will understand that he differs from the rest of us only in degree, not in kind.

DEVELOPMENTAL LIFE STAGES

Erik Erikson, a psychoanalyst who has studied the developmental process of human personality from infancy to old age, describes eight separate developmental stages in the evolution of the human personality. He sees the process of personality integration as a lifelong adventure that can be viewed as a series of tasks and crises. Drawing largely on Erikson's formulations (and from those who have worked with his ideas),[21] we summarize now some of the major tasks involved in personality integration.

Trust vs. Distrust

The infant needs to develop a sense of trust in the world—to know that someone really cares enough about him to satisfy his physical and psychological needs. He learns trust in many ways: for example, in the actual experience of being held, caressed, and cared for. Those moments constitute the biopsychological experience of *mothering*. Where those moments have been sufficient to the infant's needs, they enable him to pass safely through the critical period of of infancy. Unless he has just such attention and love, he may not be able to trust the world enough to even make contact with it.

With love and caring, the baby survives infancy and learns to trust.

Psychologists and other scientists have long known that babies who do not receive this continuing human contact, care, and attention (such as those left too long unattended in hospitals, orphanages, and poorly run day-care centers) do not develop that basic and necessary trust in the world or in themselves.[22] They tend to become sickly as a result, and have been characterized as highly "neurotic" or "apathetic." Also, they seem to die at a higher rate than those infants who have been "well mothered." For the infant, then, the basic matter is the necessity of being loved and cared for. With love and caring he survives infancy and learns to trust the world and himself. Without that basic necessary attention he may die. And if he lives somehow despite the lack, he may be a "damaged" person from the beginning.

Autonomy vs. Dependency

For the toddler, the important developmental task is learning to become autonomous: to progress from the stage of being held and fed (environmentally dependent) to being able to "walk on his own two feet," feed himself, and begin to gain control of other bodily functions (such as bladder and sphincter control).

In this second stage, the child takes its first steps in developing self-support as contrasted to being supported by and dependent on others in the environment. He must now take an active role in propelling himself toward his own needs and wants by learning how to communicate these needs and wants to others. If he does not learn this early self-support, he remains a dependent personality who expects others to take care of his needs—even in adulthood, according to Erikson. The toddler needs also to learn to control his impulsivity so that he does not destroy the things in his environment he will eventually need—such as the plant on the windowsill, or his baby brother! When he does *not* learn to integrate that kind of control into his repertory of responses, the *energy which motivates him toward action and living dominates his evolving personality.* He then can become *stubborn* and *destructive*, with a secret (unverbalized) determination to "get away" with things. Let us label that particular response pattern as a case of *underlearning.*

Overlearning at the second stage of development produces an "obsessive" personality, says Erikson—an individual who "can't see the forest for the trees." Compared to the *underlearner* (who has failed as yet to integrate impulse controls), the overlearner is overinhibited. He is so anxious to do the right thing that he sticks too closely "to the book" and thus loses access to his own creative impulsivity. Instead of being guided by the *spirit* of the law, he is dominated by and sticks to the *letter* of the law.

Initiative vs. Guilt

Autonomy leads to initiative in the preschooler. At this stage, the child moves from generalized motor activity to specific behaviors based on purpose and planning. For example, he learns to dress himself, to play games, to call on other children "to come and play," and to initiate complex "pretend games" which imitate the adult world. At this point, his personality takes a more loving, relaxed turn. He is brighter in judgment and can play cooperatively with others. He has learned, and is learning, to have confidence in himself and to feel that his place in the family is secure, and he begins to care for children younger than himself. Failure to integrate the learned behaviors of this stage results in the common "neurotic" patterns of adulthood: hysterical denial, repression, psychosomatic disease, paralysis, impotence, etc.—the all-too-common "difficulties in living" which psychotherapists and counselors work with every day.

Industry vs. Inferiority

Entrance to school brings forward the many social, intellectual, and developmental tasks which Erikson labels as "tasks of industry." At this stage the child learns to be a worker, to take pride in his productions, to learn the nature of the skills and tools he will use in his society as an adult. Whereas in the previous stage he needed to learn, for example, how to tie his shoes, he now learns how to make a telephone call, to use money for simple purchases, and to integrate the "three *R's*" into his existence as an evolving human being. Failure in school, as we all know, brings with it a sense of inferiority, of "being dumb," along with the many school problems themselves. Achievement in school and schooling provides the child with his first sense of initiation and success (or failure) in the world of his peers and of the adults outside his family circle.

Identity and Role Confusion

The adolescent's immense task is, of course, the task of sexual identification. But over and beyond that decision, the young person needs to identify himself as a *person*—that is, as someone who is part of his family circle, yet now outside it also. Interest in family concerns begins to wane, and he turns to peers and adults outside the immediate family circle for the satisfaction of his enlarging needs. The adolescent requires the freedom to move about in this larger world outside the family so he can explore models of being an adult other than the present family ones.

If he is creative, the adolescent will try out many "models" of persons, dress, speech, music, etc. before he begins to discover and integrate the blend which suits him best. But explore he must—even when his family tries to prevent him—until the time he discovers the kind of viable role-model which will prepare him for approaching adulthood.

Erikson notes that the child who has not successfully completed his previous stages of development may be overwhelmed as he enters adolescence by unresolved crises and difficulties—which is especially true in our rapidly changing society. For someone who lacks the security of an adequate interpersonal base, with its skills and competencies, the adolescent stage may become the time of the "Big Crisis." *

Intimacy vs. Isolation

Young adulthood presents the challenge of integrating a number of concurrent roles: husband, father, citizen, son, employee, etc.—or (for the female) mother, daughter, wife, housekeeper, etc. The most difficult of these roles, Erikson says, is the role of *spouse:* being a successful wife or a husband requires learning how to be intimate with another human being. By *intimacy* Erikson means not so much sexual intimacy (although it includes that, too) as emotional intimacy—that is, the ability to share one's thoughts and feelings with another, which means learning how to plan in terms of "we" instead of "I."

For that reason, young adulthood can be even more difficult a stage than adolescence. The tasks of adolescence involve primarily oneself and one's own motivations; and so it is essentially an ego-centric life style—i.e., learning how to live for oneself. Intimacy and the task of being a wife or husband demands thinking also now of another person or—if there are children—persons. This is the task which moves an individual (of whatever age) into adulthood—

* The "Big Crisis" is our formulation, not Erikson's.

Each age brings with it a new crisis and a new task.

the situation of contributing to the growth and well-being of others as well as oneself. And this whole business of living intimately and generously with other human beings in our society is not an easy task. Our growing divorce rate is testament to this.

Generation vs. Stagnation

Later adulthood brings with it the task not only of learning how to live creatively for oneself, but how to cultivate and bring forward the growth and creativity of others. As parents of older children, for example, we look out for and encourage their growing maturity and sense of self. As teachers, we foster their creative energies, their genuine desire to learn and become industrious, and (finally) to become persons. As employers, we help them to learn their vocation and to succeed. In other words, we learn to encourage the person younger than ourselves.

This contact with younger people keeps the older adult youthful and renews his vitality through the middle years of adulthood. In turn, it provides affirmation for the younger person in his search for dialogue with the world and in responsibility.

Ego Integrity vs. Despair

In later life, all of us face the reality of the limitations that come with old age: the lowering of physical vitality, slowed responses, diminished vision and hearing, etc. We also encounter at this stage, clearly and undisguised, the meaning of life once we recognize death is approaching. Old age and the peace of old age can be a highly valued experience.[23] But when we do not accept our place in the drama of the unfolding of the generations—and thus fail to sense the continuity of life—we may then view the closing of our lives with bitterness and despair.

Bitterness at being old seems to be increasing in our society. Often old persons are in despair when they remain within the family and are "tolerated," or are farmed out to "nursing homes." There has come about at last an emphasis on accepting the fact that old people are an integral part of society—a functioning part of generations, rather than an unwanted appendage. This is a beginning. We have yet to learn how to value and use the years of productive living that old people have experienced, as they do in Europe and in the East (India, China, etc.).

LIBERTY AND LICENSE

There is a hidden trap in our approach to personality, and we ask you now to consider this trap—just as we asked you to recognize the limitations of the adjustment approach to personality. The adjustment approach emphasized the necessity for individuals to aspire to a model of living based upon the expectations and demands of others in "society." The trap in that approach was that it stressed a kind of depersonalized conformity to group standards which by and large ignored the necessity of acknowledging individual uniqueness in personality development.

The trap in the growth model is that it can begin to degenerate into selfishness—the impulse to "do your own thing" first, last, and always. Thus if it is to be workable, the growth model of personality has to confront and ultimately resolve the problem of the kind of unbridled hedonism in which the person adjusts largely to his own self-interests, without regard for those other persons who share his living space. Actually, to adopt or recommend this kind of overweening self-centeredness is to misapprehend the growth model, to harbor a mistaken notion of what the growth model is all about. As we shall see in Chapter 2, the "highly integrated" personality seeks not only his own growth, but the growth also of others who share and participate in his life. That he values his own liberty to grow does not mean that he takes the license of doing absolutely whatever he wants. Here, as elsewhere, the distinction between *liberty* and *license* is crucial. License lacks the essential ingredient of responsibility, whereas *liberty assumes* self-governance.

RECOMMENDED READINGS

The following works are recommended to the student not only because they are relevant to this chapter's discussion, but also because they are highly readable and interesting and, moreover, they are available in paperback (and so within the student's price range).

BUGENTAL, JAMES F. T., ed. *Challenges of Humanistic Psychology.* New York: McGraw-Hill, 1967 (paperback).

There has been very little organized writing on humanistic psychology as an approach, but this book at least brings together some of the major personality theorists as they work their way toward understanding just what this approach is all about. In this book are gathered some of the most famous names in humanistic psychology: Sidney Jourard, Herbert Otto, Hobart Thomas, Carl Whitaker, John Warkentin, James Clark, and of course Abraham Maslow and Carl Rogers. The editor has tried to make this a very human book, and the authors have revealed themselves as very human persons.

ERIKSON, ERIK H. *Childhood and Society.* 2nd ed. New York: Norton, 1950 (paperback).

Erik Erikson's ability to lay out the panorama of human existence and its dramatic acts from birth to death is in the best tradition of the great visionaries of history. Originally from Denmark, he has that added insight into our culture that comes from having grown up in another one.

FROMM, ERICH. *Escape From Freedom.* New York: Avon, 1965 (paperback). First published by Holt, Rinehart (New York, 1941).

Like Erikson, Fromm has the advantage of comparing several cultures. Born in Germany, he came to this country during the rise of nazism. He trained in psychoanalysis and has been practicing and writing ever since. His thesis in this book is that the growing understanding of individual freedom is something that modern man has difficulty contending with. Consequently he escapes from freedom by surrendering to dictators or by transforming himself into a "well-fed, well-clothed . . . automaton."

GORER, GEOFFREY. *The American People: A Study in National Character.* Rev. ed. New York: Norton, 1964 (paperback).

We sometimes get to know ourselves, both our strengths and limitations, through feedback from others—that is to say, when others tell us how we seem to them. And just how do we seem to others? This little book will let us know how we seem to one cultured Englishman who admires us for our strengths and isn't shy about telling us about our faults either.

LAING, R. D. *The Politics of Experience.* New York: Ballantine, 1967 (paperback).

Laing is probably one of the most radical psychiatrists in the Western world. Each of his books sends shock waves into the mental health community. We illustrate with a quotation from his book, which should speak for itself: "What we call 'normal' is a product of repression, denial, splitting, projection, introjection and other forms of destructive action on experience. . . . The more one sees this, the more senseless it is to continue with generalized descriptions of supposedly specifically schizoid, schizophrenic, hysterical 'mechanisms.'"

MEAD, MARGARET. *Coming of Age in Samoa.* New York: Dell, 1967 (paperback). First published by Morrow (New York, 1923).

If the student still believes that human beings are by nature aggressive and competitive, he really should read this classic, still fresh reading today, about a gentle Samoan tribe and how they live and love and grow.

MOUSTAKAS, CLARK. *Creativity and Conformity.* Princeton, N.J.: Van Nostrand, 1967 (paperback).

This small book expands the thesis that is mentioned early in this chapter—namely, that conformity (excess adherence to externally imposed standards of behavior) destroys creative aspects in the person. This book is a series of essays on the way creativity is threatened by pretense, distortion, rules and regulations, and "meaningless standards and conventions."

NEILL, A. S. *Freedom—Not License!* New York: Hart, 1966 (paperback).

Neill is famous for having founded an experimental school in England which emphasizes students' freedom of choice. In this book, a reply to the many Americans who misconstrued his ideas about the nature of freedom, Neill clearly distinguishes between *freedom* and *license.* The book is excellent for present or prospective parents who are bewildered by the changing times. This book should be read to understand how to avoid the trap in the personality integration approach briefly discussed at the end of the chapter.

SZASZ, THOMAS S. *The Manufacture of Madness.* New York: Dell, 1970 (paperback).

Szasz has made a crusade out of his continuing theme that we are a society *producing* insanity by means of our insane labeling process. His fierce indictments of psychiatry and psychology have forced professionals to reexamine their adjustment concepts. A psychiatrist himself, Szasz accuses his own profession of recreating the witch hunts of the sixteenth and seventeenth centuries.

THE INTEGRATED PERSON: FOREVER IN PROCESS

The memorable persons in history have always been *originals*. Think of some of the names that still excite us: Einstein, Picasso, Maimonides, George Sand, Kierkegaard, Gandhi, Leonardo da Vinci, Martin Buber, Joan of Arc, Michelangelo, Bach, Shakespeare, Freud, Beethoven, Socrates, Darwin, Margaret Sanger, Goethe—the list is long, very long. These persons stand out from their society like stars in the sky so that we are struck always by the originality of their thinking, the depth of their feelings, and the unique way in which their personalities manifested themselves. As artists, they perceived the world in ways such that the rest of us could rediscover its reality. As philosophers, they formulated ideas that did not until then exist. As musicians, they made us aware of sound and of silence—the harmonies that stir the "soul." As reformers, they risked their very lives for their vision of what man is and what he can become. As scientists, they were ruthless in their search for knowledge that would dispel superstition, darkness, and ignorance.

They were men and women of spirit and passion. They dedicated their lives to self-awareness and for the greater awareness of us all. In Carl Rogers's muted phrase, they were "persons in process" —mankind evolving—and by their example and works, we too can evolve with them.

We do not expect that you will necessarily become a Socrates, or a Gandhi, or a Beethoven. These are the giants of recorded history. Each of us, however, can evolve in our own existence, and we can further our personality integration to "higher levels of consciousness" than we are able to live right now. Indeed, the present growth movement in psychology rests on just that assumption: that each person can evolve more creative and unique ways of being-in-the-world—if you want to work at it!

For that reason, we refuse to tell you what to do with your life. We refuse to tell you what kinds of goals you "should" have. That is your task, your choice. Our task is to provide ways for you to develop your self-understanding and your awareness of what life is and can be so that you can determine, *for yourself,* how you want to live. Instead of telling you what you should be like, we will instead discuss those personality growth processes that have been observed in persons who have gone a long way in their personality integration.

It is all very well to hold up as models of personality integration the memorable originals mentioned above. We can all learn something from these famous men and women if we wish to. But in one respect these men and women are idealized concepts: there is something of the folk hero in each of them. For example, we know Socrates only through the reverent pen of his student, Plato. And we know he was a man of great wisdom and courage. But it is reported also that Socrates may have been an extremely lazy person who neglected his wife and family. Similarly, we are acquainted less with the flesh-and-blood everyday person of Leonardo da Vinci than with his extraordinary and versatile productions: his paintings, his inventions, his architecture, and his writings. Beethoven and Michelangelo achieved heights of grandeur in music and art, but their tempers and fits of depression were also said to be grand. There were no psychologists in those days to study these memorable origi-

The first systematic attempts to understand personality integration were made by physicians such as Freud through the interpretation of dreams.

nals. If there had been, we might have had a more detailed picture of their essential humanity.

APPROACHES TO UNDERSTANDING PERSONALITY

An understanding of the process of personality integration must come from scientific observation of real persons, not from legends of folk heroes. We have begun that kind of observation only within the last century, and already there are some breakthroughs in our understanding of what the process of personality integration is.

I. The first systematic attempt to understand the process of personality integration (or rather personality *dis*integration) was made by physicians in the middle nineteenth century. Before the pioneering efforts of these workers, it was thought that mentally disturbed persons were possessed by demons and evil spirits or were being punished by God for their sins and they were frequently put in insane asylums where methods of "treatment" were often cruel and torturous. It was these early psychiatrists who first understood that hospitalized "mental" patients were not radically different from the people in the everyday world, that their unhappiness and confusions were only sharper in outline and more easily observed. They understood that by studying these mentally ill persons, they could get an insight into the problems of all people.

Take, for example, the symptom of depression. Anyone can feel depressed. A person who must be confined to a mental institution for a "psychotic" depression may suffer depression for days, even months, and feel so worthless that he blames himself for every misfortune that has happened to him, his family, and the world. He may be literally unable to move, rigid in his entire body, refusing to eat. This is the kind of depression that ones sees sometimes in the state institutions. Yet we have all experienced depression and have felt ourselves to be worthless for a day or so, unable to cope with everyday living. The difference between persons in the mental institution and us is a difference in degree, not kind.

Sigmund Freud was one of those nineteenth-century physicians who helped us to understand not only the "psychotic," in ourselves, but also that side of personality called "neurotic." [1] But there were others.

II. A second source of information on personality and its integrating functions is the research which compares groups of persons who share certain characteristics. For example, social scientists have studied the kind of personality integration which exhibits a high degree of "authoritarian personality" or "fascistic" orientation as compared with persons who show more "democratic" personality integration.[2] Other studies have taken a closer look at creative scientists, artists and engineers, as well as highly successful business executives and the "gifted." [3]

The most famous of these studies is the one undertaken by Abraham Maslow.[4] Maslow, an American psychologist who seems to us to be one of the true originals, studied what he called the "self-actualized person": the kind of person who can apparently live according to his beliefs and his goals, representing the "healthiest" type of personality in our society. Maslow chose his subjects from among personal acquaintances and friends, as well as "public" and "historical" persons. He also attempted to find "self-actualized" persons among college students, but found only one he could safely say was "growing well." Maslow concluded that the "self-actualized" person is the product of many years of conscious search and striving.

III. A third source of data for the understanding of highly evolved personalities—what we are calling highly integrated persons —comes to us from the persons who have undertaken to administer some form of psychotherapy—personal counseling, group therapy, or encounter groups. Carl Rogers is the best-known proponent of this kind of approach.[5] Rogers is a psychologist who believes that persons have within them the motivation to grow healthier if they are but given a safe climate in which to do so. He has described what happens in the "growth process" when persons who are only "partly-functioning" begin to become more fully-functioning"—i.e., they become happier and more self-directed, do what they want to do, etc.

PROCESSES INVOLVED
IN PERSONALITY INTEGRATION

Rather than discuss separately the many research findings in these areas of personality development, in this section we will summarize and combine the conclusions from these diverse sources.

There are bound to be some difficulties in trying to do this. For example, each personality theorist has his own particular point of view and methodology. Second, the terminology, manner of description, and definitions of each varies somewhat from the others'. For example, the famous psychiatrist and psychoanalyst Carl Jung, used the terms *individuated person* and *modern man* to describe the highly integrated person,[6] while Carl Rogers uses the term *fully-functioning*, Maslow uses the term *self-actualized*, and so forth. We begin with the assumption that all of these persons are describing what we are calling the highly integrated person.

Underlying all these descriptions, it seems to us, lie four basic processes common not only to all highly integrated persons but to all of us—processes which we are engaged in from birth to death, although the highly integrated person is more *intensely* concerned with them. The four processes are:

I. *The development of intellectual understanding of the world and of ourselves.*

II. *The purposeful furthering of emotional awareness.*

III. *The striving always to direct one's own destiny.*

IV. *The quest to relate oneself to one's world.*

These are fancy phrases, indeed, which we shall now do our best to describe more fully. (See also the box.)

The Four Basic Processes
Involved in Personality Integration

Processes	*Expressed As:*
I. The Development of Intellectual Understanding of the World and of Ourselves	a. Continuing to learn all throughout one's life
	b. Learning to perceive the world with accuracy
	c. Learning to perceive oneself with accuracy
II. The Purposeful Furthering of Emotional Awareness	a. Staying open to emotional experience
	b. Pursuing one's inner life
	c. Attending to the here-and-now
III. The Striving to Direct One's Own Destiny	a. Willingness to be oneself
	b. Willingness to think for oneself
	c. Willingness to accept responsibility for one's life.
IV. The Quest to Relate Oneself to One's World	a. Self-governance
	b. Commitment to the growth of others

I. The development of intellectual understanding of the world and of ourselves.   The first basic process of personality integration is the continual one of trying to understand the world around us. It is an urging that dominates man's consciousness in subtle and varied ways. As a six-week-old infant, he follows with interest the objects and persons in his near visual field. As he grows to a point of self-locomotion, he continues to explore the geography of his environment: he bites and tastes the breast, the bottle, solid food, a thumb (even his toes on occasion), objects on the floor, his blanket— all toward the purpose of investigating with the sense of taste what is or is not good to eat.

It is because of his total absorption in wanting to know and classify the phenomena of his world that the four-year-old asks his "why" and "where" and "how" questions: Why is the fire hot? Why does Daddy go to the office? Why do I have to go to sleep? Where does the sun go at night? How did I get to be born? The growing child is bombarded with events that he wants to understand and spends many years of his life in school learning about his world.

This basic process has been identified by many names. It has been called the "intellectual function," or the "thinking process." It has been seen as a "curiosity trait," or a "sensoriperceptual modal function," "problem solving," "decision making," "creativity," the "ability to analyze and synthesize." Individual success in developing this process is what is supposedly measured in tests of intellectual functioning (I.Q. tests).

This same *need to know* is manifested in the scientist's urge to investigate the universe; in the newspaper reporter's determination "to uncover the facts"; in the scholar's research into ancient civilizations; and in the philosopher's continuing search into the nature of goodness, truth, and beauty. It is the same underlying process behind your own search for answers to such questions as "Who am I?" "What is life?" and "What shall I do with my life?" It is, in fact, also the impulse behind the student's quest for knowledge; and it is society's attempts to help us answer these questions for ourselves which are, at least ideally, the sum and substance of education.

Despite this drive for intellectual awareness, many persons can settle into a routine kind of living as they grow older, and their sense of interest dims to those issues which do not touch their small, everyday world. Reading books becomes a thing of the past, and is replaced by only watching television, for example, or only reading the daily newspaper. In contrast, highly integrated persons never seem to lose their drive to deepen their apprehension of the world around them.

a. Highly integrated persons continue to learn all their lives. Abraham Maslow's study of "self-actualized" persons reveals that his highly integrated subjects are still involved with the same "basic issues and eternal questions" which marked their student careers. Maslow regards such persons as philosophers, "however homely," for they are still seeking knowledge of themselves and their world. They are willing and eager to learn from anyone, whether student or carpenter, if they sense the person has something to teach them. Despite their profound learning, they retain a sense of humility, sure in the knowledge that they know only a little of what there is to be known. In a sense, they remain students all their lives— students who continue to value the *learning* process wherever it touches them.

b. Highly integrated persons are more willing to perceive the world accurately. Our search to understand and give meaning to the things that happen to us involves the willingness and readiness to perceive the world *as it is.* We labor sometimes under the mis-apprehension that how we interpret the world through our eyes, ears, and other sensoriperceptual mechanisms is the way the world is. Actually, the way we view the world is modified or distorted by a host of prejudices—and by that we mean not just the prejudice directed against others who are different from us in race, creed, or nationality. We speak rather of all those small, unnoticed atti-tudes that have been conditioned into us by our background and our training, and that we do not realize we possess unless someone points them out to us—in a word, our snobberies or unexamined beliefs.

If we hear a "Brooklyn accent" we may smile with amusement, no matter how well educated the person seems to be! Despite his education and his good manners, for us the accent may mark him as somehow "uncouth." "Fat" people, to take another example, may arouse in us a curious dislike at first sight, which may prevent us from discovering that beneath this bulk can lie a sharp intellect or a poetic sensitivity.

The process involved in accurate perception of the world is

"But the king doesn't have any clothes on at all!"

related to the willingness to see what is really there rather than what one has been taught to see, or what one wants to see because of one's anxiety or wishes. School psychologists occasionally encounter a parent, for example, who prefers to think his child is being "victimized" by the school when told that the child is having difficulty in getting along with others.

This kind of "selective misperception" has been demonstrated in a series of psychological experiments originated by psychologist Solomon Asch.[7] These experiments ran something like this. Five college students are shown some lines drawn on paper and asked to judge which of them is the shortest. The answer is obvious, for one line is in fact considerably shorter than the others. Much to the astonishment of the fifth subject, however, each of the first four subjects makes what appears to be an incorrect judgment! What our (genuine) subject does not know is that all the other students are "stooges"—assistants of the experimenter instructed by him to make a wrong choice. How does the true (experimental) subject handle the conflict situation? More often than not (in fact, in the majority of cases), the experimental subject ends up agreeing with the stooges; he is unsure (many times) himself about his own perceptions!

In other, similar experiments, the effects of group pressure have been found to be stronger on persons in situations which demand conformity (such as in military contexts) than on persons trained to rely on their own perceptions (such as research scientists). These studies illustrate how remarkable an achievement accurate perception really is! Many of the rest of us tend ofttimes to see what we are told to see or expect to see—as in Hans Christian Andersen's "The Emperor's New Clothes." *

Most of the research studies on creativity and creative people concur on at least one point: "creative" persons have developed their ability to perceive the world and themselves with greater accuracy than the "average" person. Maslow's "healthy" subjects could in fact describe the personalities of their professors more precisely and accurately than the "average" person. Maslow explains that his self-actualized subjects show a remarkable ability to perceive the world *as it is* as opposed to *as it should be.* Because they are able to see what is actually going on in the present, they are also more capable of predicting the future, too. They are good "prophets" of things to come. They are less frequently fooled, incidentally, by the dishonesty and the façades of others and are impatient with the spurious and the fake.

Accurate perception is an achievement: we need to work at it. Maslow suggests that the key to such achievement may lie, paradoxically, in breaking with habits of stereotyped thinking, no matter how well these habits have served us in the past. This process of ridding ourselves of our stereotypic thinking is called "emptying the mind" by the Zen teachers.[8] Learning this process of perception requires years of study and hard work before we can prevent past associations, convictions, images, and stray thoughts from weaving into one's present perception. In the West, we call this *staying in the here-and-now,* which we shall discuss a little later on.

c. Highly integrated persons are more willing to perceive themselves with accuracy. Hand in hand with the ability to perceive others more accurately goes the ability to perceive oneself with a high degree of accuracy—that is, more objectively. Maslow's subjects did not deny their own shortcomings, even as they sought to overcome their limitations. And while they did not dwell on their imperfections, neither were they impressed by their achievements. MacKinnon and associates, studying the highly creative person, reported that their subjects were extremely candid about themselves and exhibited an extraordinary lack of defensiveness.[9] They could speak with equal frankness concerning their abilities and their

* The story of a king tricked into thinking that his new "suit of clothes" has been woven from "invisible thread" that only the most intelligent people can see. (Of course, there is no suit at all.) Not willing to admit that he cannot himself see the clothes, he pretends to see them and shows them off in a parade until a small boy shouts the truth. The emperor had no clothes on at all!

problems. Not only were they willing to reveal thoughts and feelings of the sort that others might prefer to keep to themselves, but they also showed no need for false modesty when discussing their strengths and unique abilities.

Seeing ourselves objectively involves seeing the problems that come our way objectively. The more emotionally charged the subject matter is for us personally, the less likely we are to distinguish what really is "out there" from what is a projection of our "in here" —our fears, anxieties, angers, etc. While we may not be able to know what is actually so in the heated moment of anger or in the darkness of depression, we can at least hold to the understanding that when we have returned to a more "centered" emotional state the situation may not seem as extreme as it appeared to us when we were caught up in the tidal wave of our emotions. Maslow's subjects, as a matter of fact, demonstrated a sereneness and a calmness under the severe shocks and sorrows to which we are all subject. It is almost as if they could stand back from their experiences a pace or two, and thereby avoid becoming inundated by grief or anger or pain, etc. And which may explain, in part, their ability to perceive the reality of situations more clearly!

II. The purposeful furthering of emotional awareness. Perhaps nothing is as basic to the human being as his emotional life. It begins long before he learns to think, almost as soon as he is born. Within only a few months, and sometimes even within weeks, parents can begin to distinguish different emotional conditions in their infant: contentment, distress, anger, pain, frustration, etc. It is almost as if the most primary kind of responses we are capable of are those expressing likes and dislikes.

As the human being becomes older, however, there are added to his repertory of emotions many subtler and more complex emotional tones—delight, sadness, frustration (to name but a few)—until at last he is able to experience also those rarer adult emotions of awe, ecstasy, thanksgiving—emotions that poets understand and express so well.

A repertory of complex and sensual emotions permits us to respond to musical harmonies, to the majesty of the Grand Canyon or a Gothic cathedral, and to the numerous qualities of love in all its manifestations. It is because we can experience moments of happiness and joy and thanksgiving that we are able to bear those other moments of fear, grief, disappointment, shock, and sorrow.

Most of us understand that life is a balance of both sides of the emotional spectrum, expressed so well in the title of one of Robert Frost's poems: "Happiness Makes up in Height for What it Lacks in Length."

Some of us, however, want a different kind of emotional balance. Perhaps we have experienced too many disappointments, or shocks, or sorrows. Or it may be that we have become jaded with sophistication and stimulation. Or perhaps we have developed such a low threshold for pain that we block out emotions of all kinds to avoid being hurt or being disappointed yet again. Whatever the reason, it is true that some of us live within a narrow range of emotional existence. These people seem to say: "Life may be kind of drab, but it is at least safer this way. I may not experience as much of the depth and heights that life can offer, but at least I can lay claim to less bother, and chaos, and unwelcome surprises!"

Age can bring a diminishing of those physiological (nervous and glandular) energies that once enabled us to be stirred to extremes of feeling and emotion. For example, older people sometimes begin to shy away from activities which exhaust their energies so that they can cope more adequately with the slowing down of their energies that come with increasing years. But even young people, as they situate themselves comfortably in their personal and vocational lives, lose that spontaneity they had in childhood. Other demands seem to crowd it out. ("What a lovely day to go birdwatching or for a swim—but the baby has to go to the pediatrician.") We can't enjoy the rose garden if we worry about having to pull weeds in the future. Our realization that we have to pay bills this evening can prevent us from enjoying the whole day. So little by little we close ourselves off to the present moments of joy and excitement by refusing to allow these experiences to happen to us in that moment.

The highly integrated person, however, seems to avoid the trap of emotional rigidity or coldness. And he does this, evidently, in very definite ways. One way is by pursuing new experiences and emotional understanding of these experiences.

a. The highly integrated person allows himself to stay open to emotional experiences. In other words, he allows himself to *feel* his emotions. Carl Rogers, who has studied the growth process in people actively engaged in personality integration through counseling, reports that these people not only accept their present feelings, but move away from their fear of new experiences and new emotions and toward more spontaneity in their emotions. They are less afraid to cry and to laugh and to examine their own feelings. He sees also a close similarity between his own research subjects and Maslow's "self-actualized persons" in that they (Rogers's subjects) are also more open than most people to their own bodily needs, are more aware of their own desires and impulses, and seem generally to get more out of living.

Being willing to allow oneself to experience one's own feelings entails also the willingness to experience many complex—even conflicting—emotions in a given situation. We are taught as children, for example, that we "should" love our parents, and as parents that we "should" love our children—no matter what. Yet it seems obvious that when children are spanked or otherwise disciplined by their parents, they can momentarily have feelings of anger or resentment, or even hatred. In like manner, when parents face for the hundredth time yet another instance of a child's tricks and manipulations, it is a relief for them to realize it is occasionally appropriate for them not to love their child, since they are in fact now furious with him.

Rogers's subjects after counseling discovered that it is natural to feel love, anger, frustration, and confusion (all at the same time) toward another human being. And with this discovery, they felt much less confused, since they were not repressing or denying their emotions.

Rogers also discovered that his clients became more "fluid and changeable," less in need of arriving at fixed conclusions or retreating into static emotional states. This loosening and broadening of their emotional "personality" structure may be compared with findings in studies of the authoritarian personality (see footnote 2) where a high degree of rigidity in thinking and behavior is exhibited and the person tends to experience a narrow spectrum of emotions. For such persons, the world remains dichotomized into good or bad, right or wrong, evil or virtue, masculine or feminine. This type of thinking is called *either-or thinking* and is the cause of much emotional and intellectual heartache. A person may say to himself, "Either I am right and he is wrong or he is right and I am wrong." Such "either-or" thinking leads to feelings of failure, feelings of superiority, hard feelings, inaccurate perceptions, etc.

Rogers's subjects, in comparison, show a "middle ground" in their personalities and much less of a need to come to fixed conclusions of right-or-wrong and good-or-bad.

b. The highly integrated person pursues his inner life with diligence. A comprehensive study of "creative" artists, engineers, and scientists has revealed that these persons value their inner life.[10] The subjects (all men, incidentally) were able to allow themselves a range of interests and emotions still thought at the time of the study to be "feminine" in the American culture; to allow themselves to express the "feminine" side (or emotional side) of their nature more readily than less creative individuals. Studies of

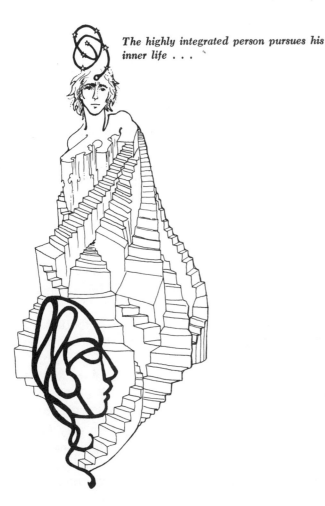

The highly integrated person pursues his inner life . . .

creative women, on the other hand, revealed them to have more "masculine" interests, and to be unafraid of expressing themselves in serious ways.

The highly integrated person studies his feelings and thoughts for enjoyment, for inspiration, and for solutions to perplexing problems. Many deep interpersonal relationships take much time and energy, and Maslow's subjects preferred to devote this time and energy to their inner world and their own growth and they needed "time out" from everyday relationships. Attention to one's inner life requires time, privacy, and motivation. Maslow's subjects showed much need for such time and privacy. Not only did they pursue their inner lives intensely, but many of them reported deep mystical experiences—what Maslow called 'peak experiences":

> . . . feelings of limitless horizons opening up to the vision, the feeling of being simultaneously more powerful and also more helpless than one ever was before, the feeling of great ecstasy and wonder and awe, the loss of placing in time and space with, finally, the conviction that something extremely important and valuable had happened, so that the subject is to some extent transformed and strengthened even in his daily life by such experiences.[11]

c. The highly integrated person attends to the here-and-now. A child is naturally spontaneous. He laughs, cries, is hungry, sleeps, or whatever from moment to moment. The young child lives in the here-and-now, and his world overflows with wonder: the feel of a caterpillar in his hand, or the sound of a squirrel chattering in the tree, or the sight of an alley cat foraging in a garbage can. He is able to focus his attention on what is here and now. And for that reason, his world is wonder-full, full of wonder and excitement and aliveness.

But so often, the boy child grows up to be a tired businessman who wakes wearily each day to go wearily to work. And the girl child grows up to be a tired housewife who dreads the daily round of routine and children. Is it in the nature of things that we must lose the excitement that we had as children?

Evidently not, for some persons never seem to lose the joyous appreciation of the moment. The artist and the poet somehow manage to hold on to the intensity of the *now* and the nearness of the *here*. Maslow and Rogers both found that their subjects had not lost their childlike ability to know joy in the present: to enjoy the scent of a flower, gain inspiration from music, experience their wives and husbands as beautiful even after many years of marriage. Somehow their senses and perceptions do not become dulled to the moments of beauty that come and go so quickly: a brilliant sunset, a child laughing, the smell of new-mown grass.

The ability to enjoy the moment (to let go of the past and avoid preoccupation with the future) has been called by Frederick Perls (and other existential therapists) as "being in the here-and-now." [12] Being in the here-and-now involves enjoyment of the senses, and Perls was well aware that many persons in our society have closed off much of their sensory functions. Perls's intuition regarding the sensory deficit in the "adjusted" man of our time is reflected also in Maslow's research findings with his self-actualizing subjects. Maslow called his self-actualizing subjects "good animals"—i.e., they allowed themselves full enjoyment of their physical senses: they ate well, slept well, played well, were able to derive strong satisfaction from loving sexual contact, and generally were able to "count their blessings." In regard to their ability to appreciate what they had, Maslow has this to say:

> I have also become convinced that getting used to our blessings is one of the most important nonevil generators of human evil, tragedy and suffering. What we take for granted we undervalue and we are therefore too apt to sell a valuable birthright for a mess of potage, leaving behind regret, remorse, and a lowering of self-esteem. Wives, husbands, children, friends are unfortunately more apt to be loved and appreciated after they have died than while they are still available. Something similar is true for psychological health, for political freedoms, for economic well-being; we learn their true value after we have lost them. . . .
>
> . . . My studies of low grumbles, high grumbles, and meta-grumbles all show that life could be vastly improved if we would count our blessings as self-actualizing people can and do and if they could retain their constant sense of good fortune and gratitude for it.[13]

Gratitude—a key ingredient in living in the here-and-now—means being able to thank someone with honesty; it involves the understanding that none of us has achieved our present level of functioning without considerable help from others. It is often amusing to listen to a young student, when asked who has helped him attain his accomplishments, reply (with innocence): "No one!" And in our time, we seem to have lost the capacity for "giving thanks" for

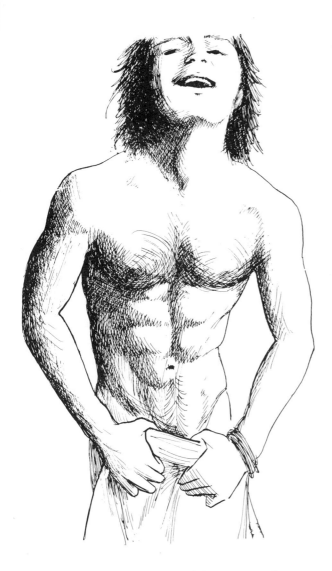

Maslow called his self-actualizing subjects "good animals."

one's good fortune, or for expressing appreciation to specific people who have helped us on the way. As Maslow says, we have grown "used to our blessings"!

III. The striving to direct one's own destiny. One aspect of our awareness of ourselves is that we can never completely direct our own destiny. We are born into a society that is not of our choosing; and we shall assuredly die when the fates will it. There are powers and events over which we have little control: the death of loved ones, natural catastrophes, and all the other events and happenings of the natural world. This is the matrix of our lives, the "human condition."

Even when we have a driving urge to master a certain skill, or to follow a certain vocation, or to attain prestige and honor, we have no guarantee this will happen for us. No matter how dedicated we are to the arts or devoted to our science, that ultimate victory of superior achievement may not be given to us. There is, then, in a certain sense, a reality to the whimsy of the ancient Greek gods when they speak of the capriciousness of "fate and fortune."

The Fates notwithstanding, there has been consistent agreement over the years regarding human personality, from the earliest "adjustment" psychologists to the present "existential" and "growth" psychologists, *on this one point:* a major characteristic of the "mature," "healthy," "self-realized," "self-actualized" person (it matters little what we call him) is that he is intent on directing his own destiny. He seeks to control his own life, pursue his essential interests, and master his environment: i.e., he is committed to being

She is less afraid to show on the "outside" what she feels herself to be on the "inside."

"the master of his fate and the captain of his own soul," no matter what the contingencies of life.

Maslow called his subjects "self-starters." They are determined to chart their own life course—despite the obstacles in the way or the setbacks received on route. In short, they take responsibility for their own lives. Indeed, there are many indications that they were sometimes so independent in the school years that they seemed rebellious as students.[14]

a. The highly integrated person is willing to be himself. Carl Rogers calls this factor the willingness "to be that self which one truly is." As each of Rogers's subjects progressed through therapy, he began to lose his fear of showing his inner self, the "real me": each became less afraid of showing on the "outside" the person he felt himself to be on the "inside"—even if that "real me" turned out to be less acceptable to others. Interestingly enough, each discovered that his "real" personality was as much, if not more, acceptable to other persons.

Rogers mentions another factor in the growth of his subjects. Each not only began to give up earlier notions of being required to live up to another person's ideas of what he was like, but also to discard his own unrealistic or overidealized image of himself. That is, subjects began to feel free of their own list of "oughts": what they should do and be. In considering the possibility that they were pleasing others at the cost of *not* pleasing themselves, they began to consider the foolishness of denying their own wishes and desires and of trying to live up to some impossibly perfect, superhuman ideal of what they should be. Psychoanalyst Karen Horney has described that particular trap as the "tyranny of the should." She says that one type of neurosis is to try to be impossibly perfect. This "neurotic" is convinced that he should exhibit

> the utmost of honesty, justice, dignity, courage, unselfishness. He should be the perfect lover, husband, teacher. He should be able to endure everything, should like everybody, should love his parents, his wife, his country, or he should not be attached to anything or anybody, nothing should matter to him, he should never feel hurt, and should always be serene and unruffled. He should enjoy life; or he should be above pleasure and enjoyment. He should be spontaneous; he should always control his feelings. He should know, understand, and foresee everything. He should be able to solve every problem of his own, or of others, in no time. He should be able to

overcome every difficulty of his as soon as he sees it. He should always be able to find a job. He should be able to do things in one hour which can only be done in two or three hours.[16]

It came as a relief to Rogers's subjects to find that they could be "just themselves" and that other people still accepted them and liked them. They didn't keep up as much of a façade and (in this way) became more like Maslow's subjects who did not like façades.

b. The highly integrated person is willing to think for himself. As Rogers's subjects gradually moved away from the endless demands of others and of themselves, they moved toward following their own desires. In doing so, they became more like Maslow's subjects again, for Maslow's subjects were self-structured, self-choosing, and self-determining. In fact, Maslow's subjects exhibited decidedly unconventional thinking and action in private life, although they could assume the cloak of convention when it suited them. These were not wild-eyed bohemians and rebels. On the contrary, they realized their unconventionality might be confusing to others, and they preferred to dress in conventional garb, speak in a conventional manner, and work in a conventional way so that they could go about the routine day-to-day tasks of working with others in slow, quiet, undramatic ways and thus achieve real progress rather than call attention to themselves.

D. W. MacKinnon's study of creative men also revealed that they are highly unconventional in their thought processes. Their center of reference is their own value system to a much greater extent than is found in the general population. MacKinnon found them more autonomous in their actions and less inclined to strive for achievement in settings where conforming behavior is expected or required.

Unconventionality in thought and perception thus seems to be a hallmark of this kind of person—to the extent that they think for themselves. They are not afraid to be original thinkers, although they may not make an open display of their originality. Certainly, the memorable originals mentioned at the beginning of this chapter not only were unconventional in their thinking, but they also displayed unconventionality, many times, in their lives.

c. The highly integrated person accepts responsibility for his own life. When Rogers's clients moved away from pleasing others and toward pleasing themselves, they did not in any way turn into hedonists or thrill seekers. On the contrary, they were more willing to be self-governing and to take responsibility for their own lives . . . and their own mistakes.

In like manner, Maslow's subjects were highly motivated to stake out their own objectives, accepting responsibility for mistakes. We have all known persons who seek to blame society, their parents, or other external factors for their present unhappiness. Maslow's subjects, highly "actualized" as they were, also found themselves occasionally in unhappy straits. But they did not blame others for their circumstances. They could be foolish, even stupid at times, but their willingness to admit their foolishness and their stupidity (and to learn from the experience) was one of the marks of their creativity and wisdom. They did not suffer any longer than necessary from their mistakes and follies; nor did they indulge themselves in endless remorse, shame, guilt, etc. They were willing to see their shortcomings realistically, but they attempted to learn from their mistakes and stupidities and to go on from there.

One of the principal obstacles in the way of many a person's progress is the fixation on past misfortunes. This particular difficulty comes up time and again in the therapeutic situation. In seeking to blame some event or person in their childhood (one parent or both, even one's teachers, or "society") for the present mess in their lives, such persons fail to see that the "blaming game" is a dead end, a vicious circle that leads nowhere except to more of the same. More important, it prevents the person from taking on responsibility for his present actions and direction—until he sees that he is thinking in a (vicious) circle.

Studies of creative individuals reveal that they too can come from a difficult home situation, and many of them seem not to have been close to their parents. Indeed, this lack of closeness may have helped them early on to establish their independence and self-support. Since they had no one to cling to and lean on, they apparently learned how to rely on themselves for support. Looking at some of the great figures of history, we discover similar circumstances. For example, Abraham Lincoln's mother died when he was eight, and it is said that his father was a rather shiftless person, as well as an indifferent father and provider. Charles Dickens, the English novelist who wrote story after story of children who suffered miserably at the hands of adults, was recalling aspects of his own early childhood.

Great men, as Maslow pointed out, seem to be no less vulnerable to "bad breaks" and "injustices" than are the rest of us. What matters is the way in which they overcome such difficulties; it is this quality which distinguishes them. Maslow's subjects knew how to remain stable in the face of life's contingencies. They, too, experienced anxiety, guilt, shame, sorrow, and grief, but they did not allow themselves to get trapped in self-pity and self-blame or blaming others.

It has often been suggested that a certain amount of pain and anxiety are necessary for developing one's personality beyond a certain point. Indeed, it does appear that pain and anxiety can be useful to us in many ways. For example, suffering can act as a warning that all is not well with us. It can become a signal to reexamine one's present situation, a motivation to grow and change, an inspiration for achievement—if only we know how to turn these experiences to use. As is well known, such events and happenings can become the route by which we discover compassion and empathy for others, or an incentive to pursue knowledge and justice. Creative individuals seem to know how to turn their suffering to constructive use. It is as if they are able to "recycle" the raw data of their experiences with the minimum necessary shame, sorrow, guilt, or conflict. Somehow they can then transcend to another level of their personality where the "larger view" of life becomes possible. We know surely that this kind of personality transformation is possible. We know much less about how to set this process in motion.

IV. The quest to relate oneself to one's world.   At the end of Chapter 1 we discussed the possible trap of the growth model. You will recall that the trap in the adjustment model was conforming to other people's standards. The possible trap in the growth model, we said, was unbridled hedonism—self-interest to the extent of exploiting or manipulating or even hurting others. Actually, we added, the trap is possible only if self-growth is misunderstood as "me *first, last,* and *always*" and if *liberty* is misinterpreted to mean *license.* The highly integrated person does not fall into this trap.

a. The highly integrated person is self-governing.   Rogers was well aware that self-interest and trusting one's own perceptions can become a handy kind of excuse for unbridled egotism. He therefore raises an essential point when he asks: Does such self-direction lead to cruelty or exploitation of others? Rogers's reply: When the person becomes more self-functioning, he also becomes more socialized; at that point he does not need to have someone else control him or inhibit his aggressive impulses—*he is in control* of his impulses, and therefore of himself. Moreover, he does not become less sensitive to others in his environment, he becomes *more* sensitive, *more* accepting of others in the world—and of himself as well.

b. The highly integrated person has a commitment to the growth of others. Maslow's research findings are similar. His subjects had a deep and abiding feeling of identification with others, a general feeling of lovingkindness, a genuine desire to help the human race. (In other walks of life, in other times, Maslow says, they may have been called "men of God.") He found them to be highly ethical, and they often had a sense of mission—what might be described as a "call" or a "vocation" to serve others.

Maslow and Rogers agree that such persons do exhibit kindness toward and patience with other human beings. This does not mean that they allow themselves to be used as doormats, for they are capable of anger and can take someone to task, especially if they believe that a person is hurting someone else or being dishonest. Yet their humor is not hostile (they have little use for the kind of "humor" which pokes fun at other people's infirmities, foibles, and limitations). It is gentle and never acid, characterized by that lack of prejudice which all men have recognized as wisdom. Maslow's example of someone who possessed that kind of good humor is Abraham Lincoln; that is, a person who realizes that folly is sometimes ever-present in human relationships.

This kind of steady love of mankind (even where we recognize individual men may disappoint us) the Romans called *caritas*, which may be loosely translated as "charity." *Caritas* is said to be the dominant quality of personality in the great saints and reformers of the world. John the Evangelist's last teaching, it is said, was "Love one another!" And Jesus of Nazareth's teaching to "Love your neighbor as yourself" is still remembered. It may well be that *caritas* —"charity," what we today call love and compassion—is a powerful force in transcending the personal difficulties and suffering of our individual lives and of attaining peace and certainty. It does seem at any rate to be the mark of certain *originals*—namely, those persons who are remembered for their "love of mankind." Today we might describe these people as loving persons.

Relating to one's world, and becoming involved with it, can take many forms of vocation. It may take the form of the prophet or the priest, or it may take the form of the statesman. It may take the form of the great reformer whose life is dedicated to sounding out the facts of life that men need to hear and few want to listen to. Or it may be in the form of a teacher, a writer, or that very tired businessman or housewife we mentioned earlier. One thing seems sure: either each of us walks the path on his own feet or the adventure that is life and growth of personality does not happen.

RECOMMENDED READINGS

ADORNO, T. W., E. FRENKEL-BRUNSWIK, D. J. LEVINSON, and R. N. SANFORD. *The Authoritarian Personality.* New York: W. W. Norton, 1950 (paperback).

In contrast to the highly integrated personality type as presented in Chapter 2, the authoritarian personality is a highly structured, highly rigid person who finds ambiguity and lack of structure extremely threatening.

BARRON, F. *Creativity and Psychological Health.* New York. Van Nostrand, 1963.

A fine account of some of the findings of a study done with "highly creative" people and their personality characteristics. It has been said that "genius is akin to madness." Barron, like others, finds that true creativity stems not from madness, nor a sublimation of neurosis, but from a different kind of healthy and integrated personality.

JUNG, C. G. *Modern Man in Search of a Soul.* Translated by W. S. Dell and Cary F. Baynes. New York: Harcourt, Brace (paperback). (First published 1933.)

Jung, the noted Swiss psychiatrist, came to the conclusion that one of the principal neuroses of persons living today is their rejection of the spiritual aspect of themselves. Material possessions, wealth, status, and worldly success is not enough for personal happiness. While the first half of one's life may indeed be occupied with advancement in the outer world, the second half of human existence is bankrupt unless the individual finds meaning to his existence.

KAGAN, JEROME, ed. *Creativity and Learning.* Boston: Beacon Press, 1970 (paperback).

Kagan, a psychologist who has studied creativity, has brought together a number of contributions to our understanding of creativity by some of the outstanding persons working in the field, including Jackson, MacKinnon, Torrance, Kubie, and Sanford.

KOESTLER, ARTHUR. *The Act of Creation.* New York: Dell, 1966 (paperback).

It will probably be said of Arthur Koestler that he was one of the most creative persons of the twentieth century. He has produced essays in philosophy, psychology, sociology, and literature. This book is a highly personal essay on the creative act.

MASLOW, ABRAHAM. *Motivation and Personality.* 2nd ed. New York: Harper and Row, 1954, 1970 (paperback).

If we want to know about the psychologically healthy person, proposed this psychologist, let us study *him* rather than the psychologically disturbed. And that is what he did. This book contains the results of his research—namely, that self-actualized people are altruistic, dedicated, spontaneously creative, etc. If the student wants to know something of what the most highly integrated and most highly evolved person is like, he should read this book.

MC CLELLAND, DAVID. *The Achieving Society.* New York: Macmillan, 1967 (paperback).

This book presents the research done by McClelland and his associates. The successful executive is marked by very special characteristics and supports some of the material presented in this book on the highly integrated personality. The material may seem to the new student generation a bit materialistic, but it still provokes a good discussion.

ROGERS, CARL R. *On Becoming a Person.* Boston: Houghton Mifflin, 1961.

Along with Maslow, Rogers is responsible for the "third force" or "humanistic" movement's early growth. Rogers, too, studies the highly evolved and integrated person, and describes him as "fully-functioning." Since Rogers always writes personally and simply reading one of his books is like getting to know him personally in a deep and significant way.

ROKEACH, MILTON. *The Open and Closed Mind.* New York: Basic Books, 1960 (paperback).

This book presents the research carried out on the nature of the highly prejudicial mind, an interesting topic in contrast to the highly integrated personality. Like the Adorno book (above), it gives an insight into the narrow, overconforming personality who needs to "narrow his awareness" in order to function.

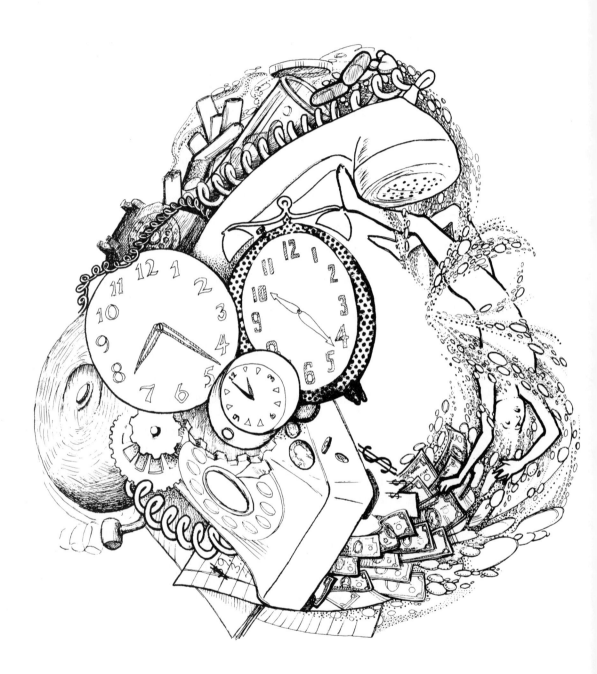

3

ANXIETY: PERSONS UNDER STRESS

In Chapter 2 we took a look at some of the research on the person who is said to have a highly integrated personality pattern—the person who others have described as "highly creative," "fully-functioning," "self-actualized," etc. These persons, in our view, seem to be deeply involved in four basic processes—processes which are common to us all, but which they utilize particularly well. The four processes are (1) becoming more intellectually aware as a life-long process (and not something that is confined to our years of formal schooling); (2) the purposeful furthering of emotional awareness, no matter how painful the process; (3) striving always to direct one's own destiny; and (4) seeking to relate to the world in terms of suprapersonal objectives.

But the question then arises: If a satisfying and viable personality is mainly the result of cultivating and actualizing those four processes, what prevents most of us from just settling down and getting on with the business of integrating our own personalities? If that is all there is to it, how come personality integration can be so difficult for so many persons?

There are as many answers to that question as there are systems of philosophy and theories of psychology. One answer to the question is that severe *anxiety* interferes with our capacity to undertake the project. Furthermore, we are today experiencing more anxiety than ever before.

ANXIETY VS. FEAR AND WORRY

Most readers will not need a definition of anxiety, since it has become a more-or-less common event in our lives. So common is the experience of anxiety that the word has passed into the vocabulary of grade-school children.

Anxiety manifests itself physiologically in diverse ways: in the fast and shallow breathing which is the mark of our time,[1] in the occasional increased rate of heartbeat, in clammy hands that bespeak excess perspiration (hot and cold), and even in the tapping of our fingers and feet which indicates we have a vague feeling that we should be doing something else, or going someplace . . . or something! Let's designate these symptoms as more-or-less "benign" forms of anxiety!

As anxiety becomes more constant and the level of stress affecting the person increases, we then begin to see the ticks or muscle spasms and cramps that say that something is wrong! The feeling of hollowness in the chest or the queasiness in the stomach may become chronic. Sometimes, the person will try to deal with this level of anxiety by overeating, overdrinking, or by smoking too much. Or he may choose to drown the anxiety in the plethora of tranquilizing pills now available. Or become engaged in frenetic activity!

Anxiety resembles fear, but it is not as specific as fear. For example, one may be afraid he will fail a test of some kind—this is a specific fear. Once the test situation is met and passed through safely the "anxiety" passes. That can be more properly regarded as understandable and normal "worry." The kind of anxiety we are discussing now is something over and beyond temporary worry. Anxiety is nonspecific. It is experienced—as one college student said to us, "Everything is so good for me right now, something is bound to go wrong any minute!"—as a vague sense of discomfort, a kind of nameless apprehension or dread which says, "Something is wrong somewhere but I don't know what," or that something undefinable is about to happen that brings on a mood of uneasiness. Continual anxiety and the prolonged stress that creates severe anxiety can lead to psychological breakdown, physical breakdown, and the kinds of personality disintegration that are not easily understood or recognized.

GLOBAL ANXIETY

The anxiety and stress we are experiencing today come from two sources. The first source is personal and involves our relationships with parents, our extended family and friends, our children, and our business associates and whether we will, for example, maintain good health, keep our jobs, make a decent living and have a good marriage, etc. These are the everyday problems of living that have existed since Adam met Eve. We shall be dealing with personal anxiety throughout the remainder of this book. Here, however, we would like to call attention to another source of anxiety, one that is becoming increasingly common in our era. We have chosen to call this level of anxiety *global anxiety,* since it looms up like the thermonuclear bomb's mushroom cloud which is, in part, the symbol of our age and time. Global anxiety has to do with the existential questions of survival of our very planet and of the peoples on it. Global anxiety hangs like a shadow over all our functioning so that our personal anxieties become even more magnified. It is well that we point out the major sources of this global anxiety.

1. The pressure to be successful. In 1961, *Time* magazine devoted several pages of copy to "angst" or "anxiety" which it saw building up after World War II.[2] It placed much of the cause of this anxiety on the American need to achieve—or to be successful. The push toward "success" can be seen in advertising inducements and articles by experts on how to stay young (don't grow old); to stay slim (don't get fat); to get ahead (don't be satisfied where you are, improve your social position); to be well informed (buy more books); to be more permissive (or less permissive) as parents; to be a rugged individualist; to adjust; not to conform; to wear the right clothes; to get a new car; to be creative and stay busy with do-it-yourself kits; to take a vacation and so forth. *Time* saw the pressure as being exerted on infants in their cradles (toys are being constructed now so that infants can learn in their cribs), and this pressure continues through our lives right up to the top and the success-driven executive.[3] William James called the success goal the "Bitch Goddess" since in his view it simply recedes farther and father, like a mirage, the nearer we get to it. We have become, *Time* summed up, a nation of driven, pressured, harassed over-achievers continually looking to future gains and accomplishments. (In so orienting ourselves, we might add, we miss the joys and our real awareness of our here-and-now blessings.)

2. *The shadow of World War III.* Since the dropping of the first (and so far only) atomic bombs to be used in warfare, in 1945, the people of the world have been living on the brink of nightmare concerning the next bomb that may be dropped. We go to bed at night never quite sure whether we will wake up in the morning. We turn on the radio or television wondering uneasily what new war has cropped up in what little-known country—a "little" war that may trigger the Big War. Small nations wonder nervously if their larger neighbors will accidentally explode a nuclear bomb. Unlike previous times, a small border eruption in some far-off place on the globe can now have immediate reverberations in Grand Forks, North Dakota.

As a result of the crumbling of world empires and the eruption of civil wars, there has been a steady loss of confidence that Western civilization as we know it will continue.[4] Because of our instant on-the-spot news media, wars and rumors of wars, mass mutilations, mass murders, etc. are almost continually assaulting our senses with anxiety-provoking stimulation.[5] All of this the average citizen (you and me) hears as he drinks his morning coffee and sits down to his evening meal.

3. *Disillusionment with the "American Dream."* World War II veterans returned from overseas glad the war was over and hopeful that they had finally made the world "safe for democracy." It was an era of optimism. The economy was expansive; millions of veterans went back to school to get a college education and to "get

We face another kind of anxiety today—global anxiety.

ahead." They were eager to begin the long trek toward success and the even longer trek out to the suburbs so that their children could grow up in a decent environment. It seemed the epitome of the "American Dream."

It is history now that the dream of peace and of the "great society" began to come undone very soon after 1950 and was finally shattered in the sixties. It was shattered by shock waves of violence: first a president of the United States was assassinated, and within days his assassin was shot to death in front of millions of TV viewers. There followed the assassination of a black peace-advocating leader and the assassinations and attempted assassinations have still not ceased. Assassination stalks every political candidate as he or she campaigns across the country, and now seems to be becoming a fact of political life in our country.

In the meantime, the black ghettos of the big cities, steaming in the hot summers, began to boil over in uprisings and lootings. The street slaying of a girl in New York City within screaming distance of dozens of New Yorkers who chose to ignore her cries for help astonished the rest of the nation. Mass murders in Chicago and California horrified American citizens, and these same citizens began to double-lock their doors at night and to stay off the streets after dark.

The affluent generation of veterans, older now, reacted with bewilderment as their children revolted against their parents' world and values. The student population shunned their parents' affluence, traded short hair for long, donned colorful and often bizarre clothes, invented a drug and rock music culture that seemed to mock all the values their parents held, and gathered around the marijuana peace pipe in different kinds of get-togethers.

Instead of a peaceful "one world," society seemed to be fragmenting: blacks vs. whites, children vs. parents, radicals vs. conservatives, hippies vs. hardhats, hawks vs. doves, women vs. men, etc. The American Dream had shattered, and Americans had to take a look at what was wrong and at what could be done.

4. From the rape of the planet: guilt and fear of survival. Rachel Carson sounded the first alarm over the state of our ecology in 1952 with the publication of her now-classic book *Silent Spring.*[6] In the first chapter she depicts the future of a North American town in which, as a result of the contamination and pollution of the water and the earth, biological reproduction is no longer possible, where cattle mysteriously become sick and die, and where people come down with strange maladies. Hens lay eggs from which no chicks are hatched, and streams are lifeless because all their fish have died. It is a strangely quiet town where "no birds sing," for even they have fled.

Carson's book was not simply an alarmist's overreaction. She believed even then that the poisons already unleashed upon the waters and earth of this planet—such as DDT and the strontium-90 fallout from atomic blasts—had released a "chain reaction of evil" that was largely irreversible. Her hope was that we would realize how devastating had become our poisoning of the planet and that we would take steps to at least prevent further destruction. She explained that the chemicals in fertilizers and poisons in pesticides sprayed on croplands or forests or gardens lie long in soil, entering into living organisms, passing from one to another in a chain of poisoning and death. Or they pass mysteriously by underground streams until they emerge and, through the alchemy of air and sunlight, combine into new forms that kill vegetations, sicken cattle, and work unknown harm on those who drink from once-pure wells.[7]

The impact of *Silent Spring* and of subsequent books (by Carson and others) has been such that whole communities have begun to take up organic gardening (growing crops without the use of chemical poisons); even citydwellers now strive to produce organically grown tomatoes on their apartment balconies. But the rest of us sometimes gingerly pick up an apple and wonder what we are taking into our systems by eating this "poisoned apple."

The whole ecological movement has now been taken up by every segment of the population—big businesses and consumers, conservatives and liberals, teenagers and the elderly, etc. It is perhaps the one theme unifying our splintered special-interest groups. Titles of other books on the ecology crisis are also designed to depress the average, already unhappy citizen who feels almost impotent to help repair his environment.

5. The pace and alienation of modern life. We are living at a dizzying pace. We fly, drive, eat, live at an intense rate. We move our households, our families, and our lives across this huge country at an average rate of once every five years. Such moves and changes

---

Books Currently Available on the Crisis in Ecology

Carson, Rachel. *Silent Spring.* Boston: Houghton Mifflin, 1962.

Ehrlich, Paul. *The Population Bomb.* New York: Ballantine Books, 1968.

Esposito, John C. *Vanishing Air.* New York: Grossman, 1970.

Laycock, George. *The Diligent Destroyers.* New York: Grossman, 1970.

Marine, Gene. *America, the Raped.* New York: Simon and Schuster, 1969.

Marx, Wesley. *The Frail Ocean.* New York: Ballantine Books, 1970.

Ng, Larry K., and Stewart Mudd. *The Population Crisis.*

Osborn, Fairfield. *Our Plundered Planet.* Boston: Little, Brown, 1948.

Paddock, William and Paul. *Famine, 1975.* Boston: Little, Brown, 1948.

Editors of *Ramparts. Eco-Catastrophe.* San Francisco: Canfield Press, 1970.

Taylor, Gordon R. *Doomsday Book.* New York: World, 1970.

have an immense impact upon the world of the individual person. He must say goodbye to his friends, to his neighborhood, to the house he has bought and improved by dint of his own labor, to his co-workers—in fact, to all he has known first-hand. He must begin yet again the painful labor of forging out a new place for himself, an effort which requires a considerable amount of physical and psychological energy. No wonder the quiet, peaceful image of a New England covered bridge and a nineteenth-century snow-covered landscape evokes in us a sad nostalgia and a sense that we could have been happier in an age that was less frantic, in which one had fewer things to do and more time in which to enjoy doing them.

We are an uprooted nation; individuals are separated from their parents, their children, their grandchildren, their sisters and brothers and cousins. Consider the European by contrast. An Irish-man is seldom more than a day's drive from his relatives even if he lives on one coast and they on the other. Paris is in northern France, but any Parisian can spend a weekend with a relative who lives even at the extreme southern end simply by taking a day's drive or trainride. The sheer size of our country, and our willingness to make transcontinental moves, often result in grandparents who seldom see their grandchildren and cousins who never see each other at all. By the second generation, all contact is often lost. (Not so with Europeans who are pleased to be able to stay in touch with their families, since the distance is not so great and contact can more easily be maintained.)

6. The plastic society.   As we become increasingly urban, we lose our sense of communion with nature, of belonging, of our relationship to plants and other animals, to the earth. City streets without trees and suburban tracts without wildlife separate us from the biology of things: how animals are born, grow, mate, give birth, and die; how plants take root, bloom, grow fruit, and reseed; how our existence—even our technologically processed and glamorously packaged foods—ultimately depend upon the underlying soil and the rains from above. We are out of contact with Nature. We have lost the connection between ourselves and our Earth, a loss which at the same time puts us out of touch with our history and our past, which makes us lose sight of the fact that our sophisticated civilization could never have existed at all had not man first learned to raise crops and breed animals.

It has been suggested that this loss of our sense of the past, our broken link with Nature, accounts for our nostalgia toward the symbols of the past: the fireplace and the hearth, the covered bridge, the time when one had time, the self-contained rural households and closely knit neighborhoods, and above all that intimate relation with the elements—with soil, stream, and forest, with wind, rain, and snow, with sun, moon, and stars.[8]

7. The impact of great social change. You have probably heard it said that we are living in a time of great technological and social change. In fact, you have probably heard this phrase so often that it is in danger of becoming trite. Trite or otherwise, it is nonetheless true. And the devastating truth of this kind of social and technological change is nowhere more clearly evidenced than in its effects on the individual. To assimilate change in his physical environment, the individual must expend a lot of energy making adjustments to it. Moreover, change—even a little change—creates anxiety.

Psychologists who work in industry are well aware that change in an organization, particularly a big change, creates anxiety in the organization.[9] If, for example, an executive resigns from his position, anxiety becomes extremely high among those persons who are intimately associated with him. Will they get on with the new executive? Are their jobs secure? What kind of changes will he bring with him? Even transfer from one department to another may arouse the anxiety-suspicion of a staff member until he is made to understand that the transfer is not a demotion.

The types and frequency of changes that people are now facing, however, are far greater and more intense than in any previous time in history. In just the last two decades, for example, we are being asked to consider radical departures in styles of living and loving: communal living, group marriage, marriage between members of the same sex, and parenthood without marriage at all. *Newsweek* quotes an elderly woman as saying, "Things I used to confess as sins are no longer sins." And a man from Kansas reports he is "so confused I don't know what to think. Things we were taught we would go to Hell for are all right now." [10]

In addition to the change in moral and ethical values, there are the inventions and discoveries undreamt of only a few decades ago which are beginning to change even our concepts of human life. Successful kidney and eye transplants seemed miraculous enough, but now there are heart transplants, which suggest that human life can be extended simply by transplanting one vital organ after another. Some scientists have even suggested that one day there may be no need to "die" at all, that life may be extended indefinitely if medical technology continues its discoveries. In anticipation of this event, some people are keeping loved ones literally frozen rather than burying them—in the hope that they can one day be brought back to life and their fatal ailments cured. Moreover, the possibility of test tube babies is no longer just the science fiction writer's idea, but is being considered a theoretical possibility by scientists. Summarizing the year 1971, *Life* magazine ran the headline, "We Learn to Tolerate the Bizarre and Intolerable." [11]

In 1965 Alvin Toffler coined the phrase "future shock" in an attempt to describe the attendant disorientation and psychological breakdown when individuals are subjected to "too much change in too short a time." [12] By 1970 Toffler had concluded that this "disease of change" was no longer a future danger but a present one. Toffler distinguishes between "culture shock" (for those familiar with this sociological term) and "future shock" in the following way.

> Culture shock is the effect that immersion in a strange culture has on the unprepared visitor. Peace Corps volunteers suffer from it in Borneo or Brazil. Marco Polo probably suffered from it in Cathay. Culture shock is what happens when a traveler suddenly finds himself in a place where yes may mean no, where a "fixed price" is negotiable, . . . where laughter may signify anger. It is what happens when the familiar psychological cues that help an individual to function in society are suddenly withdrawn and replaced by new ones that are strange or incomprehensible.
>
> The culture shock phenomenon accounts for much of the bewilderment, frustration, and disorientation that plagues Americans in their dealings with other societies. It causes a breakdown in communication, a misreading of reality, an inability to cope. Yet culture shock is relatively mild in comparison with the much more serious malady, future shock. Future shock is the dizzying disorientation brought on by the premature arrival of the future . . .
>
> . . . Unless intelligent steps are taken to combat it, millions of human beings will find themselves increasingly disoriented, progressively incompetent to deal rationally with their environments. The malaise, mass neurosis, irrationality, and free-floating violence

already apparent in contemporary life are merely a foretaste of what may lie ahead unless we come to understand and treat this disease. . . . Change is avalanching on our heads and we are unprepared to cope with it.[13]

It may not be as bad as Toffler suggests. Nevertheless, the number and quality of changes and the swiftness with which they are descending on us are reality. All change tends to provoke disequilibrium in the organism, and from disequilibrium eventually can come growth. But too much disequilibrium produces physical and psychological breakdown, as we shall soon see.

PERSONAL ANXIETY

We have known for a long time now that prolonged personal anxiety and environmental pressures can hasten and even produce psychological breakdown. *Psychological breakdown* is a convenient way of describing what happens when a person is subjected to stresses

Future shock is what happens when individuals are subjected to "too much change in too short a time."

beyond the point where he can function in an adequate fashion. In the First World War (1914–18), soldiers sometimes developed "shell shock"; in the Second World War (1939–45) when soldiers could no longer cope, they were said to be suffering from "battle fatigue." From reported experiences of prisoners-of-war in the Korean conflict, we learned that anyone can experience psychological and moral disintegration if stress is continued long enough.[14]

When we take a look at it, it seems natural enough for a man to experience psychological breakdown under wartime conditions. Take a man from his home, his friends, his parents, his wife and children; take him away from the only life he's ever known and transplant him into a new country, into a rigid and mechanical life style; take away his sense of his own individuality and worth—and he becomes vulnerable to psychological stress and even the breakdown of his present personality patterning if the stress is excessive, and the situation too widely different from his previous life style.[15] An instance where isolation and continued environmental pressure produced such loss of personal identity occurred during the Korean War when some American soldiers confined in North Korean prisons confessed to crimes they had not committed to escape further brainwashing by their jailers.[16]

In civilian life, the inability of a person to cope with the pressures of his life situation can sometimes be just as great as that of the wartime soldier who is involved in raw survival. Take, for example, the executive whose ulcers are finally killing him; or the mother of three who feels unable to deal with her children because she still feels much like a child herself. Any one of us could be these persons and cease to function as we encounter continuing pressures and demands. There are even instances where a person may decide to end chronic and apparently irreconcilable conflict by annihilating the tension altogether—i.e., by committing suicide.

A less extreme form of flight from pressures is visible in the person variously called "insane," "psychotic," "neurotic"—or just plain "crazy." The main thing we notice about all such "flights from reality" and all such "nervous breakdowns" is that the person seems no longer able to cope, no longer able to channel his energies coherently in the directions he had been traveling.

"Breakdown" in personality functioning can take many forms. An individual may become so depressed that he is literally unable to move from his bed. He may sit, for example, in a chair all day with his head bowed down—as it were, by the weight of his guilt,

Inability to cope can be just as critical in civilian life as in military life.

or shame, or anger, or any of the myriad things with which he can torment himself. Or he may suddenly become *manic* (excessively enthusiastic) and begin to turn everything upside-down in his life. He may suddenly get "dressed up" in loud, emphatic, even bizarre clothing, go on extravagant shopping sprees and spend money far above his present ability to pay. Or he may decide to become a dancer, a writer, a singer—something obviously the opposite of what he has been so far.

From the vantage point of our temporary position of safety, it is easy for us to see that such persons are dealing essentially in physical metaphors: "I can't go on like this!" "I've got to do something with my life!" "Things around me have got to change!" Yet we can see also that their efforts to change their lives are largely ineffective, destructive to others, and apparently also destructive of themselves. Unless we are quite insensitive, we can't help noticing that such persons are nonetheless attempting, however ineffectively, to break down a situation which to them seems almost impossible to resolve rationally. Suicide and (very likely) some other forms of violence, particularly extreme violence to oneself or others, are physical events which express just being at the limit of desperation with one's present existence.

PHYSICAL BREAKDOWN

Prolonged and severe stress (such as constant anxiety) can bring on physical breakdown just as easily as it can bring on psychological breakdown. Intense anxiety that is not resolved can eventually result in an ulcerated stomach or an overburdened heart which finally "blows up" in a coronary attack. These are instances in which persons having reached their limit, rather than going psychotic, express the conflict and pressure through their physical bodies.

It is well known, for example, that physical illness and death are associated with contagious diseases, inadequate shelter, and exposure to extreme temperatures, and that starvation diets in concentration camps have led to lasting changes in a person's ability to cope and grow thereafter. What is perhaps not so well known is that the death rate of survivors of prisoner-of-war and concentration camps continued to remain higher than normal during the first six years after their liberation. It was to be expected that the ex-prisoners' physical resistance to diseases such as tuberculosis and intestinal disorders would be lower than in a nonprisoner population because of the stresses in their previous imprisonment. Investigators were not even too surprised to find that liberated prisoners continued to commit suicide at a higher rate than normal ("His camp experiences must have proved too much for him"). But they had not expected to find *twice the normal incidence of death from cancer in ex-prisoners, and three times the normal incidence of death by accidents.* This is not to say that the investigaotrs think stress causes cancer, but rather that persons become more vulnerable to cancer after prolonged environmental stress.[17]

Physical breakdown of bodily functions can also occur even when there is provision for adequate diet and other life necessities. There is mounting evidence that if physical care and security is present but *psychological security is absent,* there is a significantly higher incidence of disease and mortality. We have already mentioned that babies in orphanages, hospitals, or inadequate day-care centers (who may receive adequate food and physical care but do not get adequate mothering, caressing, holding, and other kinds of personal attention) have a higher incidence of disease and death than babies who do get adequate "mothering." [18]

We are beginning to acknowledge also that aged persons who are put into nursing homes can succumb to death sooner than those aged persons who are taken care of in their own homes by their own families. Absence of love and the feeling of belonging to someone seems somewhere to be a definite consideration in the failure of physical health; if this lack of attention becomes great, the person can become "ill—even unto the point of death."

PSYCHOSOMATIC MEDICINE

The study of the interrelationships or balance between the psychological conditions of a person's life and his physical health is known today as *psychosomatic medicine.* And it is well at this point to clarify two other terms which are often confused with *psychosomatic illness*—namely, *hypochondria* and *malingering.*

Malingering is pretense. A malingerer is not sick, nor is he in pain, nor does he believe he is sick. Malingering is, pure and simple, a put-on. Many a young man has feigned poor physical health or a psychiatric condition to avoid the draft or to get out of the army. That is malingering. Such is the case also with the child who feigns a stomach ache to avoid going to school or the wife who feigns a headache to avoid sexual relationships with her husband. In malingering the person is not ill and he knows it. What keeps the malingerer going, of course, is that there is no one so far who has called his bluff—who sees that a good piece of acting is going on.

Hypochondria is not a pretense. The hypochondriac really believes (at some level of awareness) that he is ill. Sometimes he genuinely suffers pain and has other symptoms. The symptoms may take the form of "vague faintness" or a "general weakness" or a "feeling" that he is "coming down with a cold." The hypochondriac takes his temperature frequently, doses himself continually with drugstore medicines, and even stays away from work because he is sure that "the cold is becoming pneumonia."

In others, hypochondria may take the form of a secret conviction that one has cancer—even when all his physicians assure him that they find no evidence of it. Such a person is not malingering, he is

Hypochondria is not a pretense. The person really believes he is ill.

a hypochondriac! * The problem with the hypochondriac is that he is a complainer; and he continues to complain of his fears, his symptoms, or whatever until someone finally convinces him that he looks in the best of health. This can brighten his outlook for a moment, but only for a moment. Then comes that inevitable nagging fear that he has contracted some dread illness—one which physicians have not yet recognized, one of those fatal "rare tropical" diseases!

The malingerer is a con-man trying to use "illness" as an excuse to avoid unpleasant situations. The hypochondriac, on the other hand, is a person ill-at-ease with himself who channels his tensions and his feelings of uneasiness into his fantasy and imagines how he can become sick and die of dis-ease. He is "ill"—but in a different way.

Psychosomatic Disease

In the *psychosomatic* situation, we meet the genuinely ill person. A psychosomatic disease is very real, indeed. The person is sick and knows he is sick. The illness is actual: an ulcer, high blood pressure, asthma, etc. The distinguishing characteristic of psychosomatic illness is, however, that while the discomfort or pain stems from a bodily condition, the condition itself has its origins in the person's psychological adaptation to his situation and/or environment. In other words, his high level of anxiety and the pressures in his living result in *physical* breakdown of bodily adaptation.

By the 1930s the first psychosomatic diseases had been identified: the tension headache, the upset stomach (including ulcers), and some of the allergies, including hay fever. Since then, other psychosomatic illnesses, such as essential hypertension, and certain heart ailments have been shown to have a psychosomatic component. Even some of the illnesses which are known to be germ-related are now beginning to be investigated from the psychosomatic viewpoint, since they seem to occur more frequently under situations of prolonged psychological and social stress. Tuberculosis, diseases of the kidneys and liver, and even the common cold, cancer, and accident proneness (as mentioned earlier) occur with a higher frequency among people under severe psychological and physiological stress.[19]

It is important at this juncture that the reader understand this point very clearly. When we say that some forms of cancer show a

---

* The standard joke is that the hypochondriac generally lives to a ripe old age, even outliving his physician and many of his family—simply because he takes such very good care of himself!

definite psychosomatic component, we do not intend that a person treat his cancer through psychological means. Cancer is a very definite physical illness, as is the stomach ulcer. Persons with these conditions are in need of immediate medical help (surgery, radium or cobalt treatments, rest, etc.), and it matters little, once a condition has developed, what "stresses" produced it: what count are the physical skills and knowledge of the physician who can save one's life. How a person came to get the ulcer is something that can be examined later on, when the immediate, organic crisis has been dealt with.

What *psychosomatic* means is that the disease occurs more frequently under prolonged stress—stress which can be "psychological" rather than "physical." Or to put it more precisely, the distinction between "psychological" stress and "physical" stress becomes more and more arbitrary, as we shall soon see.*

There is mounting evidence also that certain types of personalities are more susceptible than others to certain kinds of disease. These findings have led to a kind of psychological "profile" among psychosomatic diseases.

Ulcers.   Ulcer patients, for example, are "worriers." As a group, they are constantly anxious lest they not always do their best, but they can also be a little afraid that their best is not going to be good enough. Because they are worriers, they are often overconscientious and may be more methodical than they need to be in order to avoid mistakes. Their worries "gnaw away" at them in the meantime. And as their worrying continues overtime, their stomach acids become so potent that they begin to erode a section from the stomach lining until the pain and nausea of ulcers result. Ulcers have even been produced experimentally in animals by subjecting them to intermittent emotional and physical stress.[20]

Heart Disease.   Heart disease patients seem to do their worrying on a different level of the *soma* (body). As a group they tend to show a calm and serene exterior as well as a steady and unified personality. They are often committed to completing a job, no matter what the pressure! So they are often committed (whether

---

* If stress is the natural "wear-and-tear" on the body, stressors are any agents that produce wear-and-tear. Stressors can be starvation, fatigue (lack of rest), or toxic substances, of course. But they can also be emotional impact or too much excitement. A visit from one's mother-in-law or a busy over-fun-filled vacation can both be stressors!

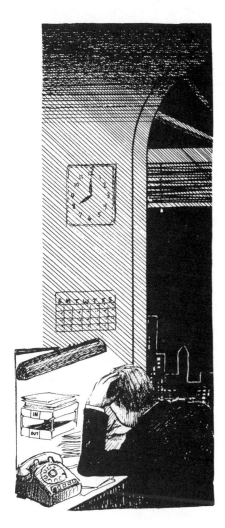

The person who breaks down with a heart disease has often demonstrated a pattern of working long hours and the inability to relax off the job.

they want to admit it or not) to working long hours on a job with fewer and fewer vacations and with less and less recreational time and, in the end, without even the ability to relax "off the job." The heart disease patient is the truly committed person who "puts his heart into his job" until the pressure begins to kill him. His calm exterior belies the internal stress and pressure that he experiences, yet he can continue to overwork and suppress his anger and anxiety until that moment when the internal stress "blows up" in the coronary artery. By then, the pressure is not so much a psychological difficulty as a medical emergency!

Asthma. Asthma is the psychosomatic response wherein the person experiences an extreme degree of difficulty in breathing. In the asthma attack the person feels as if he may suffocate at any moment. Sometimes the attack may last for hours, and the wheezing and coughing can continue until the person feels exhausted. An asthma attack frequently ends with convulsive coughing, an experience no one wants to repeat once he has experienced it. Asthma attacks are now acknowledged to be intimately related to emotional upset. For example, asthma in children is found mostly in extremely anxious and insecure children who feel rejected or "smothered" by one or both of their parents. If the asthmatic child continues to grow up as an "asthmatic," his asthma attacks can become his principal method of expressing anger, hostility, resentment, and general unhappiness. When he gets into a tight, emotional spot he feels he cannot cope with, he may get out of it by having an asthmatic attack right then and there. This response is calculated to bring on others' concern, guilt feelings, and eventually the physical attention he feels he needs to survive.

Accident-proneness.   Accident-proneness (the tendency to have a higher-than-average frequency of accidents) is recognized now as a definite syndrome related to emotional instability. Investigators have found, for example, that automobile accidents are more frequent among the young, the aggressive, the maladjusted, and those from larger families or broken homes.[21] Apparently, these children have not received enough feelings of love and caring from others, and so they do not develop love and caring for themselves, with the result that they mutilate themselves via "accidents," or whatever.

Other investigators believe that this self-mutilation is actually an expression of hostility and anger toward an uncaring world—only that it is turned inward, against the self. At any rate, the evidence seems to suggest that there is more truth than poetry in the saying, "There goes an accident looking for a place to happen," when we see an automobile racing far above normal speeds.

Karl Menninger writes of an example of self-mutilation in a man who had become so angry with his brother

> that he consciously contemplated killing him; he restrained himself, however, not only on account of the law and other such consequences but because, for his mother's sake, he felt a deep protective obligation to this brother. He became so remorseful that he made several attempts at suicide, all of which barely failed. For reasons not entirely clear to him, he then began to drive his car with a reckless abandon which seemed certain to result disastrously. But in spite of several serious accidents he was not killed. Next he conceived the

notion of exposing himself to some disease that would kill him and deliberately tried to get syphilis by repeated exposures.[22]

The common cold.   It has been maintained for some time that 50 percent (or more) of the physical ailments which physicians treat in their offices are psychosomatic in origin. Many physical complaints, in other words, seem to be due to the pressures and anxieties of everyday living which individuals are not able to resolve. Unresolved anxieties can provoke bodily conditions that break down body tissues. Even that famous symptom the common cold is now suspected to be a specific kind of psychosomatic response to unresolved difficulties. Therapists oftentimes view the symptoms of a cold as unexpressed crying. The person does not weep for one reason or another; instead, he "contracts a cold," which has all the physical symptoms of weeping: watery eyes, sniffling, blowing one's nose, a red face, and puffy eyes. In this way, these clinicians say, the body is able to do the weeping it needs to do even when the person (out of pride or even denial that he feels hurt or wounded) does not permit himslf the needed release of weeping or crying.

THE GERM THEORY OF DISEASE

The concepts of psychosomatic medicine may be hard to accept. We have been conditioned all our lives to the idea that "germs cause disease." But if germs cause disease (as we have been taught from Grade 1 on), how, then, can the same disease have a psychosomatic component?

The germ theory of disease was first formulated in the middle of the nineteenth century. We owe much to Robert Koch, Robert Lister, Louis Pasteur, and other nineteenth-century scientists who helped to disprove the idea that disease was caused by "evil spirits." The "evil spirits" turned out to be natural phenomena: tiny microorganisms—bacilli, bacteria, viruses, etc., loosely called "germs."

But these scientists also discovered that each disease has a specific "causal" microorganism. In other words, tuberculosis is caused by the tubercle bacillus, and the tubercle bacillus results only in tuberculosis and not in mumps, measles, or smallpox. This principle is the *doctrine of specific etiology*, which has been taught for generations in beginning science classes. In fact, schoolchildren grow up so conditioned to this belief that they scarcely think that there may be anything wrong with this theory.

Scientists began to realize in the late twenties that while the doctrine of specific etiology is a powerful predictive tool, it does not account for all the factors involved in contracting a disease. How is it that one person may get a severe case of tuberculosis, for example, and another person, apparently exposed to the same germs, may respond with a mild case of the disease and recover quickly—*or even not get the disease at all?* Then there is the situation of the person who seems to get one cold after another as compared with the person who even in a "cold epidemic" seems to remain free of the infection.

As science began to uncover more of the facts regarding our natural biological environment, scientists came to acknowledge that the world is full of germs and microorganisms of all kinds. Indeed, the interior of our bodies is now known to be a virtual "hothouse" for bacteria. In fact if our digestive tract did not literally team with (helpful) bacteria, we would have a hard time digesting the food we eat and eliminating what we no longer need. Moreover, the germs which "cause" various diseases abound in our atmosphere. Thus, the common cold virus, for example, is everywhere. Why, then, scientists kept wondering, do we only become ill from certain germs at certain times and not at others? Also, why is a person seemingly more vulnerable to sickness at certain times in his life and not at others? Obviously, there must be something more to the infecting process than just contact with a particular germ. And to say that someone is immune to this or that germ, or vulnerable because he is "run down," only begs the question.

The question that is being "begged" is the question of the *necessary and sufficient conditions* for a process to occur. For example, "germs" of some kind need to be present for an infection process to occur: they are a *necessary* condition. Without the tubercle bacillus there can be no tuberculosis infection.

The *sufficient* conditions are more complex, since they deal with a variety of "environmental" matters—such as the present state of health of the person, his psychological stability, and his life history. "Germs" may be a *necessary* part of an infectious disease, but they do not account *sufficiently* for all the conditions. This is a psychosomatic theory.

THE GENERAL ADAPTATION SYNDROME

The Swiss physiologist Hans Selye pondered these questions for more than thirty years.[23] Even as a young medical student he noticed that most common infectious diseases, whether the common cold, measles, mumps, tuberculosis, or chicken pox, all seem to begin in much the same fashion. There is fever and a sore throat, a runny nose, aches and pains, and a headache. *No matter what "disease"* these symptoms finally reflect, most infectious diseases nonetheless seem to have *the same set of beginning symptoms.* Selye called this the "just-sick" or the "not well" syndrome.

Many years of training and work were to elapse before Selye got his chance to research his original intuition. In Montreal, Canada, he discovered that prolonged stress of any kind produces disease (dis-ease); and if continued, stress assuredly results in death—the complete cessation of all life functions. He made these discoveries primarily through his work with experimental animals. There he saw that stressors such as extreme cold, repeated electric shock, poison, and inadequate diet all resulted in a set of symptoms (a *syndrome*). Selye found that the animal always died when the stress situation was prolonged enough. He discovered also that the experimental animals could suffer from many of the same diseases human persons can die from: ulcers, hypertension, and diseases of the kidneys, liver, and other vital organs. He found clear evidence that these diseases are the consequents of irritants other than germs. But he also found that the contraction of many infectious diseases as well is facilitated by prolonged stress.

The general adaptation syndrome is the term Selye used to describe what happens when an organism experiences a dangerous amount of stress.

The beginning of the *stress syndrome* always seemed to involve a primary period he called the *alarm reaction.* With further stress, the *stage of resistance* appeared. If stress at this level continued, the animal's abilities to cope diminished, and the final stage, the *stage of exhaustion,* would appear, and ultimately death would occur.

1. The alarm reaction. When an experimental animal is first subjected to physical or psychological stress (electrical shock, extreme cold, poison, etc.), the animal's body reacts by increasing the rate of production of certain hormones and the levels of certain sugars and salts. All of these secretions strengthen the body's defense system against the oncoming stressors. Such a response is the body's normal method of meeting an emergency, since these increased levels of body chemicals (hormones, salts, sugars) increase one's strength and endurance. Newspapers often carry stories of persons who react with seemingly superhuman strength in times of crisis. It may be no more than a six-line item describing how John Jones lifted the front end of his sports car to free a loved one pinned underneath. Or someone may have jumped from the second-floor window of a burning building and landed unhurt. In such situations the body reacts to the emergency stress with a kind of total psychophysiological response that is clearly beyond our usual capacities to function.

Walter B. Cannon, one of the early and great workers in psychosomatic medicine, called this emergency reaction of the organism the *fight-or-flight syndrome*.[24] Cannon observed that once an animal perceives a threat in his environment, his body reacts in specific ways which enable him to meet the emergency. Rate of respiration, heart rate, and sugar production increase markedly. Thus, more energy becomes quickly available so the animal can prepare himself to stand and fight the "enemy"—or to take flight if that is the more appropriate action. The pupils of the eyes also dilate (improving vision), and the blood tends to withdraw from the body surface, thereby protecting the animal against bruising and bleeding of the skin and increasing the supply of blood to the vital organs. Blood-clotting capacity also increases, as does also the tension in the striated muscles, providing for more rapid behavior response when needed.

Selye's alarm reaction is somewhat different from Cannon's fight-or-flight reaction. The latter response refers generally to a brief period of intense stress where the organism is "deciding" whether to flee from the perceived danger or to stand and fight. In the stress reaction Selye describes, the fight-or-flight reaction

When confronted with a threat, the organism reacts with the flight-or-fight syndrome.

continues over time; thus, the situation is one of *prolonged* stress. In the alarm reaction the animal continues to secrete sugars, salts, and hormones (to defend itself against the emergency stressor) for so long that the animal's body functions begin to break down, as Selye's research shows, in the form of a withered thymus, diseased adrenal glands, bleeding ulcers, etc.

2. Stage of resistance.   If the stressor (physical or emotional) is not too severe and the animal does not die, the animal seems to be able to recover from the first-stage alarm reaction pattern. His adrenal glands return to normal size, although they continue to function at abnormally high levels of secretion. The ulcerative condition also disappears, and the thymus returns to a normal state. In the *stage of resistance,* the animal's body thus *seems* to be adapting to the stressful condition by maintaining certain physiological defenses—for example, an increased production of white blood cells to defend against noxious germs and viruses. On the surface, everything appears to have returned to normal. Indeed, it was sometimes hard for Selye to tell the experimental animals (the animals under stress) from the control animals (the animals not subjected to the stressor). All seems well . . . for a while.

3. Stage of exhaustion.   But the apparent adaptation of Selye's experimental animals did not last for more than a few weeks. After that the animals got progressively weaker, their internal organs became dangerously diseased again, sugar and chloride production fell again to dangerously low levels, and the animals began to die within a month. In other words, the organism can sustain the supercharged defense rate for only so long. Its defenses or resistances then collapse and life ceases. The *stage of exhaustion,* by the way, is similar to the initial alarm reaction in that the same sets of responses are present and the same syndrome can be seen.

One more finding: in the stage of resistance, the body's defenses are marshaled only against the original stressor—for example, extreme cold. If the animal survives the alarm reaction stage and manages to achieve an adequate defense in the stage of resistance, it is a defense against only that one stressor condition. If the experimenters now add another stressor at the same time (say, electrical shock, which is considered an emotional stressor), the animal collapses immediately. Selye thereby demonstrated conclusively that as the number of stressful conditions in the environment increases the organism is correspondingly less able to cope (or even survive).

What does this mean for human existence? Well, let's take a theoretical application from the life of a young man who is doing his best to earn a living and provide for his wife and baby. He is having problems at his job which cause him some difficulty, but he manages to cope and live through this first stage of alarm. His body gears itself up to working under stressful conditions; as a result he is able to pass through the stage of alarm and is reacting with the stage of resistance. However, just as he thinks he is beginning to get on top of the mess at the job, his mother-in-law comes to visit and makes life hell for him at home as well. This additional stressor may very well be just enough to crack his stage of resistance, and he may then break down as revealed by some physical symptom —maybe a cold in the head or the flu, etc!

Selye makes very clear that *stress* is simply part of the natural "wear and tear" of life on the tissues of organisms. We cannot escape natural stress even if we wanted to, and who would want to lead such a dull life, if that were possible? But he does point out that an excess of stress or prolonged stress of any kind can do more than the normal wear and tear—it can break down body tissue in an injurious way!

Intoxication by stress.   Selye concluded that stress is the everyday "wear and tear" of life: it is the "common feature of biological activities." Stress cannot be avoided, he says, for even excitement and enjoyable recreation produce wear and tear on our bodies. But by understanding that contracting disease is made more likely by exaggerated responses on the level of some hormone-producing glands, we can at least try to eliminate those stressful situations in living which bring about such a condition. Selye expands Socrates' injunction to "know thyself" to apply not only to one's mind and emotions, but also to one's body. We need to recognize when we are getting too "keyed up" (those feelings of jitteryness and tingling sensations), to acknowledge when we are not getting enough rest, and to listen to our bodies when we begin to feel "on edge" or "all tensed up." Selye says a man can become intoxicated by his own hormone production, and it is wise to be aware also of the signs of *overstimulation.* Even when the stimulation at hand is enjoyable and exciting, long life and bodily health may require us to break off the interaction before it becomes stressful. To become aware of our critical stress level—and to watch that it does not exceed the level we can safely handle—is just as essential to good health as monitoring our intake of alcohol and food. *Intoxication by stress* is usually insidious simply because it may actually be enjoyable: we can become "addicted" to it. It is not always so easy to turn down the level of stimulation of one's body as it is to turn down the volume on TV. We can find that a stimulus, instead of being fun, is now a bother or even unpleasant, yet we are so tied to the stimulus that we are unable to prevent our bodies from reacting. Selye says we must therefore provide for relaxation in our daily lives. And relaxation does not necessarily mean play, for play can be taken too seriously, we can become overexcited, and we are again trapped in overproduction of hormones.

It is no exaggeration to call present Western civilization over-stimulating and overexciting. There is an almost constant barrage of information of all kinds being fed into our senses by television, motion pictures, newspapers, and radio. While we may temporarily adapt somehow to this complex of stimulation, Selye's findings regarding the stress syndrome do raise profound questions regarding the wisdom of that way of living. It is perhaps no accident that we now find an increasing interest in methods of relaxation in our culture. Yoga, meditation, and other mind- and muscle-relaxation techniques all attempt to eliminate these high levels of excitability and anxiety. By training the person to withdraw "inside" himself, they offer a method of sustaining bodily health and a sorely needed respite from the chronic high level of stress and tension which our present civilization continues to induce in its members. (These methods are further discussed in Chapter 13.)

The Effects of Life Change and Life Crisis upon Health

Selye studied the stress syndrome as it appeared in experimental animals and then extrapolated from these findings to the effects of stress on humans. His work seems to us of fundamental importance in psychosomatic theory. More recently there have been some equally challenging studies of stress as it appears in the form of change. This work was done with humans, and the researchers discovered that *change alone*—even when it is seen as beneficial or "happy"—can have ill effects upon a person's psychosomatic balance, on his health. Two researchers, T. H. Holmes, and R. H. Rahe, developed a "life-change units scale," which measures how much change an individual has been subjected to over a given period of time.[25] Some of the items in their scale take note of obviously hurtful and traumatic events—the death of a loved one, being fired from a job, a painful divorce, being flunked out of school, etc. What is thought-provoking about their research findings is that even agreeable changes in one's situation—marriage, birth of a baby, promotion, a vacation—are considered emotionally stressful.* This was found to be the case not only with American subjects, but with Europeans and Japanese also.

Holmes and Rahe began to see that persons with many life changes—those with high *life crises units* (LCU) scores—were more likely to suffer from ill health than those with lower LCU scores. Moreover, there seemed to be a definite additive aspect to the scale: the higher the LCU score, the more likely the person was to come down with an abrupt and serious illness.

Of the crises rated by Holmes and Rahe, the death of a spouse is assigned the highest LCU score (100). This makes sense, for the death of a spouse involves not only the sense of personal loss and grief which follows, but also severe dislocations in personal habits (such as eating and sleeping) and the continued stress of learning to adapt to social relations as a single person rather than as a couple.

Any kind of externally imposed change in accustomed habit patterns can result in an increase in one's LCU score: going away to college, moving to another place, going into the army—all of these can be stressful because of the changes in eating, sleeping, relaxation, and recreation habits, not to mention giving up old friends and the effort in finding new ones.

There is also, in some cases, the pressure of adapting to new places, new smells, new feelings. "Bumming around" the country can be a form of recreation for our youth, and it seems carefree and fun, at least on the surface. Frequent changes in eating, sleeping, and environment can nonetheless produce considerable stress.

Holmes and Rahe's early research showed there was a marked correlation—i.e., a definite relationship—between a high LCU score

---

* These findings are not so surprising once we consider what is involved in a change—any change—in our situation. Consider, for example, the advent of a vacation traveling by car to a distant place for a couple and their two young children. Almost any parent will admit that many hours of driving are a lot easier on the nerves if the children are not along. We are reminded of their wanting to stop for frequent rest periods and complaints that they are hungry. Then think of the mother's attempts to keep the children from getting bored and from fighting, and we immediately understand how vacation trips sometimes can be less happy and more tiring than one originally hoped and fantasied.

and an abrupt and serious change in a person's health. *Within eighteen months* of registering such a score, persons came down with major illnesses: tuberculosis, mononucleosis, cancer, leukemia, etc. Further research revealed that even short-term periods (of 2 or 3 days) of high LCU scores resulted in minor aches, pains, colds, and other discomforts.[26] What this means is that the everyday minor illnesses we take for granted, such as the common cold, appear more often when we are stressed for even just a couple of days. Headaches are more frequent when there is tension in our environment; stomach aches, hay-fever, and other allergies are more likely to reappear in times of duress, or where there are major changes in our physical or psychological state.

Stress factors are the obvious problems which we encounter repeatedly in our present working and living situations. They involve all the kinds of adjustment difficulties in new situations, such as moving to another city, taking a new job, going to college. They may also involve family problems, unhappy work relationships, high-pressure jobs, continued worry about one's family and relatives —any and all of these can function as the kind of *profound* stress which makes for equally pronounced changes in the psychophysiological balance of the body.

But there is evidence, also, that subtle pressures can create stress and anxiety and, in time, create equally profound changes in the body. For example, promotion of an executive to a higher position may be welcomed, yet it can cause ill health and instability, particularly among men with only a high-school education as compared with men who have some college background.[27]

Research shows there is more frequent ill health among minority-group members in the United States than among white middle-class Protestants, and more physical and nervous breakdowns occur among the unemployed than among those who are steadily employed.[28] Tension regarding the security of one's social status and concern about being discriminated against can and do work as profound stressors. But let us not forget also that the anger and resentment a person may feel because of his insecurity in a supposedly egalitarian society can also cause psychosomatic reactions.

A SUMMARY AND SOME CONCLUSIONS

In the first part of this chapter we pointed out how we are facing more anxiety than the generations which have preceded ours. Today we also have to learn to deal with general global anxiety as well as our personal anxieties. In the second part of the chapter, we discussed some of the effects of anxiety and stress on our emotional lives and physical well-being.

Some of the obvious concomitants of anxiety and stress are now well known: nervous tension, headaches, ulcers, etc. But other kinds of infectious diseases, such as tuberculosis and the common cold, are also associated with stressful conditions.

The general adaptation syndrome suggests that we can build up defenses against profound stress and that we can thereby cope and function for a period of time. That level of adaptation, however, turns out to be a kind of supercharged bodily defense mechanism which cannot be maintained for very long. Running a machine at 100 percent power eventually results in the machine "burning up." Selye's research has shown that much the same kind of thing happens with the human organism: if we demand that we function at peak levels for more than a short period of time, our defense system eventually collapses and the body then falls prey to disease. And this effect is cumulative: as the numbers of stressors increase, the greater the likelihood that one's body will "break down"—it is sometimes as simple as that!

Related to the stress levels in health and disease is the paradoxical consideration that overstimulation and excitement can become a form of intoxication which feeds on itself—i.e., we can become "addicted" to being overstimulated or "high." For that reason each person must learn to know himself, what are his essential needs for food, rest, and relaxation, and even what variety he requires in his relationships with the world (slowed down one day, bright and lively the next, etc.). Knowing our essential needs includes learning our unique anxiety reactions—what they are, when they occur, and how we seem to adapt to their causes.

Finally, change—particularly a major change in one's life situation—is a stressor that cannot be safely ignored. Not only does traumatic (painful) change affect a person's balance and health, but even so-called happy or beneficial changes can be stressful, creating a crisis for the individual.

We live in a time of great sociological and technical change; we are being continually subjected to new inventions, new styles of dress, new modes of living, new forms of marriage and child rearing, and all of these experiments in relationships can become stressful, provoking emotional imbalances in one's everyday adaptation and thus enabling a "disease process" to attack the organism when they are prolonged. It behooves us, then, to learn "new" ways of meeting and dealing with our anxieties—getting to recognize and understand them and ultimately finding ways to cope with and transcend them.

Can a person live a completely "anxiety-free" existence in our time? Possibly, but we do not know anyone who does. The persons we know who for the most part function well and happily are those who have looked their anxieties "in the eye" and have learned to cope. They seem to us well disciplined in the sense of knowing what they want, who they are, and where they belong. They seem also aware of the tolerance limits of their bodies and are more able thereby to arrive at a balance between boredom and over-stimulation, lethargy and frenzy, dependence and independence. In a sense, they have come to terms with their world: they acknowledge what it is like, and they have learned how to find viable lifestyles for themselves despite the stresses and tensions they are seemingly exposed to in their day-to-day living.

RECOMMENDED READINGS

ALTIZER, THOMAS J. and WILLIAM HAMILTON. *Radical Theology and the Death of God.* Indianapolis, Ind.: Bobbs-Merrill, 1966 (paperback). This book broke on the reading public as a series of shock waves. Written by two Protestant theologians, it proclaims a new approach to theological understanding and a methodology for living as Christian atheists.

BOORSTIN, DANIEL. *The Image: A Guide to Pseudo-Events in America.* New York: Harper & Row, 1964 (paperback). Boorstin has created a new term in the area of communication: the *pseudo-event.* A pseudo-event is not real: it is a preplanned, blown-up news item. It is not so much a segment of reality as an illusion of a real event designed to satiate our demand for sensationalism. A pseudo-event is contrived more to make headlines than to represent real events. Boorstin applies this term to the many facets of our mass media which he says cause us to be inundated with phony, exaggerated, sometimes fictional "news" stories. He levels his criticisms at our newspapers, magazines, television, advertising and travel agencies, publishing houses, movies, etc., in that the very media we have invented to enlarge our vision have now become "deceivers" and "obstructors" to our vision: "There is a crime of deception being committed in America today and each of us is the principal."

CANNON, WALTER B. *The Wisdom of the Body*. Rev. ed. New York: W. W. Norton, 1939 (paperback, 1963).

Cannon gave the scientific world a profound understanding of how the body reacts to emergency situations. Although his book deals with various physiological functions and changes within the organism, he wrote this book for the benefit of nonscientists. It is consequently excellent background reading for those who wish to know more about our internal homeostatic processes. It is particularly recommended for students of nursing and other health-related professions.

CARSON, RACHEL. *Silent Spring*. New York: Fawcett World Library, 1970 (paperback).

Carson was the first to sound the ecological fire alarm loud enough to be heard by the citizens of the Western world. She predicted that unless we take heed of how we are poisoning the earth, there shall come a time when all life shall cease to exist. Utilizing her background as a scientist and her innate writing ability, she documented her case with deadly conviction.

GREEN, HANNAH. *I Never Promised You a Rose Garden*. New York: Signet Books, 1964 (paperback).

In this chapter we spoke of psychological breakdown as a severe reaction to stress. This book is a novel about a sixteen-year-old girl who shares with us her outer life of conflict and torment and her inner world of madness to which she flees to make up for the disappointments and painful experiences in her family life. This book gives an insight into the world of madness and is a literary masterpiece as well.

KENISTON, KENNETH. *The Uncommitted: Alienated Youth in American Society*. New York: Dell, 1960, 1965 (paperback).

Through extensive in-depth interviews with young people, Keniston reveals some of the lack of personal satisfaction that caused post-World War II youth to become disenchanted with American society, disillusioned about the world situation, and alienated from the values of their parents. It is a fairly large book despite the fact that it is a paperback, and therefore recommended for people who like to read.

PACKARD, VANCE. *The Pyramid Climbers*. New York: McGraw-Hill, 1962 (hardcover). New York: Fawcett, 1964 (paperback).

Packard has been widely heralded for his vivid portrayal of businessmen's experiences and tactics as they travel the road of social mobility.

He likens the upward struggle of young executives to the task of climbing a pyramid—the apex of which is aptly titled the "bitch goddess, Success." He describes the ascent as "assaulting the slippery, crevice ridden slopes" as executives "learn the secret love of negotiating difficult passages. They sharpen some very special traits, such as maze-solving ability, which help them survive and advance." Packard elaborates on the climb by describing the "screening, grooming, and pruning" processes, the "well-packaged executive," certain "strategies and incentives," as well as "hazards and harrassments."

SELYE, HANS. *The Stress of Life.* New York: McGraw-Hill, 1956 (hardcover—also available in paperback).

Selye is one scientist who can talk and write simply while dealing with a complex subject. Reading this book is a rewarding experience for the lay person and advanced student alike. Because Selye writes so intimately of his successes, failures, and perplexities, the reader gains an understanding not only of the stress syndrome, but of the personal drama of the scientific quest as well.

TOFFLER, ALVIN. *Future Shock.* New York: Bantam Books, 1971 (paperback).

The quickening pace at which we conduct our lives and are forced to contend with technological and societal changes is bearing down on the human mind and body like that of an avalanche. The result of this speeded-up process of living is that we are losing our sense of time and reality. Future shock is no longer a distant, potential danger, says Toffler; rather, it is here and now. Future shock is a disease of change. This former best-seller is a shocker in itself.

When physical pain overwhelms us, we defend ourselves by losing consciousness; when psychological pain threatens to overwhelm us, we resort to analogous defense mechanisms.

4

DEFENDING MECHANISMS: A CONTINUING PROCESS OF SURVIVAL AND GROWTH

Each of us can stand just so much physical pain. When pain becomes too intense we lose consciousness (faint, black out) and thereby effectively block out the further conscious experience of pain. "Losing" consciousness, then, is one of the ways we defend ourselves against overwhelming forms of painful stimulation. Physical pain is one such stimulus, anxiety another.

Anxiety, then, is a form of pain. We tend to think of anxiety as "psychological pain," and so it is. But anxiety also has physiological symptoms, such as trembling, sweating, rapid heartbeat, blushing, etc. In its psychological aspect, anxiety can be experienced also in many forms: from shame and guilt feelings to feelings of self-doubt and unworthiness, to name just a few.

The study of anxiety is exceedingly complex, but let us begin with the very important consideration that, just as with physical pain, each one of us can stand only just so much anxiety. When that point is reached, we reach a psychological "trigger point" where we begin to defend ourselves against further painful stimulation. The methods by which we ward off these intense experiences of psychological pain are called *defense mechanisms*.

DEFENSE MECHANISMS AS A MEANS OF SURVIVAL

In some circles it has become a kind of verbal one-upmanship, or in-fighting technique, to confront someone with the statement, "You're being defensive!" That kind of confrontation implies that the speaker is himself free of defenses—which is illogical and absurd. No one is free of defenses. We all have defenses; we need them to survive both psychologically and physically as an organism. And that applies to everyone—even to the most enlightened among us. We need to have recourse to patterns of behavior with which to cope with the world and its problems. The real question is not whether we in fact have defense mechanisms, but how well do our defense mechanisms work.

DEFENSE MECHANISMS AS BARRIERS TO GROWTH

Although all our defense mechanisms are aimed at helping the organism survive, some defensive operations can become so dominating and self-perpetuating that they block psychological growth. For example, a certain defensive maneuver may have been a means of coping with frustrating and threatening situations when we were children, but when continued in adulthood it may create difficulties for us because the behavior is no longer appropriate to adult life. Take, for example, the child who has learned how to get his mother's attention by whining or throwing temper tantrums. He has found that pattern of behavior a fairly successful way of getting attention when he needs it. If he continues to rely on whining as he grows up, however, he prevents himself from developing more adult ways of interacting with others. Such a person will be called "immature" or "childish," and he will eventually discover that rather than getting him what he wants, his behavior is self-defeating, that it prevents him from getting what he wants.

Our defense mechanisms impose a barrier to personality integration insofar as they blur our vision of the world, deafen our ears to what others are saying to us, and generally distort or confuse our perceptions of everyday experiences. Two psychologists put it very bluntly: our defense mechanisms make us "dumb," so that we do not demonstrate our intelligence.[1] Some people have a tendency to react to a chance remark as if it were designed to slight or attack them when no such offense was intended. Feelings of hurt, anger, or resentment aroused in us by such an imagined slight can then block our ability to view reality. We may then spend unnecessary hours of pain and anxiety indulging in real or fanciful acts of revenge, retorts, or salving our own wounds—hours that could have been put to better, more creative use.

Knowledge of the major defense mechanisms and learning to recognize them and how and when we use them is therefore a use-

Defense mechanisms are ways of protecting ourselves, but they can also weigh us down in our striving for further personality growth.

ful technique in any search for self-knowledge and personality integration. This project can be extremely difficult for the beginning student of personality, particularly when he is attempting to study and observe his own set of defenses. Just as color-blind persons may never realize that they cannot see certain colors until this is pointed out to them, we may not be aware of certain of our defense mechanisms until someone else brings them to our attention. As has been said, it is easier to see the mote in another's eye than in one's own. Becoming aware of our defenses is therefore a matter of continued study and devotion to learning *who* we are and *how* we act in many situations.

THE RIGHT TO MAINTAIN DEFENSES

None of us has to go in for needless self-recrimination or time-wasting apologies because of our defense mechanisms. All of us have them. Or rather, the defense mechanisms "have us"! And it is often sufficient, therefore, to say, "Oh, I've discovered one of the blocks to my growth!" One can be justifiably proud of just that statement. We can then choose to work on that defense mechanism. Or we can choose not to do anything further on it just now. There are moments when your authors concede that the stress is so great and their ability to cope so strained, they'll take every defense mechanism they can get! The right to maintain one's defense implies, therefore, some kind of democratic environment in which the person is allowed to discover his capabilities and his limitations at his own pace and his own rhythm.

TYPES OF DEFENSE MECHANISMS

Defense mechanisms can be categorized as different ways of reacting and responding, but it is always well to remember that no matter how *aggressive* the defense mechanism appears to be, it is always a *defending behavior* against pain. Since adults generally have more sophisticated levels of defense, we shall start off by illustrating how defense mechanisms work in children.

Let us suppose a little boy sees a little girl holding a toy which he wants, but which the girl refuses to give up. The child then has several options open to him by which he can deal with his painful frustration. He may become angry and attack the girl by hitting her. Or he may take the toy from her by force. Both of these examples are *direct expressions* of his frustration.

There are other, more subtle means, however, of getting what he wants. He can, for example, begin to cry in an attempt to make the little girl feel sorry enough for him that she gives him the toy. He can also resort to a temper tantrum; or he may choose a common childhood phrase, "All right, for you! I won't play with you again," a kind of children's blackmail technique.

He can also resort to defense mechanisms which turn away from the attempt to secure the desired object. He can simply retreat into "self-pity" and nurse his hurt feelings. Or he can deny that he really wants the toy and emulate Aesop's fox by saying (to himself or aloud), "Well, it isn't much of a toy anyway!" Or he can substitute an imaginary toy for the real one and engage in a dramatic daydream that will diminish his feeling of frustration. Finally, he may decide to compromise by finding something else to play with, even if the substitute object does not interest him too much at the moment.

Defending by Attack

As in the example of the boy who first tries to take the toy away from the girl by force, attack is the most aggressive form of defense— at least it is certainly the most uninhibited form of defense. The need to strike back has been studied under experimental conditions by Nathan Azrin,[2] who believes this response to be a basic instinctual reflex in animals. Azrin observed that when animals are shocked by electric current they will immediately attack another animal close by. If there is no other animal to attack, a shocked animal will bite and attack an inanimate object, such as a ball. Should there be nothing else to vent their rage response upon, the animal may even bite himself. Azrin concluded that this pain-attack response is a kind of "pushbutton" response with the same sequence, shock-pain-attack, following always in rapid order. Furthermore, there seemed to be no lessening of the attack response over time: the animal attacks every time, ad infinitum! Many a reader will recognize this response if he's ever had an injured dog. When the owner bends down to help him, the dog may even bite his beloved master. What Azrin's experiments suggest is that any kind of intense pain is a total organismic sensation, and that the organism—be it animal or man—tends to react to the intense stressor by striking back at the closest convenient object.

Scapegoating. Scapegoating is one of the more subtle and less direct forms of attack. The word itself comes from the biblical custom of symbolically heaping the sins of the community onto a goat, which was then sent into the wilderness, thereby relieving the people of the burden of their anxieties. More recently, *scapegoating* has come to mean blaming a particular person or group for the misfortunes of oneself, one's group, or even one's entire nation or race. For example, Adolf Hitler, who had a profound understanding of

Scapegoating is the attacking of a certain person or group of people in order to feel cleansed of feelings of unhappiness, sinfulness, dissatisfaction, etc.

group psychology, directed his own sense of frustration and failure into anti-Semitism and proceeded to plan and carry through a pogrom the likes of which the civilized world had never seen.* No leader of a nation, whether an authoritarian dictator or a democratic prime minister or president, can long carry out a major policy that the populace does not accept. In Hitler's case, he merely channeled and orchestrated the already-present anti-Semitism in Germany.

Scapegoating takes many forms. In the United States our own particular form has been the scapegoating of the black race by white society. We struggle and attempt now to amend these inequities through social legislation. This is a measure of our capacities to grow as a nation—as a community which still believes that certain truths are self-evident, or need to be. We are left meanwhile with the residues of scapegoating in our language nonetheless. Such words as *nigger, wop, redneck, gook, kike, spik* are examples of our everyday testament to name-calling—which are the surface manifestations of scapegoating: a more subtle form of attack that has to do with verbal rather than physical assault.[3]

Verbal aggression.   Some persons become so sensitive to actual or imagined insults that they adopt the kind of "acid" defense called *sarcasm*. In some groups, particularly among adolescents, verbal insult is relied upon as a way of relating to others, as when they feel unable to reveal friendship feelings. For the high school student, sarcasm may even denote friendship for another person. In that case, much of the obvious sarcasm is merely a front for the dynamic that goes something like, "I'll cut you down before you do it to me . . . in fact, I'll cut myself down before you do it to me!"

The person who in later life still relies on acid remarks as a way of relating and defending himself is adopting the life style of *verbal aggression*. He may continue to experience himself as "winning" battles with his associates. Indeed, his associates may adopt behaviors aimed at appeasing him—such as letting him have his own way to avoid the acid comment that reduces oneself to nothing. They may even "cozy up" to him in the mistaken belief that ap-

---

* Before Hitler's anti-Semitism had run its course 5 to 6 million Jews were sacrificed in the gas chambers of Dachau, Auschwitz, and other concentration camps. The horror of that event has not yet been integrated into our understanding of ourselves as contemporary men. We speak of Hitler's understanding of group psychology as being *profound* in the sense that he was able to so manage a law-abiding people— through neopagan rituals and mass meetings in the late evening (when people are tired and therefore more impressionable) so they would come to accept his thesis: the Jews are responsible for Germany's misfortune!

peasement is the way to avoid attack. Though such a person may seem to have a "keen wit," may even consider himself competent and successful in everyday living, what he does not realize is the extent of his loneliness, his lack of genuine friendship. He may sense that others do not trust him, that they may actually fear him and dislike him. Yet he is caught in the vicious cycle of his verbal aggression wherein wit does not ease, but makes for uneasiness and distance. So the cycle spirals, culminating in the anecdotal situation of the person who shouts at his therapist, "I said, 'I don't know why I don't have any friends.' Why don't you listen, you blockhead!"

Projection.   Projection is one of the more frequent defense mechanisms in our world today. It is a powerful way of defending ourselves from insight into our own motivations. In its simplest meaning, projection means attributing the emotions, feelings, and motivations *we* experience to the environment—in particular to other persons. We have already discussed one form of projection—scapegoating. We are here speaking of projection that is of the more personal type.

Projecting our feelings onto others is a natural way we have of understanding other people. Because of this ability, it is possible to identify with another's joys and his sorrows, and so help him to grow. Because of his empathic ability to project his feelings and insights, the novelist, poet, or playwright (who help us to understand our own motivations more fully) can create great works of art. It is only where projection becomes a barrier to growth that it is a negative force rather than a positive one.

An example will help. The husband who, for instance, is secretly eager to have affairs with other women may attribute his own motivations to his wife and even accuse her of seeking or actually having an affair with other men when she is simply being friendly toward them. He is not able to come to grips with his own desires to dally with other women and thus he projects these impulses onto his wife, who in this instance is blameless. Or projection may explain the behavior of a mother who has not faced up to her own earlier promiscuity and now suspects her adolescent daughter of being promiscuous—granted, again, that there is no reality to the mother's suspicion.

Projection as a form of defending the self against inadmissible impulses and desires is a *powerful* defense mechanism. Its power resides in the fact that we disown or deny that these very impulses and needs are part of our own ongoing personality. Yet the impulses and needs are there, and may not be repressed with impunity. It is well for us to acknowledge their existence. And that acknowledgment leads us to the insight that we are not so much looking through a window into the world of others so much as we are looking into a mirror and seeing ourselves!

Defending by Withdrawal

Instead of aggressing against another, the human being can withdraw when the pain of anxiety or frustration is too much to bear and when he cannot cope with it in an aggressive way. This form of defense is easily seen in children, who may turn away and pout, or cry, or start fantasizing that they have a toy that is even better than the one they are denied. Withdrawal is a kind of "giving up" in the face of an overwhelming environment.

Introjection. *Introjection* can be considered the opposite side of the coin to projection. In projection, we attribute our own motivations to others. In introjection, we take into ourselves ideas, beliefs about the world and society and ourselves, and make those beliefs and experiences part of our own living. Introjection is not to be confused with the process, as we grow up, of incorporating into ourselves the values of our parents and others. When a particular value fits into our living and understanding of ourselves, when it is a useful and beneficial value, then we have *identified* with that value and made it our own. It is only when the value that we have taken into ourselves is incompletely assimilated (swallowed whole, as it were, and lodged uncomfortably within us) that it is an *introjection*. An example may help. A student of our acquaintance came for counseling help because, she said, she was "overly dependent on others." Every time she began to feel close to someone, she withdrew from the relationship: her impulse evidenced to her that she was indeed, once again, looking to be dependent on others. Yet as we got to know her over a period of time, we were impressed by what she had managed to do for herself in overcoming great environmental odds. She had come from a poor background, and had worked nights as a waitress so that she could put herself through two years of school. In addition to that, she lived by herself, saved money by making her own clothes, and was determined to "make something of herself." When we pointed out to her that this was rather unusual and hardly in keeping with the dependent type of personality, she was vastly relieved. In high school, evidently, she had been told by someone she respected that she was too dependent on others, and she had introjected this belief about herself so thoroughly that she denied herself any close relationships. She was able to rid herself of this introjected idea and go on to have a more satisfying personal life. Our advice to the reader: Beware of introjecting anyone else's ideas about you. Do not accept them as gospel unless you really agree with the statement.

The example we have given is relatively benign. A more severe example is of a man who had introjected the hatred his parents had had for each other and for their children. His guilt feelings about being alive were manifested in many ways. One of these manifestations was a highly apologetic manner. As an adult, he showed great hesitation in affirming himself and his own beliefs, views, and values. "If you don't mind my saying so . . ." "I'm awfully sorry to disagree . . ." "Of course, I don't know as much about this area as you do, but . . ."—these were the kind of preparatory defenses he used to anticipate the imagined and feared hatred of others. In the course of therapeutic treatment, he was able to disengage his own understanding of himself from his parents' hatred of one another.

Prisoners-of-war in the concentration camps of World War II provide a telling example of introjection as a defense, this time of a notable and more alarming nature. Some of the Jews responded to the confinement and the humiliation of scapegoating by scapegoating other Jews. They had introjected the hatred of their persecutors and the authoritarian values of their guards. They then became, in turn, as tyrannical toward their fellow prisoners as their oppressors.

Identification.   This is the process whereby individuals assimilate those values, attitudes, behavior patterns, etc. which seem to fit one's mold. Children tend to assimilate the attitudes and behavior patterns of the parent or other adults they feel most identified with. Identification differs from introjection in that introjected values seem to be taken in whole, without examination, sometimes without even liking them—somewhat like a foreign substance that manages to get underneath the skin. The values that are assimilated through the process of identification have been digested and become part of the person's own character structure—but always adapted to the person himself!

The martyrdom complex. The martyrdom complex is quite another kind of approach to the disappointment one may suffer in life. In the martyrdom complex we are speaking of the person who martyrs himself needlessly, since this suffering does little good for himself, for others, or for society. In truth, his "martyrdom" is a game which serves only to increase the present interpersonal difficulty of his life and of those around him.

A classic example of the martyrdom game or complex is the woman who allows her husband and children to dominate her. She does not fight overtly against that domination; in fact, she may even encourage it in subtle ways, and she seems to obtain a kind of solace from her suffering. She may believe that it is her fate in life to have no joy and happiness. She is intent, that is, on sacrificing her happiness for the happiness of others. Would she like to go on an outing with the family? "No," she tells them, "you go and have a good time; I'll be all right"—and then she adds in a tone that is meant to make them feel guilty, "and I'll have a nice dinner ready when you come back."

The martyred wife continues to pick up after her husband and children, and she cleans and scours daily—all the while imagining that some day she will be rewarded for her "good behavior." In the meantime, her spouse and children may come to understand that all this suffering and martyrdom, and their own sense of being indulged, is meant to make them all feel somehow guilty and ashamed of themselves. Eventually they may begin to strike back at this kind of blackmail, and they become resentful and sullen (and more manipulative). So the cycle continues: for after all, she is supposed to accept that kind of resentment, too!

Men can also engage in the martyrdom game. For example, men who are alcoholics withdraw from reality by dulling their anxieties through the bottle often assume the function of martyr in the family. There are other examples as well: the man who gives up his personal happiness for some noble cause; or the milquetoast who works needless extra hours at his office without recompense. Even the statesman or the civil rights leader can be involved in subtle forms of the martyrdom complex, envisioning themselves as sacrificing fulfillment in their personal lives for the "cause."

It is particularly informative and necessary to understand how the martyrdom game gets started in a family. These functions or roles, how they are chosen or assigned, are never accidental or arbitrary. They are a subtle and expressive representation of the state of a particular family's balance and health. The *need* for a martyr in the family is primarily that—someone needs to take on the function of being unhappy and unfulfilled, and the other members of that family need to go along with the game. As a form of withdrawal, it is often based on low self-esteem and on previous conditioning in which one comes to experience oneself as unworthy. The consequence of the game is always the unexpressed, yet surely experienced, resentment and guilt feelings which cast a pall over everyone.

Flight into failure. A series of experiments several years ago studied the effects of failure on achievement. They revealed that *when we fail in some task or project we tend to lower our goals.*[4] These experiments confirm the observations of school psychologists that some students just seem to make up their minds in advance to fail—and apparently so they won't be disappointed when they *do fail.* Thus, avoiding success is yet another method of insulating ourselves against the fear of failure. We see this sort of behavior in the student who avoids studying for a test. If he passes the test he can congratulate himself doubly:—first, for achieving a passing grade, and secondly, for the knowledge that he could have gotten a higher grade if he had studied. If he fails, on the other hand, he can console himself with the fantasy that he would have passed if he had studied.

Human beings are amazingly resourceful and creative on occasion and can flee into failure via many routes. One may use alcohol to such an extent that he becomes a chronic alcoholic and loses his friends, his job, the affection of his children, his wife, and even his family. Or he may choose to go the drug route, a common form of flight today. Or he may choose to become the eternal nomad, a drifter who changes jobs and residence frequently and never stays in one place long enough to succeed at anything (except being a drifter). Or he may direct his tensions and conflicts into psychosomatic illnesses, thereby closing off and limiting his capacities to deal with everyday life.

One of the more subtle (and ultimately destructive) forms of flight into failure is to choose a marriage partner, maybe even several in succession, who see to it that one never achieves his goals. Some men will deliberately select the kind of wife who will nag him, belittle him, fiercely compete with him, and point out his failures. A first marriage of that kind can be put down to inexperience. But when such a man gets a divorce and then, so to say, walks down

There are many paths to failure; among them are chronic alcoholism, nomadism, and drug abuse.

the street and marries a second wife just like his first, we can rightfully suspect that while the choice seems accidental, the goal (failure) is not.

There are indeed limitations to our abilities, and it is well we recognize them. But all too often we can become frightened by our own possibilities of success, and then we begin to flee into failure on a fantasy level—by thinking failure, imagining difficulties, etc.

Fear of success and flight into failure are quite common in our competitive society, in which we stress the values of succeeding, of getting on top and accumulating money and goods of all kinds. To avoid the stress and strain of our intensely competitive society, we may choose the path of failure. Flight into failure is often manifested in feelings of inadequacy. Where this pattern of flight has become characteristic of the person, we can speak then of an "inadequate personality." This form of defense can be extremely difficult to modify, for the person seems intent on failing no matter what anyone attempts to do for and with him.

Repression, denial, amnesia, and "forgetting." Sometimes when an event happens to us that is so overwhelming and bewildering that we are just not able to face it, we need to blot the event out of our consciousness and awareness. We can turn then to repression, denial, amnesia, or "forgetting" as ways of protecting ourselves from unbearable overstimulation. Freud believed that *repression* is the basic defense out of which all the other defensive maneuvers come.[5] When we use repression to reduce pain or other kinds of stimulation, we tighten up our awareness and refuse to see what is there. The result, then, is that we are not *conscious* of the event. Let's take the event where a child is injured and dies in her mother's arms. If the mother at that moment cannot face the

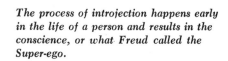

The process of introjection happens early in the life of a person and results in the conscience, or what Freud called the Super-ego.

reality of the situation, she may insist for a time that her child is still alive, and then rage at those around her for not doing something to help her child. She is saying, in effect, "I cannot, I *will* not believe this event is happening. This awful thing cannot be happening to me. I refuse to accept the truth."

A particularly poignant example of repression and denial is found in Margaret Mitchell's fine novel *Gone With the Wind*. Gerald O'Hara's plantation has been looted by Union soldiers, his daughters are without food, his beloved wife Ellen is dead, and his whole way of life has literally gone up in smoke. There is a scene where Gerald O'Hara and his daughter, Scarlett, have a disagreement, and he is scolding her for yelling at the servants and making the house slaves work in the fields. She retorts, in exasperation, that she is not asking anything more of them than she is doing herself. She tells him that all of them have come to desperate straits, that if they do not get enough money soon to pay the taxes they may even lose their house and home. She asks his advice about what to do, and it is then that Scarlett realizes that her father has retreated from the reality of the present situation, for he replies "I'll ask Mrs. O'Hara about the matter tomorrow." Thus, he is defending against the pain of acknowledging the disasters that have befallen him by resorting to denial and retreat into *amnesia*.

Young children often resort to *denial*. And parents sometimes mistake this defense for lying. For example, a child is asked if he did something, and he replies, in all innocence, that he has not. He may be conclusively lying, for children do lie on occasion; but he can also be telling the parent (and himself) that he "could not do such a thing!" Thus, the mere act of saying that he did not do something begins to be the truth for him. This is an example of denial in action.

Amnesia is another form of denial, but in amnesia the "forgetting" (or repression) is used not just to cloud one's awareness of a specific event, but to keep anything associated with it out of conciousness. Soldiers in combat, for example, have been known to reach such a peak of fear, anxiety, and exhaustion that they can no longer function and they collapse suddenly with "battle fatigue." At such times, they can also become amnesic and block out of consciousness the events which led up to their physical breakdown. In like manner, a person who has killed someone may not remember the event, since knowing himself to be a murderer may be more than he can integrate into his conscious awareness of himself. So he "forgets" the killing, i.e., he represses the knowledge of that event.

Any one of us can "forget" or "repress" or "deny" as ways of blocking off unpleasant experiences. For example, a person who fears going to the dentist may discover he has "accidentally" forgotten a dental appointment the day after. In like manner, we may "forget" to pay a particularly large bill or that we had to prepare for a test. "Forgetting a person's name" may be the equivalent (psychologically) of wanting to forget the person—particularly if he happens to be disagreeable.

Freud mentions many such examples of forgetting and repression in everyday life.[6] He helped us understand that these defenses are present not only in neurosis and psychosis, but with persons who seem to be getting along fairly well in their everyday lives. Some difficulties in bridging the so-called generation gap can arise when older persons repress memories of their own childhood experiences, particularly of things they might now be ashamed of. Thus, when young people begin to experiment with similar behaviors, their elders condemn them as unusually "irresponsible" or "undisciplined," and wonder what the younger generation is coming to.

Rationalization

Rationalization about ourselves, our acts, or our motivations is another one of the more commonly met defense mechanisms. Compared to other sets of defensive mechanisms, rationalizing is a relatively mild way of protecting our identities from pain. To rationalize (in the sense we are using it here) means to give a logical but false and self-serving explanation for something. For example, a student who gets a failing grade on an exam and can't or won't acknowledge his own responsibility in the matter may rationalize it by claiming that he and the teacher have a personality clash and that the teacher failed him out of spite, or that the exam didn't cover the course material, or any other number of ways. Rather than face up to his own (real) lack of preparation, he rationalizes—attributes his failure to some other factor. This defense mechanism always resorts to spurious reasons, explanations, and alibis. For example, a parent may rationalize a child's misbehavior in school on the grounds that he is being "picked on" by teachers, or that his teacher does not understand him. When a parent finds reasons like this for what is happening to the child, the child's misbehavior may be not only rationalized (given a reasonable basis), but even rationalized away (denied entirely).

Although rationalization is less self-crippling than other defense mechanisms, it is still a defensive maneuver that prevents us from seeing something of ourselves. It needs looking into, therefore, if we are honest in our desire to learn how to integrate our personality. Alibis, alibis, always alibis—this is the key to the person who uses rationalization as a major defense. Instead of doing a job, he gives an alibi why it isn't done.

The "sour grapes" form of rationalization is found in Aesop's fable about the fox and the grapes. The fox tries unsuccessfully to reach the grapes on the vine. After many attempts, he finally gives up, and as he unsatisfiedly walks away he mutters to himself, "The grapes were probably sour anyway!" A young man who fails to make

Aesop's fables illustrate many foibles of human nature. This fable illustrates the "sour grapes" defense.

the football team may rationalize his failure by telling himself that he did not *really* want to play on the team—he would probably get injured anyway.

The "sweet lemon" form of rationalization, on the other hand, is when a person extracts a positive result from his frustration and disappointment in meeting with painful situations. The wife whose husband is annoyingly jealous may tell herself that his behavior is really proof of his love for her. Or a student who does not get the part she seeks in a play may comfort herself by saying that she now has more time to study. Sweet lemons is not the same as maintaining a cheerful, optimistic attitude toward life. Optimism and cheerfulness have to do with not becoming so cynical that one ignores the good this complex world has to offer even though there is also a painful aspect to living. Sweet lemons has to do with denying the pain altogether and twisting any situation around so that it is ultimately (on the surface) a positive event. This is in direct contrast to the highly integrated person who acknowledges his feelings, trusts them, and acts on them.

Reaction Formation

In reaction formation, we defend ourselves against feelings, thoughts, and wishes by repressing these impulses and then developing opposite or polar behaviors. For example, a child may have feelings of jealousy and hatred for a baby brother because he feels "displaced" by him as the object of the parents' affection. The child might directly express how he feels by fighting with his brother or finding various ways of making him miserable. Suppose, however, that the child begins to be frightened by the depth of his hatred and that he even wishes (unconsciously) that his brother would die. Let's suppose also that the parents do not realize how he is feeling—that they do not appreciate the inner conflict he is experiencing—and that they forbid him to hurt his brother. The child can deal with this complex of feelings and needs in many ways, but if he resorts to reaction formation to reduce his anxiety, he will repress his hatred and jealousy and become solicitous, perhaps overly so, of his brother's welfare. Outwardly he no longer feels hatred, but a concern for his brother's welfare. To that end, he may watch out for his brother, make sure "nothing bad" happens to him. But over-solicitous behavior is not the same as affection, and it has different results. No matter how "good" the older boy is to his little brother (seeming even sometimes to be a second father), the younger child's life is still a misery. When playing with his big brother, somehow the little boy gets hurt. Or he gets "lost" when going somewhere with his big brother. "Accidents" seem to happen whenever the two children are together. The repressed hatred and jealousy emerge in subtle, almost unrecognizable forms . . . but emerge they do.

Other examples of reaction formation can be seen in the over-solicitous attention a man gives to his dominating mother in order to make up for his own wishes for her death; or in the seemingly loving care a man may give to an outrageously nagging wife, putting up with her nonsense or even bringing home flowers as a way to convince himself that he does not secretly want to get rid of her. But again, such attentions only *resemble* love and affection. Actually, there is not the freedom and spontaneity that exists where there is real love. There is too much politeness, too much pussy-footing, in these relationships. One feels as if one were walking on eggs.

Insulation

Another way we defend ourselves against feelings of horror, shame, or guilt is to prevent ourselves from feeling it at all. We turn off, so to say, the recognition that this present event has anything to do with us! We do not deny the experience, nor do we react against it. What we do instead is to build a zone of nonfeeling into our understanding of the experience.

Persons who work at predominantly intellectual (cognitive) pursuits seem to rely often on that kind of defense if they begin to discover that they are unable to manage the emotional situations and strains of the usual family life. Such a person might rely on insulation to defend against the stresses of being in direct contact with his wife and children: that is, he divorces himself emotionally from what is taking place around him in the family. He is present in the bodily sense of being around the home physically, but his attention and interest are directed somewhere else. For example, he may spend considerable time at the office "doing research," or he may retreat into his study when at home to "get some work done." He may also spend vast periods of time reading so as to prevent interpersonal contact, and so on.

It has been suggested that insulation is becoming one of the major defenses in our time, that we are beginning to rely on this defense more and more to protect ourselves from direct knowledge of the violence in our society and in the world. One of the thought-provoking examples of insulation is the case of Kitty Genovese in New York City in the early 1960s. Several dozen persons heard her cries for help, yet no one came to her aid. Some persons are actually said to have witnessed Kitty Genovese's struggles with her attacker and then to have turned away and gone about their own business. Field studies of the witnesses to the attack revealed that they had insulated themselves from the reality of what was happening—the fact that a woman was actually being murdered! They managed that insulation by suppressing or inhibiting their own "honest" impulses about what was going on before their eyes. By dodging their responsibility in the situation they seem to have concluded that nothing of any importance *to them* was happening.[7]

We see a similar kind of defense at work in how we continue to isolate elderly persons in "rest homes" and "nursing homes"—almost as if the adage "Out of sight, out of mind" will dismiss our present responsibility to the older generation. We have, in like manner, insulated ourselves for years to the tragic, morally reprehensible things that white men have done to the native American Indians. Many of the German people insulated themselves against realizing what was taking place in the concentration camps of Germany during the years 1938–1945. Middle-class America is beginning to awaken from its insulated lack of awareness about urban ghettos, but we are still insulating ourselves even now against the reality that our world may be, in fact, dying from pollution and over-crowding. And so we continue to pollute our rivers, land, and oceans with chemicals that poison life even when the research evidence is mounting that we may already have reached the point of no return! "It can't be really that bad," we say to ourselves. Or we decide, "Scientists will figure out a way to take care of the mess, and then everything will be okay again." These are only a few examples of insulation.

Magical Thinking and Rituals

When we say to ourselves, as above, that *someone* is going to take care of the pollution problem, we are also engaging in *magical thinking,* a defense we adopt particularly when faced with situations that seem to defy our present abilities to understand and grasp reality. Magical thinking can take many different forms throughout the world. In Ireland, for example, it was once a common thing to set out a saucer of milk "for the wee folk" so that they would not pull their mischievous pranks—such as curdle the milk in the cow, or blow the wash off the line, or blow out the fire in the hearth. Setting out the saucer of milk was thus a magical ritual, done in the hope and belief that evil would then pass one by. The Pennsylvania Dutch painted "hex" signs on their barns and houses to ward off evil spirits who might harm their carefully harvested hay and crops, and to protect those crops now gathered into barns for safekeeping.

We sometimes still unwittingly carry these kinds of magical rituals and thinking into our everyday life. Think for a moment of the handwashing behavior of Lady Macbeth after she has taken part in the murders of Duncan and Banquo in Shakespeare's play. It can be a haunting experience to watch her wash her hands again and again, as if to wash the imaginary blood from her hands.

In our own times we find persons who need to wash themselves and their surroundings, not of blood, but of *dirt.* And the same ritualized cleansing is to be seen even as it was with Lady Macbeth. The prototype of that kind of ritualized washing is the housewife who seems to spend most of her life "cleaning up." Let there be the slightest indication of dust or a cobweb and she has no choice but to run for the mop or the duster. A guest in her house may even be startled to discover her emptying the ashtray after only a single cigarette. A psychotherapist colleague of ours several years ago successfully treated a woman who was obsessed with cleaning her toilet. She had been using one of the readily available potions for that ritual, and the skin of her hands had become so raw that she was no longer able to hold the container.

Most of us are relatively free of that level of anxiety and worry, though we sometimes nonetheless show other forms of magical ritual. For example, the authors had a colleague who could not go to sleep unless he went through a certain well-defined ritual at bedtime. His ritual was to make sure the door was locked, the stove was off, the fireplace was safe, tomorrow's clothes were set out, etc. At that point he could take a bath and get ready for sleep. If one of these ritual steps was missing, he would be unable to sleep and would have to get up and go through the entire ritual yet again. Sometimes it was many hours before he would feel safe enough to lapse into sleep. And sleeping at someone else's house or in a hotel was a horrendous experience for him. Psychotherapists call this particular style of behavior an *obsessive-compulsive neurosis.*

The essential points to remember regarding magical thinking and its rituals are the following: (1) in magical thinking, *thought becomes the substitute for action;* (2) nonproductive action behaviors are substituted for productive and appropriate responses; and (3) underlying these magical types of acts is an inherent assumption that wishing something to be so puts it into action. The highly integrated person, on the other hand, knows it is up to himself to get where he wants to go and do what he wants to do.

SOME "HEALTHIER" DEFENDING OPERATIONS

Are there any really "healthy" defense mechanisms? Well, in a sense all defense mechanisms are healthy at some point in that they help the person to survive; but in another sense no defense is "healthy," since all defenses interfere with our vision and understanding of what is really occurring from moment to moment. But in the sense that they are more "benign" (less injurious), three ways of coping with anxiety can be mentioned that tend to have more rather than less positive results: *substitution, overcompensation,* and *sublimation.*

Substitution

We are taking a path to the city, and our way is blocked; most of us will simply find another path and get around the obstacle if we can. This is a simple example of the process of substitution. If a young man cannot take one young woman to the movie, he finds another girl who can go. Simple, yes? but some people do not seem always to manage their frustrations so simply. In running into interference, they seem so stereotyped in their behavior that they cannot substitute one goal for another or one method for another. Their own understanding of themselves is so precarious or so overdetermined that they cannot make changes in direction or goal easily. They become so frustrated by their failure that they lose sight of the fact that there are many ways to solve a problem. Or their behavior is so *stereotyped* (we speak further of this in Chapter 8) that they cannot seem to find another way of operating.

Substitution becomes malignant, on the other hand, when a person uses it to excess and continually changes his direction, his goal, his method—and thereby never carries anything to completion, when he seems to have no native push to succeed in something, but follows the path of least resistance.

Overcompensation

Sometimes a person reacts to inadequacy or inferiority (imaginary or real) by refusing to admit defeat. Overcompensation can sometimes result in astonishingly productive results. Demosthenes was one of the greatest orators of Greek antiquity, yet it is said that he stammered as a child and even as a young man. The manner in which he overcame his infirmity, according to legend, was by practicing orating everyday on the beach, where he would fill his mouth with pebbles and try to shout his exercises above the roar of the ocean. In this way—by overcompensating—he learned to speak not only clearly, but commandingly.

Biographers of great athletes sometimes note a similar kind of compensation. As children, they may not have been well-endowed physically; indeed, they may have been relatively puny in stature

It is said that Demosthenes overcame his stammering by shouting above the roar of the ocean and thus became a great orator. This kind of overcompensation can produce beneficial results.

and musculature, and relatively small for their age. As "handi-capped" persons in childhood, they learned to adapt early to their environment, but always with the acknowledged understanding that they had no intention of submitting to their "fate." In fact, they reacted against their limitations by developing a degree of physical prowess and endurance that no one expected them to attain. Once weak, they become strong; once apparently incapable, they become models of capability—demonstrating what a person can do once he sets his mind to the task.

Overcompensation can be malignant, too, as when an older

person must keep proving to himself that he is still young—so while working out at the gym he tries to keep up with much younger men, or wears clothes that are more appropriate for a younger age group.

It is very likely no accident that many of the dictators of olden and modern times have been men of small stature. Napoleon Bonaparte—from whose career we get the idea of the "Napoleonic complex"—was small in stature, yet he became a military genius who almost succeeded in imposing his will on all of Europe. Was it his small size that set him upon a path of proving his superiority? We cannot answer that question now, for we do not know all the facts which combined to create him. We do know, however, that small boys sometimes seemingly overcompensate by "acting tough" and gaining a reputation as "scrappers." One such case is described in Chapter 6.

Sublimation can be said to be among the more productive defense mechanisms.

Sublimation

As in the other defense mechanisms, sublimation functions on the unconscious level of the personality. As defined by Freud, sublimation refers to the redirection of the libido, or sexual energy, into constructive channels. Freud believed that sublimation is one of the main defenses responsible for creative and artistic production, and we continue to accept his definition though we no longer believe that great art comes into being solely because of rechannelling so-called neurotic drives and needs.

Sublimation can provide an important function in personality integration: by means of this defense a person attempts to redirect his frustrated or antisocial impulses into socially acceptable and constructive behaviors. Anna Freud, Sigmund Freud's daughter and an analyst in her own right, called sublimation the "normal" defense.[8]

You will understand how sublimation functions in your personality if you begin to notice the "art forms" and "leisure activities" or choice of vocations that appeal to you; how you attempt to give expression to certain basic needs via poetry, storytelling, painting, or physical projects of any kind. A childless woman may adopt children or breed animals. A "bossy" individual may find satisfaction in executive management. A young man unrequited in love may turn that experience into a work of art.

Sublimation is a "tidy" kind of defense and one that bears close examination if you want to allow for your dreams and yet are hemmed in with the compromises of reality.

SUMMARY

The first thing to remember about defense mechanisms is that everyone has them. So no one has to be defensive about his or her defense mechanisms.

Defense mechanisms are ways of defending ourselves from overstimulation from the environment, particularly painful overstimulation. As such, they help us to survive.

Defense mechanisms are not static states (as they appear in texts, even ours), but real behaviors that we are acting out every day, here and now. In a sense, we do not so much "have" defense mechanisms as our defending mechanisms "have" us or run us when we are not aware of how these defending behaviors of ours are working.

Some persons have more defense mechanisms than others: they seem more defensive than other persons, more chary of opening themselves to interpersonal involvement, of discussing themselves and their thoughts and feelings easily. These persons seem to need to defend themselves more consistently and strongly. Telling such a person that he is "defensive," however, is not a good idea. We do not help anyone by challenging him at his weakest point, where he is most insecure and least able to cope!

While most of us have a pattern of defensive mechanisms—i.e., tend to handle our anxiety by aggressive means or by defensive means—no doubt most of us have used all the defenses mentioned in this chapter at one time or another. Each person's pattern of defending operations is one aspect of what is called "character" or "personality," of which we shall talk in the later chapters.

It is in the above ways that we ask you to think of defense mechanisms in general and of your own particular ways of defending your own psychic integrity. To manage that kind of understanding of defense mechanisms will take time and work on your part. But we hope you will never again take your or another person's defenses for granted.

This chapter has described some of the ways we learn to survive and cope with the increasing complexity of pressures and demands of our society. But there is another whole universe of stimuli that operates upon our sensibilities—the world of our sensory and physiological reality—which we discuss in the next chapter.

RECOMMENDED READINGS

ADLER, ALFRED. *Understanding Human Nature.* Translated by W. Beran Wolfe. New York: Humanities Press. Reprint of 1928 ed. (hardcover.) New York: Fawcett World Library, 1968 (paperback).

Adler, like Freud, was a physician who became interested in the mental aspect of sickness. A prominent member of Freud's psycho-analytic Congress of Vienna, he later broke away from the strictly sexual orientation of the Freudians. He is best known for his development of the concept of inferiority and how people use various defense mechanisms to offset it. This book is especially recommended for the advanced student.

BERNE, ERIC. *Games People Play.* New York: Grove Press, 1964 (paperback).

This book gives insights into the way people manipulate each other and get caught up in each other's "games." Berne's transactional analysis rests on the idea that all people maintain three ego states: their Parent-ego state, their Adult-ego state, and their Child-ego state. At any moment they may be operating in any one of these ego states and interacting with others who also may be operating in any one of these states. This book is highly readable and entertaining as well as a learning experience.

BISCH, LOUIS. *Be Glad You're Neurotic.* New York: McGraw-Hill, 1946.

Why should you be glad you're neurotic? Well, at least you are not psychotic, but struggling like all of us. This is an informative but lighthearted book that seeks to simplify the mysterious-sounding neuroses of our day. Like your authors, Bisch believes that neuroses have very definite utility when put to constructive use!

GROTJAHN, MARTIN. *Beyond Laughter.* New York: McGraw-Hill, 1957.

We have not said too much (as yet) about how to overcome one's defenses. That comes in the latter part of the book. Dr. Grotjahn has an answer for us. He recommends cultivating laughter. Like other theorists (among them Darwin and Arthur Koestler), Grotjahn believes that laughter is a purgative expression of the unconscious expression of anxiety and a help in attaining freedom and maturity.

HOFFER, ERIC. *The True Believer.* New York: Harper & Row, 1966 (paperback).

Hoffer is an ex-longshoreman–turned–philosopher and writer. Although he is not a psychologist, he writes convincingly on the psychology of one of the most malevolent of all neuroses: the True Believer, the fanatic who seeks causes to worship and die for. He is, says Hoffer, the "mortal enemy of things-as-they-are" and ready to die for an impossible dream, a man who will, for a cause, give up his personal freedom, even his life, the lives of his family and friends . . . or anyone else to carry out his ends.

LAING, R. D. *The Politics of the Family and Other Essays.* New York: Ballantine Books, 1967 (paperback).

Laing, a leading psychoanalyst and psychiatrist, considers the family as "marvellous when it works and, as everyone knows, absolutely hell when it doesn't." The politics of the family can and does breed neurosis on the unfortunate member who does not realize how subtle the forms of defense mechanisms can be. A real shocker and eye-opener!

LINDNER, ROBERT. *The Fifty-Minute Hour.* New York: Bantam Books, 1956 (paperback).

Dr. Lindner's life was cut tragically short, but before he died he bequeathed some of the most humanistic psychoanalytic literature available. In this book, Lindner introduces us to several case studies and the torments these people face as they try to break through their maladaptive defense systems and neuroses.

LORENZ, KONRAD. *On Aggression.* New York: Bantam Books, 1966 (paperback).

Lorenz is one of the outstanding naturalists of our day. He has written several well-known books, among them *King Solomon's Mines.* Because he writes well, his books are always an important event. His contention in this book is that aggression is instinctive in man and that unexpressed aggression results in neurosis. Our problem, then, is to find ways to handle the aggression within ourselves without hurting others.

MC NEIL, ELTON B. *The Quiet Furies.* Englewood Cliffs, N.J.: Prentice-Hall, 1967 (paperback).

In a beautifully illustrated book, McNeil has written up twenty case studies which demonstrate both how our personality inadequacies work and how we defend against feeling inadequate. Some of the case symptoms discussed are the obsessive-compulsive neurosis, chronic alcoholism, psychosomatic migraine, and drug addiction.

PUTNEY, SNELL, and GAIL J. PUTNEY. *The Adjusted American: Normal Neuroses in the Individual and Society.* New York: Harper & Row, 1966 (paperback).

The Putneys write about neuroses which they call "normal" but which are peculiarly American. The problem with "normal neuroses," they say, is that they are so "normal" in our society—that is, shared by so many Americans—that it is difficult to become aware of them. Some of the neurotic American personality types they describe are the Martyr, the Wolf, the "Dutiful" family member, the Little Tin God, and the Jealous Wife. The book can be read quickly in a few hours' time.

It is via our bodily senses that we come to know the physical world that surrounds us and the internal world of feelings and emotions.

5

BECOMING AWARE
OF
OUR SENSES

Self-awareness begins in the experience of being at ease and open to experiencing one's body. A person's body is the vehicle, the vessel, the medium through which he comes into contact with two worlds: the "external" world which comes to him through surface sense receptors (and which has been traditionally called "reality"); and the "inner" world of experience, feelings, thoughts, sensations, and dreams which each one of us comes to know and codify as his "internal" sense of reality.

It is via the body we first come to experience, sense, and know both of these worlds and thus come to know ourselves. Our *senses* consist of the many sense receptors which lie on or near the surface of the skin or buried deeply within our tissues; and it is via these sense receptors that we "take in" the "physical" properties of our external universe. Millions of sensitive receptors located all over the body are being stimulated constantly by light, sound, temperature, taste, smell, and pressure changes of all kinds. This complex of stimulation is taken in and coded by our central nervous system until it is eventually translated into the higher brain functions of vision, hearing, and our other perceptions of the universe.[1]

We understand our world because we see it, hear it, feel it, smell it, taste it, and experience ourselves as "standing up" or "lying down" or as having our head "tilted" or "straight," etc. Indeed, we are immersed in a world of stimuli which is impinging on us continually from many sources. And it is precisely our capacity to see, feel, and otherwise take in the world that is "out there"—and to integrate it into our ongoing experience of ourselves—which is a mark of the sensing (integrating) personality. Such a person is able to take note of the subtle variations of yellow among a cluster of flowers even as he is about to enter the stolid grayness of his concrete office building. He is able, even amid the tumult of family life, to enjoy a few minutes' conversation on the back porch with a son or daughter. He and she can enter into the sexual act with full appreciation of one's body and the presence of the partner. In like manner, that person can enjoy the tastes of a well-prepared full-course dinner, or the taste of one single juicy and tart apple. His body works well for him: it keeps him in touch with his own nature and the (larger) Nature of which he is a part. Because that person is at ease with his body, he is better able to be at ease with other humans and to contemplate their present bodily existence as well. He is, in Maslow's apt phrase, "a healthy animal." [2]

VICTORIAN REPRESSION OF SENSORY AWARENESS

The importance of bodily awareness and the necessity for accepting that awareness is illustrated by what happens to a person when he is sick: his perceptions of the world then are "tilt." When one is sick or in pain, the glorious sunlight streaming in through the window may only increase one's blinding headache. If, on the other hand, one is sick with anxiety or dread, the sounds and harmonies of music may only serve to set a particular nerve more "on edge." It is in the sensory body (bodily awareness) that one lives and moves and has one's being. Yet we human personalities (in contrast to other animals) can get strangely out of touch with our closest and most intimate physical environment—our bodies. For example, we have lost touch with our ability to heal ourselves when sick by eating certain grasses —behavior that cats still show when ill. We are still a part of nature, but now also apart from it.*

In extreme instances of departure from nature and from what is natural, we can become so divorced from our sensory awareness that we are actually "unaware" of the richness of "reality." When a person is cut off from "bodily self"—from the capacity for sensuality and bodily awareness—he is also cut off from many possibilities of personality. Sigmund Freud's initial psychological discoveries were made largely in just this area. Freud was able to demonstrate, for example, that Viennese society for all its self-satisfaction, was largely a "sick" society—manifested, for example, by Victorian clothing, which was generally uncomfortably restricting: a man's collar mostly choked him, and a woman's corset was often so tightly laced that she "swooned." When Freud's Victorians went swimming, they did so in so many clothes that they seem now to us to have been fully dressed—not only uncomfortable but dangerous! The Viennese Victorian era, Freud pointed out, was marked by suppression of sexual understanding and sensory awareness. It was considered improper for the woman to look at her naked reflection in the mirror; and if by chance she accidentally caught a glimpse of herself, she was expected to blush at the sight. This is an attitude we are hard-pressed to comprehend today.

The Victorian woman was expected also to enter the state of marriage more-or-less ignorant of the sexual act, and she was not expected to experience "sexual feelings." † Indeed, the woman who experienced passionate feelings during sexual intercourse, even after many years of marriage and the birth of several children, might have been suspected of having a "lewd and lascivious nature." Frigidity (total lack of interest in sex) seems to have been the norm for upper-class Victorian women. The lack of bodily awareness and continuing repression of basic sexual needs such as accepted and approved by Victorian society, Freud said, can result only in illness—the illness he called "neurosis." Freud showed how neuroses can be expressed

---

* We have borrowed this phrase: credit is due to Erich Fromm, author of *Escape From Freedom, Man for Himself,* and *The Forgotten Language.*

† An excellent description of the sexual naïveté of the gentlewoman can be found in Margaret Mitchell's *Gone With the Wind* in that part of the novel that deals with the betrothal of Scarlett O'Hara's parents. Although GWTW is set in the antebellum South, the upbringing of a genteel female was quite Victorian.

in many forms: physical paralysis, amnesia, hysteria, lethargy, insomnia, neurasthenia (depression and hypersensitivity), and other physical and emotional states.

We seem more knowledgeable today regarding the sexual nature of the human animal and therefore freer in acknowledging the sexual side of our sensory reality. At least, we seem more enlightened there than our Victorian predecessors. In areas other than sex, however, our understanding of our bodies (and the physiology thereof) is no less naïve than that of our Victorian parents, and we are in many ways cut off from much of the information our bodies are sending us via *sensory* channels of information. We shall come back to that difficulty later on.

The Victorian era was sick insofar as bodily feelings were repressed, a tendency manifested by the fact that the body was kept hidden under strait-laced clothes.

REPRESSION VS. STAYING OPEN

The body's nervous system can be likened to an extremely intricate and sophisticated transmitter-receiver in which messages to the individual's consciousness are being sent every second. As sensory organisms, we literally vibrate with sensory data all the time. But in times of pain or anxiety a person can turn off or tune out certain messages and thus prevent them from getting through to his conscious awareness. This tuning-out or blocking behavior Freud called "repression"—the exclusion from conscious awareness of sensations, thoughts, ideas, and bodily reactions by means of what he called "defense mechanisms."

Learning to know oneself, then, is in part, learning how to become receptive to and "understand" the signals one's body is sending to one's consciousness—even in those moments when these signals may be painful or damaging to one's self-esteem (feelings of worthiness and dignity). But when someone chooses to close off signals and information from his senses, he closes off part of his aliveness. When, however, a person manages to remain open to the signals and information that his body receives from the world, he can then integrate these experiences into the ongoing development of his personality—even when these sensory experiences may seem painful and unpleasant. Thus, although staying open to the world and to one's own feelings may sometimes be a painful experience, the highly integrated person we spoke of in Chapter 2 is better able and more willing to do this even when it means suffering pain as well as experiencing joy.

The ways in which people block off sensory awareness are many and various (and even curious), and the greater part of this chapter is devoted to examining these mechanisms. First, however, we shall briefly discuss the human senses themselves.

THE MANY SENSES OF MAN

Aristotle once proposed that man has five senses—the ones every schoolchild knows by heart: vision, hearing, taste, smell, and touch. Actually, we have many more senses than five! The human organism is teeming with sense receptor nerve cells over the entire surface of the body and even within it. We are receiving messages not only about what is "out there in the world," but also about how we are responding internally to the bits of information we are receiving.

Vision

Vision in man is composed of not one but *two* systems, which though they act conjointly are actually different kinds of structures. The primary system allows us to see *black-and-white* and accounts for our ability to see at night. This system is composed of the rodlike structures that are found around the periphery of the retina. The other system is composed of conelike structures in the center of our retinal tissue and permits us to see color. There have been some very interesting speculations about color vision. First of all, some animals do not possess this double visual system—it seems to be an evolutionary development that came later on in the emerging differentiation of the higher species. Thus, many animals are virtually colorblind. As we all know, some humans are also colorblind, and it is obvious that their perception of the world is somewhat different from our own. Another interesting fact is that when people have severe emotional problems (schizophrenic episodes, etc.), their ability to see color is diminished, as well as certain other visual perceptions such as depth and variation in texture.

The ability to "see" what is out there in the world, therefore, is dependent not only upon the functioning of the physiology of the eye, but also upon emotional states and past experiences. The more integrated one's personality, the better able is one to sense the color and variety of the many surfaces in daily living. Artists, of course, have developed their ability to see very fine differences of tone and shade in flesh colors and other manifestations of reality. Sailors can look at a seemingly even body of water and tell by subtle differences in surface texture where the wind is coming from. Thus, our sense of sight is in large measure dependent upon our psychological maturity, our past conditioning, our experiences in the world, and our educational background.[3]

Hearing

Hearing depends on a series of complex structures which respond to vibrations of a different order from light vibrations, but which (like light waves) are a form of energy. We will not go into the physiological mechanism of hearing, but rather concentrate on the varying levels of hearing which we all experience but do not usually consider consciously.

First, there is the *conversational level* of hearing where persons simply exchange words and sentences with each other in a shared language. This is the social realm of shared verbal communication and is peculiar to *Homo sapiens*. There is also the *emergency level* of hearing—for example, where the siren of a fire truck, ambulance, or police car alerts our hearing system to pay immediate attention. This level of hearing takes over at once, reducing the importance of and cutting through conversation or any other activity. Thus, a mother might sleep soundly through a thunderstorm, yet awaken to the sound of her child gently coughing in the next room. The third level of hearing is one of *background sound*, such as the noise of automobiles in the street below or the shuffling of papers in an office, or the birds singing, or the sound of a plane overhead or of footsteps down a corridor, etc. This level of hearing is important and necessary to us even though we may be largely unaware of it—as demonstrated by the testimony of army veterans who have suddenly lost their hearing. They report that what is most depressing about their loss is the absence of precisely this third level of hearing—the background noises of everyday life which are going on around us all the time. We become accustomed to cues, on this level of hearing, and we orient ourselves more than we realize on that level—until we lose it in the deafening noise of battle or other high-noise environments where our hearing is literally bombarded into nonexistence.

But even when someone's hearing is adequate within the "normal" range for all these levels, his perception of hearing depends again on his emotional state, educational level, and *motivation to hear*.[4] Every mother and teacher can verify that a child will hear when he wants to hear and turn off his listening mechanism when he doesn't. Research evidence suggests that a person will interpret a speech in the direction of his own political beliefs and biases.[5] It is extremely uncomfortable for the average person to hear or listen to something he doesn't agree with or doesn't want to know about.

We can think much, much faster than we can speak. Therefore, when we listen to someone speaking, we can think rings around his words and still "understand" what he is saying. However, most of us have become so used to thinking our own thoughts while someone else is speaking that we do not really know how to listen to others. Half the job of the trained psychotherapist (a "professional listener," if you will) is to still his own thoughts so he can really hear what his patient is saying.[6]

Hearing and *listening*, then, are not the same thing! The reader may ask at this point: "But can't we make the same distinction for vision?" Yes, in fact, we can: we can *look* at the world, but we may not really *perceive* or *see* what is really there! In a way, our senses are more-or-less prejudiced in that all our previous experiences influence what we perceive with our eyes or hear with our ears. Thus, becoming a trained observer (the job of the scientist) requires learning how to see and hear what is really there with a minimum of interference from what one hopes or expects to find there!

Taste and Smell

The senses of taste and smell are not two, but many. Taste buds are really composed of four separate taste receptors (which react to bitter, sweet, sour, and salt) located on different parts of the tongue, and the sense of smell depends on several different kinds of sensory receptors (there is some dispute on how many, with estimates ranging from four to eight or more). To complicate the picture just a bit more, the senses of taste and smell are closely interrelated. For example, there would be little difference in taste among the foods we eat if we could not smell our food as we ate it. Anyone who has had a stuffy nose from a cold can testify to the loss of taste in his food.

The olfactory (smell) sense receptors are located in the nose, and not as much is known about how these receptors work as is known about the sense of taste. *Smell* is, in terms of evolution, one of the oldest sensory experiences—one we still share with animals, although for the latter this sense is still more acute, intimately involved as it is in survival behaviors. Even though there are still persons who have not "lost" the sense of smell, many individuals today—particularly those who live in large cities with pollution—do seem to have lost touch with their noses, almost as if in defense against the smells of car exhausts and other pollutants which have blanketed out the organic odors of natural environments.

One specialized kind of sense receptor in the membranes of the nasal passages detects the presence of foreign particles in the air we inhale, after a certain point provoking the reaction of sneezing and thus expelling these substances before they have the opportunity to infiltrate our lungs.

The Senses of the Skin

The skin may well be our most basic and most important sense organ, according to at least one anthropologist.[7] It is the most primitive sense organ we possess: it begins to appear very early in evolutionary and embryonic development, long before the other sense organs arise.

The skin is a vast, intricate, and elegant computer of the most advanced possible design. One's skin and one's self are commonly equated in one's consciousness; thus, the skin represents a very high level of sensory awareness for man. The skin is involved with such diverse experiences as perception of the weather, the act of making love, caring for children, and even basic survival (as in sensing pain).

The skin surface contains at least two different kinds of receptors

The many senses of the skin may be our most basic, most primitive, and deepest sensory modality.

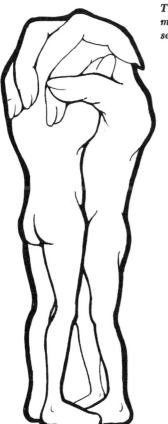

for temperature (hot and cold), and one each for pain and for pressure (touch). Remember also that a person's skin is relatively large, it is the organ that weighs the most, and it is the one organ that is in continual direct and intimate contact with the external environment. The sense perceptors in the skin, extending from the top of the head to the soles of the feet, are sending messages of many kinds to us every moment, both waking and sleeping.

Other sense receptors called proprioceptors are located in muscles, joints, and tendons. These, too, are transmitting impulses to us all the time about posture and our movements. They tell us whether the head is erect, let us know what our hands are doing (even when we aren't looking at them), enable us to walk without falling and to squeeze in between narrow spaces, etc. One's sense of balance (equilibrium) is also aided by the feedback of sensory information from structures located in the inner ear, which enable one to know whether he is standing up, sitting down, or lying horizontally. When a child turns himself around and around until he feels dizzy, it is this organ that he has overstimulated and which now "causes" him to feel dizzy. What the child has unwittingly done is to so disturb the liquid inside the inner ear that it continues moving even after he has stopped whirling around.

Internal Sense Receptors

In addition to the proprioceptors that send us information about our posture and movements, there are other sense receptors within the body sending us information about the interior of the body, especially the vital organs. For example, stomach contractions tell us it is time to eat; and pressure in the receptors of the bladder and bowel areas say it is time to pay attention to elimination. There are also thousands of pressure and pain signalers we are mostly unaware of until trouble arises for the organism. The body, then, is an amazingly complex and sensitive system of stimulation-recognition networks which enable the individual to perceive or become consciously aware of the world around him and himself as a part of it.

From Sensory Reception to
Conscious Perception

The millions of sensory receptors of the body we have just discussed are being "bombarded" with stimulation both from the interior of the body and from the external environment. At one moment of time, a person can perceive or become aware of standing on a concrete sidewalk (pressure receptors on the soles of the feet), of being warm and perspiring (warm spots on the skin), of watching a child play (visual receptors in the retina), of smelling dinner cooking inside the house (olfactory-gustatory receptors), of being hungry (sensory data from the stomach), of being disturbed by a slight headache (pain receptors in the temple-jaw area), and of detecting the faint sound of a buzzing bee coming too close for comfort (the sense of hearing). The order in which he becomes aware of these various stimuli is directly associated with the primacy or importance of each stimulus for him personally at that moment. If the person normally has an allergic (exaggerated) reaction to bee stings, all other sensory information will be crowded out by the sound of the bee and he will make his own beeline to escape. If he is not afraid of bees, then he might turn his attention to the other sensory data he is receiving—perhaps the smell of food, if he is very hungry. Therefore, above and beyond the complex, computerlike processes going on within the body as the nervous system interprets the sensory information, one's *perception* of the world and its events is highly influenced by the so-called psychological factors of human personality. Too many of us perceive only what we want to perceive —or what we need to perceive for the sake of survival, or what our background prejudices us to perceive.

In contrast, the highly integrated person is better able (that is, *more willing*) to perceive the world and himself accurately—i.e., *as it is*, and not how he wishes it to be or fears that it is.

Each of us can use his sensory-perceiving self to become conscious and aware of himself and the universe if he is so motivated; then we are on our way to becoming determined psychonauts. Or we can actually use our central nervous system to block off perception of the world and its events. "Neurosis" can be said to be a form of defending oneself against perceiving what is actually the case— a case of psychological blindness, deafness, and dumbness, if you will. As we strip away our defending mechanisms, we become more alert, more "seeing," more "hearing," and generally more intelligent.

HYSTERICAL REACTIONS

In Chapter 4 we discussed the various mechanisms through which the mind-body organism defends against the psychological pain variously called guilt, embarrassment, disappointment, anger, or shame. But when we deny such feelings, we are also suppressing, blocking out, the sensory data which our muscles, joints, tendons, and skin are sending out toward consciousness. This defending operation is best understood when viewed as a continuum with awareness (or consciousness) at one end and unawareness (or unconsciousness) at the other. When we are unconscious of our feelings because we have repressed them, or view the world inaccurately because of our prejudices, we can be said to be largely *unconscious* or *unaware*. But if we are able to see ourselves and others accurately, to that extent we have become conscious and integrated persons.

When Freud began his psychiatric investigations of neurosis, he came upon two key behavior patterns: *suppression* (holding back an impulse of which we are aware) and *repression* (holding back even *awareness* of an emotion or impulse). He noted that suppression and repression of sensual feelings and impulses and of aggressive feelings and impulses are prime factors underlying neuroses. He called the symptoms of such patterns of behavior *hysterical reactions*. As used by therapists today, this term is not to be confused with the state of crying, screaming, and general "hysterics" which is the usual sign of an overwrought person. Hysteria, or an hysterical reaction (as used by therapists), refers only to how a person cuts himself off from sensing and perceiving feelings in certain parts of his body. In other words, hysteria refers to how a person has made himself unaware or unconscious of some areas of his bodily needs and impulses.

In Freud's time, hysterical reactions were quite common. We believe that this was so because the Viennese milieu (the society in which Freud grew up and whose folkways he attempted to study) was heavily committed to defending itself against both sexuality and the emancipation of women. Small wonder, then, that some women in that culture began to express—in symptoms—what the culture was doing to them . . . quite specifically! Part of the sickness of that society had to do with the suppression and repression of sexuality—particularly feminine sexuality, or sensuality. Men also experienced hysterical reactions, but in more subtle forms. The authors, however, had occasion recently to work with a man who was suffering from what is an almost classic example of an hysterical reaction.

Mr. Smith, as we shall call him, was a man of exceeding "moral" fiber, and his conduct in business was ethical to an extreme. Mr.

Smith treated his employees with unusual diplomacy and dignity, and they in turn were loyal to the firm and to him. His friends were many, and he was, as he himself admitted, a very friendly and genial person. His home life seemed to him eminently satisfying. He liked his wife and children, who happened to be intelligent and doing well in school and elsewhere. But one day, to his astonishment, he had woken up paralyzed in his right arm. He had already made the rounds of family physician, internist, neurologist, etc., all of whom concluded there was nothing wrong with his arm neurologically or anatomically. They had suggested to him that his trouble might be "psychological" in nature, and that maybe he would do well to investigate undergoing psychotherapy. The thought that there could be anything wrong with him psychologically obviously seemed somewhat amusing to him as he sat in our office that first day of our acquaintance, but he was willing to try anything to get cured—even psychotherapy!

After a time in psychotherapy, he became gradually aware that all was not as "ideal" in his life as he had supposed, particularly in his relationship with his wife. He began to realize that while he deeply respected his wife—who was intelligent, capable, and a good mother in the bargain—she was also a source of irritation for him. He began to remember situations where her nagging had "got to" him, and as he recalled those instances again, he began to feel and remember the headaches that resulted.

These confessions were often extremely painful for Mr. Smith. He felt "disloyal" to his wife in looking at her shortcomings—let alone discussing those shortcomings with anyone else!

He was asked to consider the proposition that it is "normal" to have several feelings in regard to a person, even to have all these feelings at the same time. For example, it is possible for us to be irritated with someone we love and respect—even temporarily to feel, *"I hate you!"* This feeling is not a sign of "moral degeneracy"; it is simply evidence of being a human person among other human persons—of being imperfect, in other words. An understanding of this proposition came to Mr. Smith as a form of relief, and he left the office in a seemingly more cheerful frame of mind.

When he returned the following week, he was no longer paralyzed in his right arm. He demonstrated the use of his arm as he talked, and spoke of his gratitude for the help he had received. Then, in a somewhat embarrassed tone, he explained how his arm had begun suddenly to "unlock" one evening: his wife had been nagging him, but instead of letting his feelings of irritation turn into a headache he had allowed himself to feel his irritation fully. With that, his arm began to ease. Then he was able to tell his wife, "Be quiet!" and the moment he did so he was able to move his arm again!

In the time still left in the therapeutic session, Mr. Smith was able to "remember" what had led to his paralysis. The night before his arm had become paralyzed, his wife had been (in his words) "giving him hell," and he had raised his arm to strike her. At the last moment he realized what he was doing, and he stopped himself and left the house. He had been "horrified" to realize that he could be capable of "such violence." After suffering some moments of guilt and shame (gentlemen don't hit women!), he was able to return to the house, apologize to his wife for his behavior, and go to bed with a headache. The next morning his arm was paralyzed.

"The strange thing," he said with a smile of remembrance, "was that I had forgotten the incident of the previous night—both the disagreement with my wife and my impulsive urge to hit her."

We cannot always demonstrate cause-and-effect relationships in interpersonal affairs in the way that physicists, for example, can interpret their data. Yet there seem to be enough facts in "Mr. Smith's" case to demonstrate a definite relationship between his feelings of guilt and shame over his violent feelings, his repression of the incident with his wife, and the subsequent paralysis of his arm. Not only had he repressed the memory of his anger, but he had closed off all feeling from his right arm to the extent of paralysis.

Hysterical Blindness and Deafness

In *hysterical blindness* (or *hysterical deafness*), the person is, for all intents and purposes, blind (or deaf) in the sense of not being able to see (or hear). There is nothing the matter with the physiology or neuroanatomical structures in the central and peripheral nervous systems. But the person nonetheless does not see (or hear): he is effectively tuning out his senses. In *amnesia,* a further example of this kind of repressive defense mechanism, the memory of an event or series of events—sometimes even the knowledge of one's name and memories of past associations—is no longer available to consciousness. Hysterical reactions also include hysterical muteness (the inability to speak), hysterical paralysis of the legs, etc. Hysterical reactions are a powerful and perennial form of defense which some persons fall back on when all interpersonal avenues seem closed and inaccessible. Such reactions are dramatic in the effects they can have both on the person who experiences them and on those who live with him: *they are guaranteed attention-getters*—which is quite in line with the basic level of personality integration of these persons.

PERCEPTUAL DEFENSE

A more common form of blocking of sensory awareness is to be found in *perceptual defense*. Perceptual defending occurs in several small ways in our daily lives, but primarily as "selective (in)attention." Rather than blocking off whole sensory *modalities*,* as in hysterical blindness or deafness, we simply "screen out" the particular items or stimuli we do not wish to see, hear, or feel. For example, a child learns to screen out his mother's "nagging" if she suggests, for example, that he clean his room or mow the lawn. We can all remember the child who responds with "What?" every time he is asked to do something like that, as if he had some kind of hearing defect. But let the mother mention that a delicious dessert is waiting for him in the refrigerator, and the child then seems able to hear the message very well indeed.

By the time we enter school, most of us have become experts in perceptual defense. We hear the complaint among teachers, "He seems to let everything go in one ear and out the other." Or we can practice a kind of selective (in)attention when we no longer want to listen to someone: we give him, so to say, "half an ear," and then go on thinking our own thoughts. All of these forms of selective (in)attention are forms of perceptual defense.

In a lighter vein, young people in love commonly see their beloved through a veil of adoration. A boyfriend may have a wart on his face, or buck teeth, or a very large nose, but in the flush of romantic love his girl knows only that he seems to appear good-looking to her, and she may even be unaware of his minor blemishes: love is blind, as the maxim goes. Likewise, in the initial passion of romance one may avoid acknowledging—and not really see—that the loved one is in reality a mite stingy or a bit dominating. If he appears overly jealous and suspicious, that only proves the depth of his love and so to marriage. Alas! it is only after some months of marriage, when the fire of sexual hunger has somewhat abated, that one

* A sensory modality is a sense category such as vision or hearing.

can "see" the wart on the beloved's nose, or the slightly protruding teeth, or the stinginess—and become irritated by unreasonable and unwarranted jealousy. If love is blind—another saying goes—then marriage is an eye-opener!

Perceptual defense systems can cause other kinds of difficulties —for instance, in work relationships. A corporation executive, for example, may avoid recognizing (*refuse to see*) the significance of the symptoms of job dissatisfaction and low morale among the employees of his company. He might attribute their attitude to such factors as the "present recession" or blame the unions for "stirring the men up again so as to get another pay raise." Any and all of his interpretations may in fact be true. But what the executive does *not* see is his employees' basic dissatisfaction with their immediate job situation. He has "tuned out" what his employees are saying. In other words, he has become psychologically deaf, blind, and stupid.

BASIC NEEDS AND DRIVES

On the basis of a series of studies of human needs and motivations, Abraham Maslow proposed a *hierarchical* model of motivations for human personality. Maslow says the first and most basic need level in the human hierarchy includes the satisfaction of bodily needs for food, water, sleep, oxygen, shelter, protection from cold, pain, and anxiety.[8] These basic needs must first be satisfied before the second, or "higher order," need system (such as personality integration) can come to the fore and be given attention.

If we accept Maslow's hypothesis, and then think of the number of people who still struggle with hunger, cold, and lack of shelter, we can see that poverty-stricken persons are less likely to attain personality integration than those more fortunate persons whose basic bodily needs are being met and satisfied. The man without enough food is struggling with his environment just to stay alive; the well-fed person has the time and the energy to cultivate the so-called higher values in his culture since he does not have to devote so much of his attention and energy just to staying alive.

It would be a mistake to assume that everyone in a wealthy and flourishing culture knows how to take care of his bodily needs—or even knows what these basic and essential needs are. How else explain why so many of us have ulcers, heart trouble, and the other psychosomatic diseases which we know are brought on by psychological stress? The prevalence of such disorders seems to indicate that many of us do not fully realize what our basic physical needs are. Indeed, one group of psychotherapists believe that man in modern industrial societies has become so unaware of his body's needs that he does not even give adequate attention to the basics of sleep, rest, eating, and breathing.

Getting in touch with our bodies, then, first requires *understanding* what our basic needs and drives are and *being able to recognize* those signals our bodies send out telling us that "all is not well." For example, instead of trying to cover up a headache with an aspirin, why not see if you can first track down the tension-producing agent which is getting you in the head—or "giving you a headache."

We are remarkably out of touch with our bodies. Try this as an experiment. At some appropriate time ask some friends if they would like to eat lunch with you, and then simply observe how many of them consult their watches instead of their stomachs. We have lost touch even with our need for food.

Very briefly, we are going to discuss some of these basic needs and drives. As we do so, see if you have given them enough attention in your life. Chances are you haven't, for we are caught up, by and large, in a frantic pace which does not enable us to focus on our simple but basic bodily needs.

The Need for Air

Our most basic need as a living organism is for air (oxygen). This is an ongoing need from conception to death. Without air, we die in short order. Without oxygen, the cells of the body begin to die, even within a few minutes. If these injured or dead cells happen in the brain, a cerebral vascular attack (stroke) occurs, and there can be eventual paralysis and even sensory numbness to the body, coma and death. Air is therefore a vital need essential to our well-being—to our very survival. Accidents leading to a lack of oxygen continue to kill miners, firefighters, caisson workers, and scuba divers. Babies can be asphyxiated at birth or suffer irreparable neural damage just from the lack of oxygen that can result from a prolonged and difficult labor. Our need for air is absolute, constant, and intense. Our need for air cannot be overemphasized, for the oxygen balance of the organism is critical.

We are probably less aware of our need for air than for any of our other basic needs. It seems incredible that we scarcely pay attention to our breathing when we are living during what is surely one of the most "breath-taking" times in man's evolution. Too many of us who live in a complex civilization breathe too often in a shallow way and too quickly: we don't give ourselves enough breathing room!

If this seems surprising, just compare for a moment your ability to sustain a single breath with someone who sings or acts—someone who has developed and trained his breathing apparatus. Our breathing, we soon find out, is much less well sustained, less deep, less even, and much more unbalanced.

Pranayama or breath control is the yoga way to psychological awareness.

How is it that civilized man in our times has developed this kind of shallow breathing? Psychoanalysts attribute this breathing behavior to our desire to avoid pain. Alexander Lowen, for example, notes that children seeking to avoid the pain of a spanking or whipping consciously hold their breath in and tighten or "deaden" their bodies.[9] Has our civilization, then, become so painful for us that we have adopted this shallow breathing pattern in order to survive? Maybe so. But there are consequences. In tightening up the diaphragm, one of the basic structures in the breathing apparatus, we begin a circular pattern of bodily desensitization to feelings and other bodily sensations, until we eventually live for much of the time on the edge of minor distress because of lack of oxygen. Lack of oxygen itself is one of the primary factors in the anxiety in modern man.

Frederick Perls, the first Gestalt therapist, recognized our present inadequate breathing pattern as one of the several desensitization procedures that modern man relies on to avoid pain.[10] Perls worked continually to help his patients and friends realize that they were not breathing adequately, that they held their breath in artificially, particularly in moments of anxiety. In other words, at precisely those times when they most needed to insure an adequate supply of oxygen, they "forgot" to breathe. According to Perls, the experience of anxiety is related to the absence of an adequate oxygen supply in the body. The more stressful the present moment, the more the person needs to turn his attention to breathing. Indeed, in Perl's view, the so-called anxiety neurosis is an instance of chronic lack of breathing; and the first steps in resolving the neurosis will consist of teaching the person how to breathe well and fully yet again.

It is never completely accidental when a particular emphasis or approach in psychology appears and becomes popular. Inadequate breathing patterns are to be found often in our contemporary society, and it follows that sooner or later someone is going to take note of that fact and to begin to prescribe for the difficulty. The Gestalt therapy approach is one method of personality development which stresses the influence of breathing, and Yoga is another. In the yoga view—and this is to take only one aspect of its comprehensive approach—calm, slow breathing itself deepens psychological awareness. This type of breathing is called *pranayama*, but it is never advised to practice this discipline without a competent teacher. When we deal with breathing, we deal with life itself, and the consequences of tampering with this most basic bodily process could be extremely dangerous. Nevertheless, the practice of a few very simple, calm breaths daily does enable the person to continue breathing adequately when anxiety threatens to overwhelm him.

Hunger

How do we know when we are hungry? Most of us would answer that question by saying: "because of hunger pangs!" Research, however, has indicated that the sensation or "knowledge" of hunger does not depend solely on contractions of the stomach; other factors, such as the blood salt and sugar levels, as well as emotional and physical factors, may also play a part in making one experience hunger. A person may eat, not in response to hunger pangs, but just because he is tired, or upset, or bored—or even when he is actually thirsty or cold instead. So the symptoms of experienced hunger are not limited just to "hunger pangs." In one experiment demonstrating this phenomenon, animals without stomachs (their esophagus tubes were surgically connected to their intestines) still exhibited "hunger" behavior—in fact, just as strongly as control animals whose stomachs were left intact.[11]

Obviously, then, "hunger" stems from something else besides contractions of the stomach. Yet many still hold to the myth that how we feel hunger is through "hunger pangs." But give a group of persons a list of other possible symptoms of hunger, and they soon begin to identify (some for the first time in their lives) their own hunger-warning symptoms. Some persons, for example, get irritable and "touchy," whereas others become more active (actually, hyperactive). Still others begin to feel drowsy and slightly sick; while yet others begin to feel "cool" without realizing it. Of course, there are still those who never feel hunger at all—they know only that it is "time" to eat.

Changes in modern "civilized" man's feeding habits have had a lot to do with his losing touch with his hunger. For example, we consume *more* starch, *more* fat, and *more* protein than ever before. And we are getting fat on it all: fat on the food intake, and fat on our lack of exercise. Being overweight has become a nationwide problem in some industrialized societies, and in such cases dieting becomes inevitably a national pastime. Being overweight, we know now with some assurance, not only adds to the likelihood of heart problems, but is also associated with diseases of the liver, kidneys, and other vital organs. Moreover, when we are overweight and have more bulk to carry around, we have less energy available to us for other pursuits and we become tired more easily.

Stuffing ourselves with food makes us less responsive and less alert—anyone who has had the joy of a really full and delicious meal knows that! After a big meal, the processes of digestion divert so much blood away from other parts of the body (including the brain) that we are less capable of paying attention to the external world. We feel sluggish and apathetic, and unwilling to attend to anything other than the job of digestion.

Fasting. Fasting (cutting down radically on the intake of fluids and solids) may well be a needed discipline for a person glutted with food and fat. Aside from a way of getting back in touch with the balance of bodily functions, fasting has been periodically recommended by religious communities as a means of conducting the search for religious understanding and mystical communion. Fasting undoubtedly does sharpen the bodily senses, and it can trigger profound insights into the essence of oneself—that is, increase sensitivity to one's inner life and one's surroundings. One psy-

Obesity has become a national disease; and fasting has become another way to get in touch with a healthier body.

chologist argues that fasting is a more natural avenue to an altered state of consciousness than drugs.[12] This method of inducing altered states of consciousness has been practiced in many societies other than our own—including the Hindu, Zen, Judaic, Christian, and Islamic religions. The Indians of North and South America learned to fast as part of their traditional "rites of passage," as did natives of other "primitive" societies. Since childhood, Americans have been fed the myth that a hearty breakfast is imperative for everyone. Actually, many people feel uncomfortable when they eat a large breakfast; they prefer to break their night fast later on in the day, after they have been up and around for a few hours. For others, eating is necessary in the morning just to be able to completely wake up. We do not recommend that anyone undertake a radical program of fasting except under the supervision of a qualified physician. The risks are too great that tampering with one's accustomed dietary habits will trigger—not a feeling of ease and growth—but a profound physical crisis with equally serious psychological consequences.

The only myth involved here, of course, is that what is good for one is good for all. On the other hand, what we ask you to consider here is that we are *individually* different. And so developing a more integrated personality in part requires that each of us discover how he differs in his physiology and psychology from others—in other words, find out what is best for oneself, and develop a life style that is therapeutic for oneself, provided, of course that that life style harms no one else.

Thirst

In some respects, our need for water is more intense than our need for food. A person can live for weeks, even months, without food; but lack of water will eventually render him unconscious within a few days, and he then dies soon after. Unlike hunger, whose symptoms tend to diminish after a time of fasting, thirst increases in intensity over time until the desire for water completely dominates the person's thinking, feeling, and perceptions: thirst can eventually drive a person literally "insane."

As with hunger, we know now that thirst depends on more than just the perception of dryness in the throat and mouth and on the lips. Like hunger, thirst is triggered by an imbalance of chemical substances in the blood and by other hormonal-neuronal effectors. Our need for water is more easily appreciated when it is pointed out that more than 98 percent of our body cells are composed of water. For example, our blood, lymph system, and the interior of our cell bodies all function in fluid balance. In addition, we give back water to the environment through sweat, tears, and urine. The intake of salt increases our need for water, as does warmth. In one sense, we may be land creatures, but we still need fluids to survive. It's a primary need.

The Need for Rest and Sleep

Our need for periodic rest and sleep are other examples of the dynamic balance of the body. Although we still do not know too much about the physiological bases of fatigue or exactly why we need to spend approximately one-third of our life in sleep, we do know that the effects of sleeplessness can be devastating. For example, persons who go without sleep for long periods of time begin to exhibit a wide range of behaviors: lowered reaction time, poor judgment and confused thinking, hallucinations, and other symptoms which have been labeled "psychotic." [13]

It has been suggested that some of the symptoms of senility (disorganized thinking in elderly people) are due partly to their chronic insomnia. Worried (perhaps) by an awareness of approaching death, or kept awake because of physical aches and pains, elderly people often suffer from some form of sleep deprivation. When given sedatives that enable them to sleep, much of their pain and anxiety disappears and there is marked improvement in their thinking and memory. Even adolescents and young adults who appear to be going through a similar form of "schizophrenic" episode may be actually exhibiting the disorientation that occurs after weeks and weeks of intermittent sleeplessness due to worry and anxiety.

Sleep disturbances seem to occur at certain life stages and in response to certain crises—failure in school, fear of being fired, illness in or danger to a loved one, financial pressure, disappointment and hurt in one's love life. We may then begin to suffer from insomnia because our daytime difficulties dominate our thoughts and, in truth, "will not let us sleep." Or we may be afraid to go to sleep, to let go of our conscious controls and slip into unconsciousness. For some persons, sleep can be a frightening experience—when, for example, dreams keep getting more and more disturbing. Ironically, crisis periods in which we begin to lose sleep are the very times we need sleep even more than usual.

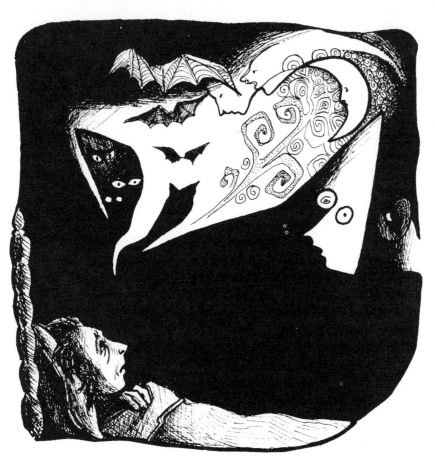

Older people suffer from insomnia, which increases their senility (confused thinking) and their worries and fears; by the use of drugs, many older people are enabled to get more sleep and their condition improves markedly. But we all need sleep.

Avoidance of Pain

Pain comes to us in many ways, both physiologically and psychologically. Moreover, the escape from pain (the "pain reflex") can be so instantaneous that there is little doubt that it happens on a more "primitive" level of our physiology, far, far below the level of conscious awareness.

Consider, for example, what happens when someone accidentally puts his hand too close to a flame: he reacts to the pain by withdrawing his hand even before he realizes what has happened. The pain-avoidance reflex is evidently such a basic survival mechanism of the organism that the pain-avoidance signals do not have to go to consciousness for interpretation, as do other "higher function" signals. The sensory impulses of pain go simply to the spinal cord, where the messages are received and coded and other messages are sent back to the muscles to "get the hell away from all this by all possible and available means!" This transaction happens so quickly that one is aware of the pain and of jumping away from the source of the pain all in the same moment. For all this while, traveling at a slower rate, another message has been traveling up the spinal cord to the brain to inform the consciousness that there was a pain experienced in that part of the body and to indicate what was done about it. The experience of the pain and the realization of what was done about the pain both occur *after* the events themselves simply because the reflex to avoid pain is faster, simpler, and travels a shorter route.

Our avoidance of psychological pain seems to be almost as swift. Pain (both psychological and physical) constitutes a warning system: it informs us that all is not well within our internal universe. We have receptors for touch and pain, warmth and cold, proprioceptors, etc. throughout the whole body (inside and out) which can be likened to giant antennae bringing information that things are safe and well, or unsafe and not well. Lately, we have taken to anesthetizing this early warning system with drugs (aspirin, codeine, tranquilizers, psychedelic drugs, etc.). Such readiness to take drugs which are essentially painkillers and tension reducers results, however, not only in diminishing the experience of the pain itself, but also in the more pertinent effect of taking our attention away from the effects of the pain. Pain is a signal not to be ignored, any more than the blinking red and yellow traffic lights which say "Stop!" "Slow Down!" "Proceed with caution!" "Yield!" Attention to all levels of our sensory awareness is one of the primary avenues to personality integration—which means that we need to learn to pay attention to our pain signals and to "stay" with those symptoms of our anxiety. This is a most difficult task, since the impulse to avoid pain is so instinctively fast that we hardly have time to focus on what is causing us pain before we run from it! Yet if we are able to focus in on this pain or that anxiety, the resulting awareness can tell us something about our present living.

In other words, when you begin to sense a headache, or a cold, or a back pain, you can learn to pay attention to the body language that is being expressed by your symptoms. Just saying, "Pain in the neck!" can help you find out *who* you think is being a "pain in the neck" to you. Or if you come down with a cold, you might ask yourself, "What is it that I want to cry about?" or, "Who do I want to feel sorry for me?" If you find yourself with a skin problem, discover what you are feeling "touchy" or "irritated" about. Who is the person that is making you touchy and irritable?

If you are doubled over with cramps and are pretty sure that it can't be something you ate, ask yourself whether you feel as if someone had kicked you in the belly or punched you in the solar plexus. If these kinds of formulations sound right to you, your next job is to discover *who* it was during the day who said or did something (it may have been something seemingly kind or innocent) that only now you are experiencing fully (in that you are now doubled over with pain as a result).

The exact (suppressed or repressed) reactions that later manifest themselves in physical symptoms may at first be difficult to pinpoint. Recognizing who or what has made you feel the way you do is often painful in itself. If you had been ready to recognize that person's hostility or "knifing," you would have sensed it immediately. But you may consider that person a friend, or he may be a close and trusted loved one, and up to this moment you may not have wanted to believe that the hostile remark or double-dealing could have come from him. And so you may have denied consciously what your body and your senses were telling you. Yet if you had been "all there," in touch with your sensory awareness of what was actually happening, you would very likely have responded differently: rather than denying what was taking place, finding evasions for the unpleasant reality, you might have confronted it. At any rate you would have been in touch with your *body language*, which is the matter we take up in the next chapter.

RECOMMENDED READINGS

ELLIS, HAVELOCK. *The Psychology of Sex.* New York: New American Library, 1954.

This book, first published in 1938, is one of the pioneering classics. Havelock Ellis was the first man to deal in a straightforward manner with both the psychology and physiology of sex. As Ellis himself explained, the book is a *student's manual.* As such, it surpasses even some of the more recent "swinging" sex manuals.

BIRREN, FABER. *Color Psychology and Color Therapy*. New Hyde Park, N.Y.: University Books, 1950 (hardcover), 1961 (paperback).

Seeing color is one of man's most unusual senses. In this book Birren discusses what color means to us and how various colors unconsciously affect us. Feel depressed? Tired? Can't relax? This book may help you understand how colors can energize us, calm us—and perhaps even heal us. Birren presents some fascinating research on the use of color in clothing, in home decorating, and in industry, hospitals, and schools.

Birren has also written a paperback, *Color in Your World* (New York: MacMillan, 1966), that discusses many of the same subjects as the above title.

GREGORY, R. L. *Eye and Brain: The Psychology of Seeing*. New York: McGraw-Hill, 1966 (paperback).

The eye is not just a sense organ, according to many: it is also a literal extension of the brain. By studying the eye, then, we are studying part of the brain itself. Gregory's book is an almost definitive introduction to the visual sense, presenting the most recent understandings and speculations about the eye.

HUXLEY, ALDOUS. *The Doors of Perception*. New York: Harper & Brothers 1954 (hardcover), 1970 (paperback).

In this small book, Huxley, whose physical vision was not good, reports his altered states of consciousness after having taken a dose of mescalin. Of particular interest is the heightened sense of sight he experienced—not of objects of fantasy, but of the real world. He tells us that he became aware of *really seeing* and realized that his semi-blindness had been half-physical, half-psychological.

ITARD, JEAN-MARC-GASPARD. *The Wild Boy of Aveyron*. Translated by George and Muriel Humphrey. New York: Appleton-Century-Crofts, 1962 (paperback).

This book is a translation of the French classic about a youngster who was found running naked on all fours in the forests of Aveyron, France, around the turn of the nineteenth century. He seemed more animal than human, and apparently lacked the ordinary sensory characteristics of civilized human beings. He seemed to be indifferent to extreme cold and heat, could run for hours on end without tiring, and had a much higher tolerance for what would be painful sensations for others. His only means of verbal communication were guttural barks. Itard took him out of the cage in which he was imprisoned and for several years attempted to teach him the ways of civilized man. The sections on the sensory and perceptual training Itard gave the boy are fascinating.

Psychological opinion now prevailing about this boy is that he was autistic—i.e., out of contact with the normal shared experience of being *human*. Other books that deal with the strange and lonely world of autism are Bruno Bettelheim's *Love Is Not Enough* and Virginia Axline's *Dibs in Search of Self*, both of which provide fascinating, thought-provoking reading.

KELLER, HELEN. *The Story of My Life*. New York: Dell, 1902 (hardcover), 1961 (paperback).

Understanding what it is like to live without certain senses makes us appreciate how those senses function in the physical world. Helen Keller was a remarkable individual who was blind and deaf from birth. Her autobiography gives us an insight into her "silent, dayless life" and into the worlds of meaning that came into existence for her when she learned to associate meanings with her perceptions of touching, tasting, and smelling.

LANDSBERG, H. E. *Weather and Health: An Introduction to Biometerology*. Garden City, N.Y.: Doubleday, 1969.

Animals mate, migrate, and hibernate according to certain time cycles or the dictates of local atmospheric conditions. Although we like to think that humans have gained some independence from the material forces of nature, we, too, are governed by weather: our health, our psychological well-being, our performance are all influenced by weather and climate conditions. Cities with towering buildings that cut off cooling breezes and refreshing air and fill the atmosphere with pollutants not only promote specific diseases, says Landsberg, but also result in a poisoning of the body and mind conducive to urban riots and suicide.

MONTAGU, ASHLEY. *Touching: The Human Significance of the Skin*. New York: Columbia University Press, 1971. Also available in paperback as *Touching* (New York: Harper & Row, 1972).

The skin, the largest sense organ of our body, is involved in the whole area of touching, feeling, pain, tickling, warmth, cold, sensuality, sexuality—even in the processes of birth and physiological development of the newborn. Montagu's book is astonishing if only because of the questions it raises regarding our approach to childbearing, labor, and postnatal care.

NICHOLS, RALPH G., and LEONARD A. STEVENS. *Are You Listening?* New York: McGraw-Hill, 1957.

Although this book is a hardcover, it is highly recommended to the student for improving one's listening ability. We have been discussing in this chapter the fact that although man is a sensing animal, he has a tendency at times to become psychologically blind and deaf. This book, written for the layman, presents some of the research findings on how little we really use our hearing sense.

RUESCH, JURGEN, and WELDON KEES. *Nonverbal Communication: Notes on the Visual Perception of Human Relations.* 2nd ed. Berkeley, Calif.: University of California Press, 1972.

First published in 1956, this book illustrates civilization's many forms of nonverbal communication which act as sensory stimuli and affect our perceptions. The book's many photographs depict how even our physical and social environment imposes on us a definite "set" (attitude of mind). City streets, store windows, furniture placement, street signs—all communicate many messages of which we are unaware but which nevertheless influence us.

SCHEFFER, VICTOR B. *The Year of the Whale.* New York: Charles Scribner's Sons, 1969.

This book provides an offbeat approach to the psychology of the more primitive senses (touch, feeling, smell) and helps give a deeper understanding of our biological natures. A biologist with the U.S. Fish and Wildlife Service in Alaska for thirty years, Sheffer presents a year in the life of a female sperm whale and describes how she responds to what Aldous Huxley called the "categorical imperatives": the urges to court, mate, nurse, battle, and journey for many miles in the Pacific Ocean currents. Awarded the John Burroughs Medal in 1970 for the best book in the field of natural history, this book (together with its sequel, *The Year of the Seal*) is a unique literary experience that enables us to get in touch with *our* deeper primitive sensory experiences.

Learning involves all of those activities, formal and informal, which result in a relatively permanent change in behavior.

BECOMING AWARE OF OUR CONDITIONING

LEARNING

Learning is generally defined by psychologists as an *activity resulting in relatively permanent change in behavior.* That definition may come as a surprise to the reader who may have been taught to think of learning as something that happens in a classroom where a teacher directs a student's activities toward increasing his skills in reading, writing and arithmetic.

Actually, classroom learning is only one kind of learning, a rather *formal* kind of learning; and it is sometimes one of the *least* efficient ways of conveying information and changing behavior. One reason classroom learning is relatively inefficient is because of the artificiality of the classroom situation itself. For example, it is one thing to look at pictures of the anatomy of the human body in a textbook or even to study a skeleton and attempt to memorize the bones of the body, but it can be quite another thing to learn and understand how the body is put together while one is working in a hospital with persons suffering from bone injuries. That is why the internship of the physician is considered one of the essential aspects of medical training, and why it has begun to spread to other professions: psychology, counseling, education, etc. It is in just that reality context of working with actual events and real persons that formal textbook learning comes together and becomes real.

To take another example, an American can spend two, three, or even four years taking French courses in high school and still be barely able to speak more than a few words, while an American who spends less than a year in France and who is forced to speak French will learn to speak the language quite fluently. Thus, there is a difference between the isolated, theoretical learning of a language in the classroom (especially when, as is usually the case, one rarely uses it outside the classroom) and the necessity of having to learn to communicate in a country where few speak one's native tongue.

In contrast to the formal learning which takes place in the classroom, we learn many things very quickly in the everyday world of living and working and playing with other persons. This kind of learning begins very early in life. We *learn* to speak, to walk, to smile (or not to smile), to cry and whine, and to have good manners—or to be aggressive and rude to others. We also learn to have a "bad temper" or to "control ourselves." We *learn* to act "like Mommy and Daddy," and even to be prejudiced or tolerant. In like manner, we *learn* to hate or to be loving, to value certain things and to despise others. We *learn* our "attitudes," our likes and dislikes; and we *learn* to dress, to walk, to be respectful toward others or to be "acid" in our speech patterns. We *learn* to dominate others, or to cringe in the face of disapproval. And we may *learn* also when to be healthy and unhealthy—as if somewhere in the experience of growing up in a family we discover that "being sickly" gains us certain satisfactions, such as sympathy and attention from others or simply the right to be left alone.

We *learn* many of our behaviors—many of our *response patterns* —at a "lower" or "subliminal" level of consciousness than we realize.

For example, we adopt the opinions of others and consider them our own without awareness, often at a very early age, and sometimes even before the acquisition of words and language. As Freud pointed out, we learn many of our defense mechanisms and much of our life style before the age of six years—for example, to approach others with confidence and optimism, or to retreat from them so as to avoid anticipated "problems." If as children we received real caring and support from adults, we may have learned in that way to trust adults and those in authority. On the other hand, if the adults in our early years engendered fear, we may have learned to fear and distrust adults and authority in general.

Freud maintained that a person's character is the result of his experiences with his parents and siblings and those fortunes or misfortunes of fate (death of a parent, early sickness, poverty, etc.) which any child may have to confront. However, it was not until Pavlov's classic experiments with a laboratory dog that psychologists found (began to develop) a rudimentary "scientific" method for studying the ways we learn these early skills, behaviors, and characters.

CLASSICAL CONDITIONING

The Russian scientist Ivan Pavlov is rightly considered the discoverer of one of the great psychological principles in learning. Oddly enough, Pavlov was not a psychologist but a physiologist, and his discovery of the laws of classical conditioning was one of those serendipitous (chance) events which happen occasionally in science.

Pavlov's main interest was in measuring the gastric secretions and other digestive processes in animals. In one experiment, he and his assistants had strapped down a large dog to measure the increase in the salivary reflex (amount of saliva secreted) when food was presented to the animal. A difficulty arose, however, when it appeared that the animal could not be made to begin salivating at a regular time.

The first few times the experiment was conducted, the animal began salivating when he *smelled the food* as it was being set down in front of him. After a few trials (runthroughs), however, he would begin to salivate when he *saw the laboratory assistant* approaching him with the food. Then he began to salivate every time *the door to the laboratory opened.* Finally, the dog would begin to salivate when he *heard the approaching footsteps* of the assistant coming down the hall to the laboratory. These responses perplexed Pavlov; moreover, the intended experiment was being obstructed by the increasingly earlier onset of salivation. In other words, the assistants could not seem to get a consistent starting time for the onset of salivation, and it was thus impossible to measure accurately how much fluid the animal's salivary glands were secreting—the very purpose of the experiment!

It was Pavlov's genius to recognize that here in front of his eyes a phenomenon of "learning" was taking place; and he went on to study the "processes" which were at work. In time, he even began to understand some of the abiding laws of these processes. Pavlov realized at that time that he may have stumbled on a method of studying

Pavlov's famous dog.

learning which could be generalized to those higher intellectual processes called "education," "habits," and "training." [1] Pavlov's reasoning was approximately as follows. A dog does not have to learn to salivate at the sight and/or smell of food since he is born with this reflex—a type of reflex Pavlov called an *unconditioned response* (UR). Thus, anything which arouses an unconditioned response (UR) can be termed an *unconditioned stimulus* (US). What kinds of stimuli provoke the unconditioned response of salivation? For a dog, the presence of meat, milk, or water arouse the UR of salivation, so in this situation these particular stimuli are *unconditioned stimuli.* Now, ordinarily, if a bell is sounded in a dog's presence, the animal will perhaps prick up its ears and listen to it, but a dog will not ordinarily salivate simply at the sound of a bell. The bell, therefore, is not an unconditioned stimulus for the response of salivation—it is a *neutral stimulus* (NS). But then Pavlov rang a bell at the same time food was presented to the dog several times—a type of procedure now called *pairing the neutral stimulus and the unconditioned stimulus*—he observed a very interesting phenomenon: when the previously neutral stimulus of the bell was then sounded by itself (*without* the US of food), the dog began to salivate. Oh! You mean the bell was no longer a neutral stimulus for salivation, since the dog had *learned* to salivate upon *hearing it* (without the accompanying food). Pavlov said that *the neutral stimulus (NS) had now become a conditioned stimulus (CS).* In "psychological," we might say that the dog had learned to "associate" the idea of food with bell-ringing, although psychologists prefer to speak in terms of "conditioning" and "stimulus" and "response."

Conditioning and "Unconscious" Prejudice

Part of the importance of the facts of conditioning for our purposes here lies in the fact that many of our likes and dislikes, our fears, phobias, and anxieties, as well as many of our preferences for certain kinds of life situations, are conditioned (i.e., acquired) at an early age.

For example, Pavlov's further experiments illustrate that if a dog was continually subjected to a shock (US) every time a bell (NS) was sounded, the dog very easily became conditioned to fear the *sound of the bell* by itself: when the bell was sounded, the dog demonstrated all the outward behavior of extreme stress and fear, as if he were being shocked!

In just such ways, say present-day psychologists, we may have been conditioned to dislike blacks or whites. Consider, for example, a white child growing up in a "prejudiced" white family. If no one conditions the child, he may eventually begin to walk home from school with a black child with whom he has become friends. The mother in this hypothetical family sees the two walking home, and she is immediately horrified; she calls the child into the house and then proceeds to deal with the child in an "emotionally fearful" way. Behavioral psychologists would say that the parent has given the child his first "pairing" of the stimulus *black person* (a previously neutral stimulus) with the stimulus *bad/horror/shame/negative/guilt.* As he continues to grow up, the child learns also that his father says "damn" everytime he uses the word "nigger" (in tones of contempt or hatred). Slowly, even without anyone telling him how to think or react to blacks, the child is being conditioned to dislike, distrust, and avoid associating with persons who have black skins.

A similar thing can, of course, go on in black families that carry forward hatred and resentment of whites. The children in those black families grow up in like manner to fear and/or hate all whites as the result of conditioning in their early lives. Our prejudices against Jews, "spics," "kikes," "rednecks," Communists, Democrats, Republicans, or whatever, are early-learned responses over which we have had, by-and-large, very little control. In childhood, we can be conditioned *directly* because we do not yet understand the sub-

tlety of *nonverbal language,* i.e., *"the sound of the bell which equals fear,"* and so on. It is hard for any of us to trace where or how we learned prejudice—how to appreciate one set of values while deprecating particular races, groups, beliefs, or values.

Stimulus Generalization and "Unreasonable Fears"

Further work in classical conditioning revealed another interesting phenomenon. Suppose an animal is conditioned to respond to a particular tone (say middle C) of a tuning fork. He can learn, for example, to salivate to the tone of middle C after some pairings of that tone with food. If another tone is sounded which is higher or lower than the original tone (say high C or low C), *the animal will most probably salivate to those tones also* (although not with the same intensity as in response to the original tone).[2] The animal will probably also salivate to other sounds which differ significantly from the original neutral stimulus: he may salivate to a buzzer, an alarm clock, a doorbell, etc. In other words, psychologists discovered that the conditioned stimulus can be *generalized* to other stimuli which are similar to it—and without any more "pairing" with the unconditioned stimulus.

An American psychologist, John Watson, carried out an interesting experiment which illustrates this point very well in the now-famous case of "Albert."[3] Watson encountered Albert as a healthy, "normal" child of nine months. When various objects were placed in Albert's crib (such as a very hairy mask, a piece of cotton, a rabbit, a dog, etc.) Albert showed no signs of fear. He did not even show fear when a white rat was put into the crib. On the contrary, he leaned forward to touch it. He did show fear, however, when a loud noise was made close to him.

In Watson's experiment, when Albert was almost one year old a white rat was placed in his crib and a loud noise was made nearby *as he leaned forward to touch it.* In fact, the loud noise was made every time Albert leaned forward to touch the rat on subsequent days. After this series of pairings, Albert began to cry when the rat was placed in his crib even when the loud sound was not made. The rat, which had previously been a neutral stimulus, had now become a conditioned stimulus capable of arousing the conditioned response of fear and crying in poor Albert!

Not only was Albert now afraid of the rat, but *he was also afraid of anything else that was white or furry*—as, for example, a white rabbit, white cotton, a dog, or a mask with a beard on it. None of those objects had evoked fear in their original presentation to Albert; they had rather sparked his interest and delight. The fear stimulus (sound of a loud noise close by) that was associated to a specific object (white rat) had now become "generalized" (associated) with any object that was white and furry. This is what is meant by *stimulus generalization*. We don't know what happened to "Albert" as he grew up. He may have continued to evince intense fear when he saw a bearded man—and without knowing why. Or he may have become phobic about rats! Or it might be that he had a peculiar dislike for Santa Claus and everything connected with that jolly old man at Christmastime. And he may not even know why.

A fear without a recognizable cause or "rational" explanation is called a *phobia*. Watson and his colleague, R. Raynor, were fairly sure that direct conditioning and stimulus generalization probably "caused" some phobias, *particularly if the fears were engendered in the child before the advent of language*—in other words, before we have enough words to make "sense" out of the thousands of events (stimuli) that are impinging on us from birth to two or three years. Human beings, therefore, can suffer from many seemingly "unreasonable" phobias: fear of cats, fear of birds, fear of closed spaces, fear of heights, etc. And *it may be that one severely traumatic event* in one's life at an early age (or several less severe events) *can call forth a generalized fear to other kinds of similar "objects" or situations*, as in the case of little Albert. Far from being "unreasonable," a phobia is simply a conditioned fear of great size—of some stimulus that happened in the remote and "silent" period of infancy.

Classical Conditioning and Our Present State of Being

In classical conditioning experiments, a first step in the precise measurement of what we call learning was made. And classical conditioning seems to account indeed for some kinds of learning, particularly those learnings and behaviors that deal with the so-called involuntary reflexes and functions: salivation, eyelid blinking, muscle tension, heart rate, etc. It may also account for why we have pleasant reactions to certain objects while others have unpleasant reactions to the same objects. Since loud sirens have been associated with accidents, sickness, and death for so long, many of us still experience a rush of fear or find our hearts "skipping a beat" when we hear one in the distance. An acquaintance of the authors lived through the 1941 blitz in London as a young child, during the "Battle of Britain." Even now, she reports, the sound of an airplane flying overhead fills her with dread, even though she has not experienced anything but pleasure in traveling by airplane herself since she was ten years old.

Someone else, a man in therapy with the authors, felt "unreasonable" hostility toward his employer, who happened to be a woman. Although he professed to subscribe to the principle of equal rights for women, he could not tolerate having a woman in charge—that is, until he recognized that his boss resembled an aunt whom he had disliked as a child. The dislike of his aunt had faded from his memory, but his negative childhood responses had been "recorded" and were still there. He was acting out that resentment now toward his woman employer, who was evidently a kind of generalized stimulus for the aunt he disliked.

One of the principal goals of psychotherapists is to enable a person to achieve in the therapeutic situation the recognition that much of his behavior and emotional response to others is simply a generalized conditioned response to new but similar stimuli. Many men are unable to deal with women as individuals since they are, in fact, reacting to them as they once reacted to their own mothers, sisters, daughters, etc. If they liked their mother, their response toward other women will be generally favorable. If they disliked their mothers, they may be working out (or actually unleashing) their long-stored-up anger, resentment, guilt, etc.—not upon their mother, but upon the other women in their lives.

The same principle, of course, works in reverse. If a woman as a child had doted on her father, she may look for someone to dote on for a husband. Or if she disliked her father, she may seek revenge on men in ways she does not understand and may not be aware of.

First Impressions

Favorable and unfavorable first impressions of people may also in part be accounted for as *generalized responses* to *generalized stimuli*. Suppose your mother (of whom you were very fond) had a preference for blue and wore a certain pleasant perfume. And suppose you meet one day an attractive lady wearing a blue dress and enveloped in an aura of similar perfume. Would it not create in you a most delightful first impression? And, of course, since she has created just such a delightful impression on you, you will convey this response to her in verbal and nonverbal ways as you communicate with each other. The fact that you find her so charming, no doubt, works a chemical magic in her, and she responds quite favorably to you . . . and so you fall in love.

On the other side of the learning continuum, it is also true that you may have a very negative first impression of someone because of some association in your past, and then you manage to convey this instant "dislike" to the person, which of course sets up a "negative valence" (corresponding reaction) in him. Your responses to each other in that kind of situation are then suspicious and in general "negative." The moment the person does something you dislike, you may then say to yourself, "Ah, I *knew* he was a nasty character the moment I set eyes on him"!

Conditioning and Personality Patterns

You may have noticed that the classical conditioning process requires two stimuli presented contiguously (at approximately the same time). The appearance of the feeding bottle (stimulus 1) to an infant soon becomes associated with the sight of Mommy (stimulus 2), and the baby soon smiles upon the appearance of Mommy herself—with or without the bottle, rather like Pavlov's dog. We could say that the baby has been conditioned to expect being held, cuddled, fed, changed, played with, and all those delicious things that go on in a good mother-child relationship, and he has learned to associate these things with the very *sight* of Mommy. Or the opposite response could be conditioned: the sight of Mommy could arouse fear and anxiety in the baby. And when this happens, particularly for a long time, there is a good chance the child will grow up highly anxious, or what is called "neurotic." He may even grow up with a psychotic pattern—some severe lacks or aspects in his personality.

"Sally," a nine-year-old black child, had come to expect "trouble" (derision, hitting, name-calling) from *all* white children because a *few* white children had treated her in this way. Accordingly, she distrusted the friendly advances of other whites. She evidenced a negative, suspicious, hostile attitude toward all whites and kept otherwise friendly whites from trying to establish communication with her. In other words, she had not only developed a generalized response to *white* people, she even began to condition them to dislike her and stay away from her.

Experimental Extinction and
Spontaneous Recovery

Two other principles of conditioned behavior that Pavlov was responsible for first formulating are *experimental extinction* and *spontaneous recovery*. Going back to Pavlov's dog, the reader will remember that after the bell and the food had been "paired" (presented together) several times, the dog would salivate to the sound of the bell alone—that is, the dog was now conditioned to expect food at the sound of the bell. What would happen, Pavlov wondered, if over a long period of time only the bell were sounded—without food being given? You have probably guessed it: eventually, the dog stopped salivating to the sound of the bell—he "learned" that there was no food forthcoming and thus did not "expect" any. In psychological terminology, this phenomenon is called *experimental extinction;* that is to say, the conditioned response of salivating at the sound of a bell had been *extinguished*. All very well, indeed! We can say that while we can learn almost anything, it is possible to "unlearn" it as well.

However, there is a "catch!" The "catch" is the phenomenon known as *spontaneous recovery*. Some time after the dog was no longer salivating to the bell (i.e., after experimental extinction had been achieved), the bell was accidentally sounded one day and (much to the surprise of everyone involved) the dog salivated again! To put it in psychological language, after a response has been extinguished and a period of time has elapsed, the conditioned response may spontaneously recover—regain some of its strength without additional conditioning. The whys and wherefores of this phenomenon are totally speculative. Suffice it to say here that knowledge of this phenomenon can aid the person in understanding why some of his fears, phobias, resentments, and jealousies may flare up long after he thought the embers had died out. If the person then learns not to "feed" (further condition) these negative emotions, eventually the response patterns will be extinguished once and for all. (This is more fully discussed in Part II.)

OPERANT CONDITIONING

The examples of the conditioning process that we have discussed so far all have one important feature: the simultaneous appearance of two stimuli in the environment which instills in us a conditioned (learned) response. That is, the various environments we encounter condition us to behave in certain ways: to act, think, and feel, and to believe that given *this* event or person, *that* event will follow.

This model of learning seems to propose that we are nothing more than passive organisms reacting to the environment, a model more appropriate to the jellyfish that is carried along by the current until it comes up against another organism which it can eat (or which can eat it). Human persons and other higher animals, however, learn in another way: through their own conscious energetic interactions with their environment.

The leading proponent of this second conditioning model, the American psychologist B. F. Skinner, calls this approach *operant conditioning*, so as to account for the fact that animals learn also by *operating* on their environment as well as by responding to it.[4] In a typical operant conditioning experiment, a rat is put into a *Skinner box*—usually a cage equipped with certain mechanical devices. When first put into the cage, the rat will engage in *exploratory behavior;* i.e., he runs around the cage, sniffs, stretches, cleans himself, and runs around again and exhibits various other exploratory behaviors.

There is a bar in the cage which, when pressed, activates a mechanism that drops a food pellet down a shute to the rat. In the course of his explorator behavior, sooner or later the rat is bound to accidentally touch the bar, whereupon a food pellet is immediately released. The rat eats it (rather eagerly, we assume, if he is hungry) and looks around for some more. When he doesn't find any more food, he may go to the opposite end of the cage, sniff, wander around aimlessly. Eventually, however, he does manage to hit the bar again and is *reinforced* (rewarded) by another food pellet. This process is repeated over and over, and eventually the rat discovers that a certain action or behavior on his part (pressing the bar) produces a reward—namely, food. The animal's behavior then becomes less random and more purposeful, and he quickly engages in pressing the bar and eating the released food pellets until he has had enough. This method of conditioning relies more on self-learning than does the classical conditioning approach.

A human baby, too, is not just a passive organism. When he begins to engage in exploratory behavior, he indulges in all kinds of trial-and-error learning. Since a baby tends to discover his environment by touching and tasting things, he soon finds out that certain things taste good (food) but other things do not (such as a piece of lint off the floor). He also discovers that the kitten will scratch sometimes, and he begins to learn these facts through his own experience. He may discover, for example, that if he crawls over to his mother and looks up at her engagingly, she will pick him up and cuddle him.

As the child grows up, he operates on his environment and experiments with a variety of behaviors. Some of these behaviors are reinforced and others punished by the environment. The "baby" of a large family indulges in "cute" behavior at the dinner table, and to his delight discovers that he is the focus of attention and laughter. The child has now been reinforced for acting in such a droll way. He tries it again, and again, and each time he is filled with those familiar sensations of laughter and applause. When he tries out his jokes at school, his classmates also enjoy his antics. He has discovered for himself a way of eliciting that longed-for applause from his audience, a pattern of reinforcement that could one day result in his becoming a stand-up comic.

George was a rowdy little boy whose parents had not taught him to respect other people's property. In kindergarten, his lack of awareness that children do not like their possessions taken away from them or destroyed created difficulties for him in class. He was surprised and highly irritated when his teacher disciplined him. His displeasure was expressed as anger and resentment against his teachers, behavior which often eventually necessitated removing him from the classroom. By the time George was in second grade, he had established for himself a resentful attitude toward school and his teachers. Since he had no awareness that it was *his* behavior which called forth antagonism in others, he assumed that the teachers and the school were "out to get him."

Free Will vs. Determinism

Since this is not a textbook on general psychology, we have discussed only a few of the principles of learning theory and conditioning. What we want to underline now regarding the conditioning of behaviors is that much of an individual's basic conditioning or learning takes place at an early age, when the personality is still relatively unformed and the child *is not aware* of how he is learning to be the way *he is*. (Being shaped or molded without being aware of it is what we call *determinism*.) Such conditioning may account for adult behaviors which seem, on the surface, to be self-destructive, yet which also have a secondary reward system built in. For example, suppose a girl has grown up in a family where the mother was mysteriously "sick" off and on. Whether through imitation or trial-or-error learning, the girl grows conditioned to the idea that when one is "sick," people tend to be indulgent and attentive. Now being sick is not pleasant in itself; moreover one is then excluded from many things going on in the world. So being sick can be a lonely, unpleasant experience. On the other hand, when this girl (now grown to womanhood) cannot get what she wants from her husband and children or wishes to avoid quarrels, she has already learned (at some level of herself) that by getting sick—really sick—she will be left alone, not quarreled with, even, in fact, taken care of. As she gets older, she can come to rely on "sicknesses" as a method of controlling other people's behavior. A classic example of such control is the woman who has a sudden "heart attack" when her son begins to talk about getting married.

These are examples of how complex conditioning and the learning of response patterns can be. The point we want to make is simply that awareness equals freedom and nonawareness is the equivalent of being determined. The less we are aware of what's going on, the more likely it is that our freedom to determine ourselves is being lessened . . . and determined by someone else.

One of the perennial and most intensely debated philosophical questions is whether man is *predetermined* to act as he does or is able to operate on the basis of *free will*. This dichotomy can be resolved once we place it in the context of whether or not a person is *aware* that he has been conditioned to think in certain ways, to value certain things, and to respond (behave) to his environment in certain ways. We learn our habits of eating, our habits of sleeping, our habits of talking and interacting and responding through the various thousands of conditioning experiences we have undergone, both reinforcing and painful. When we are completely unaware that many of our behavior patterns are indeed conditioned, we may then be considered *determined*—controlled ultimately by our past experiences and therefore "unfree." For example, when we are unaware of the choices available to us at a given moment and behave with old conditioned responses to a "new" situation, at that point and to that extent we are more like automatons and machines—that is to say, *predictable* because we repeat old responses over and over like a machine.

English philosopher and novelist Colin Wilson describes this conditioned aspect of the human personality as that part of oneself which is like a robot, nonhuman.[5] Wilson points out how his own robot (the conditioned part of himself) is very useful. For example, he doesn't have to *think* about walking, or about driving a car or about typing, since the response patterns for these behaviors are "programmed" into the nervous system, and his robot allows him to do these things more-or-less automatically. Extra energy is thus available which can be directed into the creative aspects of himself—thinking, reasoning, deliberating.

But the robot in one's personality also imposes one enormous disadvantage (among others). To quote Wilson:

> If I discover a new symphony that moves me deeply, or a poem or a painting, this bloody robot promptly insists on getting in the act. And when I listen to the symphony for the third time, *he* begins to anticipate every note. He listens to it automatically, and I lose all the pleasure. He is most annoying when I am tired, because then he tends to take over most of my functions without even asking me. I have even caught him making love to my wife.[6]

Wilson's point is well taken. There is a needed economy in conditioned and fixed behavior patterns, and we need that kind of learning to be "robotlike," or we would have to relearn to drive a car everytime we got into it or work a typewriter over and over again. Being determined and "unfree" on those levels of experience is desirable and all to our good. It's when the robot or the "computer" begins to take over our lives, particularly where conscious choice

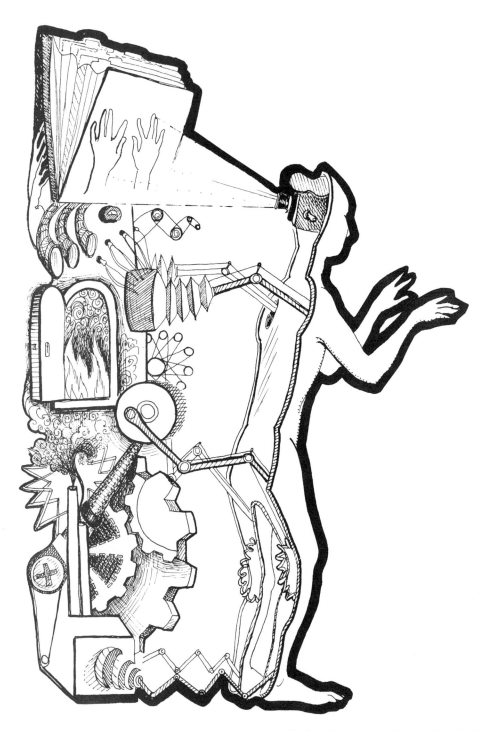

To the extent that one is controlled and unaware of his conditioning he is nonhuman, a robot.

and awareness are indeed demanded and needed, that it becomes not a blessing, but a hindrance to growth. Then we have become "pseudopersons" who continue to do the same things just because we are unaware of the choices available to us. One woman of the authors' acquaintance comes to mind: she never accepted an invitation if it fell on a Monday, because Monday was the day she did the wash.

Thus, we continue to do the same things, say the same things, speak the same clichés, accede to the same demands from our environment—without question and without awareness. In Freud's terminology, this is the "unconscious" (unaware) aspect of ourselves. Whatever term we use to describe such behavior, it is astonishing how many of our responses are predetermined in ways we are unaware. Let us give some examples to clarify this question.

The Case of Michael

One of the authors' children, Michael, has been (since he was adopted by us) an exceptionally strong, lithe, and well-coordinated person for his age and size. Michael has received much reinforcement from his environment in the area of sports, so he has a certain amount of self-esteem and confidence on the athletic field. However, he has always been somewhat small in stature, and that continues to be a point of insecurity in his personality development. When he was in the lower elementary grades, Michael was hauled off the recess field several times because of fighting. As we investigated each incident, we discovered a common element in many of his fights: someone had called him a name which made him angry. These names generally referred to his small size: "shorty," "small-fry," "pipsqueak," "shortstop," "peanuts," etc. Michael's reaction to these stimulus words was to prove to the name-caller that he may be short, but he sure was tough!—and not someone to mess around with too often!

Consider, now, that Michael's behavior was so automatic that any casual reference to his size resulted in the inner command, "Fight!" As long as he had no other response but "Fight!" to the stimulus words, he was not in control of his own behavior. He was conditioned to respond in just one way. As long as anyone could arouse his anger and call forth the fight response in him through the stimulus words, that person was more in control of Michael's behavior than Michael was himself!

We have control of our behavior only when we have *at least two* (significantly different) *choices available*. Michael, seemingly (most of the time) had only one choice available, and that was the pushbutton reaction to fight when called one of these "painful" names, rather like the animals in Arzin's experiments (Chapter 4). In his robotlike conditioned response (fight), Michael was as unfree as any other animal who attacks, after a pain stimulus. That is what we wanted him to see and understand.

We have already discussed how conditioning generalizes to other stimuli. For example, in the case discussed earlier, Albert showed signs of fear not only when a rat was put in his crib, but also when a rabbit or a muff or a fur coat was placed near him. Let us see how Michael's conditioned response generalized to other situations.

Once Michael began to realize how automatic and robotlike his fight reaction was to the stimulus words, his fight response began to diminish somewhat. Yet the conditioned behavior was still present, and it began to show itself in other ways. For example, if he saw a large boy and a small boy fighting, he would now immediately jump to the smaller boy's rescue. He became a kind of champion of the underdog! Very noble indeed—and especially when the large boy was being a bully! In one case, however, it was clear that the younger boy had started the fight and was actually bullying the taller boy. The taller boy was only trying to defend himself. Though he knew that he had a tendency to side with someone just because he seemed the underdog, Michael continued for a while to leap in and rescue any small boy—without first determining what was going on. For him, any small boy was now a stimulus substitute for himself, conscious as he was of his own small status. In psychoanalytic theory, this process is called *identification*.

Up until recently, Michael's chief resentment was in being told what to do as if he were still the small boy he used to be. For a while he tended to hang around with bigger boys because (he told us) he felt stronger around them. Also, he would sometimes befriend boys who reacted aggressively to the adult word, for Michael still identified with anyone who was even symbolically an underdog.

Like Michael in his fighting stage, adults frequently jump into a fracas on one side or another without seriously examining the issues. When this happens, the person may be exhibiting a conditioned response rather than a response based upon deliberation and free will. He may be reacting to some kind of previous conditioning of which he is unaware. Such behavior is then predetermined *because it is not based on choice.*

Our Conditioned Patterns

Many of our values have been conditioned much to our own disadvantage. "Thomas," a student, wants to be a better student. He probably has the capacity to get through college, but he lacks the motivation to study or even take his courses seriously. Thomas comes from a family which placed little value on education. His father used to take him on fishing and hunting trips and encouraged him to go out for the football team, and they had a most gratifying father-son relationship. His father never got past junior high school, however, and Thomas has frequently heard his father condescendingly refer to the university population as "eggheads." Thomas was conditioned early to value the "manly" things his father approved of, such as hunting and fishing; and he was conditioned also to look down on the pursuit of intellectual knowledge.

"Garry" travels in a drug crowd. Several of his friends have been picked up by the police, and one was hurt (perhaps purposely so). Now Garry refers to all policemen as "pigs," and the very sight (stimulus) of a policeman engenders in him the generalized response of anger. He hastens to join any demonstration, even without knowing what issues may be involved. He gets a reinforcement because, as he says, everytime he shouts an obscenity at a policeman or participates in a demonstration, he feels he has "gotten one in" for his friend.

Shaping Behavior

We are conditioned in many subtle ways by other persons' responses to us. B. F. Skinner, the psychologist who formulated the concept of operant conditioning, has illustrated how behavior can be shaped in a series of steps. If one wants to train a pigeon to peck at a table tennis ball, he begins by giving the pigeon a kernel of food everytime the animal *approaches* the ball. Soon the pigeon is

We reinforce any behavior we give attention to.

walking toward the ball, and again he is reinforced (given more food). The next step is to reinforce the pigeon with food only when the bird gets so close to the ball that it is *almost touching* the ball; now the pigeon will not move away from the ball. The final step in the reinforcement process is to reinforce the bird *only when he touches the ball.* And in short order, the trainer has the pigeon pecking at the ball every time the animal wants something to eat.

Many animal acts are trained using just this kind of method of *shaping behavior.* In fact, two psychologists have made a business of training animals to perform at such places as Marineland, Florida, simply by shaping these animals' behaviors in the desired directions by a series of small learning steps.[7]

But the insightful fact that we ask you to consider is how we consciously and unconsciously shape other persons' behavior, particularly the response patterns of our children. We are well aware, of course, that we attempt to shape their behavior when we teach children to say "Please" and "Thank you" and when we correct them for jumping on the couch or interrupting someone else. What we perhaps do not realize, however, is how we may be unwittingly shaping their behavior in ways we do not really want to.

In one nursery school, teachers devoted considerable time and attention to one apparently immature and withdrawn child who spent most of her time on the floor. When they failed to get the child adapted to the school routine, they called in a consultant for advice and help. They discovered then that they had actually been reinforcing the child's withdrawn behavior by constantly giving her attention while she was on the floor and playing by herself. The consultant suggested that the first step toward enabling the child to interact with the other children (and to get the child up off the floor) was to stop paying attention to her (stop the reinforcement) when she was on the floor and *to give reinforcement* (smile at the child, talk to her and pat her) *only when she got up to a standing position.* In a few days the child was standing for much of the time, and in two weeks she was behaving in a manner that was indistinguishable from the other children in the nursery.[8] Furthermore, the teachers then proceeded to reverse the previous conditioning and reinforced the child only when she was down on the floor, playing by herself. In a few days, she was again withdrawn and staying on the floor for much of the time. As if that were not enough demonstration, the psychologists again reversed the reinforcement patterns (giving reinforcers again for *standing* behavior), and the child was standing on her feet, happily playing, within a few hours.

As we go the daily round of our everyday lives, we are often reinforcing undesirable behaviors of people around us. There was a woman who was concerned for her oldest daughter who did not eat enough and was therefore "too thin for her age." Being a guest at their dinner table was very instructive. Both parents and all four children were sitting at the table busily eating, except for the oldest girl. This behavior, as usual, aroused the anxiety of the mother, who reacted by constantly urging the child to eat or asking her whether she would prefer something else instead of the food on her plate. The mother also attempted to "coax" her—i.e., attempted to reinforce the *eating* behavior of her daughter—by telling her she could have a delicious dessert if she would finish her food. In other words, the mother was not aware that she was giving her daughter attention, which she wanted and which she did not receive at other times—that she was in effect continuing to reinforce her daughter's *noneating* behavior at mealtime. We do not know how the family eventually dealt with the situation, but what was clear at the time was that the mother and daughter were both caught up in a series of reinforcements which strengthened *noneating* behavior.

In much the same way, parents can sometimes reinforce the syndrome of "being sick." A couple of generations ago, when a child became ill, he was put into a room by himself, the blinds were drawn, the child was given evil-smelling, foul-tasting medicine, and other children were not allowed to visit him. In general, treatment of the illness was sometimes considerably more unpleasant than being sick.

Nowadays, parents are advised to treat a sick child differently —for example, to fix up special meals in pretty packages and to keep the child occupied and happy while convalescing. Many of our medicines today are made to taste like candy. A child may even get special little gifts from the family and friends, and if the illness is protracted, he may even receive letters from his classmates at school.

Although we do question the severity of the older approach, it does seem nonetheless *not* to provide reinforcement for "sick" behavior. The limitation of the apparently more humane contemporary approach is that it may unwittingly reward "sick" behavior, thus providing reinforcement. A balance between these two approaches

—where adequate attention is given but the child is still not rewarded for being sick—is very likely a much more reasonable approach to illness.

Husbands and wives can get trapped in similar vicious cycles of reinforcing behavior that inhibits interpersonal growth. John and Patti have been married for a number of years. During the early years of the marriage, Patti discovered that John on occasion awoke like a bear, a cross and irritable bear. To forestall that irritability, which she came to dread, Patti would prepare an especially tempting breakfast on those days and an equally fine meal when John came home from work. In the beginning, this pattern of reinforcement seemed to work very well in placating the husband's crossness and irritability. Over the years of marriage, however, Patti noticed that her husband's morning irritability had become more frequent, even though he seemed to be pacified and made more mellow by the fine breakfast each morning. What she did not realize was how she was in fact reinforcing her husband's "negative" behavior in the morning: she did not realize that she served her *best* meals on the days that John was at his *most* irritable and cranky.

Patti might serve both her own and John's best interests if she prepared her delicious meals on the days when he was *not* irritable. In that way, at least, she would be attempting to reinforce his "good" moods, and it might be possible to shape his morning behavior gradually away from irritability and crossness altogether.

Shaping "Positive" Behavior

The research on reward versus punishment as behavior shapers reveals a most interesting fact: by and large, *rewarding positive behavior is a far more efficient method of conditioning "teaching" than is punishing negative behavior.*

True, there are situations in which, at least according to research data, punishment *seems* to be necessary—as in stressing to a small child that he must not go on busy highways, where he may be run down by an unobservant motorist. At such times, punishment, such as a good whack on the rear end, may be necessary. Or then, we may choose to shake the child (really shake him hard) to emphasize that he is not, under any circumstances, to go on the highway by himself.

We observed just the latter form of teaching by a permissive psychologist father many years ago. And when we questioned him about his unaccustomed sternness and his punishment of his young son, he replied, "It's hardly a good thing to let him learn how dangerous the street can be by allowing him to get himself killed."

There are many instances where such punishment will serve to inhibit the proscribed behavior for only a moment—whereupon the impulse may reappear when the child believes *it is safe to respond* to his wish to cross the street. (When the cat's away, the mice will play!)

Furthermore, although punishment may *stop* the particular behavior for the moment, it does not teach a new way of behavior which is desired by the environment (i.e., parents, teachers, society)—and this is one of the *basic limitations* of *punishment* as a motivator of *behavior*.

Take, for example, a behavior parents commonly complain about—that their children seem to *whine* for attention. Let's suppose a mother is talking with a friend, either in the home or on the phone, and her child comes into the room demanding attention—attention the mother is now directing elsewhere. The child may pull on the mother's dress or interrupt in some other way to get the attention for himself. And if those behaviors do not get him what he wants, he may begin to whine and complain, even to throw himself on the floor and launch into a most impressive temper tantrum. The mother can deal with the pressure in any number of ways. She may slap him and tell him to be quiet, which is the punishing approach; but he still got what he wanted—attention. She may give him a cookie to distract him, which is a reward and therefore a reinforcer of his present behavior. Or she can tell him firmly to wait until she is finished with her conversation—again, attention!

The undesirable behavior in this instance is interrupting the mother and the subsequent whining when the child does not get attention he seeks. The desired behavior, on the other hand, might be that the child, seeing his mother is occupied, either waits or plays until she has finished her conversation.

How can the mother encourage the child to wait for attention and not to rely on whining when attention is not forthcoming immediately? There are many possibilities of "positive reinforcers," and in the instance of this child the mother will be intent on showing the child clearly what behavior is being desired of him. For example, she may give him a coloring book (if he is still very young) or a special toy he can play with provided he remains quiet and does not interrupt. When he begins to engage in the desired behavior, she can then further reinforce the behavior by remarking how well he is now behaving, how he no longer interrupts and gets caught up in the "whining game." Verbal compliments are also strong reinforcers.

Let's suppose that the child is not yet ready for this approach to his ongoing behavior pattern and still wants to have his way with the world despite the cost. For example, suppose he begins to interrupt yet again and then to whine. The parent at that point had best simply ignore the child's behavior. But at the first moment he begins to play quietly, a compliment is then indicated.

Of course, the child can still express his frustration in not getting what he wants by returning to the temper tantrum behavior. And in that event, the mother can simply walk away from the uproar. Or she can firmly remove the child to his room, telling him quietly, "I understand that you are not feeling well. I want you to stay in your room until you begin to feel calmer and better. Then you can play [use your coloring book, etc.] again. . . ." Of course, at this point he may throw his final tantrum. He can even go in for blackmail—for example, "holding his breath"—as some children seem to do. But whatever the "defensive" behavior the child may choose to utilize in dealing with his present frustration, the primary consideration now for the parent is that the child *realize something is being expected of him*—and that he can do it the "easy way" or the "hard way"!

The "hard" way of learning how to grow and evolve personally is through the experience of *suffering or punishment*. The "easy" way of learning how to grow and to evolve our "selves" is by understanding that persons really are "caring" about our growth sometimes and that frustration of some of our wishes is necessary for the "common good," no less than for the growth of each individual personality. (This approach has been called the *self awareness* approach.)

The shaping of behavior through positive reinforcement has proved useful, even in its still-rudimentary stage of development with human persons, in enabling "backward psychotics" to get up and move around. Some writers have even advanced a theory of society in which sooner or later most persons would decide to "give up" punishment altogether and simply decide to enable others to grow through positive reinforcement.[9]

Verbal and Nonverbal Conditioning

Much of the conditioning that takes place between persons, according to Erich Fromm, H. S. Sullivan, and other clinicians, takes place on the "nonverbal level." The nonverbal level is the level of the musculature, the deep organs of the body—where we can really begin to feel those "nagging pains" that do not go away. The nonverbal level is, also, the level of "body language," where the body "begins to speak" in symptoms—such as "ulcers," "cancer," or the more common symptoms we all share—and in the many subtle ways we sit, move toward and away from each other, and convey our present experiences to each other.

In one revealing experiment a psychologist posed as a guidance counselor, and every time a student he was "counseling" began a statement with "I think . . . ," "It seems to me . . . ," "In my opinion . . . ," or a similar phrase, the experimenter (counselor) reinforced those statements by agreeing with the student. When the student did not preface his statements in those ways, the experimenter said nothing. In other words, he did not punish the student—he simply did not reinforce him. At the end of the "counseling" experiment, the frequency of the opinion statements had significantly increased.

This apparently simple experiment demonstrates how powerful nonverbal reinforcement can be. In that experiment, by not reinforcing anything verbally except the opinion statements, and remaining silent otherwise, the counselor-experimenter began to shape the student's behavior in the directions he (the counselor) wished.

In our daily social interactions, we may be unwittingly reinforcing behaviors in others that we do not want or like—simply by responding to those behaviors on the *verbal* level. Do you have a friend or coworker, for example, who is constantly unloading his or her problems on you? If you don't want to put up with the "nonverbal" demand of that situation ("Let me complain to you about my life . . ." or "Give me attention even when I am beginning to exhaust you . . ."), then don't reinforce that person by giving him or her your attention. Instead, remain silent, look away, maintain an "unsmiling face" until the person begins to turn to topics of a "positive" nature. In the interpersonal adult world, nonverbal conditioning does not happen all at once, and the person may resist being shaped by your silence, your turning away. In that event, if there is a resurgence of the look-what-a-hard-life-I've-got behavior, then other responses may be needed. You may be moved to interrupt the person, for example, and say you have to make a telephone call and politely excuse yourself.

Some persons get that message relatively quickly. Others are more determined, like the child with the temper tantrums who is going to get attention any way he can. In the adult world, the counterpart of the child's "immature" power play is trying to provoke anxiety in us, or guilt feelings, or feelings of "responsibility." In the case of the person we are speaking of now, if he or she is determined to have our attention and comes back for more attention no matter how we fail to reinforce, very likely that person needs a professional listener—a psychotherapist or counselor of some kind who does the listening at a set time, for a fee. (That could have been the nonverbal message being sent out all along!)

Persons who are naggers or complainers have been conditioned to be that way. That does not mean we have to reinforce them in that behavior. We do have a choice not to reward these behaviors —that is, if we are willing to allow our own "self-esteem" to rest in ourselves, and not solely in the "good opinion" of others (*their* reinforcement of our "self-esteem" system).

One more example of the nonverbal level of conditioning before we leave this section. Suppose your teenage son leaves his clothes all over the house. You have spent much time trying to get him to pick up after himself; and all of this time and effort seems to change the situation not at all. Yet you don't want to have to continue to pick up after him.

Say nothing from now on. But you can do something to extinguish (not reinforce) the "sloppy" behavior. Pick up everything he has dropped around the house and put them in a box somewhere out of the way, where he cannot find them easily. When he asks where some of his clothing is, simply say that you have picked his clothes up all over the house, that they are in a box, and suggest he look for the box. The new situation then requires that he expend energy and attention finding his clothing. He may also find some of the other things that have been "missing" in the same box. A few of these incidents (without nagging) will create a self-interested change in his behavior.

There can be a "next time," as there was in the two instances we mentioned above. And if the son in that family gradually slips back into his original behavior pattern, start the picking-up again. But this time, place the box outside the house in the garage or, in extreme circumstances, outside the garage, where the contents can be affected by the rain and sun. If his "special shirt" has become stained by these circumstances—then more's the pity! If his pants are now so wrinkled that he cannot wear them without ironing, then that is his "problem"! If he eventually has "nothing to wear," he will have to figure that situation out for himself; he may eventually learn, if the parents are determined enough!

Learning is not all just "positive" reinforcement, but it is *positive* for the person's *learning*, particularly when learning has to do with the nonverbal levels of personality. The point to remember now about operant conditioning and learning, both verbal and nonverbal, is that we need to know what we want of the other person, that we need to convey our messages clearly to the person, without nagging and verbal noise. Operant conditioning is a "nonviolent" method of shaping behavior in the sense that it recognizes punishment is inefficient as a shaper of abiding behavior patterns and relies on reinforcement and nonreinforcement. For that reason, it requires patience, a quality many of us occasionally lack. But when we lack the patience to be a nonpunishing person, more often than not we can give in to our own frustrations and pass them on to the other person.

RECOMMENDED READINGS

FRIEDAN, BETTY. *The Feminine Mystique.* New York: Dell, 1970 (paperback).

Friedan is one of the first of the women's liberation writers. One of her theses is that the American woman has been molded into nonentity by many forces and factors in our culture, one of the greatest being the typical "woman's magazine" with its image of a rouged and powdered doll who lives only for the pleasure of working for her husband and children.

GRIFFITH, JOHN HOWARD. *Black Like Me.* Boston: Houghton Mifflin, 1960 (paperback).

Griffin is a white man who through a kind of tatooing process turned his skin black in order to experience living as a black person. The book describes his experiences as he is *conditioned* to adopt a negative self-concept: to become suspicious of white people, to expect rudeness, sarcasm, hostility, and physical violence, to adopt a passive, shuffling manner around whites. This book gets enthusiastic responses from college students.

HALL, EDWARD T. *The Silent Language.* Greenwich, Conn.: Fawcett Publications, 1961 (paperback).

We speak with more than just words. In fact, even when we say nothing at all we speak and are spoken to all the time. The way we treat time and keep appointments, how we relate to others formally or informally, how we laugh, sit, stand, and dress—all these things speak volumes to others. We learn them as part of our conditioning process. But these signals are different from culture to culture. And in this era of international relations, we can gain much by learning the "silent languages" of other nations and cultures.

HOLLAND, JAMES, and B. F. SKINNER. *Principles of Behavior Analysis.* New York: McGraw-Hill, 1961.

For the serious student who wishes to learn something more about programmed learning based on operant conditioning, this is a very interesting book to investigate. It teaches the student about programmed learning and conditioning by using itself as an example.

IBSEN, HENRIK. *A Doll's House.* (Many editions available.)

We include this classic play here because we want to remind the reader that one of the earliest woman's lib advocates of the modern era was the nineteenth-century Norwegian playwright Henrik Ibsen. In this much-anthologized play, which can be very easily found in many libraries, the heroine, Nora revolts against a basic idea that was conditioned into people by Victorian culture—that women shouldn't be thinkers, but rather should find fulfillment within the confines of the household.

KRISHNAMURTI. *You Are the World.* New York: Harper & Row, 1972.

Not an easy book to read, and therefore recommended here primarily for students with a background of reading in psychology and philosophy, this volume is a collection of conversations between Krishnamurti, a Hindu, and students at various universities. Krishnamurti's essential message is that we must become aware of how we have been conditioned to be violent, dominating, afraid, aggressive, jealous, possessive, tense, and nationalistic. The world will not change until we ourselves change—i.e., until we become aware of our conditioning and break out of the prison of our own violence making.

LARSEN, OTTO N., ed. *Violence and the Mass Media.* New York: Harper & Row, 1968.

If much of our learning (conditioning) is through informal education (the type that is going on all the time even though we don't realize it), then it follows that TV is one of the prime conditioners of children's values and thinking. If we allow our children to watch the blood and violence so prevalent on TV, argues Larsen, then we are perpetrating the conditioning of violence into our children's personalities.

MALOTT, RICHARD W. *Contingency Management.* 2nd ed. Kalamazoo, Mich.: Behaviordelia, 1972. (Available from Behaviordelia, P.O. Box 1044, Kalamazoo, Mich. 49001.)

For another really off-beat approach to the principles of learning and the management of behavior, try this "text." Actually, it is a 250-page comic book, but its intent is perfectly serious: to illustrate the principles of learning clearly and understandably. A lot of fun, it is perhaps better to read after serious learning for the purpose of reinforcing the material rather than for actually learning the material.

SKINNER, B. F. *Walden Two.* New York: Macmillan, 1960 (paperback).

Now that the reader has some idea about operant conditioning he may very well enjoy this novel written by the man who first formulated some of its principles. *Walden,* the reader may remember, is the account of how the American philosopher Henry Thoreau retreated from civilization and attempted to find the good life by living alone in the woods. *Walden Two* takes off from there and describes a utopia based upon the principles of operant conditioning. This is "must" reading for the earnest student of education, sociology, or psychology.

SKINNER, B. F. *Beyond Freedom and Dignity.* New York: Bantam Books, 1971 (paperback).

Skinner here proposes that our society can be successfully run by introducing a technology of behavior based on certain of his principles of positive operant conditioning. In an era when so much of our literature is concerned with freedom from control and escape from our cultural and personal conditionings, Skinner's book represents a rather provocative (to some, shocking) counterproposal.

WILSON, COLIN. *The Mind Parasites.* Sauk City, Wisc.: Arkham House, 1967. This deadly serious book concerning our enslavement by our own conditioned fears and phobias is disguised as science fiction. It emerges as an engaging philosophical treatise in readable form of what the next step in the development of the human race might be.

7

BECOMING AWARE OF OURSELVES IN SOCIETY

A person's emerging understanding of himself and others can be likened to the ever-widening ripples that emanate from a stone thrown into a smooth-surfaced pond. In the beginning, one's knowledge of society is composed of a single person (the mother) who is the center of his existence. In fact, one might say she *is* the infant's society. She takes care of all his wants and needs. She centers all her attention on him. He needs and wants no one but her. She is the first person he recognizes, and he clings to her when he is frightened.

Later, however, the child becomes aware of his father and his sisters and brothers—the members of his family, in other words. He finds, sometimes, to his astonishment, that not everyone treats him with such regard or attention as his mother. He may find that he has to fight for his niche in the wider circle of his family society.

The ripples widen even more as the child learns to venture outside the family circle into the neighborhood and into that great and sometimes painful society called "school." There he has even less protection than in his family, and he finds that he has to compete with his peers for his place in the sun.

Thus, our knowledge of our society ripples out until it encompasses "our" town, then "our" country, and finally those who speak "our" language or who share "our" religious and/or political beliefs. The more highly evolved persons of our time have come to accept as their society the whole family of man who inhabit this earth. But this is a hard concept and one that most of us must grow toward.

Coming to know ourselves as persons, therefore, is the result of a complex of factors: the parents we are born to, the family patterning, our struggles with our siblings, our biological inheritance as it interacts with our society, and finally, our ethnic background and heritage. This complex of interactions is called the *socialization process*, and it is through this process that each of us comes to know himself as a person in society.

OUR EMERGING EMOTIONS

We are not born with an adult set of emotions any more than we are born with the adult capacity to think. In 1932, an extensive study of sixty-two infants in the Montreal Foundling and Baby Hospital determined that infants do not start life with anything that resembles adult emotions.[1] On the contrary, when the neonate (newborn infant) is not sleeping, the investigators could observe only a *generalized excitement*—a state in which the baby was awake and agitated as compared to being asleep. When hungry or awakened by some kind of stimulus (loud sounds, pinching, bright light), the infant's reactions seemed not to be ones of fear or anger, but more simply a generalized state of excitement manifested in increased muscular tonus, slight kicking movements, and quickened breathing. The investigators concluded that the only emotional state a newborn infant is capable of is an undifferentiated agitation or excited reaction, and that this awake state of generalized excitement is the original emotion of the human being.

It is only after a period of two to four weeks that this primitive emotional state of generalized excitement begins to differentiate

Our emerging emotional behavior develops slowly from a generalized waking excitement.

into anything resembling adult emotions. The first specific emotion that is differentiated is *distress,* which emerges at about the age of three weeks. A few weeks later, sometimes as late as three months, the baby begins to show the emotion of delight: he kicks, breathes faster, smiles fleetlingly, etc.

From these two emotions of distress and delight, there emerge over the next twenty-one months other distinguishable emotions. From distress, there emerge anger, disgust, fear, and jealousy, and in that order. From delight, there emerge joy, elation, and affection, again in that order.

The special importance of this field study, it seems to us, is that it shows that *emotional behavior is a slowly emerging and differentiating* process and that *the wide and subtle repertory of emotions of the mature person is an achievement, not an inborn attribute.* There is a kind of folklore in American literature and the literature of other countries which says that children are somehow more sensitive, wiser, more intelligent, and more creative than adults. (Consider, for example, Huckleberry Finn, Holden Caulfield, and the Little Prince.) Some of this folklore seems even to have crept into psychology and education. While it may be true that some children are seemingly more intelligent, more sensitive, and more creative than the adults around them, this is the exception to the rule. *Wisdom*, as Maslow has pointed out (Chapter 2) *is something that comes with years*.[2] A sensitive child (by and large) becomes more sensitive, not less so, when he becomes an adult. Thus, the finely tuned emotional repertory of the *Portrait of the Artist as a Young Man* (as portrayed by James Joyce) is something the person grows toward rather than a gift he has somehow been given at birth.

The above-mentioned research on infants also indicated that the "positive" emotions emerge a little later than the "negative" emotions. It would seem that positive emotions are even more of an achievement than are our negative emotions. For a child, at any rate, it seems to be easier to cry than to laugh, although the reverse can be true once we get into adulthood. Developing the positive emotions and evolving increasingly more "adult" and deeper emotional variations of behavior is one end we can work toward. The evidence from persons who have undertaken personal psychotherapy, or have involved themselves in a continuing-growth group situation, demonstrates the validity of this concept. They do, indeed, seem to find that they are capable of more subtle variations of emotional response and to function more of the time at the so-called positive end of the emotional continuum.[3]

MAN'S "HIGHER" EMOTIONAL NEEDS

It becomes apparent that even in his early infancy, man's emotional behavior is very much richer than even the highest of the other primates (the group of mammals including man and the apes). But because our emotional repertory *is* so much more complex, our emotional growth is fraught with more dangers than our biological growth. Unless interrupted by a severe illness, our biological growth proceeds in more-or-less orderly fashion from birth to death. In order to grow into a physically mature individual, the human being needs a modicum of adequate diet, adequate shelter, some genuine mothering, and not much else. The development of an individual's emotional maturity, on the other hand, depends on many more factors, many of which involve society's support and approval at every life stage between the crib and the grave.

Early psychologists (that is, the leading psychologists of twenty, thirty, and forty years ago) built a model of man that went something like this: a person has certain basic needs (air, food, water, and all those factors we discussed in Chapter 5), and these needs drive him to satisfy them. In the course of seeking to satisfy these needs, man learns better ways of doing things: building houses instead of hiding in caves; raising crops and tending herds instead of hunting wild animals; weaving and sewing cloth instead of wearing animal hides. By this model, once a person is in a position of homeostasis (all bodily needs satisfied and balanced) he initiates no further activity until one of his needs drives him to do so.

Freud was apparently among those who had this view of man. Freud further postulated that most of man's creative works result from his sublimating neurotic or destructive wishes and fantasies. (This model of man led one present-day anthropologist to concoct a view of man and his society as nothing more than a naked ape in civilized clothing living in a human zoo! [4]) And for a long time many personality theorists seemed to go along with this point of view. But observations of children and animals began to reveal that they engage in certain behaviors without any apparent need-satisfying. In 1928, a psychologist noticed that young children play without any apparent purpose that could be attached to tension reduction.[5] And later, another psychologist called attention to the fact that rats will

One model of man asserts that he is nothing more than a naked ape in civilized clothing.

leave their safe and familiar nests simply to explore new objects in their environment. Furthermore, they will do so even if it is a dangerous thing to do—for example, they will even undergo electric shock in order to investigate the new objects. Other interesting phenomena began to be observed in animals.[6] Monkeys, for example, can be reinforced to repeat a certain behavior over and over for the mere pleasure of being able to peer out an open window at the researchers!

These and other data began to suggest that higher animals have drives other than those that are simply directed at hunger, thirst, sex, etc. And if true of the higher animals, how much more true it must be of the human species. Various kinds of "drives" were hypothesized to account for man's urges to create and to explore, including drives to "mastery" (or "competence") and "curiosity."

Abraham Maslow summed up all of this speculation in his self-actualization theory, which postulates that there is a graduated hierarchy to our needs (see diagram on p. 185). Maslow pointed out that all humans share certain basic needs with other members of the animal kingdom, such as the need for food, air, and sex, as well as those other physiological needs already discussed in Chapter 5.[7] Although we share these needs with the rest of the animal kingdom, these are only the most basic and primitive needs in the human personality; they are necessary, but not sufficient, for a person to come into full awareness of what being human is.

Humans need more than food and water and sex for satisfaction, however. They need to feel belongingness and love, a sense of "family," of identity, a sense of "we-ness." Moving up the hierarchy, when a person's needs for "belonging" have been somewhat satisfied, there remains the *esteem* needs—those involving recognition from others as well as pride in one's own accomplishments. Esteem can come in the form of fame, honors, and awards or it can be a simple feeling of self-confidence and mastery of skills for better coping with one's environment.

According to Maslow's scheme, man's "highest" need is that for self-actualization, which must be satisfied if a person is to become fully human. Furthermore, the self-actualized person is so in touch with himself, so integrated in personality, that he can afford to expend some of his energy to help others. He has a rich emotional life and the ability to direct his own destiny. His life is filled with meaning and satisfaction.

Maslow's Hierarchy of Needs*

```
NEED FOR SELF-ACTUALIZATION

Self-mastery, desire to help others,
ability to direct one's own life,
rich emotional experiences, a sense
of meaning to one's life.
```

```
ESTEEM NEEDS

Self-esteem, esteem of others, achievement,
recognition, dignity, appreciation,
self-confidence, mastery of oneself and one's
environment.
```

```
BELONGINGNESS AND LOVE NEEDS

Love, affection, belongingness  need for
family, friends, group, clan, territorial imperative;
community.
```

```
SAFETY NEEDS

Security, stability, dependency, protection; freedom from
fear, anxiety, chaos; need for structure, order, limits, etc.
```

```
PHYSIOLOGICAL NEEDS

Homeostasis; specific hungers  sex, food, water; air, shelter,
and general survival.
```

It can be seen that the growth-potential movement in psychology is moving explicitly toward a more expansive understanding of human nature. Where once we talked mainly of needs and tension reduction, we now speak also of those other motives which we sense but which we cannot always name—those vague yearnings and desires to explore something new, or to understand something now only dimly perceived, or to achieve a new level of consciousness, or to create some new thing under the sun. There is in man a desire to reach for something just beyond his grasp, sometimes just beyond his awareness. That is the need for self-actualization.

It is a long way from the person's early total emotional dependence on others to self-actualization where he has learned to discern his own emotional needs and goals and can orient his activities toward them. The obstacle course that the person encounters on this life journey is the socialization process—the compromise between what *he* needs and wants and the wants and needs of *others* (soci-

* Adapted from Abraham Maslow, *Motivation and Personality* (New York: Harper and Row, 1954).

ety). As Erikson has noted, every twist and turn of this journey has its special life tasks, crises, and dangers (as noted in Chapter 1). These conflicts and tasks begin very early in the child's life. We are indebted to Freud for his understanding of these early crises, and it is this understanding that we shall look at first.

PERSONALITY FORMATION

The Id, the Ego, and the Superego

Freud divided the personality into three functions which he called the *id*, the *ego*, and the *superego*.[8] A newborn baby has no sense of "I." In fact, he has not much sense of anything except, perhaps, that sometimes he feels good and sometimes he feels bad. Freud called this baby-consciousness (or unconsciousness, perhaps) an "it" or "id" (the Latin word for "it"). The id can be thought of as an organism of undifferentiated energy which strives only for growth and pleasure. In the early days of his evolution as a personality, the infant is largely dependent for his nourishment on his mother's breast or attention. When he gets that attention (mothering), he feels pleasure; if he does not, he feels displeasure. Far from possessing anything that approaches the rationality of adulthood, the infant, according to Freud, is a cauldron of seething and primitive emotions and instincts. (Note the similarity between Freud's concept of id and the findings cited earlier of generalized excitement as the original emotion.)

Since the infant still lacks a sense of separateness from the environment (his *self*), except in the most rudimentary sense, he is largely an "unconscious" being. Freud said that the id level of personality functioning is, by its very nature, impulsive, blind, irrational, and pleasure-seeking. Very simply, the baby cries when he is frustrated and responds with delight to attention. The id stage of personality is essentially self-centered, oriented only toward pleasure and the avoidance of pain.

This life of having his every wish indulged cannot continue forever, since eventually he comes up against the realistic fact that there are other persons in the world than himself. For example, as he crawls around he discovers he is not allowed to touch certain objects unless he wants his hand slapped. He is taught also, when the times comes, that he may not urinate or defecate whenever and wherever he feels the need to do so. He is taught now that he must urinate and defecate at certain times in this certain place (the "potty"). He discovers also—sometimes to his surprise and displeasure—that he may not hit his little sister without running the risk of getting hit in return. In other words, he is being initiated into the socialization process.

Most of the prohibitions and social learnings in the human family begin in late infancy and early childhood, and some of these prohibitions are not at all to the child's liking. He's being expected to control himself, his impulses, to "mediate" his id strivings and find other ways of getting satisfactions for himself. This is the beginning of the infant's encounter with the power which resides in the "outside world." And more often than not, he rails against the limitations that are being imposed on him. He sulks, pouts, whines, and engages in any kind of maneuver which will enable him to continue to get his own way.

According to Freud, these early confrontations or encounters with the "outside world" (the parents and other members of his family) constitute an important stage in the socialization process of the human personality. For it is the continuing encounter with the demands of significant adults in one's life which results in the development of the *superego*. The superego is thus the result of socialization. In learning to become socialized, to become a member of a group or family, the child identifies with or introjects the values of the parents, and eventually the values of the society itself. He learns: *this* is the right thing to do and *that* is the wrong thing to do. According to Freud, the superego is the basis of our conscience, and is one of the enduring aspects of personality throughout the adult life in one form or another.

Whereas at the level of the "blind," instinctual id we simply say, "I will do what I want to do," the superego is the power of parents and society which says, "You may do this; you may not do that." The infant or child is therefore confronted by two possibilities, and it is from mediating the directives from the id ("I will . . .") and the superego ("You may or may not . . .") that the child's sense of "self" eventually comes into being. It is through these experiences that the child begins to understand and to acknowledge that he is a separate person—an individual entity, who is indeed separate from his mother and his physical surroundings. This (beginning) sense of self Freud called the *ego* (Latin, meaning "I"). The ego is therefore the conscious level of personality, that part of ourselves of which we are aware and which we identify as the seat of reason, intelligence, self-knowledge, etc.

Freud saw the ego as a kind of battlefield between the id and the superego. The ego must somehow discover a balance between the demands of society (and its capacity to punish for "wrongdoing") and the enduring biophysiological needs of the id. The ego, or sense of selfness, can therefore be caught in seemingly irreconcilable conflicts.

Freud says that much of the fate of each individual life style is often decided in these early years in one's family. If the socialization process in the family is essentially human, caring of the child, and relatively consistent in teaching what prohibitions are demanded, the ego of the child becomes relatively healthy and aware of reality, and the person learns how to function according to the *reality principle*.

Fixated Behaviors

If the child, however, is not cared for, if he is neglected or treated inconsistently in these early years (indulged too often, or frustrated too often, or both at various times), the child's "ego" can then become fixated at certain "crisis" points. These crisis points, according to Freud, may occur during the oral and anal development stage. In the oral stage, the child is totally dependent on the environment and relates to the world mainly through tasting it (the baby puts everything in his mouth); during this stage he behaves solely according to the *pleasure principle*—his *own* pleasure. If a personality is fixated at this level, even as an adult he will lack those societal standards whereby one recognizes that *other* people have feelings, rights, and needs as well as oneself. Such a person is said then to be either a *passive-dependent* personality who wishes to be taken care of all his life or perhaps a *psychopath* or *sociopath* who has little feeling for others and calmly sets out to "do them in" to his own benefit.

If the child has been overdisciplined (instead of overindulged), then he may grow up constantly concerned about not doing the "right" thing. The danger of overdisciplining occurs at the anal stage, when the child learns to "do his duty" in the "potty" instead of in his pants. It is also during this stage that one is asked to give up the pleasure principle—not to hit one's sister when one wants to, throw food on the floor, etc. A certain amount of discipline develops character; too much instills endless guilt, remorse, and feelings of inferiority—in other words, the "neurotic anxieties" of our times.

Inconsistent handling of the child, alternating indulgence and rejections, results in the so-called psychotic disturbances which in the last analysis are a matter of confused thinking, feeling, and disorientation induced by the parents.

The "mature" stage Freud called the "phallic" stage, in which the person is able to relate as a psychologically and sexually mature person to another of the opposite sex.

Examples of fixation. A person may be able to operate in many (even most) areas of his everyday life in an *integrated* manner, yet "have fixations" in other areas where he functions less well because of conflicts and unfinished situations stemming from early life. How do we recognize a "fixated" behavior? By its uncreativeness and/or its highly repetitive nature. The fixated person, in contrast to the highly integrated person of Chapter 2, responds in essentially the same stereotyped manner to a given stimulus every time. He seems to lack a wide repertory of emotional responses to a certain category of situations. He just keeps doing or saying the same kinds of things over and over again. His behavior is simply uncreative, monotonous, and predictable. An example may serve to illustrate.

A man of our acquaintance is highly creative in his work and job, gets along well with his associates, has an apparently satisfying relationship with his wife and children, yet he has an unreasoning, irrational, and highly prejudicial emotional reaction to policemen, lawyers, judges, administrators—anyone distinctly representative of authority. His behavior toward "them" (and he often talks about "the Establishment") is highly stereotyped; that is to say, he reacts to "them" more-or-less always in the same way: with fear, hatred, resentment, feelings of persecution. Any mention of the "law" or the police provokes in him verbal abuse, harangues against "corruption" or "the government"—just as if someone had "pushed his button" (remember the Azrin pain-attack pushbutton response?). At these moments, his coworkers, friends, and relatives brace themselves for a sermon (which they have heard many times before) or quietly excuse themselves.

A fixation is an area of our personality that has stopped growing, has become blocked off, so to speak, so that we respond to certain situations with the limited primitive and stereotyped patterns of our infantile personality.

A person can also become fixated in so many areas of his development that he presents a constellation of behaviors known as the "inadequate personality." Such a person tends to be overly passive in his orientation toward living, unsure of himself in relation to the opposite sex, and can be a virtual milquetoast at work and at home. He is that one who is ignored in conversation because he does not know how to pay attention to others; he is the one whom others forget to invite to a party or to an evening out; and somehow his deserved salary increases always get overlooked.

The inadequate woman hardly knows how to function as a mother, wife, and citizen. As a hostess, she worries endlessly about what to serve; when going out she frets about what she will wear; and since every small decision is a major event in her life, she asks advice of everyone, all of which gets lost and misunderstood when she is given different types of answers—which, of course, only adds to her confusion. Such persons are often treated as children by others—and with good reason, for they *are* children emotionally—which only serves to compound their own understanding of their inadequacies.

It is clearly evident that the socialization process by parents and parent-substitutes has an abiding influence on a child's future approach to the world, which can be timid and self-effacing at one extreme and aggressive and dominating at the other with many possible variations in between.

Channeling of emotions.   Adults sometimes indulge in forms of fixated or stereotyped behavior when they are confronted with situations they cannot deal with comfortably. When a situation calls forth an emotion that is uncomfortable for them, they seem to switch into some other emotional gear, one which is quite inappropriate. This is called *channeling of emotions.* One young professor of our acquaintance is very comfortable in situations requiring confrontation and political in-fighting. He is able to use his anger as an energizer and to give himself the self-support needed in situations which would be overwhelming for more timid souls. He can put himself "on the line" in situations, therefore, which require courage and stamina. At the same time, however, he distrusts even the smallest signs of affection and tenderness and interprets these emotions by others as "manipulative devices." Since he is fixated at the level of aggression and has not developed the "tender side" of himself, he reacts (in these situations) by channeling most of his emotions into his most comfortable emotional response—anger. His students and colleagues are sometimes rather taken aback when, after expressing their feelings of admiration for him, he reacts to them angrily and with distrust. He cannot handle their tender feelings for him except through his safest emotional response—anger.

Perhaps a more serious example of channeling of emotions is the man who "sexualizes" his social interactions with women: any sign of courtesy, interest, or hospitality from a woman he immediately interprets as an attempt to seduce him. (Women can also react similarly toward the attentions of men.) His own approach to women, in the meantime, is so sexualized that he finds it difficult to conceive of any woman as having any intellectual capacity or any interests other than being a convenient and impersonal bed partner. He addresses himself to females generally in a seductive fashion, and his speech is replete with *double entendres* (statements which seem innocent on the surface but which also have a sexual meaning). To deal with women as *persons* is highly uncomfortable for him, since he regards them as less than human. Intelligent women who reject his pseudo-sexual approach confuse and infuriate him.

Another common example of stereotyped behavior is seen in the "whining child" syndrome. Such a child has not been able to secure what he wants from his parents except by incessant whining. To shut the child up, his parents respond to his whining by giving him what he wants—anything, everything to stop the whining. This child stands a good chance of growing up to become that most pathetic of creatures—the nagging wife or the whining husband. Incessant whining and nagging eventually results in selective deafness in the persons subjected to it, just as the constant noise of traffic causes us eventually to tune it out. And so the "whiner" or "nagger" gets listened to less and less, which of course increases his desperation to be heard. He steps up the noise level of whining and nagging, and in turn his family becomes even more deaf to his noise—and so the cycle spirals on and on to the point where meaningful communication ceases almost completely.

Some clinical research has been done which tends to support

Freud's theories of fixation and stereotyped behavior (with its in-
ferred emotional channeling). Experiments in which rats are given
inconsistent handling and/or harsh treatment seems to result in
stereotyped patterns of behavior in the rats. In these experiments,
the rats finally "broke down" and made the same response over and
over again through hundreds of trials, no matter whether that response was punished or rewarded.[9] The results of these experiments
seem to confirm the field-study observations of children who are
raised in institutions and who have (presumably) been given less
than adequate psychological care. These children have been found
to be less intelligent, less capable of coping with stress, more prone
to physical breakdown—and less adaptable in their emotional responses.[10] In other words, their repertory of emotional behaviors is
limited and fixated at the early levels of functioning—presumably
because of the deprivation of their early years. Persons with severe
channeling of emotions and stereotyped behaviors act as if they did
not realize there are alternative ways of responding, more than one
form of behavior open to them. As the Greeks said, "There is always
a third alternative." And maybe a fourth, and a fifth . . . if we can
bear to become aware of the alternatives.

Child, Parent, Adult Ego States

A leading psychoanalyst, Eric Berne, has developed an interesting therapeutic approach which is an extension of Freud's theory of
the id, ego, and superego.[11] Berne maintains that no matter how old
we are, everyone past early childhood carries within him a "Child"
—a complex of feeling and experiences he had as he was growing
up in the first years of life: his hurts, angers, affections, spontaneity,
etc. Although we continue to grow toward adulthood, we cannot
erase the recordings of these experiences of childhood. At the same
time, each of us is also incorporating into his personality a Parent
(one or both or more), our elder siblings, and any of the significant
adults in our environment we listened to. Our Parent permanently
records the admonitions, looks, gestures, what-to-do's, etc. of these
significant adults. Thus, according to Berne, each person constantly
carries with him three ego states: his Child, his Parent, and also his
present Adult state. Each person alternates between his three ego
states without being aware of it. In our Parent-ego state, we tend to
reprove, punish, or make value judgments regarding other persons.

In our Child-ego state, we tend to strike back or one-up another in self-defense. In Berne's approach, which he calls *transactional analysis,* therapy consists of becoming aware of how one is operating and, by so doing, learning increasingly to keep operational one's Adult-ego state, which is constructive and growth-producing for oneself and for others. In our Adult-ego state, we seek information, ask questions, weigh alternatives, and react with composure and nonthreatening statements when confronted with punitive or angry statements from others.

But the issue is not to erase the Child or the Parent—we can't anyway!—but to use these ego states constructively.[12] Our Child contains our good feelings as well as our bad feelings and is the spontaneous, creative aspect of ourselves which is alive and excited by the world, full of zest for living. Our Parent also contains positive aspects. Our Parent can be the repository of the wisdom of society —ethics, truth, life-saving injunctions, and basic survival judgments— and thus saves us from having to relearn all this by ourselves. But if we operate predominantly in our Child-ego state, the result is that we are in a position of continuous rebellion, fighting, and agitation. If we operate continually in our Parent-ego state, we may act predominantly in a conforming way. The Adult state seeks to evaluate and make choices out of the alternate possibilities that he sees before him. (But your authors would like to add that the Adult-ego state can also seem a bit of a bore and lifeless.) Harris points out that these three ego states

> are not roles, but psychological realities. Berne says that "Parent, Adult, and Child are not concepts like Superego, Ego, and Id . . . but phenomenological realities." The state is produced by the playback of recorded data of events in the past, involving real people, real times, real places, real decisions, and real feelings.[13]

For purposes of an example of how these ego states work, we give the following (imaginary) interchange:

HUSBAND (*operating in Adult state*): What happened to my cufflinks?

WIFE (*operating defensively in Child state*): How would I know where they are!

HUSBAND (*operating reprovingly in Parent state*): Because you borrowed them and I knew then you wouldn't put them back!

WIFE (*operating in "bad news" Parent state*): Just like all men, you always blame things on women!

HUSBAND (*operating now in his Child state*): Oh, so now you're on a women's lib kick!

WIFE (*suddenly emerging in her Adult state*): I'm being silly! I guess I meant to put them back and didn't. I must have put them in my jewelry-box. I'll come upstairs and look.

HUSBAND (*now returning to his Adult state*): I guess I got my back up, too. Don't bother to come upstairs. I'm right here! Yeah, here they are.

Berne's group therapy attempts to enable each member of the group to recognize when he is being his Child or his Parent and to use them constructively. In that way, group members learn not to channel all their emotional conflicts through earlier fixated levels of responding and gain the opportunity to escape stereotyped behaviors. Thus, they have more clear choices available to them while interacting with others, who may be functioning at more primitive levels of responding.

The Effects of Sibling Order

In addition to his relationship with his parents (particularly his mother), the child's early emotional reactions are determined and shaped in his relationship with his siblings—his brothers and sisters (or lack of them).

Freud believed that *sibling rivalry* is one of the basic conflicts of childhood.[14] The newborn baby, he postulated, is the crown prince of his family. He is petted and feted, made much of, and generally feels himself to be the center of the world (which he sometimes is in a family or household). When a second child is born, the first child now finds it difficult to move over and allow the new baby to share the spotlight and attention. Venting his childish emotions, he rages and pouts; he feels rejected, jealous, etc. But these feelings and actions are directed not so much against the parents (who have withdrawn some of their attention from him) as toward the new addition to the family who is threatening "his" place. He secretely hopes that the new baby will disappear, and may even have fantasies of helping it to some dire end (flush it down the toilet along with his feces). He may even hit the baby or otherwise try to do him some harm. Many books now available on the early childhood experience describe in detail this process of socialization. Parents these days are consequently less concerned, since they now know that most children can suddenly "regress" in behavior after the birth of a new baby. For example, the child may take the baby's bottle for his own, or revert to thumb-sucking, or demand to be held in Mommy's lap more often (only for a while in most cases).

But the child may also react against his "infantile" wish to be the baby again by trying to be a "mother" or "father" figure to the new child. That is, according to Freud, if the child cannot regain his central role by regressing, he may seek approval by acts of caring, by becoming a second "little mother" or "little father."

Central to Freud's concept of rivalry in our early sibling relationships is that these jealousies and conflicts are reflected and repeated in our adult relationships with peers and working associates. For example, the child who never feels quite secure in his family may later not know how to compete successfully in the adult world; and the child who gains attention from parents by crowding out his brothers and sisters may, as an adult, be fiercely competitive and jealous of any honour or promotion that comes to a coworker.

There has been some interesting research on the personality characteristics of only children, older children, younger children, and children who come from large families summarized in a little book, *The Sibling*.[15] We can only touch here on a few of these findings; the interested reader is urged to consult the book itself.

Sex Status Effects

Considerable research has been conducted, for example, on the effects of same- and opposite-sex siblings in two-child families. Thus, a boy who has a brother tends, on the average, to have more "masculine" interests than does a boy with a sister. Similar findings apply to families with two girls—such girls were found to have distinctly more "feminine" interests than girls with brothers. It seems natural enough that a boy or girl with an opposite-sex sibling would have a wider spread of interests, since they play together, talk together, and take an interest in what the other is doing. Thus, a boy with a sister tends to show fewer strictly athletic interests and a greater interest in "strategy" games such as chess, scrabble, puzzles, etc. A girl with a brother is more interested in "heterosexual" activities and is more aggressive. In other words, it appears that a family with a sister and brother has the effect of cross-fertilizing interests and activities. This finding is of interest when we remember that studies

Having opposite-sexed siblings results in a wider diversity of interests. Girls with male siblings, for example, tend to become more skilled in athletics and in other activities associated with their brothers.

of highly creative men showed they are more open to their feminine aspects and are thus more imaginative than their "less creative" counterparts (Chapter 2).[16]

An interesting secondary finding, however, is that a single male child with two sisters shows a *counteractive behavior;* that is, he seems to evidence more "masculine" behavior (in terms of interests and playmates) than does a boy with only one sister. Evidently, a single boy with more than one sister may feel in danger of being overwhelmed by the feminine side of the home environment and escapes (or is encouraged to escape by his parents) into a world of masculine interests.

Birth Order

The order of birth in the family seems to have a direct bearing on one's eventual orientation to the world. It is not surprising to find, of course, that first-born children are perceived as more bossy, more

There are differences in motivation and achievement in the first-born compared to the later-born.

verbally aggressive, generally more able to use their authority, and that they use their "oldest" status as a means to secure their ends. They also try more to use reason, logic, and other forms of intellectual persuasion. Younger children, on the other hand, have learned to use a low-powered technique to get what they want: crying, pouting, tattling, even threats. But younger children also learn to be more conciliatory and to rely more on "help techniques": compromise, flattery, pleading, and giving in. Younger children also learn to switch between many roles to get what they want. (In the view of I. D. Harris, first-born children see their function in the family as authoritative, even messianic, while the later-born view themselves as agitators who harass and challenge the "established authority." [17])

Another point the authors of *The Sibling* make is that while first-born children (of either sex) are highly influenced by their parents, younger children are more influenced by their older siblings—in other words, these children grow up in different environmental conditions from the older child. Adler suggested that later-born children become power seekers as a result of their long years of subjugation.[18] The research evidence does seem to indicate that younger children are more physically aggressive, less docile, less amenable to reason than oldest children, and that the latter tend to identify with their parents' values and roles—and that oldest children in a family are more often given an opportunity to function as parent-substitutes and given delegated legitimate authority.

First-Born and Achievement

In terms of achievement, first-born seem to have the advantage. Studies of highly gifted children reveal a predominance of first-born. National Merit Scholars, for example, show a significant predominance of first-born children in their samples—that is, more than would be expected on the basis of chance. First-born are overrepresented in *Who's Who*, and even our astronauts seem to be first-born children primarily.

The reasons behind the eminence of first-born children is probably not so much related to biology (inherited superiority) as it is to the "sociological" structure of the family. The family generally gives to the first-born a degree of exclusive time and attention impossible for subsequent children. The first-born thus generally has greater access to family resources; he (or she), for example, is more likely to receive a college education. As many a parent can testify, by the time the younger children come along, the parents are more relaxed in their "parenting," and they can also be somewhat weary. Thus, standards (both academic and behavior) are often more lenient. Older children are frequently heard to say, "Boy, I wasn't allowed to get away with that when I was *his* [or *her*] age." Furthermore, with one or more children already in college, the later-born children may not be pushed as hard in the same direction, if only because of a shortage in the family exchequer.

The Only Child

By and large, an only child resembles the oldest child. Like the oldest child, he is more highly verbal, and he seems to adopt the standards of the "adult" society more readily than do children with siblings. This may be because the parents take him more places, include him in more of their activities, and talk to him more frequently. It is easier to include one child in the parents' activities than it is to include two, three, or more.

At the same time, both the oldest child and the only child can be more dependent upon approval of the adults in their society. Since they more readily identify with the adult world rather than with their peer group, they will conform more to adult standards and accept them as their own more readily and at an earlier age. They also tend to use their brains more than their brawn, show more anxiety in the face of threat, evince more need for succor (nurturance and reinforcement from others), and are more conscientious and reliable in carrying out their duties. Since they have a greater sense of responsibility than later-born, they thus tend later to take positions of responsibility and authority in the world at large, which perhaps helps to explain their eminence in *Who's Who*, etc.

Individual Differences

Before Freud, a person's adult character was thought to be the result of his hereditary makeup—those traits inherited from his parents and grandparents. A person of "dubious" character was thought to have come from "bad blood." For example, a boy might turn out to be a renegade—"*just* like his father." A favorite theme in the literature of the nineteenth century was the sudden surfacing of a hitherto hidden "trait"—such as "madness"—which was supposedly passed on from father to son—as, for example, in Ibsen's play *The Wild Duck*.

Once Freud's theory of personality development began to gain acceptance, the pendulum swung the other way. Personality theorists then began to emphasize the effects of early environmental experiences, and the child's conflicts with the family became the focus of personality theory, sometimes almost to the exclusion of "hereditary" characteristics. The controversy between advocates of the "hereditary" school of intelligence and personality and the advocates of the "environmental" approach to human growth continues even into our own day, with the former maintaining that "nature" is the decisive factor in what "personality" can become and the latter (the "nurture" or social-interpersonal growth) group contending that personality is primarily a *social* phenomenon. As is often the case in such arguments, both sides in the "nature-nurture" discussion have "a piece of the truth," in the authors' opinion: that is, we are the product of both our heredity and our sociology (and of other things besides).

Research studies tend to show that children who are reared in impoverished and isolated environments, generally perform at lower levels of "intellectual functioning" than the children who are reared in culturally rich and provocative environments.[19] Experimental animal studies show much the same results—that animals show increased learning capacity when reared in "culturally rich" environments.[20] The research data with animal "intelligence" are now so numerous that only a skeptic can doubt the effects of environment on personality or intelligence.

But what about those evident and "innate differences" among persons. There is evidence accumulating now from long-term child studies that the newborn child is not simply a lump of malleable flesh and bone whose intelligence and personality will be determined solely by the environment of his early years. Each child does indeed seem to come into the world with a "personality" all of his own and quite different from others.[21] It is obvious, of course, that we differ from each other in color of hair, eyes, skin; that we can be long and thin, or short and stocky; that we are more or less muscular, more or less fat than others; that the shape of our faces and various parts of our body differ from each other. Physically, each of us represents quite a different set of physical structures from any other man or woman on earth. It is important to realize that even these physical differences will cause the world to be slightly different for each person and thus affect his functioning. For example, a person who is color-blind perceives the world quite differently from a color-seeing person. So also, a child with farsightedness experiences the early world of learning to read quite differently than other children. A person who is left-handed makes constant adjustments in a world that is designed for right-handed people: he sits at right-handed schoolroom desks, and doors always open the "wrong way." And so directions must always be reversed (by him) in order to be rendered sensible. In school, children are generally seated so that the sun comes in the windows over their left shoulders, and so the left-handed child frequently finds himself working in his own shadow. The left-handed person learns to sit in a certain position at the table so as not to keep bumping the right-handed person sitting next to him, etc.

The fact of being born a redhead in our world may indeed have a relationship with being "hot-tempered." If it is not genetic, then the very fact that many persons believe there to be a relationship between red-headedness and hotness of temper may result in a self-fulfilling prophecy: and the redhead may allow his anger to show more openly simply because that is what is expected of him!

And surely it is also true that a boy who is small for his age or who reaches puberty later may be more prone to develop feelings of inadequacy about his strength or even his masculinity. The girl who was taller than everyone else in her grade school, on the other hand, may suffer from feelings of being a "giant" for most of her life, even though by the time she grows up she is not unusually tall. And the round shoulders she developed at an early age (to avoid seeming tall) will remain with her during her adult years. All children probably some time in their lives suffer from some aspect of feeling different, no matter what that difference may be and how seemingly unimportant it may be to others. Adults also can feel "different" or "stigmatized" if they have been identified as being diabetic, crippled, bucktoothed, etc.[22] Thus, our physical inheritance does, indeed, shape our personality in ways of which we perhaps are unaware.

Besides the effects of physical differences, there is now growing evidence that children come into the world with different emotional makeups, or what we are coming to call *behavioral dispositions*, general patterns of emotional behavior. We can observe that process in ourselves easily in our growing children. Some children are eager, spontaneous, physically energetic, outgoing, and aggressive, whereas other children seem to be quiet, preferring to play by themselves. Still other children seem to be "fretful" and generally reside in an "unhappy state." These behavioral dispositions are evident very early in life—as early as during the first three years—and they seem to continue and evolve throughout the life of the individual—to constitute an emotional set, so to speak.

But as psychologists have become more skilled in discriminating finer and finer differences in the behavioral patterns of infants, they are confirming that even babies demonstrate different "qualities" right from birth. For example, some newborn infants are active and lusty, whereas others are quiet and passive. Nine different "emotional patterns" have been discovered so far among newborn infants which seem to be relatively "stable" or "even" patterns of behaving. And these patterns have been found to continue to exist up to at least two years of age.[23]

Psychologists today seem to be discovering what most mothers have been saying about their children for many years: that this baby was "happy from the moment he was born" while that baby was always "fussy and colicky," seemingly from the day that he was born. Even here, however, we must consider the effects of such behavioral dispositions upon the parent-child relationship. An athletically inclined father will interact quite differently with a strong, robust son with whom he can play ball than with the boy who seems passive and less energetic or less interested in sports. Or consider the mother who is herself emotionally subdued and passive. How does she react to an aggressive and extremely husky baby who begins to demand all her attention almost from the day of birth? The mother may soon become physically exhausted from the demands of such a child, whereas she will feel more comfortable and loving toward a child who is more subdued, more like herself. Such emotional interactions will inevitably have their effects on the child and on his rearing.

Cultural and Subcultural Differences

Before we leave this section, we should note too, that the culture (or subculture) we are born into and raised within can have a profound effect on our "emotional" development and on how we subsequently react to events and people. Anthropologists like to study small or relatively isolated societies such as those that were to be found on South Sea Islands seventy-five years ago, or that still exist in the remote jungles of South America. That kind of society still has a fairly consistent culture. Most of its members seem to share the same beliefs, the same marriage rituals, the same child-rearing practices. In that kind of culture, one grows up in a society where most people feel, think, and behave like most others in one's immediate environment. One has a model to follow. If the young wife suffers the tragic loss of her husband, she knows exactly how to react, to mourn, how long to wait before choosing another husband, etc. The model has been set in former generations by the tribe in which she lives. There is some comfort in following an established tradition even where one's emotional reactions are concerned.

And societies differ drastically in their models and expectations of behavior. A Polynesian eight-year-old thinks nothing of suddenly being given the care of her three- or four-year-old sibling to tote around all day, bathe, feed, and mother. A child in our society might be expected to play with a sibling for a while, but the all-day care of one's little brother or sister would be viewed as persecution by an American eight-year-old.

Our Western societies are more complex than the isolated societies that most anthropologists study, and there are wider emotional reactions and models to choose from. Nevertheless, even nationalities within the Western world show definite cultural differences. The French have been found to be more like other Frenchmen than they are like Englishmen. Even if we erase the stereotyped traits associated with certain nationalities, Frenchmen do seem more emotionally "expressive"! Englishmen do seem more "reserved" in extending friendship, although they usually extend cordiality very easily. Germans, on the other hand, do seem to be more patriarchal and "masculine"-oriented, whereas the Irish do tend to produce strong women who become martriarchs in their particular families.

These "cultural" differences have an effect on all of us, and they have had an effect on you and your emotional behavior. For example, if you have had an emotionally reserved father and an "Italian" mother who openly displays emotions and affection, you will tend to model yourself after the parent for whom you have greater regard. It may be that as a boy you came to feel that emotion is "feminine" and thus identified yourself with your "masculine" father. Of course, if your father was so reserved that no "relationship" was possible with him at all, then very likely you favored your mother's warmth and affection; and her reality became your model of "emotional behavior."

In a like manner, if you are a second- or even third-generation "American" in an affluent society, if your parents or grandparents came from, say, Scotland, then you may still carry forward the "frugal" tendencies of your forebears who became acquainted with reality in the Scottish Highlands—where only "oats, peas, beans and barley" grow.

On the other hand, if you are of Italian ancestry, you may still need to "use your hands" to express the complexity of life and the feeling of being a human person with others. Anyone who has ever seen a "French shrug" or observed the fluidity with which Italian-Americans express the love of life "in their hands" knows what we are attempting to state in words.

North America has been peopled by almost every conceivable nationality under the sun, and the process is still not completed. We are, as a continent, still receiving "immigrants," even as we realize we may be running out of "living space" and want to close our doors to those who want to come and live with us. But we are not merely a "melting pot," nor are we a single "nation." Rather, we are a curious mixture of Scandinavian, French, German, Armenian, African, Italian, Russian, Chinese, Japanese, and Dutch cultures, not to mention the English and the Irish and the Jews, and those others who have brought their heritage to our shores and stayed to become citizens of our country.

We may still become a "melting pot" in the sense that interracial and interethnic marriage are increasing and producing an ever-wider range of "role models" of personality, ones which we or our children are attempting to integrate and understand. We *seem* to have a fluid kind of awareness of what personality is, and we seem still to have no national norms of what "personality" is. We are experiencing a wide variety of behaviors among our friends, peers, and associates. It's as if there were, right now, no "just-right" way to behave, or be, and it is that which makes us still a melting pot, a place and occasion where growth and evolution are still happening.

Let us not be overawed or impressed by the phenomenon of personality in our own culture. We are only one nation, attempting to discover for ourselves where we are going, what kinds of emotional responses we can try out in safety, and how these responses will determine what the next generation may be and what coming generations will have to contend with as a result of our "mistakes" in child rearing, the socialization process, and the process of "emotional" development.

We end this chapter on that note. Only a multivolume work could encompass the near-infinite variety of emotional responses that are possible within "human" personality. Personality is an "open-ended" phenomenon in our time.

RECOMMENDED READINGS

ERIKSON, ERIK. *Identity: Youth and Crisis.* New York: W. W. Norton, 1968 (paperback).

A well-known psychoanalyst, Erikson has devoted much of his clinical research to studying children and adolescents. He considers one of the major developmental tasks of youth to be that of identity. He sees the acting-out, confused, self-conscious behavior of the adolescent as symptomatic of "identity crisis." Although identity has been an acknowledged factor of human development for longer than we know, now more than ever the adolescent seems to be behaving in bizarre ways in attempting both to achieve a distinct identity divorced from that of his parents and to purposely avoid identity by "dropping out."

GOFFMAN, ERVING. *Stigma: Notes on the Management of Spoiled Identity.* Englewood Cliffs, N.J.: Prentice-Hall, 1963 (paperback).

A stigma is a bodily sign which indicates a blemished person. When a person has a stigma (such as a scar, stuttering, deafness, protruding teeth, etc.), it influences (and reflects) how he sees himself and ultimately his whole personality. This book will sensitize the college student to the embarrassments and fears that stigmatized persons suffer from and the methods they use to keep from being discovered.

HARRIS, IRVING D. *The Promised Seed.* New York: Macmillan, 1964 (hardcover).

More theoretical than research-based, this provocative book offers the thesis that the first-born child identifies with the prevailing establishment (his parents and other significant adults) and uses his power to influence his younger siblings and thus maintain the status quo. The later-born, however, resent this power and do everything they can, both as children and later as adults, to unseat the establishment. Harris uses the lives of historical figures to support his thesis. A fascinating book.

HARRIS, THOMAS A. *I'm OK—You're OK: A Practical Guide to Transactional Analysis.* New York: Harper & Row, 1967 (hardcover).

In highly readable and simple language, Harris lays out the fundamentals of transactional analysis including the child-ego state, the parent-ego state, and the adult-ego state. We have recommended this book to many people and have received enthusiastic comments back. A presentation of this material to a class has generally met with a comment like, "Why didn't you tell us about this before? I could have used it last night when I got into a stupid argument with my roommate!"

JAMES, MURIEL, and DOROTHY JONGEWARD. *Born to Win: Transactional Analysis with Gestalt Experiments.* Reading, Mass.: Addison-Wesley, 1971 (hardcover).

Here is another book based on Berne's transactional analysis. A word of explanation is needed as to why we don't cite Berne himself. Berne wrote his transactional therapy manuals for the professional psychiatrist or psychotherapist. This book and the Thomas Harris book (above) are written more for the intelligent layman and the beginning professional worker. It is filled with many exercises and projects for self-understanding.

MORRIS, DESMOND.. *The Naked Ape.* New York: McGraw-Hill, 1967 (hardcover). New York: Dell, 1967 (paperback).

If you really take a good look at man, says Desmond Morris, you have to see him as the most fully developed of the primates: an upright, hunting, weapon-toting, territorial, neotonous, brainy, naked ape—a primate by ancestry and a carnivore by adoption . . . a new and experimental departure from his progenitors and, like many new models, one with a few imperfections. Although culturally civilized, he is genetically still a primate—and his animal nature causes him problems.

SPIRO, MELFOR E. *Children of the Kibbutz: A Study in Child Training and Personality.* New York: Schocken, 1965 (paperback).

Most of the material in this chapter is based on our Western concepts of the nuclear family and the personality types and problems that are the result of the nuclear family society. For an interesting insight into what results when children are not raised by "mothers and fathers" as we know them, read this book. The kibbutz is the Israeli commune unit. There the children are raised by group parents in separate lodgings from their biological parents, who visit them two hours each day—not to discipline them or to nag them but to love them. The result: the *Sabra* (native Israeli)—an interesting personality type.

SUTTON-SMITH, BRIAN, and B. G. ROSENBERG. *The Sibling.* New York: Holt, Rinehart and Winston, 1970.

This book is a summary of the major findings of investigations into the influence of birth-order and sex on character, personality, and achievement. There is an overrepresentation of the first-born among geniuses, Ph.D.'s, eminent scientists, and political leaders. Other differences between first-borns and later-borns makes it clear that there are factors involved in shaping a personality other than parent-child relationships. This is not too easy a book to read, but the advanced student will get much from it.

VAN GENNEP, ARNOLD. *The Rites of Passage.* Chicago: University of Chicago Press, 1962 (paperback).

This book has become a classic for the serious student of the social sciences. Van Gennep observes that any transition from one stage of life to another is, in most cultures, marked by a "rite of passage." These transitions include pregnancy, birth, initiation into adulthood, marriage, and death. The three major phases of the rites of passage include (1) separation from one's previous role, (2) transition, and (3) reincorporation into the flow of one's new role. The phenomenon has relevance for us in that we need to develop new rites of passage in our changing society.

8

OUR MANY SELVES: BECOMING AWARE OF EMOTIONS AND FEELINGS

OUR BEWILDERING EMOTIONS

Sometimes, perhaps you have caught yourself doing something that wasn't characteristic of your "usual self." Or perhaps you have heard other people make remarks such as: "I was so overwrought I didn't know what I was doing," or "I knew I was saying the wrong things but I just couldn't help myself," or "He didn't seem to be himself." And on occasion, one in fact doesn't seem to be "one's self." We feel "out of sorts" or "at our wit's end"—phrases implying we are "off our center," bedeviled, driven (so to speak) by forces we are only dimly conscious of.

Sometimes, we may even be driven to emotional excess. We feel full of confidence on one day, even the life of the party, and the next day we feel inadequate and wonder why we put so much effort into things that aren't worth it after all. Or we may find ourselves caught up in the onslaught of changing moods, wishing desperately to be centered somewhere.

It is no wonder, then, that our moods and feelings very often confuse and bewilder us. No wonder that we often feel conflicted, "of two minds," "divided." The truth is that personality integration, if and when it is achieved, is a truly remarkable event. We grow in spurts and lopsidedly for the most part.

OUR MANY EMOTIONAL SELVES

The experience of doing or saying something that is not like your usual self is quite common. Most of us have experienced just that. The truth is that, emotionally, we frequently feel as if there were several personalities within us which come out at various times.

Many personality theorists have confirmed this in their clinical observations. In Chapter 7, you read how Freud divided the human personality into three functions: the id, the ego, and the superego. You read also how Berne demonstrated to his patients that they sometimes acted their own Adult (mature) self, but also the Child self and the Parent self.

Topdog and Underdog

Fritz Perls, the founder of Gestalt therapy, liked to call the conflicting personalities in us Topdog and Underdog.[1] The Topdog personality in the human being (according to Perls) is roughly equivalent to the superego of Freud and the Parent-ego state of Berne. He's the one we see on the outside and who seems to be in charge. Topdog shouts orders to Underdog (our inner, more frightened, "weaker" personality) much the way Papa shouted at Mama, etc. We have incorporated this struggle within us, Perls said, and we act out the conflicts of our parents all by ourselves. Consequently, we have at least two subpersonalities (besides the "I" that we know) within us. Therapy sessions with Perls often proved to be surprisingly amusing and dramatic, for it would frequently turn out that the roles were actually reversed—that the mild-mannered Underdog personality was more in control of the person that the huff-and-puff Topdog.

The Persona and the Shadow

Splits in our personality can be viewed from another viewpoint, such as Jung's; and then we speak of the Shadow and the Persona.[2] The Persona and Shadow are *archetypes* for Jung. An archetype, as defined by Webster, is a representation or copy. The following discussion will clarify what Jung meant by this concept. For now, think of a mold from which something can be made in a particular shape, such as a coin, an automobile part, or even a person. Though each of these individualities can be recognized as belonging to the type and mold from whence it came, there are often subtle and individual differences within each type. Such individual differences within a type allows for the possibility of individual personality and freedom in the psychological sense.

The Persona and the Shadow are only two of the complementary archetypal forces in the personality. They are polar to each other, at opposite ends of a continuum. The Shadow is the "dark" or hidden side of personality: those parts of ourselves we do not want to acknowledge, and thus the parts about which we remain "in the dark." The Persona is the other side of that shadow face we see in the mirror. The Persona is also the face others see. It is the "personality" we put on when we are being merely "social"—that is, involved in some kind of role-playing activity, such as being a "lawyer," or a "doctor," or a "New York taxi driver," or a "psychologist," or a "Jew," or "a black," or "a liberal." (Or a schizophrenic.) (Persona, from the Latin, originally meant a character in a play, i.e. someone who puts on a mask to portray a certain character.) Most of us, once we begin to develop social personas, or personalities, have difficulty in admitting to these masks and games—the little dishonest behaviors by which we evade the truth about ourselves. Any and all these conscious evasions constellate an oppositional set of tendencies in the unconscious side of personality, says Jung. He called the oppositional archetype of the Persona the Shadow.

The Shadow. The Shadow is the unliked, the unappreciated, the unacknowledged, even the hated side of ourselves which we are not willing to admit into consciousness. As with the real shadow that one's body casts when the sun is shining, a person cannot escape his Shadow. It is always there accompanying him and her (if silently) in the background. It can remain forever in the background of one's awareness in the waking state; but in dreams sometimes the Shadow appears, and then it can be a frightening experience, particularly if the person has been out of touch with his real behavior in the world. For example, a person may dream of a monster, or a frightening witch, or some other kind of overwhelming figure. A woman, for example, who is repressing her sexuality in the way women did in the Victorian age may find a female figure in her dreams behaving in sexual ways that horrify her. Such a figure may then change into a gorilla, implying some biological aspect of herself she is presently ignoring. Or a man who prides himself overly about his "wisdom" may dream of a clown. These are polarities.

The persons we have been just describing want to deny, according to their dreams, the "negative" side of their personality: they don't want to admit their shortcomings. Oddly enough, there are

The shadow is that aspect of ourselves we deny but that we cannot get away from.

some persons with the opposite difficulty—they don't want to admit to their *virtues*, the so-called positive side of themselves. Let us explain: A man who prides himself on being "tough-minded" in business may have a dream in which he is clearly portrayed as foolishly charitable, even "saintly." This is his Shadow, the part of himself he is ashamed of. A woman who sees herself as unattractive may dream of a Shadow self filled with light, joy, and expressiveness. This also is she—her Shadow side that she can't bring herself to accept.

One of the difficulties in denying such possibilities in oneself is that we are then vulnerable to attributing our "Shadow side" to others. In Chapter 4, we called this *projection*. A man who does not trust himself will not be able to trust others. A man who denies his own "femininity" will get nervous, even angry, when he sees some other man behaving in a way that seems "too feminine." A man who denies his own need for power for too long can come in time to view others as "power-hungry." And so on.

In Jung's postulation of the Shadow, it is related always to the Persona as a kind of balancing phenomenon: the Persona is the public (in the light, visible) side of self, whereas the Shadow is the hidden (in the darkness, not easily seen) aspect of ourselves. And remember: these possibilities are polar aspects; they go hand-in-hand, always together.

The Shadow-Persona archetype is not the only subpersonality system within us, according to Jung. Within the collective unconscious there are many other archetypes to be identified, and we discuss some of these in Chapters 10 and 12.

MULTIPLE PERSONALITY

Sometimes a person is so fearful of the "dark" possibilities in his personality that he attempts to repress all knowledge of their existence. These repressed emotions and feelings are still present in his personality even though he may be unaware of them consciously. When repression is complete and successful, the person remains largely unaware of these "dark" impulses in himself. But should these repressing defenses begin to fail, or even to break down, the "dark" impulses can then begin to emerge in an actual and distinct personality with a separate identity, and not just as another aspect of personality. That would be an archetypal event, according to Jung.

Literature abounds in stories with the theme of multiple personality, as illustrated by Robert Louis Stevenson's novella *The Strange Case of Dr. Jekyll and Mr. Hyde* and Oscar Wilde's *Portrait of Dorian Gray*. In Stevenson's story, Dr. Jekyll, a humanitarian physician, drinks an elixir which transforms him into his opposite—an irresponsible, pleasure-loving man who does as he wants. Wilde's Dorian Gray, on the other hand, literally projects his psychological degeneration onto a portrait of himself. The figure in the portrait ages, taking on the jaded and evil aspects of Dorian Gray's inner self, while Gray himself remains outwardly young and beautiful. German literature abounds also in tales of the "doppelganger"—the double, the mirror-image of oneself which portends death.

There have been actual cases of multiple personality recorded in medical history. One is discussed in a thoroughly absorbing book, *The Three Faces of Eve,* in which two psychiatrists describe their amazement and perplexity in discovering that a rather attractive but colorless housewife in her mid-twenties was harboring a repressed personality quite different from her public personality.[3] The public personality was completely unaware of her second personality, which emerged during periods of "headaches" and "blackouts." This second personality was cocky, brazen, aggressive, spontaneous, voluptuous—everything, in fact, that her public personality held to be unacceptable. While the public personality, "Eve White," could not bring herself to admit to certain emotions (feelings of sexuality, disliking her husband, boredom in being a mother, etc.), her alternate personality, "Eve Black," had no such inhibitions. Indeed, "Eve Black" tried to act out some of the impulses "Eve White" would not admit to herself. The third "face" was Jane, who the psychiatrists believed to be the integrating force in Eve's personality.

Recently another, even more striking example of multiple personality has been reported in the book *Sybil*. "Sybil" (a pseudonym) had been victimized by some of the most severe child abuse in the annals of child psychology.[4] As a way of managing these childhood traumata, Sybil created for herself sixteen different personalities with distinctly different identities, interests, and even sexes. Although all of the sixteen identities were aware of the others and of Sybil, Sybil herself was unaware of their existence. The story of Sybil is at once the most fascinating and the most grizzly of multiple-personality case histories.

THE WIDE RANGE OF EMOTIONAL PATTERNS

In addition to the multiple-personality pattern, there are other kinds of life styles that are considered so deviant that they are known as "psychoses" or "mental illness." We shall discuss only a few of them. But the thing to remember as you read about them is that these so-called psychoses are simply ways for persons to manage emotions which are ordinarily too uncomfortable for them to recognize and to "own."

The "Manic-depressive" Personality

Another pattern that shows wide variation in personality is that known as the "manic-depressive psychosis." A person with this personality pattern exhibits, not two or more distinct personalities as in the multiple-personality syndrome, but rather pronounced extremes in mood. At first glance, such a person may seem as normal as you and I—perhaps with just a trifle more extreme swings in their mood. They can be very warm on the surface, friendly and self-confident; and they may seem to experience the same kinds of emotions you do. What, then, is wrong?

As you get to know them, you become aware that their emotional reactions are far out of proportion to events. A minor incident can arouse an oppressive down-in-the-dumps reaction that can last several days, even weeks. Then suddenly and without apparent reason they can revert to an elated, happy-go-lucky mood, full of self-confidence and vigor, in which they may go on a reckless shopping spree, or decide to completely alter their life style, or undertake a project—such as composing a symphony—for which they have no talent whatsoever. Their emotions are exaggerated and seem unstable. In a word, they are overemotional! They exhaust us by just being around, for their emotions control them and threaten to overwhelm us, too. Such is the manic-depressive personality pattern.

The "Schizophrenic" Personality

In the so-called schizophrenic forms of deviancy the person seems to be out of contact with the normal, commonly shared experience of what it is to be a human person. Schizophrenia is not, as commonly believed, "split personality." When we become schizophrenic, our behaviors and thought patterns seem strange and at times bizarre to other persons (sometimes also to ourselves). Sometimes, in fact, our emotional response pattern undergoes such a "sea change" that we seem to be "turned inside-out." A schizophrenic may giggle inanely when he is confronted with a frightening situation, and he can just as easily (and as unpredictably) become morose and withdrawn—a "dead man" who refuses to allow further stimulation from his environment to get through to him. Such a person may even become *catatonic*—he may sit for hours without moving, or he may not eat or walk for long periods of time. He does not seem to be aware of things around him and may stand statuelike in an awkward position. The schizophrenic has other curious (to us) emotional responses: he can become morose where other persons seem to encounter situations of joy—for example, at holiday celebrations. And he can deviate in other directions thought "abnormal" by many in society.

Most of the severely disturbed schizophrenic personalities were once confined to state hospitals. With advances in drug therapy, that percentage is now gratifyingly lower.

The "Schizoid" Personality

The "schizoid" personality appears to function even as all of us do. He works and supports himself and his family. He interacts with other persons in the everyday world apparently without too much conflict. And he seems to carry on his daily round of activities with an apparent sense of direction.

The mark of the schizoid personality is that he seems to operate more effectively and completely than he really does. What distinguishes the schizoid life style is his "cool" and detached way of living with others. For example, he seldom seems to engage in spontaneous laughter, and many persons eventually come to experience him as aloof, withdrawn, emotionally disengaged. Such persons seem to prefer to work more with machines than with people, and they seldom have intimate relationships—the kind of relationships where one is free to share one's inner thoughts and feelings. It's as if their trust in other persons is totally lacking. They do not seem to feel trust or derive joy from human relationships the way most of us seem to. The schizoid personality can therefore appear to be withdrawn in company: for he says little and shows few "emotional responses." He may seem on the surface nonetheless to have everything in hand.

Though such personalities can be highly developed on the "intellectual" level of their personality, and do well (even brilliantly) in their careers, they do not seem to enjoy or encourage the company of other persons too much. According to one personality theorist, their posture and facial expressions are characteristically stiff, mechanical, even robotlike, and their smiles seem masklike.[5]

Sociopathic Personality

In the emotional deviancies we have been talking about, the person has found some method (as bizarre as it may seem to us) to handle his conflicting emotions. There is another kind of pattern which seems to be one of an *underdevelopment* of emotional behavior, called the *sociopathic* or (sometimes) the *psychopathic* personality.

The sociopath appears to value human life so little that he can snuff out another person's life much as we would slap down a mosquito—and with about as little sense of relationship with his victim! Interviews with psychopathic murderers seem to reveal just this curious lack of affect or feeling. They do not shoot or stab a victim in anger or rage or fear. Nor do they kill him while under the influence of alcohol or drugs or "voices"—as does the psychotic personality most often. The sociopath simply shoots his victim, or stabs him, or runs him down with an automobile, or pushes him out of a window—in cold blood. The sociopath is the extreme deviant.

Of course, there are "milder" forms of sociopathy. The sociopath may not murder his next door neighbor, but he might "do him in" in other ways. He may sell him a car that is a "lemon" with full knowledge (and no remorse) that he has cheated the man. He may become an actual "carney" whose only object in life seems to be to fleece a "mark"—the general public. He may "borrow" money from a friend with no intention of paying it back, although he says he will when he "gets the bread." Or he may be a professional (physician, attorney, engineer, etc.) who is not living up to his code of ethics.

The Range of "Normal" Human Emotions

Although we have been describing emotional deviancy, there is probably not one of us that has not experienced something of all of them! Who has not, for example, experienced as an adolescent the emotional extremes of the manic-depressive personality? Who among us has not occasionally experienced depressions so deep that we were drained of the ability to do anything but lie on our beds? Or who has not experienced giggling inanely after a shock or become hysterical after an accident? Or who has not injured (physically or emotionally) another person without caring?

Our emotions, then, can be a source of pain and anxiety. They can cause us to suffer, and when we take our pain and anxiety out on others they can cause others around us to suffer. In fact, unless we can become aware of our emotional pain, we will *tend* to pass our pain along to someone else. After a period of stormy interpersonal strife, one young college student said recently, "Life would be a lot less hectic if we didn't have emotions!"

EMOTIONS AS MOTIVATORS

But very few people would want to live without emotions. One psychologist has pointed out that "a life without emotion would be a life without motion.." [6] Even though our emotions can be (and often are) a source of confusion and anxiety for us, they also can be (and are) the basic substance of our deepest satisfactions. One source of emotional satisfaction comes to us through our senses: the texture and taste of an apple, the feel of cool water on a hot summer's day, the scent of pine woods, or the nostalgic sound of rain pattering on a roof. These are part of our emotional heritage.

Our emotions provide us with pleasures in other ways as well: in the act of sexual fulfillment when two persons meet each other lovingly; or in that sense of possession and control of one's physical body—say, after skiing a mountain slope; or after a real meeting of skills on the tennis court. We gain emotional fulfillment also from satisfying our needs for achievement and in sharing the personal achievements of our children, our students, our friends, our associates, and even of organizations with which we choose to affiliate.

Emotions, in other words, are one of the processes that motivate us and energize our being, that move us to know ourselves and others better.

When our emotions are constructive, we are moved toward other people in friendship, in work and partnership. Our emotions are the "fuel" we use to direct and channel our energies as we create order and beauty, in writing a letter or a book, in painting a picture, making love, embracing a friend, rearranging furniture, creating an architecturally exciting building, or wearing and designing descriptive clothing. Emotions at their highest level are the wellsprings of the artist's painting, the poet's word-music, the dramatist's play, the philosopher's utopia. Freud identified this need to express ourselves (to create, to achieve, to discover our universe) as the process of *sublimation.* Freud called basic emotional energy *libido,* that primitive biological energy from which all life is created and which seeks to grow and express itself, to reproduce and to derive pleasure from the world. (This is as simple a formulation as we can make of what Freud intended when he spoke of the *pleasure principle.*) [7] Sublimation of the pleasure principle, therefore, involves the energy of the libidinal force in secondary ways, and is always involved in the act of creation.

EMOTIONS AND CIVILIZATION

Emotional energy, then, is that deep and basic part of biological survival which the human species shares with the "lower" animals. The rapidity of our retaliate-or-run responses enabled us to survive in prehistoric times, when our stone-age ancestors had to be on the alert for the giant mastodons and other monsters who inhabited the very ancient world. And in one sense, our *emotional* self *is* a more primitive part of our personality structure than our *intellectual* self (that cool and rational process by which we think, make judgments, evaluate, etc.). The primitiveness of our emotional responses can be seen quickly when we observe two boys haul off to fight each other over an apparently minor incident or a dispute about their territorial rights. Our emotional reactions are often so quick, and sometimes so unreasoning, that we often lash out before we realize what we are doing.

We are no longer living, however, under conditions which allow us to express our flight-or-fight reactions so unmistakably and so visibly. When an employer snaps at us, for example, we can hardly afford to haul off and sock him in the jaw; or even snap back at him. Neither can we afford to allow our primitive emotional reactions to overwhelm us when some driver on the road begins to play childish but very dangerous games with us. We might in fantasy "teach him a lesson," but we know that to do so in actuality would be to court dire consequences. Freud understood this, and that is why he said that civilization is based on the *reality principle.*[8] Thus, civilization itself prevents expression of these primitive emotional reactions and sometimes savage urges.

Absorbing, Blaming and Channeling of Emotions versus Understanding Them

Since civilization does not permit us free license in acting out our emotions, the intellectual part of ourselves tries to evolve more rational ways to deal with conflict and frustration. But what happens to our urge to strike back or run away when neither of these emotional responses are going to aid us? Well, many things happen. But

they can be classified generally under two rubrics or classes. The first is that we can take the insults and injuries and assaults into our being—we can *absorb* them, so to speak. When we do this, however, the repressed and unrecognized emotional reactions run underground and begin to emerge in other ways—as, for example, the personal and global anxiety discussed in Chapter 3. The unexpressed rage, anger, resentment, jealousy, etc. may also turn into the physical complaints and psychosomatic reactions of headache, gnawing ulcers, and hypertension also discussed in Chapter 3.

The second possibility is that we can deny the negative emotions. In so doing, however, these emotions emerge in ways we may not realize: in general irritability (when one can't pinpoint what is wrong), in depression (feeling that everything is going wrong), in hostility toward others (sometimes seen as "wit" at the expense of someone else), in general "malaise," in "boredom" (sometimes a cover-up for other, more frightening emotions), in "whining" (motivated by a feeling that if we complain more, someone will help us out of our problems), in manipulation (motivated by the feeling that the only way to get what we want is to use others, since "no one really looks out for anybody but himself"), and so on through the defense mechanisms, some of which were discussed in Chapter 4.

What we are doing in such cases, it appears, is disassociating ourselves from our original negative emotions and then channeling these emotions into other kinds of reactions and responses. Much of this channeling reemerges eventually as "blaming" behavior. Examples: "The reason I have to nag is because no one listens to me." "Yes, I'm short-tempered, but it's been so damned hot, I can't help it." "I wouldn't be so jealous if I were sure of my husband." "My children do everything they can to upset me." "My parents didn't love me."

It is via such statements and communications that we defend ourselves from an important insight—and that is that the dilemma of our unhappiness lies within us. Our irritability, our nagging, our whining, and all the other ways our negative emotions are channeled—all these prevent us from *owning our emotions*. The key to resolving the dilemma of emotions, according to Carl Rogers, is simply to *own* them—that is, to "own up" to the fact that these emotions and behaviors are ours, that *we are creating them*, and that all the "blaming" in the world will help us not one iota. The only way to get over whining and nagging and jealousy is to own them and then to decide to work on ourselves to change ourselves—not others.

Denial, Diassociation, and Demonism

When we deny the existence of our negative emotions, they begin to control us, to run amuck in the sense that they become "unconscious" motivators of our behavior (and all the more insidious because we are unaware of them). Carl Gustav Jung, the noted Swiss psychoanalyst, points out that as long as a person is unable to control his moods and emotions, or to be conscious of them, they control him and affect his decisions. He is certainly, then, not his own master! Jung likens these unconscious emotional impulses to the primitive tribal beliefs in demonology: namely, the belief that my unhappiness is due to some bad spirit, malevolent demon, or jealous god who is deliberately making evil and thus causing unhappiness. The end result of demonism, as Jung has pointed out, is the placating of the demon, the spirits, or gods by human sacrifice.[9] In the sixteenth and seventeenth centuries, as Aldous Huxley has pointed out, a man's personal unhappiness, particularly if it took the form of sexual impotence, was frequently attributed to the malevolence of some woman, who may then have been burned as a witch. Huxley has estimated that over a million women were so burned.[10]

If we believe that we are that much more advanced in self-understanding than these medieval folk, we have only to make note of Nazi Germany of thirty years ago, and how that nation became engaged in a wholesale slaughter of six million Jews—because Hitler said Germany and the world would be better off without them. In our own country, sociological evidence continues to point up the relationship between acts of violence and personal unhappiness. In the southern United States before World War II, for example, whenever the price of cotton dropped and there was a temporary economic recession, the number of lynchings of black persons increased.

In the Middle Ages, men often blamed their impotence on women, accusing them of being witches.

Jung says Eastern and Western cultures are locked up now into a kind of "demonic insanity" in which each threatens to destroy each other and the world. And this demonism is based on the assumption that the evil and pain in the world is due primarily to the existence of the opposite culture. Capitalism, according to the Communists, is the tyranny of the few over the many, and the world would become a paradise if it could be liberated from the domination of the capitalists. Our expression of this demonism is summarized in a slogan which was popular some years ago: "Better dead than Red!"

THE INTEGRATION OF PERSONALITY

Throughout this chapter you have come across examples of personality disintegration and the many subpersonalities hypothetically part and parcel of the human experience. We have all experienced a strange assortment of emotional selves from time to time. You may find yourself behaving quite differently with your friends than you do with your parents. Or your personality may vary markedly as you go from role to role, from son to husband, father, employee, lover, and citizen—or similarly, from daughter to wife, mother, employee, lover, and citizen.

We are not saying that you should not vary your pattern of responding according to different situations. On the contrary, different situations and different persons evoke in us different feelings and prompt different behaviors. The important questions to ask yourself as you look at all your roles are: Are you happy with them for the most part? Are you happy with all of them or none of them? Is there one role in which you find that you feel "not yourself," for example? Would you like to become less of a "child" when you are with your parents or your "employer"? Would you like to become less punitive as a father? Are you on top of all your emotions, or do they run you up and down in mood like a roller coaster? Or are you somehow less feeling and involved with others than you would like to be—as if you were aware that you are missing out on some of the richness that goes with deep interpersonal relationships?

The process of personality integration involves the recognition of one's subpersonalities and the assimilation of these aspects of oneself into a more harmonic whole being. It may be that the moment of perfect integration is the moment of the "peak" experience that Maslow has talked about, or of the "mystic" experience that abounds in religious literature. It is the moment when we become no longer divided within ourselves or feel alien and apart from the world around us—when we are One.

How can we go about the process of integrating these many possibilities in our personality and ourselves?

There are many paths to that goal. One approach is through psychotherapy. Another is through learning to interpret our dreams, for our dream self is frequently astonishingly different from our daytime awareness of our self. Another approach involves the study of our personal mythological truth, for, as Jung says, we are all acting out archetypal roles of which we are frequently unaware. Still another approach is through any of the various sensory and physical therapies now becoming popular. There are many routes, many pathways available now to the person who earnestly seeks integration of his personality. And we begin to discuss some of these routes and pathways in Part II of this book, which begins with the next chapter.

RECOMMENDED READINGS

DARWIN, CHARLES. *The Expression of the Emotions in Man and Animals.* Chicago: University of Chicago Press, 1965 (paperback).

First published in 1872, this book is as exciting and up-to-date now as it was then. Darwin traces some of our emotions and expressions to our early anthropoid genesis or to species further back along the evolutionary scale. Fascinating reading.

JOURARD, SIDNEY M. *The Transparent Self.* Princeton, N.J.: D. Van Nostrand, 1964 (paperback).

This book was largely responsible for popularizing the term *self-disclosure*. As Jourard describes it, because we are afraid of rejection, hurt, or criticism, we hide behind various masks which prevent us from knowing one another. "But such protection," he says, "is purchased at a steep price. We are then never able to be truly ourselves to someone else." The choice is ours: Shall we wear our masks or shall we reveal our true faces? Some of us come from cultural backgrounds that inhibit self-disclosure. Students usually get a lot from this book.

JUNG, CARL. *The Undiscovered Self.* New York: Mentor, 1959 (paperback).

Each of us wears a mask, says Jung, which he called the *Persona*. The Persona is the public face we wear which others see and which we see when we look in the mirror. But there is another self, which we deny most of the time and which Jung called the Shadow. We may deny it, but it clings to us like our real shadow and often takes over when we don't know it. We each have a *real* self also, but it takes work to get to know it—this is the undiscovered self.

MC NEIL, ELTON B. *The Quiet Furies.* Englewood Cliffs, N.J.: Prentice-Hall, 1967 (paperback).

We have not discussed the various aspects of extreme emotional deviancy to a great extent. Students who would like an insight into various types of emotional deviancy such as alcoholism, suicidal tendencies, the manic-depressive syndrome, sexual deviation, drug addiction, etc. will find this book highly readable. McNeil presents case studies of various emotional deviancy in highly dramatic and informative style. The illustrations alone are extraordinary in their symbolic presentation.

MONTAGU, ASHLEY. *Man and Aggression.* Fairlawn, N.J.: Oxford University Press, 1968 (paperback).

Unlike many anthropologists and psychologists, Montagu refuses to believe that man's basic nature is "bestial." Highly readable and well-documented, this book maintains that inner man is essentially a cooperative and peaceable animal. This is an interesting contrast to such person books as Konrad Lorenz's *On Aggression* and Robert Ardrey's *African Genesis* and *The Territorial Imperative.*

PERLS, FREDERICK S. *In and Out the Garbage Pail.* Lafayette, Cal.: Real People Press, 1969 (hardcover).

In this remarkable autobiography, Perls discusses himself in frank detail. People either love this book or hate it. The illustrations are very apropos and humorous and aid the text. Your authors knew Perls well and declare this book to reveal him as he was: exhibition-istic, courageous, shocking, outrageous, brilliant, honest, remarkable—but never boring.

ROGERS, CARL R. *On Becoming a Person.* 2nd ed. Boston: Houghton Mifflin, 1961 (paperback).

Rogers developed a therapy for enabling persons to drop their masks and to become more themselves. He calls it the "real me" feeling, and describes the process of discovering the "real me" as learning to be a person—that is, "to be the self which one truly is." He discusses the ways in which a person may discover, under the mask he wears, his real self: the real emotions he feels and the real thoughts he thinks.

ROKEACH, MILTON, ed. *The Open and Closed Mind.* New York: Basic Books, 1960 (hardcover).

Rokeach studied the person who has a "closed" mind—who has "fix-ated" on certain ideas intellectually and who could be said to be the opposite of the creative person. Using a "dogmatism scale," he deals with such questions as: Are closedminded people more authoritarian? How does the closed mind develop during childhood? Recommended for the serious student, since it is heavily data-oriented.

SCHREIBER, FLORA RHETA. *Sybil.* Chicago: Henry Regnery, 1973 (hardcover).

One of the most extreme examples of multiple personalities yet reported is to be found in this book. With a schizophrenic and sadistic mother who abused her to the point of amnesiac retreat, Sybil was able to manage the physical and psychological traumata she experienced only by fleeing into sixteen different personalities.

THIGPEN, CORBETT H., and HARVEY M. CLECKLEY. *The Three Faces of Eve.* New York: Popular Library, 1957 (paperback). Hardcover edition—New York: McGraw-Hill, 1957.

This book describes the case of a young married woman who has three different personalities. The surface, conscious personality was unaware of the existence of the other two. An utterly engrossing book as we follow the author-psychiatrists in their attempt to enable Eve to integrate her varying personalities.

INTEGRATING OUR PERSONALITY PATTERNS

PART II

9

APPROACHES TO PERSONAL GROWTH: PSYCHOTHERAPY, COUNSELING, AND GROWTH GROUPS

In Chapter 2 we noted that the highly integrated personality is able to assess his strengths without undue modesty and evaluate his limitations without excess shame, embarrassment, or "judging." He is aware, that is, of his particular gifts and the style of life that is his own. Upon making a mistake, he has the wisdom often to acknowledge it and to move on from there. The highly integrated personality, therefore, does not go in for the "blaming game." We can do no better than to follow that example and teaching.

When we "take stock" of ourselves, we in effect draw ourselves a "personality profile"—which tells us where we are, so to say—and then we can go on to survey those new dimensions in our selves and the world we wish to explore. Assuming you have taken stock of yourself in that way, you now face the situation of becoming the kind of person you would like to be, want to be, and need to be. There are many paths to that place.

One of the best-established paths to fulfill that kind of need today is called the *therapeutic* situation. The words *therapy* and *therapeutic* come from a Greek word which loosely means "to heal," and our *psychotherapy* today is in that sense the art and science of healing ills and suffering on the *psychological* plane. Much of that healing attention is now being focused on enabling persons to cope with the pressures and tensions of our industrialized civilization.

For example, there can come a time for any of us when the difficulties in our lives have become so burdensome, or where we find ourselves so prone to anxiety, that we feel emotionally crippled and unable to cope. At times like these we need some form of psychotherapy, no matter what we call it.

Most of us have heard about psychotherapy from other persons. They may have told us, for example, about their own therapy, or about someone else who was in therapy, etc. Yet unless we have personally experienced the psychotherapy *process* for ourselves, we do not know what is really involved in that situation.

For some persons, the very idea of undergoing psychotherapy is as anxiety-provoking as it is for others to go to a physician with a long-undiagnosed physical complaint. You may have heard the remark that "anyone who goes to a 'head-shrinker' ought to have his head examined"! We know that we have! You may be puzzled also by how "just talking to someone" can enable a person with real problems to change his living pattern for the better. These are only a few of the reservations that can be expressed concerning psychotherapy. So you will need enough information to answer those questions for yourself. And that is why you need to know something of how psychotherapy in our time has developed.

It matters little by what name personality disintegration has been called—"madness," "schizophrenia," "insanity," or whatever—in any event we are involved here in a severe crisis of some kind. And personality disintegration has existed since the beginning of recorded history. For example, Nebuchadnezzar in biblical times is said to have ended his days eating grass and roots from the earth. And Saul, king of Judah and Israel, is known to have suffered from severe depressions and to have become violent and even homicidal at times. In some cultures—for example, among the American Indians—a person who was "mad" was treated with respect, since he was thought to be touched by the gods. In Europe in the Middle Ages, on the other hand, persons who were "insane" were thought to have lost their reason and sometimes even were thought to be possessed by demons. Since the devil was the personification of the "evil" principle, "insane" persons were sometimes whipped, starved, or branded with hot irons in the belief that punishing the devil (who had taken over the personality) would persuade the evil spirit to leave.

Many of the mentally ill roamed the streets and byways in the latter years of the Middle Ages and just starved to death or became victims of ridicule and cruel treatment. Some were even burned as witches or warlocks.

A small step forward occurred in the treatment of severe personality problems when "insane" persons were placed in asylums. Unfortunately, these places were often not much better than prisons, and their inmates were frequently chained to the walls like other criminals. The word *bedlam*—which has come to mean "a place of wild confusion and noise"—is actually a contraction of the name of a former insane asylum in Southwark, London: the Hospital of St. Mary of Bethlehem (Bedlam). The screaming of Bedlam patients could be heard clearly by passers-by, and the patients were sometimes exhibited like zoo animals (for a fee) to the curious and the thrill seekers.

Many kinds of treatments once used to heal the personality disintegration of persons now seem to us almost barbarous if not outright inhuman. In the snake-pit treatment, for example, the unfortunate patient was lowered by ropes into a pit full of snakes in the belief that the fright of the experience would shock him back into sensibility.

Treatment of insane personalities showed an improvement in France after the Revolution. A remarkable physician, Philippe Pinel, was then put in charge of La Bicetre, an insane asylum in Paris. To the astonishment of his colleagues and despite their ridicule, Pinel insisted on changing the environmental conditions of the inmates. He removed their chains, cleaned up the dung and filth, and let the sun shine into the dungeons where the inmates were housed. Pinel treated his disorganized personalities not as "witless" creatures, but with the same kindness and consideration he showed to other persons. His approach resulted in the improvement and release of

234

many patients who otherwise might have remained in the asylum for the rest of their lives.[1]

Pierre Charcot, another French physician, made a further step forward in the treatment of the mentally disturbed when in the late nineteenth century he demonstrated that the apparently bizarre symptoms of stuttering, trembling, or the inability to walk and talk could be relieved under hypnosis. Charcot's discoveries in hypnosis and treatment of the mentally ill constitute one of the really big breakthroughs in psychiatric treatment. He demonstrated, for example, that many of the *physical* symptoms and disabilities of the insane can have an underlying *psychological* cause, and that if the cause is "psychological," then the condition might be treated "psychologically." [2]

PSYCHOANALYSIS

Among the students who gathered around Charcot in Paris was a young Viennese physician named Sigmund Freud. Freud was already deeply interested in the problems of treating severe neurotic conditions, and he had come to Paris specifically to study under Charcot and learn of his hypnotherapy. Upon his return to Vienna, Freud began to work with a colleague's patient, Anna O., a young woman suffering from "hysteria." This patient was a virtual cripple. Anna not only had trouble eating and sleeping, but she had been suffering from frightening dreams at night and equally frightening delusions during the day. Using Charcot's hypnotic method, Freud enabled Anna to remember certain traumatic events in her earlier life, and as she began to remember those "lost" experiences in her life her symptoms began to decrease in intensity.

One day, Freud was unable to put Anna into a hypnotic trance. To enable her to work out a dream she had had the previous night, Freud suggested that instead of being hypnotized she speak consciously of everything she was thinking and feeling about her dream. That was the beginning of Freud's method of free association.* What Freud had discovered was a "talking cure" for the neuroses of his day.[3] We are still building and adding onto Freud's original discoveries, as we shall see in a moment.

* In Freud's method of free association the person is supposed to be relaxed enough to speak of everything that comes into his "mind," his present awareness. That kind of honesty is bound to provoke change and growth, as Freud demonstrated in his treatment of many persons.

But how does talking to a psychoanalyst seem to enable a person to cope with the difficulties in living in a more efficient way? The answer to this depends on determining what interferes with a person's ability to grow in the first place. For Freud—who was then involved in building a psychological theory of interpersonal relations—the basic factor that interferes with growth was *anxiety: How much* anxiety did the person experience? *With whom* was the anxiety experienced? and *How* did the person deal with that interpersonal situation?

In his original theory of personality development, which he subsequently modified and extended, Freud said that the child who experiences too much anxiety or trauma (pain) has little choice other than to repress the conscious memory of these experiences —he tries to "forget" them, in other words. These traumatic and painful interchanges with others are, however, not forgotten—they simply go "underground"—are "buried" or repressed in what Freud called the "unconscious mind." Repression demands a great deal of our psychic energy. When too much of the psychic energy is directed toward repression, the person can eventually feel emotionally drained and mentally exhausted. He may even become so split off from himself that he is no longer aware of his former thoughts, feelings, and experiences.

The person who is involved in the vicious circle of repression may not realize exactly what is the matter with him. All he knows consciously is that he feels tired and weak, or that he seems to suffer from feelings of shame and guilt; he can also be obsessed with fears and phobias; or he may begin to experience similar kinds of nightmares and delusions as Anna O. On the other hand, he may need to go through a certain complicated ritual every night before he can go to sleep. Or he may find that he is unable to sleep more than a few hours a day—or that he needs ten to twelve hours sleep, etc. When one's life becomes frightening or painful, Freud said, look to the unconscious memory and the anxiety which is bound up in that memory. That, in simple form, was Freud's original understanding of neurosis.

One reason our early childhood memories can be so frightening to encounter is that they represent a *child's* understanding of the world rather than the feelings and understanding of the adult state of awareness. What happens in the psychoanalytic relationship is that these previous memories—and the anxiety and suffering attached thereto—are slowly and cautiously uncovered by the therapist and patient so they can be worked through and assimilated into one's present understanding of the self. Thus, they become not so frightening or shocking for the adult personality as they were for us as children. Suppose, for example, that a child whose parents take care to protect their privacy sees them engaged in sexual intercourse. That event may have seemed a violent struggle, and sexuality then may have been associated with anger and hostility and subsequently with anxiety and shame. If he can recall that repressed childhood memory as an adult, however, he is better able to understand that what he saw was not physical violence but a part of the natural sexual order of things (which he is now ready to share in).

In his work with emotionally handicapped persons, Freud developed the theory and approach of *psychoanalysis*. Our contemporary approaches to personality disintegration are modifications and variations of Freud's basic approach. In the classical form of psychoanalytic treatment, developed by Freud, the patient came to the therapist's office three to five times a week for an hour. Generally, he lay down on a couch so he could be comfortable and relaxed, and so better able to free-associate, discuss his dreams, and reconstruct his daily problems. In that way the patient was able to get in touch with those experiential aspects of his personality from which he had cut himself off. (The analyst, in Freud's method, sat behind the person.) In working these experiences through ("finishing" them), the person in psychoanalysis became thereby a more integrated personality. And Freud (and later, his colleagues) demonstrated that his treatment approach worked—not with everyone, but with many tortured souls.*

INDIVIDUAL PSYCHOTHERAPY
AND COUNSELING

The kind of classical psychoanalysis that Freud and his students practiced has been modified to some extent over the past half-century. Psychoanalysis is still available today for those who can afford it and who need the continuous support of this approach while

---

* A person no longer has to lie on a couch to engage in psychoanalysis. Psychoanalysis is a much broader term and has a less precise meaning than in the classical period of Freud's time. Today psychoanalysis denotes any therapy that systematically investigates a person's early memories and experiences and their effect on his present life style.

working through personality conflicts. Other types of individual psychotherapy are available today besides classical psychoanalysis.

Freud had been a neurologist and still considered himself a physician; in fact, he treated people so emotionally confused that they were often physically ill or crippled. Freud treated them as patients. He saw them regularly sometimes for an hour daily. He gave them instructions to lie down on the couch and give voice to everything, anything, that came into their minds. He interpreted their neurotic symptoms in much the same way any physician interprets symptoms today, and he gave them advice on what to do in much the same way a physician today advises his patient what to do to get better. It was essentially a doctor-patient relationship.

Psychoanalysis, transplanted to the United States in the twenties and thirties, was essentially more suited to the European aristocrat with plenty of time and money on his hands. And it took an American psychoanalyst, Harry Stack Sullivan, to advance the idea that a person who enters psychoanalytic psychotherapy is not necessarily "ill" or "sick"—he is, more simply, experiencing difficulties in his interpersonal relationships.[4]

With Sullivan, American psychoanalysis became analytic psychotherapy, or depth psychotherapy, and a more practical, once-a-week event in which two persons—the therapist (not "doctor") and the patient (or person)—sat together for an hour speaking to each other. The person no longer lay down on a couch and the therapist was in full view rather than, as in psychoanalysis, seated behind the patient. Since the person was not required to come to the therapy several times a week, this approach also placed the therapy within the financial reach of many who could not afford psychoanalsis.

Carl Rogers took this idea even further and eliminated the word *patient* and replaced it with the word *client*. Both Sullivan and Rogers viewed themselves as consultants whose primary skill was in being able to be with other persons as they discuss the specific personal difficulties that bring them into counseling or therapy.

Carl Rogers says that each person has a "healthy" aspect within himself that influences him to find his own directions and conclusions. The therapist's role, in Rogers's approach, is to act not as a "doctor" but as a sounding board, to reflect the person's feelings, thoughts, and concerns so he sees for himself what he is actually saying, feeling and doing. An advantage of Rogers's "client-centered" approach to therapy has been that it encourages the person to grow toward self-direction: to find out for himself what he wants to do and be, rather than depending solely on the judgments of his therapist. Rogers believes that when a person comes to trust his *own* perceptions, his *own* feelings, his *own* thoughts, that he comes also to *value himself* as a reliable center of consciousness capable of deciding what he wants to do with his life.[5]

It might be well to mention now that it takes someone trained in listening to simply reflect another's thoughts and feelings and to keep his own personal likes and dislikes out of the ongoing conversation. Can any one of us act as a "therapist" for another on that level of listening? Well, theoretically, we can—particularly if we know *how* to listen. Friendship involves that kind of sympathetic listening, and many of us have experienced that true sense of relief and release when we have been able finally to pour out our hearts to another human being who is listening—simply listening without interfering. But sympathetic listening is a great skill, and for most of us it is not easily come by since it involves the kind of "impersonal attention" which is free of judgments, and the willingness to

Psychotherapy is largely the art of listening.

listen without getting caught up in the other person's difficulties. Furthermore, a lay ("nonprofessional") person who listens to us may end up giving us "advice" that goes in one ear and out the other.

What is different about psychotherapy or therapeutic listening is that they provide the kind of situation where we are able to speak of many things normally thought "taboo" in ordinary conversation. For example, such subjects as suicidal thoughts and feelings, masturbation, incestuous feelings or acts, feelings of inadequacy and loneliness are still topics not usually shared in our everyday conversation. A person's fears and feelings of "going mad" are often diminished radically in simply being able to speak of these stress points in a climate of safety and understanding. Freud called this experience *catharsis* (from the Greek meaning "to purge")—i.e., cleaning out the "mess" in our lives now and then; to speak to another of our secret anxieties and conflicts that we bottle up within us. Many a ghostly fear, secret guilt, or shameful secret dissipates itself in the sunlight of self-revealment when there is a person there with us who "understands."

In psychotherapy and counseling, as in psychoanalysis, we begin to sort out for ourselves the tangled knots and webs of our interpersonal lives. We devote our attention and energy toward finding out how to live more intelligently and creatively in our various activities. But seeing a therapist for a private session once a week can be a costly project—the going rate for an hour of private therapy is now around $35—and the approach is therefore limited even now again to those who can afford it. However, many schools and universities are beginning to provide that service to students for little or no charge, and community mental health clinics give psychotherapy and counseling for persons who could not ordinarily afford to pay for long-term individual psychotherapy.

There is a built-in limitation to individual psychotherapy. Psychotherapists are still simply human persons who can manage only so much "psychotherapeutic" stress (listening to the problems of many persons in a week *can* be stressful), and beyond that point they are not able to be effective therapists. For that reason, therapists generally can manage to see only around twenty-five persons each week if they want to maintain a sense of personal balance and health. Psychotherapy is an *intense* kind of work. It demands the kind of attention and commitment to other persons that can drain and deplete one's own resources as a personality—once the therapist goes beyond the critical point of emotional depletion. There is an additional limitation to individual psychotherapy in that there are just not enough trained psychotherapists at the present time to take care of all the people who would like to enter therapy. The complex of these factors—cost of the service, an insufficiency of trained therapists who can provide expert consultation and the built-in limitation of approximately twenty-five individual clients each week per therapist—all of these considerations have contributed to the development of other kinds of treatment and professional help.

CHEMOTHERAPY

A major breakthrough in the attempt to relieve stress and reverse the processes of personality disintegration occurred after World War II, with the widespread use of so-called psychotropic drugs. The psychotropic drugs are medicines or substances that change the chemical balance of the human body and produce noticeable changes in perception and in one's ongoing ability to deal with interpersonal relationships. The psychotropic drugs fall largely into three classes: the so-called tranquilizers, which relax the person and reduce tensions and the experience of anxiety; the psychic energizers, which are used primarily to diminish feelings of depression and other low energy states; and the so-called psychedelic or mind-expanding chemicals, such as LSD, peyote, psilocybin, etc.*

Before World War II, these chemicals were available on a limited basis only, but by 1950 the first group of chemicals, the tranquilizers, began to be used in the treatment of severely disturbed persons in the state hospitals, and they began slowly to find a place in the treatment of out-patients as an adjunct to individual psychotherapy. The effects of these medicines were indeed notable. For example, some persons who had been inaccessible and withdrawn for many years in the back wards of state hospitals were enabled to manage social relationships once again. Some of these patients could even be sent home to live on a visiting basis with their families; and many of them—if they continued to take their medicines regularly, as prescribed—did not need to return to the hospital.

In the first flush of enthusiasm of the 1950s, many thought that in the tranquilizing medicines we had at last found a solution to personality disintegration, and that personality functioning might even be understood eventually in purely chemical and biological

---

* We shall not concern ourselves here with the third group of chemicals.

terms. That enthusiasm and certainty has since diminished, and there has been a reappraisal of the value and contribution of psychotropic medications in our hurry-hurry, over-stressed society.

Let's begin with the tranquilizers and the evident and now well-known fact that these chemicals tranquilize the person: they enable the person to be more relaxed, less tense, less anxious and less on edge. Just as the correct use of dilantin reduces the frequency of epileptic seizures and enables the person to live a more reasonable life because he does not have to worry about the sudden onset of an epileptic seizure, the tranquilizing chemicals relieve some of the extreme experiences of anxiety and tension which are often found in severe psychological stress and personality disintegration. The use of tranquilizers is no longer confined to the treatment of state hospital patients; they are used widely by persons in many kinds of crisis situations to enable them to continue to function where they are, and to diminish the anxiety feelings that are associated with the pressures and conflicts of everyday living. And in that sense the tranquilizers have become a part of the technology of present day living.

The psychic energizers are used primarily to relieve depression and low energy states. These medicines provide a boost, they "energize" the person, make him feel less withdrawn, less hopeless about his life and himself; and so they enable him to "keep going," to examine his present life style which is now "getting him down." These chemicals have had considerable effect on the treatment of psychotic depressions and the melancholia which sometimes affects persons in the middle and later years of life. For example, previously electro-convulsive therapy (ECT) was often used to relieve the guilt feelings and the experience of worthlessness associated with continuous depression. The psychic energizers have now become the treatment of choice in many instances of severe depression, and they have proved to be a valuable adjunct in the treatment of psychiatric difficulties which once would have required hospitalization. Not only is it now less necessary to use ECT, but the person may not even need to enter the hospital in the first place. And in that sense the psychic energizers perform a much needed function for the persons who need their assistance.

Although the tranquilizers and the psychic energizers were developed within the last twenty-five years, these chemicals are now in widespread use and there seems to be every likelihood that there will be more reliance on them if the pressures of modern urban society continue to increase. We would add that they are prescription medicines to be taken only under the direction of a physician. Though they are used often by many persons, some of these chemicals require concurrent laboratory checks to insure the health and safety of the person who is taking them. So they are not like the aspirin one takes for the momentary headache; and one is advised always against self-treatment with these medicines. Moreover, borrowing and using someone else's tranquilizer is definitely not a wise thing to do.

GROUP THERAPY

In group psychotherapy a therapist (or a number of therapists) meets with a number of persons once a week for one to several hours at a time. In group therapy, group members interact not only with the therapist, but with each other; in fact, part of the therapist's function is to enable the group members to observe their own and others' behaviors and to encourage them to try out behaviors with each other that are more satisfactory to them personally. The group itself may vary from as few as five to as many as ten or twelve persons, or even twenty persons. The group members develop close relationships similar to a family situation. But unlike family relationships, the group members are not forced to live with each other day in and day out, so the conflicts within the therapy group have time to heal between sessions. This is one great advantage of group psychotherapy.

A second advantage is that each person has come to the group voluntarily (as he does also to individual therapy), and thus there is a marked increase in equality in the *group* compared to the relationship in *individual* psychotherapy. (In the group there are always more "patients" or "clients" than group leaders.) A young man suffering from resentment toward his parents is thus enabled to work on those resentments in the group as he interacts with his peers and older members of the group. In like manner an older person is able to appreciate the young man's difficulties *without having to be the object of his resentment*. Through many kinds of interchanges (discussion, questioning, listening, nonverbal communication, even violent disagreement sometimes) the group members gradually develop insight into their own specific difficulties. They also come to appreciate the problems other group members are living with; and it is often a blessed relief just to know that other persons have problems—that we are not alone!

When group psychotherapy was first tried, there was some concern that the group experience would "water down" the therapeutic effects of individual therapy; and so for a time group therapy was thought to be inferior to the individual approach. Such has proved not to be the case, however: the group approach is not so much better or worse than individual therapy as it is different from it. The value of the group approach is the undoubted "socialization" which takes place within the group. Members not only learn to share the group's attention with their peers, but get the opportunity to share vicariously in the work each group member does on his particular difficulties. For that reason a person may come to a group for many weeks, even months, sit quietly, and not seem to do any therapeutic work on his own difficulties, yet *still improve markedly* in his way of living.

There is finally the matter of finances: an hour of group therapy costs about one-fourth the fee for an hour of individual therapy, which means that many persons can afford the group experience who would not be able to consider individual psychotherapy. When we add up all these advantages and then consider also the advances in the techniques of group interaction in the last twenty-five years, it is easy to see why group therapy is so popular, and why the demand for it continues to grow.

GROWTH GROUPS

There are many kinds of approaches to group interaction. One approach is group psychotherapy, the kind of approach we have just discussed, in which persons with moderate to severe interpersonal difficulties seek alleviation of psychological conflicts interfering with their capacity to grow. Another approach to group dynamics is the *growth-group* method. One of the pioneer approaches in the growth-group movement is the communication laboratory developed by the National Training Laboratory (NTL) in Bethel, Maine. As it was originally planned, the NTL approach provided a place where business executives, office supervisors, plant managers and similar occupational groups could study group dynamics (how people interact together) and so become more effective leaders. In the early years of the NTL, many of the persons who came to the training groups (called "T-groups") were sponsored largely by industrial corporations as a kind of in-service training program for leadership effectiveness in corporation management. The persons who attended the NTL T-groups were already leading relatively effective and harmonious lives, and they wanted simply to further their skills in interpersonal relationships. As the effectiveness of the T-group method became known, however, it became clearer and more certain that the laboratory experience not only resulted in more effective leadership on the job, but also seemed to generalize to the T-group member's personal life as well. Such persons seemed better able to do their jobs and to be better integrated in their overall social relationships as well.[6]

Many kinds of group combinations have developed in the past decade which have been inspired by the growth group philosophy. Some of these groups specialize in working with heroin addicts, alcoholics, married couples, professional persons in the social sciences, task-oriented groups for community and volunteer workers, and so on. There are also many names for these groups, including the T-group, already mentioned, encounter groups, sensitivity groups, human-potential seminars, and leadership-training labs. Although there can be certain, sometimes subtle, differences in emphasis among these various approaches to group process, most of the practitioners of growth-group methods subscribe to what is now called "humanistic psychology."

The growth-group approach differs from traditional group psychotherapy in certain ways. First, the members of the growth group meet for longer sessions, say, a weekend, for several days, even for several weeks at a time. During that period they eat together, live and enjoy recreational activities together, besides coming together at stated intervals for the more personal-interaction group discussions. Second, the group leaders generally begin with the premise that there are no "patients," no "doctor" or "psychotherapist" in the group, and that the leader's function is to facilitate group interactions by developing a climate of trust, safety, and open communication so that group members can work on the task of becoming aware of their here-and-now experiences with each other. In the process of working in that way the groups members learn to understand themselves better and the other group members as well.

A growth group seems definitely not the place for persons with acute or chronic interpersonal difficulties that will demand continued attention from the group. (Such persons, we believe, belong in individual or group psychotherapy.) The growth group is suitable for persons who are functioning more effectively in most areas of their living; it is oriented toward those persons who are willing and able to enhance the growth of the group and the persons in the group, and without needing hours or days of the group's attention and time.

The effectiveness of growth groups in carrying out their stated goals of enhancing the growth of persons is thus dependent on the successful screening of potential members and on the skill and experience of the growth group leader(s). No matter how comprehensive the screening procedure may be, however, sooner or later some person in the group may reach the point where his interpersonal supports collapse; he will then need effective and expert "help" of some kind. A group leader does not come by that kind of expertness simply by reading books or by attending a few training groups to learn the rudimentary techniques of group leadership and practice. We thus urge anyone who is contemplating entering a growth group to investigate carefully the experience and background of the leaders.

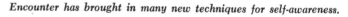

Encounter has brought in many new techniques for self-awareness.

Our belief in the necessity of knowing the approach of the leader was confirmed recently by three psychologists who performed the first extensive research on the effects and effectiveness of group encounter leaders.[7] Their finding was that the benefit derived from an encounter approach was less dependent on the particular techniques or skills of the encounter leader so much as his personal warmth and genuine caring and the amount of meaning that could be derived from the experiential process. Furthermore, dramatic and sensational group episodes, it was found, might have an emotionally stimulating effect immediately afterward, but long-lasting positive effects generally do not result from group experiences in which emotionally stimulating, less-caring leaders use such techniques as hostile confrontation. We need a climate of safety and respect for our defenses if we are to explore the growing possibilities in ourselves; moreover, each person comes forward to the growth step at his own pace, in his own time, when he is ready to make the step forward, and generally not before that time. Is warmth and caring a skill that can be learned? We believe that is so, and that is where experience and training comes in: it refines an already present capacity for liking persons, enjoying being with them as they explore their possibilities and their limitations. But skill and experience in employing that skill is necessary also, for only in that way will the encounter group leader know when and how to respond with the just-right remark and action that facilitates the ongoing growth of the person and the group. All of the capable encounter group leaders we know manifest this skill, as well as being the warm and caring individuals in whose presence persons can grow safely.

GROWTH GROUPS AND MASLOW'S HIERARCHY OF NEEDS

In Chapter 7, you read about Maslow's hierarchy of human needs. Maslow said, you will recall, that we share certain basic needs with lower animals (food, sex, air, and the other physiological needs), but that once these needs are met, the human being has certain other specific needs that come to the fore—"higher" needs. Specifically, these are safety needs, belonging and love needs, and esteem needs. Under a competent leader, growth-group members can help to satisfy some of these higher needs.

The Safety Needs

Children can frequently feel unsafe. But adults can also suffer from feelings of being unsafe. Karl Jaspers, a psychiatrist-turned-philosopher, says that in our time personality may be undergoing the experience of "shipwreck"; we are floundering, unable to put down roots, we feel estranged and alienated, without a home-place we feel to be our own. In a growth group, a person who is encountering precisely that experience of "shipwreck" can begin to risk sharing himself if a climate of safety and trust has been established in the group. For example, a shy and retiring person who has been conditioned to hold back and not express himself because of fear of criticism can begin to explore such feelings of distrust and fear; and since the climate is now supportive, he can begin to initiate assertive behaviors which do express the measure of his present reality. By being accepted for what he is, and because other persons are now interested in him for himself, he can begin to let go of his fears even as he realizes that not every adult in the world responds with criticism.

Belongingness and Love Needs

Maslow has suggested that the need to belong to someone, to feel at home someplace, may be responsible for the present popularity of T-groups and other personal growth groups. He notes that American friendships tend to be shallow, that we are a mobile society (every year 20 percent of the population move households) and that when we move, the roots we establish are pulled up and we must face (yet again) leaving our friends, our home, our place of belonging.[8] And in that sense Maslow seems to be correct—much of the success of the growth group is attributable to its status as a substitute *family:* it often has older and younger people in the same group, and both sexes, as well as a variety in the kinds of jobs represented, styles of living, and so on. Sometimes child-parent conflicts are discussed and acted out between the generations in the group, thus allowing group members to face and resolve sibling rivalries and jealousies. At other times the climate, although safe, may get very hot. But hot or cold, stormy or peaceful, the group members work toward developing a sense of belongingness with one another, if only "for this time" and "in this place."

It follows that no one is going to be outright rejected, led out the door, nor should there be demands to deal with conflicts a member is not yet ready to discuss. A person can work on something as he chooses, and he may dare to work on a conflict he might not undertake in his biological family for fear of rejection or reprisal. This is not to say that group members do not get angry with one another, nor that there are no misunderstandings, or "hurt feelings" or breakdowns in communication of the kind found in most family situations. But when a real family feeling exists in the growth group, each person knows that when the anger passes or the fighting subsides, he will still be related to the group, still a functioning member of the whole.

Esteem Needs

As our more basic biological motivations are satisfied and the needs for belongingness and safety are being met, there emerge the higher-order needs of the personality. Self-esteem is an excellent example. Although we can theorize that "self-esteem" is correlated merely with the pecking order among certain species, the human personality seems to have a wider spectrum of needs that cannot be subsumed merely under the "esteem" needs. A person needs to have a worthy opinion of himself, a feeling of self-respect, a knowledge that he "amounts to something." He needs also feedback from others in his society that assures him he is regarded and appreciated just for himself.

We have many names for the self-esteem needs: status, fame, glory, recognition, dignity, appreciation, feeling understood, and so on. As these needs begin to be satisfied, the person achieves the sense that his life has meaning, and he begins to feel more competent, more useful, better able to make choices for himself and to direct his own life. He is then on the way to what Maslow calls "self-actualization," or what Carl Rogers calls being a "fully functioning person."

Growth groups have been exploring the self-esteem needs for a long time, and this approach has enabled many persons to recognize themselves as unique individuals with certain inalienable needs and rights. Even though a person has achieved social recognition in his professional, personal, and social life, he can still feel cut off, a small boy, unloved—still lacking the real love and caring and respect he longs for. In a growth group, such a person is sometimes able to doff his "public" personality and to allow the private agony to show and be seen by others. In the "outside" world, such a person may experience expressions of respect and sentiment, but may also suspect that the deference he receives is largely due to his position and status. In the growth group, on the other hand, he allows himself to be seen without his mask, his status, his social personality; and he knows that whatever feedback he receives from the group members is given as genuine, honest, and open communication. In that way he may become more available to his "real" possibilities.

The Need for Self-Actualization

We have discussed the highly integrated personality in Chapter 2, and we have said that once a person has satisfied his basic bio-social needs the so-called higher needs in personality come to the fore. The need for self-actualization, or what Jung calls "personality individuation," is said to be one of those higher needs. Self-actualization does not mean "doing my own thing" independent of the group or shared ethnic. Nor does it mean abject conformity to group standards. The self-actualizing or fully functioning person *does dare to think for himself,* he does not need to conform passively to group standards; he conforms because that is his will and his choosing. He is therefore more available to his freedom, his capacity to choose, and better able to become the person he wants to be. In like manner, as his own sense of himself grows and is grounded in the reality of his personhood, his appreciation of others becomes richer, more positive, more enduring, more compassionate, whole, complete!

Peak Experiences

There are moment along the path to personality integration when "everything seems to come together," when one has for the moment an experience of joyfulness, peace, contentment, the realization that the world is perfect (despite the miseries which human flesh is heir to). Maslow called these moments "peak experiences." All work on the so-called lower level of personality needs contributes to the likelihood that peak experience will happen. In our personal view, "peak experiences" are the moment of ecstasy where the "splits" in the personality are for the moment transcended and we experience ourselves as integrated. Conflict-free, whole, all-of-a-piece, and being the person we really are at this moment.

Peak experiences can happen in a growth-group session itself (as the authors can testify). Sometimes they occur spontaneously for individual persons and sometimes for the whole group. When a single person in the group reaches that level of awareness, there is an in-pouring of energy into the group, and everything seems more alive, more exciting, more colorful, more available for work and consideration. A group of persons can also share a peak experience, and then there is a sense of peace in the room, a sense of awe and wonderment, even of reverence at what seems to be happening. Zen psychologists call this the moment of "going home and quietly sitting," and from our experience this is an apt formulation. For in those moments seemingly there is nothing left to do, or be, since *everything seems to be given* to the group and to all of us in the group.

Not all groups reach this level of personal and collective integration, for the peak experience is a gift that one can work toward but not necessarily receive. To that extent it is a paradoxical event, a something we can prepare ourselves for by work on ourselves, yet that we cannot apparently set out to *make happen.* Some day we will know more about these ecstatic moments, and we will provide centers where these higher functions in personality can be cultivated; and then we will be coming closer to realizing the enormous potential for growth and community realization that resides in human personality.

Psychotherapy and Growth Groups

The therapeutic methods of each age and time express the needs of the time. Our own age is remarkable in that it is an age of *psychology,* and the therapeutic approaches we have discussed in this chapter give only a brief overview of the revolution which is presently going on in our study of personality. By the way, the *name* that is given to a method does not matter. What does matter is that a person can grow in the situation, so whether he receives psychoanalysis, psychotherapy, counseling, or goes to a growth group is of small importance. There are, and always have been, forms of psychotherapy wherever there is a person or group needing healing for the ills, suffering, and dislocations which befall human personality in society. What counts ultimately is how well each approach works, if it is enhancing the individual's capacity for choice, and how dedicated it is to enabling the process of change which is the mark of growth and the growing personality.

Growth groups, however, have enabled so many in our society to find new aspects of themselves or reveal undeveloped skills, and have enabled so many others to grow in ways undreamed of, that the growth-group movement has spread all over the country. It is becoming a part of the school experience, of college education, of management training, of church work, and other areas. It is considered now an effective way for enabling persons better to learn and for societal institutions better to function. It is becoming a part of our ongoing life-education. And many persons find it a more satisfying experience to take a "trip" to their "inner space" than to a resort since the effects are so much more generalized and long-lasting. How the movement grows and develops we will be witnessing in the coming years.

In the meantime, the reader may be left wondering whether he should "try out" an encounter group. If he is, he would do well to abide by Everett Shostrum's advice for the neophyte in the encounter movement: let the buyer beware! [9] There are good groups, but there are also groups which can effect negative changes. Shostrum suggests seven considerations in choosing an encounter group. They are:

1. Never respond to a newspaper ad. The encounter group leader should be a qualified professional who probably would not resort to newspaper advertising.
2. Do not participate in a group with fewer than half a dozen participants. Too small a group won't give a person "breathing room."
3. Don't enter an encounter group on impulse. Your decision should be the result of deep consideration.
4. Do not participate in a group with close associates. You need all the privacy you can get and strangers will not interfere with your privacy when you get "back home."
5. Do not be bamboozled by pretty surroundings. The experience is an inner one.
6. Never stay with a group that has a particular ax to grind or

ideology that it seeks to convert members to. You want a broadly based experience so you can choose your own path.

7. Never participate in a group that is not allied with some sort of professional institution. Professional qualifications are your safest bet that you will receive expert leadership.

RECOMMENDED READINGS

AGEL, JEROME, ed. *The Radical Therapist*. New York: Ballantine Books, 1971 (paperback).

This book is a "manifesto" of a new approach to mental health. It considers psychotherapy a white, middle-class way of adjusting and molding people to conformity. "Radical therapy," according to Agel, seeks to put more of the therapy program under client control, encourage new techniques, and generally demystify the therapy process. Particularly excellent for the person with background in therapy either as a client or as a practitioner.

CARKHUFF, ROBERT R. *The Art of Helping: A Guide for Developing Skills for Parents, Teachers, and Counselors*. Amherst, Mass.: Human Resource Development Press (paperback).

Although Carkhuff is an internationally known therapist, he is still willing to write in simple terms. Although the title says it would be a good book for counselors, our opinion is that it is more suitable for the lay person or paraprofessional who wishes to develop his interpersonal skills.

FAGAN, JOEN, and IRMA LEE SHEPHERD, eds. *Gestalt Therapy Now: Theory, Techniques, Applications*. Palo Alto, Cal.: Science and Behavior Books, 1970 (hardcover).

For an overview of one of the more popular techniques of treatment used today, this book is excellent. Fritz Perls presents his model of therapeutic change as well as many others who have adapted Perls's essential therapeutic techniques to their own special areas. Of special interest is a chapter by Shepherd entitled "Limitations and Cautions in the Gestalt Approach."

GOFFMAN, ERVING. *Asylums: Essays on the Social Situations of Mental Patients and other Inmates*. Garden City, N.Y.: Doubleday, 1961 (paperback).

This chapter indicates some of the progress we have made in our mental institutions and in our thinking about people who have "mental problems." Goffman, however, presents a series of essays which depict how we still debase and degrade the entering mental patient and dehumanize him throughout his stay. Goffman always writes with a great deal of force, and this book is no exception.

HOWARD, JANE. *Please Touch*. New York: Dell, 1971 (paperback). Originally published in 1970 by McGraw-Hill (New York).

There has been a lot of criticism of the encounter group and growth-group movement. Writer Jane Howard decided to investigate the furor over this new movement and has written up her adventures in various growth centers in a personal, insightful, and funny way. She reveals some of the various methodologies that are used and gives the reader some warnings about the differences between the genuine and the fraudulent.

LEVY, RONALD B. *I Can Only Touch You Now*. Englewood Cliffs, N.J.: Prentice-Hall, 1972 (paperback).

It is difficult to understand just what goes on in the therapy situation and the change in a person's feelings as he becomes more self-aware. Levy does a fairly good job on a fairly difficult subject. Particularly good are the chapters explaining the here-and-now compared to the then-and-there. He also presents considerable material on the encounter situation from many viewpoints.

O'BANION, TERRY, and APRIL O'CONNELL. *The Shared Journey: An Introduction to Encounter*. Englewood Cliffs, N.J.: Prentice-Hall, 1970 (paperback).

The authors attempt to describe the experience of the encounter situation by discussing the process in a series of dialogues with one another. The reader may gain a more intimate understanding of the process of encounter as the two authors encounter each other throughout the book and discuss their own candid feelings about what it is to be human, to be lonely, the nature of happiness, and their feelings toward each other. In addition, there are included students' reactions to their experience of the growth-group situation.

RUBIN, THEODORE ISAAC. *Lisa and David*. New York: Ballantine Books, 1961 (paperback).

This is a love story involving two severely disturbed adolescents. The setting is a residential treatment center for exceptional children. Rubin describes life and treatment in such an environment, awakening the reader to two facets of human therapy—the one that medicine and counseling offer, and the one derived through a relationship in which two people are sincerely interested and involved in the welfare of one another. Through their attraction to each other, both David and Lisa succeed in breaking down the barriers of communication between them and, eventually, with those in the "outside" world.

RUITENBEEK, HENDRIK M. *The New Group Therapies.* New York: Avon
  Books, 1970 (paperback).

  This is a more in-depth discussion of the new therapies than Jane
  Howard's book (discussed above). Ruitenbeek discusses the history
  of mental treatment, and the advantages he believes have been
  gained. Some of the new therapies he reviews are Gestalt therapy,
  nude therapy, the encounter marathon, and the confrontation approach practiced by Synanon and others.

THE DISCOVERY OF THE SEXUAL AND SYMBOLIC SELF IN DREAMS: FREUD AND JUNG

10

INTRODUCTION: BAH! HUMBUG!

The nineteenth century was a century that demolished myths. One by one, long-cherished beliefs about the nature of man and our world were debunked as nineteenth-century scientific discoveries led to new theories about reality and mankind. Darwin's theory of evolution, for example, electrified the thinking world and then paved the way toward new methods of studying man through phylogenetic and comparative physiology. In the field of physics, the principle of conservation of energy, the discovery of electricity and electromagnetism, and the laws of thermodynamics put an end to the popular belief that heat and light are mysterious and unknowable qualities. Furthermore, the formulation and acceptance of the germ theory of disease put an end, once and for all, to the superstition that disease is caused by evil spirits or bad humors.

The nineteenth century was an age of rationalism. The dominant belief of the age was that all phenomena would be explained eventually in terms of logical, straightforward cause-and-effect relationships.

Even the study of dreams and dreaming came under the sway of nineteenth-century science and assigned a sensible, rational place in this neat and tidy and pragmatic world. As a consequence, dreams were explained simply as a reaction to physical distress, or as a result of one's physical disposition. For example, if a person dreamt of drowning, it was probably due to his need to urinate! If he dreamed of being guillotined, it was the result of something which had fallen on his head as he slept, or because of the bedclothes that were choking him. Scrooge, in Charles Dickens's novel *A Christmas Carol*, probably sums up the physiological theory of dreaming when he reacts to his "night visitor" as nothing more than "a bit of undigested food."

This approach to dreaming came as a relief to educated men in the nineteenth century. Since the beginning of time, dreams had been haunting men with sexual content and other confusing elements that disturbed one's peace of mind. Frightening dreams were, in fact, called "nightmares" in Old English because they were believed to be caused by monsters (*mares*). During the medieval witch-hunts, erotic dreams were seen as the work of devils (incubi and succubi) which invaded the souls of innocent men and women. And there is probably not one of us who cannot sympathize with Job's desperate cry, "You frighten me with dreams and terrify me with visions."

It was comforting, then, for people in the nineteenth century to be able to rid themselves at last of the disturbing belief that there was something real or important going on in their dreams. After all (they could say), these events and experiences happened during sleep, the "sleep of reason"! And clearly there could be little correspondence between these strange aspects and happenings of the dream self and those everyday experiences of the sensible, mature, and virtuous person in the waking state! The explanations of rational science provided just enough impetus for them to dismiss their dreams as essentially unimportant. Then Sigmund Freud happened.

FREUD AND VICTORIAN SOCIETY

Until the publication in 1900 of *The Interpretation of Dreams,* Freud was a relatively unknown physician living in Vienna. *The Interpretation of Dreams* went through eight editions during the author's lifetime; it was translated into every major language; it was to have a profound and lasting effect on our present-day thinking about the nature of man—yet it netted Freud only a few hundred dollars in royalties and gained him the opprobrium of Victorian society. For Freud was saying that the dreams of the men and women of his time who were his patients showed clearly that their society, which so prided itself on its conduct, ethics, and belief in progress through science, was producing neurosis—that is, not healthy persons, but sick people.

Freud seems to have anticipated some reaction from religious leaders, but he probably never expected the extent to which he would be ridiculed, condemned, and ostracized by his own medical and scientific colleagues. It was ten years before the six hundred copies of the first edition were all sold. Freud allows a little of his disappointment to show through in the preface to the second edition, published in 1909.

> If within ten years of the publication of this book . . . a second edition is called for, this is not due to the interest taken in it by the professional circles to whom my original preface was addressed. My psychiatric colleagues seem to have taken no trouble to overcome the initial bewilderment created by my new approach to dreams. The professional philosophers have become accustomed to polishing off the problems of dream-life (which they treat as a mere appendix to conscious states) in a few sentences—and usually in the same ones; and they have evidently failed to notice that we have something here from which a number of inferences can be drawn that are bound to transform psychological theories. The attitude adopted by reviewers in the scientific periodicals could only lead one to suppose that my work was doomed to be sunk into complete silence.[1]

Freud maintained that dreams are *not* meaningless and unimportant, but are the "royal road to the unconscious"; that is, dreams provide pathways to those levels of the self which men in every time and age have sought to ignore and keep hidden from themselves. Freud said also that dreams reveal the savage, infantile, uncivilized aspects of the self which each dreamer would prefer to ignore. He said, as well, that the lusty, exhibitionistic, and aggressive dream-self is just as valid a self as the one each man attempts to construct in the waking state. He said, finally, that the denial of the existence of this lusty and aggressive self in Victorian society was one cause of the psychological conflicts in that society.

Anyone who dares to throw down the gauntlet to his society must expect some resistance to and criticism of his views. We can say now, therefore, that it was somewhat naïve of Freud not to anticipate how difficult and threatening it would be for men of his time to accept what he himself saw so clearly. But we can also sympathize with him in retrospect for the animosity expressed toward him. That is history. What counts for us now, perhaps, is that Freud's views did prevail, that there were others outside the immediate circle of psychoanalysis who eventually listened to what he had to say and teach.

HISTORICAL ROOTS
OF DREAM INTERPRETATION

Freud's contributions to the theory of dreams, as original and monumental as they certainly were, nevertheless did not burst full-grown and independently from Freud's intellect. Ever since men became aware enough to differentiate between their waking and dreaming states, they have been fascinated by dreams. There was thus a considerable amount of literature on dreams by Freud's time, much of which Freud knew and which he quoted extensively in his book. We summarize that history briefly now to set the stage for Freud's original insights.

In the first place, the Old Testament is not only a source of accounts of dreams, but one of the first handbooks on dream interpretation. For example, Joseph's role as a dream interpreter was good enough not only to secure his release from prison but to gain him the chancellorship of the Pharaoh's court.[2] Joseph's dreams may have also been a deciding factor in his being sold into slavery, for he dared to interpret an early dream as a prediction that one day he would be a mighty lord before whom all his brothers would bow down.[3]

One of the most beautiful Old Testament stories, concerning

The Old and New Testaments of the Bible indicate that the Hebrews and early Christians relied on their dreams for guidance.

Solomon at the beginning of his reign, illustrates very clearly that the Hebrews believed that God could use the medium of dreams to appear to men.

You may remember that Solomon had not always been the heir apparent, for he was not the oldest son of King David. It must have come as a surprise to him, then, when he became successor to the throne. At any rate, God appears "in a dream" to Solomon and says: "Ask what you would like me to give you." Solomon's dream-self displays an astonishing wisdom in his reply:

> My God, you have made your servant king in succession to David, my father. But I am a very young man, unskilled in leadership. Your

servant finds himself in the midst of this people of yours that you have chosen, a people so many that its number cannot be counted or reckoned. Give your servant a heart to understand how to discern between good and evil, for who could govern this people of yours that is so great?

The Bible notes that God is pleased by this response and answers:

Since you have asked for this and not asked for long life for yourself or riches or the lives of your enemies, but have asked for a discerning judgment for yourself here and now I do what you ask. I give you a heart wise and shrewd as none before you has had and none will have after you.

But God rewards Solomon even further:

What you have not asked I shall give you too: such riches and glory as no other king ever had. And I will give you a long life, if you follow my laws and commandments as your father David followed them.

And then to remind us, the writer repeats again the setting of this dialogue: "Then Solomon awoke; it was a dream." [4]

The New Testament also provides many instances of divine revelation and guidance through the medium of dreams. For example, in the book of Matthew, when Joseph discovers that his bride-to-be, Mary, is pregnant, he is sorely distressed; but being a "man of honor" he does not want to expose her publicly, so he decides to divorce her quietly. The Lord's angel, however, Matthew goes on to say, appears to him in a dream and tells him not to be afraid to take Mary for his wife for their conception is "by the Holy Spirit." [5]

Later, the Magi, after their visit to the child Jesus, fail to inform Herod of the child's whereabouts—as he instructed them to do—for they had been "warned in a dream not to go back to Herod," and thus return to their own country by another route. [6] The Angel of the Lord appears twice more to Joseph in dreams: first to tell him to take his family and flee into Egypt, [7] and then again to tell him that it is safe to return to Israel. [8]

In the last hours of Jesus' trial, there is also that well-known moment when Pilate, ready to pass sentence on a man he realizes is not a criminal, receives a plea for mercy from his wife:

Now as he was seated in the chair of judgment, his wife sent him a

According to the Talmud, "A dream uninterpreted is like a letter that is not read."

message, "Have nothing to do with that man; I have been upset all day by a dream I had about him." [9]

Most religions we know of have recorded dreams and interpretations of dreams. In fact, the earliest extant book on dream interpretation, the so-called Chester Beatty Papyrus, dates back to 2000 B.C., from Thebes (in the ancient kingdom of Upper Egypt).

The stone inscription on the Sphinx at Giza records that Thutmose IV obeyed instruction which came to him in a dream. His instructions were to clear the statue of sand, and the inscription records that Thutmose did, indeed, carry out the commandment.[10]

The Talmud records that a certain Rabbi Hisda regarded dream interpretation as essential for personal guidance. Said he, "An uninterpreted dream is like an unread letter," [11] a point of view which the psychoanalytic school of Freud was to reiterate later on.

Mohammed, the prophet of Islam, made a practice of relating his dreams each morning to his disciples and having them relate their own dreams. The art of dream interpretation was dignified as a science by Mohammed and his followers, who considered it one of the higher orders of natural philosophy.[12]

Although Freud may not have been conversant with the dream literature of the East and Near East, he was certainly well aware of the history of the Western theories of dreams. Twice in his *The Interpretation of Dreams* he quotes Plato's dictum: "The virtuous man is content to dream what a wicked man actually does."

He quoted also Artemidorus, a second-century dream interpreter. Although it is believed now that Artemidorus wrote several books on dream interpretation, only one, the *Oneirocritica*, is extant today; and it seems likely that this book was the basis of all subsequent dream interpretation books. Artemidorus believed that dreams must be interpreted in the light of the dreamer's background. For example, dreaming of having one's head shaved would be a good omen for Egypt's priests (whose heads were clean-shaven in their priestly duties), but for Europeans accustomed to wearing long hair such a dream would portend ill fortune. Writes Artemidorus: "For we say that a man has been scalped if he has suffered a loss and been deceived by another person." [13]

During the Middle Ages dreams became associated with devils and demons, an outlook on dreams which was to continue until the eighteenth and nineteenth centuries. Yet even in those years, as Freud points out in his book, philosophers had intimations of the real meaning of dreams. (See box, pp. 266-67.)

It will perhaps be clear to the reader by now that Freud did not begin empty-handed when he undertook his master work on dreams. But it was Freud's particular genius to pull together the many diverse insights and intuitions of these other ages, and to integrate their intuitions and discoveries systematically into his own clinical work as a psychiatrist.

THE STRUGGLE WITH SELF-REVEALMENT

It was not an easy task for Freud, for the venture had definite risks. It entailed, for one thing, speaking of subject matter that was taboo in his society—namely, sexuality. We need to remember, secondly, that Freud was himself a Victorian, a gentleman and a scholar by training and nature, and somewhat timid in his interpersonal relations. He risked much, therefore, in daring to publish his book. Freud also recounted and analyzed some of his own dreams in the text, thus exposing aspects of himself and his private life to public view that were (and still are) generally kept to oneself. Moreover, Freud dared to analyze dreams which showed his own professional and personal jealousies, his anger and his sexuality! It must have been an agonizing task. If Freud sometimes fainted when on the brink of some insight, or at the moment of uncovering a repressed memory which was distasteful, it served only to underline, for us, the difficulty of daring personal integration.

In his book, Freud reported and interpreted twenty-eight of his dreams for his readers. Fortunately he was a prolific dreamer, so he had considerable material to put under the microscope of his scientific intuition. Moreover, his dreams were lengthy and rich in detail, so they demonstrated explicitly his unresolved conflicts with his own parents and colleagues, as well as his everyday difficulties with living. From this rich fabric of dreams and fantasies Freud wove his theory of the psychology of dreaming. He validated his investigations by gathering hundreds of other dreams from patients, colleagues, and even relatives. Although we are aware now that Freud's theory of dreaming was incomplete and that other investigators would extend his theory and develop still other approaches to dream theory, Freud still stands out as the father of contemporary dream theory—the benchmark against which any dream theory must be measured, examined, and understood in our times: a remarkable accomplishment of a remarkable man.

FREUD'S THEORY OF DREAMS

A basic element of the psychoanalytic theory of dreams is Freud's postulate that there are two levels to every dream. The first level is the *manifest* or surface dream, the actual pictorial-auditory dream we remember upon awakening.

The second level of the dream Freud called the *latent* content, to emphasize his belief that there is a truth hidden (or latent) behind the manifest content. In other words, we disguise the real meanings of our dreams!

Why do we disguise the real meaning of our dreams? Freud's answer: our dreams are repositories for our hidden wishes, particularly sexual wishes and aggressive impulses. Indeed, said Freud, when such thoughts, feelings, or wishes invade our conscious aware-

Excerpts from Freud's Review
of the Literature on Dream Interpretation

The following are only a very few of the many quotations Freud lists in his review of the prevailing philosophy of dream interpretation, but they suffice to show that a few philosophers and psychologists had been thinking about the real nature of dreams and that Freud had studied and drawn from them. All the quotations are drawn from The Interpretation of Dreams.

. . . Dreams carry on waking life. . . Acute observation will almost always find a thread that connects a dream with the experiences of the previous day.

(W. Weygandt, 1893)

[Dreams represent] an archaic world of vast emotions and imperfect thoughts, the study of which might reveal to us primitive stages in the evolution of mental life.

(H. Ellis, 1899)

Our dreams are a means of conserving . . . successive (earlier) personalities. *When asleep we go back to the old ways of looking at things and of feeling about them, to impulses and activities which long ago dominated us.*

(J. Sully, 1893)

A dream . . . shows us our every day fears in the ghastliest shape and turns our amusement into jokes of indescribable pungency.

(J. Sully, 1893)

[We do not] become better or more virtuous in our sleep, on the contrary conscience seems to be silent during dreams for we feel no pity in them and may commit the worst crimes—theft, violence and murder—with complete indifference and with no subsequent feelings of remorse.

(P. Jessen, 1855)

In dreams, as we are all aware, proceedings are especially unbridled in sexual matters.

(J. Volkelt, 1875)

In dreams is truth: in dreams we learn to know ourselves as we are in spite of all the disguises we wear to the world.

(F. Scholz, 1893)

Tell me some of your dreams, and I will tell you about your inner self.

(E. R. Pfaff, 1868)

> Dreams often do no more than reveal to us what we would not admit to ourselves and . . . it is therefore unfair of us to stigmatize them as liars and deceivers.
>
> (P. Radestock, 1879)
>
> Dreams have never shown me what I ought to think of a man; but I have occasionally learnt from a dream, greatly to my own astonishment, what I *do* think of a man, and how I feel towards him.
>
> (J. E. Erdmann, 1852)
>
> In dreams what is especially revealed is instinctive man.
>
> (L. F. A. Maury, 1878; trans. A. O'Connell)

ness we tend to forget them very quickly. (That is where psycho-analysis comes in: it enables people to remember forgotten material —or more explicitly, to unearth material that is not so much forgotten as *repressed*.) For Freud had discovered that "forgotten" material is simply driven below conscious awareness and "down" into what Freud called our unconscious mind. This process of forgetting he called *repression*. Repressing an idea, feeling, or wish requires a lot of effort, Freud added, for our repressed urges are constantly striving to come "up" to our conscious mind again. Repressing requires considerable psychic energy, therefore, to keep impulses below conscious awareness.

The "normal" person manages the process of repression fairly well during the day, since he is more-or-less "conscious" then. But at night, when the person is asleep, the repressing agent of the mind (Freud called this the *Censor*) is less vigilant, and repressed wishes thus have an opportunity to surface again—*but only in disguise,* as symbolic dream content. If the repressed wish were to surface in undisguised form, the Censor would be immediately on the alert and the person would wake up. The purpose of the Censor, in other words, is to protect the sleeper from waking up in reaction to the expression of his repressed impulses.

The wish to kill one's father, for example, may be transformed in a dream into seeing one's father melt away like a snowman; or the wish to expose oneself may appear in a dream as having one's clothing blown off by the wind; or the wish to have intercourse with one's mother may be expressed as making love to a woman who has no face and is therefore unrecognizable. If such desires were expressed literally in one's dreams, however, the Censor would become immediately operative, and the person would then wake up.

This translation or transformation of the latent dream experience into the symbolic manifest dream content Freud called the *dream work*. The translation process, he said, explains the bizarre and unreal quality of many dreams. That is also why dreams sometimes don't "make sense" to our conscious awareness; how peculiar and unfamiliar personages can at times appear to invade dreams; and how we can find ourselves sometimes doing things apparently alien to our waking understanding of ourselves.

Each dream is thus a kind of puzzle—a set of meanings and feelings that make sense only when we understand the essential dream work. We will discuss only three methods of the dream work Freud postulated:

"Left-over Refuse"

Freud had a gift for anticipating objections to his ideas. One of the objections he sensed would be raised to *The Interpretation of Dreams* was that dreams deal mainly with the most insignificant and common occurrences of our everyday lives—for example, walking along the street, picking flowers, bicycle riding, etc. In other words, a dream reviews the scattered and left-over memories of the just-finished day. To that objection, Freud answered that although many dreams do seem to be just the carryover of insignificant details of our everyday life (it's as if we depict the "left-over refuse" of the day once again in our dreams), these insignificant events are just convenient symbols.

This "left-over refuse," said Freud, is simply the convenient channel through which psychic energy (from the unconscious mind) can be expressed and so find representation in consciousness. For that reason, it is essential to pay attention to every single element in a dream—no matter how insignificant that element may appear to be.

Condensation

According to Freud, a dream is always economical in expression, even laconic in its manner of conveying its message. A dream expresses ideas and feelings always in the briefest way possible. For that reason, one dream symbol can stand for many things simultaneously. For example, a tall giant may stand for all the authority figures we have ever known: one's father, a policeman, a school-teacher, etc. Or a soldier may stand for an army, or a book may represent knowledge in general. These are called *collective objects* or *collective persons.*

When words are part of the dream process, they tend to be *verbal condensations.* Freud gives many examples of verbal condensation in his book, but since they involve puns on the German and/or Yiddish language, they lose much of their force in their translation into English.

One of the dreams Freud reports is an example of just such process of condensation. A medical colleague once sent a journal article he had just written to Freud. Freud thought it overwritten, as well as overrated by the author as far as its scientific value. That night, Freud had a one-sentence dream: "It's written in a positively *norekdal* style." Analysis of the word *norekdal* revealed to Freud two different condensations: First, the word *norekdal* is a play on the German word for "colossal" "and "pyramidal"; and second, the word is also a combination of two characters in Henrik Ibsen's plays: Nora in *A Doll's House* and Ekdal in *The Wild Duck.* Freud then remembered that his colleague (the author of the paper) had also written a newspaper article about Ibsen some time earlier which

Freud readily analyzed his own dreams. This dream is an example of condensation, one of the elements of dream work.

Freud had also read. Newspaper articles have a peculiar style which is actually called pyramidal, and journalistic adjectives tend toward exaggeration. Freud chooses not to make further inferences at this point—at least not in print. It is not too difficult for us to infer that the author, in Freud's opinion, had written his scientific paper in much the same exaggerated style as his previous newspaper article.

(Notice, incidentally, how much space it has taken to translate Freud's one-sentence dream—a good example of dream condensation.)

Other forms of condensation involve space and time. For example, the image in a dream of a man standing at the end of a long, winding road may indicate that he has come a long way or has a long way yet to go—depending on which way the person in the dream is headed. Several levels in a scene may represent the several stages of one's life simultaneously, and a person can thus see himself both as a child and as an adult in the same scene. As a final example, a person on a treadmill may be the symbolic representation of the individual's feeling that he is getting nowhere for all his trouble. A single picture, someone has said, is worth a thousand words.

Dream Symbols

Freud was so impressed with the universality of some of the symbols appearing in dreams that he jokingly considered the possibility of drawing up a dream book not too dissimilar to those fortune tellers use. For he recognized and admitted that symbols are very much the same wherever they surface—whether in folklore, myths, legends, dreams, parables or even jokes. The dream interpreter thus must not only know the dreamer's personal associations to his dream symbols, but also study and know the symbols of literature, mythology, religion, art, etc. He needs to be, in other words, an educated man or woman who understands the whole panorama of human existence.

Freud's was a society that was suppressing its sexuality, and as a scientist Freud reported what he saw. He therefore necessarily interpreted symbols in dreams according to the problems of his age. Accordingly—and his point of view now seems somewhat old-fashioned and outdated—he viewed elongated objects such as neckties, knives, sticks, spears, even bananas as symbolizing the male sexual organ, the penis, and boxes, chests, cupboards, and ovens as representing the female organ, the vagina. Rooms in dreams could also represent women, and so could boats, cars, and other kinds of "boxes" which carry people around. A train going through a tunnel would be an excellent symbol for intercourse, as would also be such physical activities as rocking in a chair, climbing, swimming, etc.

In a dream, a child is often symbolic of the genitals; so playing with one's child could be symbolic of masturbation, according to Freud. He noted that the male penis is sometimes called by a male name. In English, for example, the words *dick* and *peter* are used to denote the penis. Similarly, fear of castration may be represented in a dream by having a finger or a leg cut off, or even of a tooth falling out. The snake is then obviously a representation of the penis; and particularly if the dreamer is a woman who is afraid of sexual intercourse.

Freud did not confine his investigations to symbols of the human body. He saw that the animal world is, in fact, a rich source of symbols and symbolic representation. For example, the dislike children have for their brothers and sisters can be symbolized by small obnoxious animals and vermin. On the other hand, a woman who dreams that she is plagued with vermin Freud viewed as symbolic of pregnancy and as an indication of the woman's loathing of the event.

A dream concerning direction can have several meanings. *Right* and *left* are used commonly in our language in symbolic ways—e.g., the *righteous* way or the *right* way—whereas the *left* (*sinister* is from the Latin) denotes illegitimacy, even homosexuality. The directions *up* and *down* can represent success and failure, as they can also represent the sexual parts of the body, with breasts represented by "upstairs" and "downstairs" referring to the genitalia.

These few fragmentary illustrations can only begin to convey the panorama and depth of Freud's thought, how thought-provoking the objects and symbols in dreams can be for self-knowledge and the integration of personality. We hope that we have given the reader a taste of Freud, just enough "incentive" to encourage individual pursuit. Freud is highly readable, besides being a great man. He had great skill as a writer and was a master of the clear argument. Even when, to our eyes, he is clearly wrong, or where his vision is unclear or myopic, we cannot deny him his rightful place in the history of ideas.

Freud is one of the giants of the twentieth century—one of those few who reshaped our understanding of the nature of man in our time. Perhaps no one has said it better than Carl Jung, one of Freud's first and most brilliant students:

Freud's greatest achievement probably consisted in taking neurotic patients seriously and entering into their peculiar individual psychology. He had the courage to let the case material speak for itself. . . . He saw with the patient's eyes. . . . He was free of bias, courageous, and succeeded in overcoming a host of prejudices. . . . By evaluating dreams as the most important source of information concerning the unconscious processes, he gave back to mankind a tool that had seemed irretrievably lost.[14]

JUNG AND THE DISCOVERY
OF THE SYMBOLIC SELF IN DREAMS

By the time Freud got to publish the second edition of his *The Interpretation of Dreams,* a devoted group of psychoanalysts had gathered around him in Vienna. Many of these analysts were eventually to make original contributions to psychoanalytic theory and to achieve public renown in their own right; for example, Wilhelm Reich, Alfred Adler, Otto Rank, Karen Horney, Ernest Jones, Wilhelm Steckel, and Carl Gustav Jung—to mention a few. We have chosen to speak of Jung and his theories now because Jung's works, in particular his work on dreams, led psychology to a wider understanding of dream symbols.

Freud and Jung

It was common knowledge among the original psychoanalytic group that Freud considered Jung the "crown prince" who might one day take over the leadership and direction of Freud's Psychoanalytic Society. Although that was a flattering possibility, it was also a considerable burden for Jung, for he was twenty years Freud's junior and one of the youngest members of the psychoanalytic movement. Freud, however, considered Jung brilliant, and his feeling for Jung came close to that of a father for a favorite son. This period was a time of great importance in Jung's personal and professional life. He had been a relatively unknown Swiss psychiatrist who was just beginning to feel the stirrings of genius within himself when he met, in Freud, the kind of seminal teacher he needed.

Nonetheless, by 1914, Jung knew he could not unequivocally accept Freud's approach to personality. He was a more solitary individual than Freud, and he felt himself constitutionally unable to assume the function of a "crown prince". Whereas Freud was an "extravert," and so emphasized the reality of the "external" world and was more pragmatic and practical in his approach, Jung seems to have been an "introvert," a contemplative who looked into "inward" spaces of personality and told of what he encountered there. Furthermore, by 1914, Jung was also coming to feel increasingly uncomfortable with some of Freud's ideas and beliefs.[15]

SYMBOLS AND SEXUALITY

The turning point in their relationship came when Jung acknowledged he could no longer accept Freud's "exclusive sexualistic conception of dream symbols." [16] To be sure, Jung believed that dreams could convey powerful biological messages from the unconscious (as Freud taught), but Jung also believed that sexual content in the dream could itself be symbolic.

Suppose, for example, a man dreams that he is pregnant and is going to have a child. A Freudian analyst might interpret this dream at the sexual level of content, and he then might say that the dream represents a wish-fulfillment of the person, and possibly also "homosexual" overtones in the man's personality. A Jungian analyst might suggest a different interpretation of the dream. Knowing the man to be a writer or a scientist, for example he might suggest that the dream is a symbolic representation of the person's intuition that he is on the verge of "giving birth" to a literary work or a scientific discovery.

For Freud dreams are mainly *retrospective*—i.e., concerned with past unresolved, infantile conflicts and instinctual needs. For Jung, however, dreams deal also with the present and can even portend future plans, imaginings, hopes, and desires of the person.

The radical differences in temperament and outlook between Freud and Jung resulted in the eventual withdrawal of Jung from the Vienna school led by Freud. It was an event that was painful for both men, for both were geniuses, and genius is sometimes blind to its own "shortsightedness." Neither Freud nor Jung found areas for reconciliation after their break, though Jung was to acknowledge Freud's contribution to his own theory later on in his autobiography.

Jung returned to his beloved Swiss mountains and lakes and, except for journeys to the United States, England, and Africa, he remained at his home to work in comparative isolation for the remainder of his life. As he says himself, he became accustomed to being misinterpreted and merely tolerated by the psychological world.[17] And there is little doubt that, until the last decades of his life, his psychological approach to personality was considered too "mystical" for American scientists to take seriously, though his writings and theories had been respected in Europe for some time.

The confusions and suspicions that have been aroused by some of Jung's ideas is understandable. Jung is neither as clear a writer nor as systematic a thinker as Freud was; and it is indeed sometimes difficult to grasp his theories and ideas—some of which can seem, on the surface and to the uninitiated, downright spooky. He was content to wait for the verdict of history, and in that regard his faith in the validity of his own approach to personality has been justified. We see now a reappraisal of Jung's contribution to personality theory; and some of his views—once thought extreme, even outlandish or just plain wrong—are beginning to make more sense in our contemporary life.

MAN'S DUAL NATURE

Throughout the ages, philosophers, writers, theologians, and scientists have concerned themselves with the apparent duality of man's nature: our possibilities for good and evil; our sublime achievements and our equally murderous atrocities; our capacity for transcendental awareness and our biological limitations.

Freud had opened up discussion of the existence of polarity in the human personality in his theory of human bisexuality (i.e., that each person has both male and female components) and in his conception of the mind being separated into conscious and unconscious functions. This principle of opposition, or polarity, became pivotal in Jung's own psychological theory. Jung writes, for example:

> The sad truth is that man's real life consists of a complex of inexorable opposites—day and night, birth and death, happiness and misery, good and evil. We are not even sure that one will prevail against the other. Life is a battleground. It has always been and always will be; and if it were not so, existence would come to an end.[18]

But if a man is divided into oppositional tendencies, how, then, does he deal with these polarities? And, more important, *is it possible for him to reconcile his divided nature and become whole*—at peace with himself and his world?

The *whole* person (the one Jung calls an *individuated person*) is better able to integrate these polar aspects of personality into a creative and beneficial adaptation. He sets as one of his life goals the *reconciliation of those opposites* in his personality and life.

The Personal and the Collective Unconscious

Like Freud, Jung accepted the conscious and unconscious levels of personality. But whereas Freud viewed the unconscious as a kind of "repository" for repressed aggressive drives, Jung believed that the unconscious levels of personality can also be a source of psychic wisdom and insight into personality development itself. According to Jung, the unconscious also "contains" unbiased and accurate judgments about the present moment, about each individual's history, and about the history of the human race as well. This (human) *racial memory* Jung called the *collective unconscious,* and it is necessary to understand this concept since it is crucial to understanding the difference between Jung's and Freud's approaches to personality.

Taking the human fetus as an analogy, Jung points out that in the mother's womb the human body undergoes the phylogenetic history of the human race—i.e., it goes through the stages of evolution leading up to man, progressing from a one-celled organism, through a "fish" stage (complete with gill-like structures), until eventually the fetus becomes recognizable as a higher-order primate and finally resembles a human infant. And just as our *bodies* have evolved over millions of years so, too, according to Jung, our human personality has evolved psychologically—and we carry this psychological evolution in our collective unconscious.

Jung says the person who is able to tap the wellspring of his collective unconscious has at his disposal insights and understandings of our earlier ages on this planet. These "deeper" levels of personality are still there for our consideration, according to Jung, and each of us needs to integate that wisdom and knowledge into our present self if we are to appreciate who we are in reality and to attain wholeness.

Archetypes

The way to attain this wholeness, according to Jung, is for the person to get in touch with some of his subpersonalities which Jung called the *archetypes,* as we mentioned in Chapter 8. We discussed one of these archetypes in that chapter, the Shadow. Here, we will discuss a few of the other archetypes which influence our lives.

The Anima and the Animus

In every man, Jung says, there is a feminine component, the *Anima* and in every woman there is a masculine component, the *animus.* As a boy grows into manhood, he differentiates himself into the masculine mode, thus veering away from the feminine side of himself. In cultures which punish particularly the slightest trace of "femininity" in a male, or "masculinity" in the female, children of both sexes tend to split off (by social conditioning) those aspects of themselves.

For example, if a man is made ashamed of his softness and tenderness, and is taught to think of them as "feminine," he can become lopsidedly "masculine" and resent or repress the opposite emotions in himself as they come into consciousness from time to time. He will emphasize his intellectual, physical, and aggressive drives and thereby miss out on a whole dimension of experiencing. However, if he recognizes the feminine side of himself and gets into harmony with it, lets his "femaleness" speak to him occasionally, he can use these energies in productive and creative ways.

Women and men are biologically and psychologically differentiated, and a man's Anima, if he will allow himself to confront her, can provide him with insights that are only available through his "feminine" intuitional vision. The Anima provides him with those soft and tender and lovely moments of beauty and insight; and if he can enter into dialogue with that level of himself, his creative potential is immeasurably increased. You will recall from Chapter 2 that Barron, Taylor, McKinnon, and their associates discovered that the most creative architects, physicists, engineers, and poets are markedly more in touch with their feminine nature, as measured by a masculine-feminine scale. *Anima* means "soul"; and to Jung, a man is only half a person if he is without this soul aspect of himself.

When, on the other hand, a man is not in harmony with his Anima, or refuses to engage her, she can actually "possess" him; and he can react then, despite his masculine inclination, with outbursts of very feminine moodiness, "irrationality," sulkiness, and pessimism.

In the woman there is, in like manner, a coalesced male component, the *Animus. Animus* means "mind," and it represents the woman's assertive, intellectual, and aggressive side—the side of personality which women in our culture often deny or repress for fear of being thought "unfeminine." If a woman does not accept the masculine component in her nature, if she does not allow herself full independence of intellect, she can evolve into that rather pathetic creature: the colorless, uninteresting mother/housewife with no identity as a person in her own right. Her conversation centers on her children, her house, her husband, her surgery—there is nothing else of herself she can put forward. And when her children are grown up and gone, she remains for the rest of her life feeling incomplete, since so much of her identity is now gone with her departed children.

Extraversion-Introversion

Another polarity, and one which was to become well known, was Jung's concept of the polar modes of experiencing: namely, extraversion and introversion. *Extraversion* is a tendency to move toward the external world as reality, the capacity to concentrate on outside events, objects, and persons. *Introversion* is the tendency to withdraw into oneself and to study one's reactions, motivations, and "inner" psychological experiences. Ideally, the individual is able to alternate between these two modes of experiencing and achieve a harmony between both realities. Unfortunately, however, this flow and rhythm can be interrupted, and people can then tend toward an exclusive use of one mode or the other.

The extraverted type thinks, feels, and acts so as to correspond directly with objective conditions.[19] His whole consciousness looks out at the world. Since he is intensely interested in the persons and events of the outside world, his attention is centered on them and he is then less aware of his inner world. The extraverted person lives in the physical and social world with relative ease, he generally gets along well with others, is often a natural leader because he understands and is able to fit himself into experiences of others. In like manner, he is the person who is eager to please and likes to see peple get along together. He is a "people person" rather than a "loner," and goes out of his way to pay attention to others and their needs.

The introverted type, on the other hand, is governed more by subjective factors, by his own "internal" reactions to the world. Compared to the extravert, whose attention and interest is directed to the reality of the "world out there," the introverted person is more

interested in *how he feels and thinks about* that world, and his central focus is primarily on his own inward experiencing. The introverted personality can also be less at ease in social situations (such as parties), and he more often prefers small groups to be with, a few persons at a time rather than a bunch. He needs his solitude to find out who he is, and generally he prefers the kind of work that provides peace and quiet rather than noise and bustle. He does not need the frequent kind of interpersonal stimulation which the extravert seeks and needs to feel secure, though his need for love and attention can be as great, or even greater, than that of the extravert. The introvert is likely to be an independent thinker who prefers to reach his conclusions for himself; he can also be more "radical" in his philosophy, just as the extravert is prone, as a type, to be more "conservative." In like manner, the introvert can become rigid, unadaptable, stubborn, and difficult when his opinions are challenged, whereas the extravert, who is easier to get along with, is more willing to compromise, to adapt his views to the group ethic if need be.

It would be difficult in this short space to convey the complexity of the introversion-extraversion continuum. Remember, however, that few of us are "pure" types; most of us are combinations of extraversion and introversion rather than being one or the other all the time.

The Four Functions

In addition to the conscious-unconscious polarity and the extraversion-introversion polarity, Jung also postulated four additional functions of the psyche: thinking, feeling, sensation, and intuition. For Jung, thinking and feeling are polar, or opposite to each other; and so are sensation and intuition (see figure below).

What Jung says is that each person tends toward a dominant mode which is his strength and asset, i.e., a set of behaviors, responses and attitudes that he feels express who he is. If he is very dominant in one mode (for example, thinking), he may be very weak in the polar (opposite) mode (in this case, feeling). No manner of responding is superior or inferior, since we need all functions to be complete.

A schematic representation of Jung's theory of personality.

Thinking. Thinking is the intellectual faculty, the faculty which analyzes, seeks to understand, orders facts, uses logic to understand relationships. It is the logical, rational, objective faculty of the personality. Thinking makes use of reason, abstraction, and generalization. The thinking person can look at data, make acute observations about them, theorize, apply inductive and deductive logic, see holistic concepts, and at the same time observe fine dissimilarities between facts. The thinking person is at home in the scholarly world of research.

If the predominantly thinking person neglects to develop his feeling function, however, he may be acutely uncomfortable in the world of human relationships. Such a person distrusts human emotions (because he does not understand them) and prefers to use impersonal logic in relating to others. As a scientist, he may be accurate and wholly competent in his work, but he may be unable to meet the emotional needs of his wife and family.

Feeling. The feeling function is a valuing function. It is the channel through which we evaluate pleasure and pain, likes and dislikes, and the whole range of human emotional expression. The feeling function enables us to decide the value of an object, a person, or an event in relation to ourselves. If a person is predominantly a feeling type, he will be able to experience the fine gradations of human emotions (awe, delight, grandeur), which is the mark of the lyric poet. The world can be for him a passionate place to live, a constant medley of emotional interplay. Life for him is seldom dull or boring. Each moment of his existence can afford him some new emotion to be savored, distilled, and examined. On the other hand, if he is so dominated by the feeling function so that he neglects the cool clarity of his thinking function, he can become the victim of his emotions—someone who whirls from one eddy of feeling to another. He is at the mercy of his emotions, as are others in his environment as they get swept up into the currents of his roller-coaster emotional reactions. The person who is so dominated may need to take a step back into the impersonality of reflective thinking every so often so that he does not wear out other people—and himself as well. Yet if he manages to moderate and discipline this function, he becomes the "warm" personality which many are drawn to and few dislike.

Sensing. The sensation-intuition continuum involves reliance on *inner* versus *outer* "knowing" (not to be confused with introversion and extraversion). Our sensing function is the *reality* function which enables us to behold and integrate objective phenomena which are "out there." In using this function we are able to see and hear clearly what is actually out there—what exists in the external world that we perceive through our senses. A person who is predominantly a sensing personality is a highly realistic, practical person who has clear perceptions of external situations. He remembers facts, is observant, and has a firm grasp of reality. The sensor is a doer because he can see what is the case, what needs to be done with the particular situation.

The sensing personality has as his unused function the quality of intuition. If he distrusts his intuition, or is less in touch with that function, he will still be able to see external facts, but may be unable to envision possibilities for the future. In that case, he will tend to be realistic but lacking in originality and imagination. In other words, he is so "realistic" that he sees the facts, but misses the point!

Intuition. The intuition function, on the other hand, provides us with startling inspirations, revelations, and insights regarding what is not readily observable but is nevertheless true. It is the intuitive function which enables us to make the mental "jump" from the known, present facts to the unknown, still-unseen possibilities of "what can happen *if* . . ." Intuition accounts for our prophetic abilities, our "hunches," and those accurate "first impressions" we sometimes get about things and people. As contrasted with the practical, sensing personality who is able to read the data of the "external" world, the intuitive personality gets his information primarily from his inner unconscious responses.

A person who is highly intuitive may be the true visionary; but if he is greatly underdeveloped in the function of sensing, he may not know what to do with his intuitional understandings. If he lacks sensitivity in the realm of practical affairs, his intuitive knowledge will not help him pragmatically to get to where he wants to go and do what he wants to do. Such persons are often characterized as "dreamers" or "impractical visionaries."

The Search for the Neglected Function

Each one of us is generally a blend of the four functions, with one function being dominant and its two "neighboring" functions (see schematic, p. 279) contributing their particular flavor or character to our personality. The remaining function—the one polar to the dominant function—is generally unconscious, in a state of underdevelopment. Jung believed it took considerable study of oneself, as well as long and continuing effort, to enable the fourth function to come into conscious awareness. An example may clarify how the functions work in an individual's personality.

Consider a person whose dominant function is *feeling*. His polar function is thus *thinking,* and he will be very likely deficient in this domain of awareness. His neighboring functions are *sensation* and *intuition,* so he will be (approximately) a feeling-sensing-intuitive type, or a feeling-intuitive-sensing type—depending on which of the two neighboring functions he relies upon more. If, on the other hand, his dominant function is thinking, he will be deficient in the feeling realm, and so on.

The essential requirement for growth is that one identify the functions that are readily available and dominant in his personality and then develop (at least rudimentary) awareness of his inferior or neglected functions. That is more than a routine, intellectual exercise when it comes to a complex interpersonal relationship such as marriage, as the following example may show.

Let's suppose a man who is a thinking type (say, a lawyer, or accountant, or teacher by profession) has married a woman he finds attractive because of her feeling qualities. He fell in love with her in the first place because he was drawn to her gay, warm, spontaneous personality, her way of lighting up when something pleased her. She brought *feelings* into his life, which until then had been satisfactory even if a bit sterile and unexciting at times. After marriage, however, her constant "likes and dislikes," her "ups and downs," her "emotional binges" begin to weary and frustrate him.

The wife is caught up in a similar dilemma: what she admired in the man before marriage was his "cool control" of situations, a quality that gave her a comfortable feeling of security and protection which her "flighty" personality needed and lacked. After marriage, though, he seems to her "dried up"; he no longer fulfills her expectations, for he prefers intellectual pursuits to being with her and having "fun."

We can theorize that each member of this couple sought to "complete" himself and herself by marrying the quality of personality which was lacking in each person individually. A marriage that is based on these "unconscious" motivations may endure, but it can also be stressful and given to misunderstandings, and it can often lack the peace and contentment which married couples in all ages and times have sought.

For brevity's sake, we have discussed only how the polar or opposite attitudes toward living can function in this couple's relationship, and how these oppositional tendencies can produce the kind of incompatibility that sometimes, for example, leads to divorce. We did not discuss the contributory functions and attitudes the couple share which can also help to "make things manageable;" for that would demand a more extensive discussion of Jung's theory of psychological types than we can go into now. We do need to say, however, that his theory of psychological types is a subtle and complex theory of how individual personalities view their reality and that, in our view, Jung's theory is well worth study if that is your inclination. Jung recognized that wholeness, integration of personality, finding out who we are and what we can become, make a lifelong task that requires continuous effort and determination. He acknowledges that most of us come into the world with given possibilities and given limitations because of our type, and that most of us, therefore, begin the adventure of living with limitations which shall demand sometimes extraordinary effort to surmount. What about the unrealized possibilities, the unconscious functions that we do not discover and integrate into our personality?

A quote from Jung:

> We know that a man can never be everything at once, never complete; he always develops certain qualities at the expense of others, and wholeness is never attained. But what happens to those functions which are not developed by exercises and are not consciously brought into daily use? They remain in a more or less primitive and infant state, often only half-conscious, or even quite unconscious. . . . The one-sided emphasis on thinking is always accompanied by an inferiority in feeling, and differentiated sensation and intuition are mutually injurious. . . . We are always at a disadvantage in using the inferior function because we cannot direct it, being in fact even its victims.[20]

Body and Soul

The adventure that is each person's life has certain stages of development which can be more-or-less clearly marked and differentiated. First each person is an infant, then he becomes a child, then the teenage years are upon him, then he marries, has a family, learns to make a living, and settles down into the pattern of being a householder, husband or wife, and so on. Each stage of development must be lived through, and integrated before one can go on to the next stage of our development. (We mentioned these stages of life-evolution earlier, particularly when we discussed Erik Erikson.)

There is a stage in the development of personality which is sometimes neglected in our culture—some would say because we continue to emphasize and emulate the "under-thirty" approach to life. This neglected stage has been called "the middle years," and it deals primarily with the crises in personality which come upon us when we have satisfied and completed the "householder" stage and begin to approach "maturity," that is when we can now begin to cultivate the values and attitudes that have to do with the last half of life: from thirty-five years onward. Jung was one of the first psychologists to take note of this stage of personality evolution, the second half of life, and we need to discuss some of his findings in that realm of personality if our treatment of his psychology is to be anywhere near complete.

Jung says men and women are always oriented in two directions: toward the physical-biological-material world and toward the psychological-spiritual-transcending dimensions of the self. The beginning stages of our development as a personality entail the work of coming to terms with the physical-biological-material plane of existence. We begin there as newborn infants and we further and complete that plane of our growth when we marry, raise a family, and learn how to love and support them so they, in their turn, can carry on and raise children on their own.

Not all persons marry and get involved with learning how to be a "householder." These "unmarried" individuals are not thereby necessarily any less complete than someone who takes the path of family life. As some marriages can be forms of misery and nonlearning, so also there are radiant personalities who have taken "all men" as their family. We are thinking now, for example, of members of certain religious orders, and of widows and widowers and others who continue to unfold the truth of their reality without having a spouse. We have known such persons, and their "middle years" are often an example of the compassion and understanding sometimes lacking in "married" persons.

Many a person can become neurotic, Jung believes, when he

enters these "middle years" of life and the previous adaptation has been oriented solely toward the physical plane of his existence. Such a person has not allowed himself time to become aware of the urgings of the "other side" of his nature—his "soul," the "spiritual" needs of his personality. For example, the person who has concentrated his energies and attention on attaining wealth, fame, position, and success may have thereby neglected the spiritual side of his personality —that side of self that provides "meaning" in life and can make the success and fame seem worthwhile. Such persons, according to Jung, can enter their middle years psychologically unprepared to deal with the specific factors in themselves they must now encounter, as they approach the waning of their powers and the coming of old age.

A problem of modern man, again according to Jung, is often just this lack of psychological preparation for the second half of life. We put so much of our energy into the material plane of our existence—the first half of life—that we can remain perpetual "juveniles," oriented toward power, to "making it" bigger and better than anyone else! Thus, as we come upon the middle years of life, we are in a continuous state of envy and dissatisfaction with our present state, and lack the resources within our personality that we will need if we are to manage to grow and mature as we approach middle and old age.

THE COMPENSATORY FUNCTION IN PERSONALITY

In Jung's view, unity, harmony, and peaceful understanding of what living is all about comes to the person who manages to sustain the rhythmic alteration between the two poles of existence. Neurosis is the lopsided development of one of the various possibilities in personality. Integration of personality is the achievement of a well-rounded balance of our total possibilities. If we do not achieve that kind of integration, the neglected side of personality begins eventually to demand attention in our dreams and in our fantasies, and ultimately through neurotic symptoms. This process is called *compensation.*

According to Jung, there is a profound compensatory wisdom at work in all personality. Thus, if in the waking state a person has been preoccupied with routine business affairs, then his dreams and his fantasies tend to compensate for that overemphasis; for example he may find himself alone in a dream, away from people, just sitting around and doing nothing in particular. Or a woman who has allowed her intellectual function to fall into relative disuse may dream an Animus dream; or a man who has been too caught up in intellectual activities may in a dream be attracted to an unknown woman, representating his Anima. The point to remember, here, is that continued neglect of a necessary function or possibility in the *conscious* personality will constellate, or call forth, this possibility on the *unconscious* level of the self; it will begin to appear in our fantasies and eventually our dreams. That is what Jung meant by the compensatory function in personality, and he believed that when we pay attention to our fantasies and dreams we have direct and reliable feedback of the status of our present life style.

THE MANDALA SYMBOL AND THE INTEGRATION OF PERSONALITY

A mandala is generally circular in appearance though it can also appear in the form of a square, or even a "squared circle," that is a circle and a square that are integrated. Mandala drawings and paintings have appeared in many cultures in Western and Eastern societies and they have been used for meditative purposes in the religions of the East for many centuries. A mandala may appear in the form of a wheel, something akin to Ezekiel's wheel in the sky in the Bible story; or it can take the form of a four-sided cross or square, as in the medieval tradition with the Christ figure at the center and the four evangelists at the cardinal points. For examples of mandalas see the illustrations on page 287.

Jung became interested in mandala symbolism very early in his professional life as a psychotherapist, and he noticed that at certain psychological crisis points some of his patients began to have dreams, and sometimes fantasies, in which mandalas appeared. These dreams not only had great significance for these persons, but in many instances there followed also a resolution of the person's particular psychological conflict—and a notable step forward in his growth and understanding of himself—once he worked through the dream in which the mandala appeared.

In Jung's theory of personality the mandala came in time to symbolize the integrative forces at work in personality. Indeed, he believed, when these figures begin to appear in dreams, they point toward an oncoming wholeness, unity, and harmony in the personality and personal life. Jung encouraged his patients, for that reason, to work on these symbols during the therapeutic session, also to draw and paint the dream symbols in detail. For in making the dream symbol objective, out there on the canvas, a necessary distance or impersonality occurs which enables the person to understand more fully what he is presently living through. Jung painted many mandalas himself over this lifetime and he appears to have used such paintings both as a creative discipline (to "externalize" the psychological forces stirring within his personality) and to understand objectively what he was presently experiencing in his own development.

Can any one of us use the mandala symbol to aid us in our search for wholeness and integration of our personality? Or do we have to wait until these symbols appear to us in a dream? We do not have to wait for the dream symbol to occur; we can draw a circle, or a square, or a combined figure, and then, feeling who we are now, just complete the figure so as to express how we seem to be at this moment. Subsequent concentration on the completed figure—while paying attention to our fantasies, hunches, and intuitions—can provide us with new insights and understandings of where we

Two examples of mandalas: the one on the left is from the Western tradition; the one on the right is Tibetan.

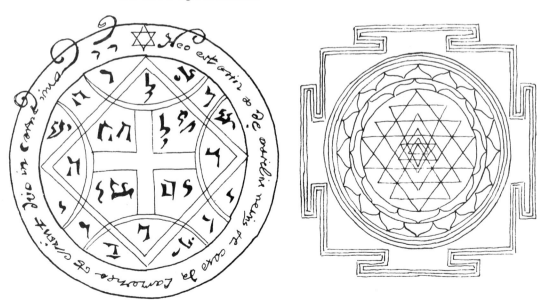

are in our present development. With practice, this method can become of considerable help in expressing objectively the forces within personality; and where we have a series of mandalas to study, we can see for ourselves not only where we were, where we are now, but even where we may be going in our development.

RECOMMENDED READINGS

ARGUELLES, JOSE, and MIRIAM ARGUELLES. *Mandala*. Berkeley and London: Shambala, 1972 (paperback).

These two artists have done an extensive treatment of the mandala across cultures and through time. They have also added their own investigations into the mandala through meditation and painting. The text is one of the most beautifully illustrated books we have come across. It is an experience.

FREUD, SIGMUND. *The Interpretation of Dreams*. Trans. J. Strackey. New York: Avon Books, 1965 (paperback).

The trouble with most people's misunderstanding of Freud is that they have not read him, but only about him. There is no substitute for the man himself. Not only was he a giant in his thinking, he was also a master writer, as this book so well demonstrates.

FROMM, ERICH. *The Forgotten Language*. New York: Grove Press, 1951 (hardcover).

Like the Mahoney book below, this is a very-easy-to-read primer on how to use dreams for guidance and self-understanding. Particularly good is Fromm's section on the historical roots of dream interpretation, especially as it relates to the Bible. The religiously inclined student might find this book a source of inspiration. It has also been used by ministers and rabbis.

HALL, CALVIN S. *The Meaning of Dreams*. New York: McGraw-Hill, 1953, 1966 (paperback).

This book is a summary of Hall's research on the nature of dreaming at his Institute of Dream Research plus some interesting information about dreamers. Easy to understand and highly readable.

JUNG, CARL G., et al. *Man and His Symbols*. New York: Dell, 1968 (paperback). Originally published in hardcover by Aldus Books, London, 1964.

This book was written with the express hope that the reading public would come to understand Jung's work, particularly his work on dreams. As a consequence, the book is far more readable than Jung's other writings. He believed that dreams offer practical advice from the unconscious mind to the conscious mind. He believed that if we learn to understand our dream symbols we will be far wiser. This book is a particularly valuable source book for understanding our dream symbols.

JUNG, CARL G. *Memories, Dreams, Reflections.* Ed. Aniela Jaffé. New York: Random House, Pantheon Books, 1961 (hardcover).

For a truly remarkable autobiography, there is none superior to Jung's, in which he discusses his interior life, including his visions and dreams. This is a "must" for the really serious student of dreaming.

MACKENZIE, NORMAN. *Dreams and Dreaming.* New York: Vanguard Press, 1965 (hardcover).

A beautifully illustrated and written book on the history of dream interpretation. Sophisticated enough for the person knowledgeable on the subject, yet written in language that the lay person can understand.

MAHONEY, MARIA. *Meaning in Dreams and Dreaming.* New York: Citadel Press, 1966 (paperback).

Jung can be pretty heavy going for the beginning student of dreams. We recommend this book for the person who would like an easy introduction to Jung's formulation of dreams. It is easy to read, and Mahoney does a good job of interpreting archetypes.

WHYTE, LANCELOT LAW. *The Unconscious Before Freud.* Garden City, N.Y.: Doubleday, 1962 (paperback).

The student who wishes to know some of the historical roots of Freud's theory of dream interpretation might want to look into this volume, which discusses the mainstream of European thought regarding the meaning of dreams and dreaming that preceded and in part influenced Freud's theories.

PRODUCING AND RECORDING DREAMS: PERLS AND THE DREAM SELF

In the years since Freud and Jung and other pioneer psychoanalysts made their studies of the dreaming experience there have been significant breakthroughs in the area of sleep and dream research. For example, we now know that all of us dream, even those among us who do not remember dreams. So the sentence, "I don't dream." would now be more accurately put as, "I don't remember my dreams."

Second, sleep and dream research have shown that, depending on what we consider to be a dream, we dream more-or-less almost all night long! [1]

Third, the fact that one is dreaming can be observed by others, for dreaming is accompanied by observable physiological changes in the body. Just as emotional reactions in the awake state can be measured with scientific instruments, so also the experience of dreaming has definite emotional reactions that can now be measured and described—with such accuracy, in fact, that the research scientist can say when a person is specifically in the "deep dream state." [2]

Dream and sleep research now tell us that we dream many times during the night when asleep, and that dreaming may account for as much as 85 percent of the sleep experience. Dreaming, therefore, accounts for almost a third of our lives (since we spend approximately a third of our lives asleep).

Some persons seem to remember their dreams better than others. If you are a nonrememberer, there is hope for you, too—if you want to put the time and energy into that project.

The guidelines which follow have been used for several years with all kinds of persons in teaching them how to remember dreams. Although they may seem rather obvious, these pointers have proved useful to many persons, and we hope they will be of use to you as well.

1. Tell yourself before you go to sleep that you want to remember your dreams.

This is one of the crucial steps in any dream-recording program, since it begins to direct your attention and energy where you want your energy to go. It is a kind of autosuggestion technique, and it may sound somewhat magical, but the approach does work if you apply yourself to it conscientiously every night.

There is a fair chance that you will dream on order the first time you attempt this approach. There is also the likelihood that you will remember nothing. You are to be congratulated if you succeed on your first trial (it's called beginner's luck!); but do not be put off, or discouraged, if your new program does not work the first night. Try again on the second night, and the third . . . until it begins to happen that you remember your dreams. The repeated instructions to yourself night after night will be necessary if you are a "nondreamer" (i.e., a "nonrememberer"), since you may have many years of resistance to overcome before the command is followed by the results you want. Practice!

2. Wake up quickly!

Dreams can be forgotten very quickly; so quickly, in fact, that they may begin to fade from "memory" in the first few seconds of waking up unless something significant occurs that will fix the dream in your conscious awareness.[3] Incidentally, this may be a partial explanation for the fact we seem to remember nightmares more easily —for we wake up then with a start! Nightmares are usually so vivid and emotional that we do not just turn over and slide off into another dream or sleep state, as with other, less terrifying dreams.

Why do our dreams seem to fade so quickly? You can demonstrate the same phenomenon if you refer to your conscious, waking state. Do you remember occasions when you have been talking to someone about something, and you have gone off on some tangent for a moment, and when you wanted to get back on your original topic you could not remember what you were saying a few seconds before? Or, as a child, you may have tried impatiently to get to say something to your parents; and then when you were given the chance, you stood there bewildered, only able to say, "I forgot what I wanted to say." Someone may have said to you at that point, "Well, it probably wasn't that important anyhow." Nonsense! It's just that our thoughts and feelings fly through us at hundreds of words per minute. (In fact, many modern writers have tried to catch this "stream of consciousness" in their works—a noteworthy example is the Irish writer James Joyce.) Our dreams move and have their existence in this same kind of environment. It is a fast and "moving" world that requires training and practice to participate in. For that reason—because it is a world of motion and time—one dream can "push" a previous dream out of reach, out of memory very quickly.

If you are a person who has difficulty waking up in the morning you may well be a person who has difficulty remembering your dreams. At wake-up time you turn over and say to yourself, "Oh, I don't want to get up yet. . . . I think I'll just turn over and give myself a few more minutes of sleep." That thought may be just the thing you do which pushes the dream experience from your memory, out of your psychological reach. Hence our next guideline for remembering your dreams.

3. Wake up earlier than usual.

Catch yourself in the middle of a dream, if you can; and then decide to wake up. If you are used to waking up at, say, 7:00 A.M., your sleep stages will gradually become lighter and lighter as that time approaches—you will begin to fade gradually into the *awake* state where your *dreaming* now turns into *early-morning thoughts.* A very valuable program to set for yourself, therefore, is to wake up slightly before your usual waking time, say 6:45 A.M. You may begin to dream then—and simply by reason of the fact you are disturbing your usual routine, which is to wake up at 7:00 A.M.!

4. Keep a notebook by your bed.

If you don't write your dream down *immediately* upon awakening, you may very well forget it before noon, or even before your morning coffee. So often people say, "I had a dream last night, and it was so vivid and clear I was sure I'd remember it—but now I can't remember." So, to repeat, as soon as you realize you are waking up from a dream, *reach for the pen and notebook you have set by your bed and write it down while it is still clear.* If you have to hunt for a pencil and paper, you may forget the dream.

Psychoanalysts, writers, and other introspective persons frequently keep a special dream-notebook beside their bed so they can record their dreams soon after they awaken. They are among the persons who take their dreaming seriously, and they do not want to miss even one clue to self-understanding.

So, simply write down whatever you *think* you remember. Don't worry at this point about details, nor if you are possibly changing things already in your memory. Just get down on the paper what you think you remember; and trust that in your "unconscious" your dreams never lie, and that each of us knows what we need to know and no more.

5. Write your dream down using the present tense.

For a long time, philosophers and psychologists argued whether a dream occurs over a period of time or instantaneously. One of the remarkable achievements of sleep research has been to confirm that dreams actually take place in time.[4] A dream may exist for a few seconds, or we may dream for twenty minutes. How did sleep researchers discover this? Simply by following the rapid eye movements (REMs) of research subjects night after night and comparing their observable eye movements with the dream subsequently related by the sleeper when he is awakened. The sleep research people discovered that the REMs correspond to the dreamer's memory of his dream. For example, if someone dreams of watching a tennis match, his eyes will move horizontally back and forth as if he were actually watching a real ball. If one dreams of watching a basketball game, there will also be up-and-down movements of the eyes. Also, a long and complicated dream will take a much longer actual period of time than a dream fragment.[5]

A dream, then, is a real experience happening in time. And a way to remember more dream details is to write down the dream in the present tense as if reliving the dream. Instead of writing, "Last night I dreamed I was at Manderlay. . . ," write, "In my dream I find myself now at the front gate of Manderlay. . . ," etc.

6. Write down every detail of the dream.

Nothing is unimportant in a dream: everything, *every fragment,* is important and can have significance. So write down the smallest detail. For example, if there is a vase of flowers, try to remember how many flowers there were—two, three, or four flowers, or a dozen. If there are colors in the dream, what colors were they? If a person in the dream has a scar on his right cheek and that's all you can remember, then write that down. In like manner, remember if a person in the dream is to your right side or to the left. And if he was walking toward you or away from you or just standing there! Write down particularly strange or bizarre elements. Does an otherwise mild acquaintance, for example, appear very violent in your dream? Does someone with a mustache remind you of a relative or friend? If you are climbing a set of stairs and you notice that the third step is missing, write that down even though it does not seem to have any special symbolic meaning right then.

7. Remember your "bad" dreams as well as your "good" dreams.

Our nightmares, or "bad" dreams, are seldom so frightening once we understand their symbolism. A student of the authors',

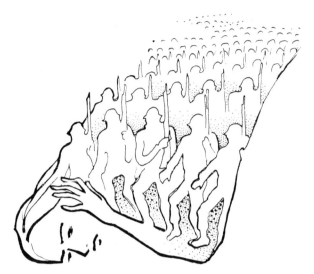

Nightmares when they are understood are
not nearly as terrifying.

for example, once dreamt of armies descending upon her, and she
awoke terrified that they would ride right over her. During the process of interpreting her dream, she gradually detected a relationship
between the armies and the relatives who visited her every Christmastime. She confessed that although she liked these relatives very
much, after a week of them "on top of her" she felt exhausted, overwhelmed by the extra work of cooking and cleaning up, irritated by
the lack of privacy, and so on. They had become for her, symbolically, an invading horde.

In like manner, death dreams also do not need to be interpreted
literally, as signs of impending physical death—at least not in the
authors' experience. For a very elderly person or someone clearly
on a self-destructive course, a death dream may have some such related significance. But in general, if you dream that a friend is
dying, it is more likely that he is "dying to you," that your relationship has become "dead," that what you once had together is now
over and done with. A dream of one's own death (again, in the
authors' experience) generally refers to the end of some aspect of
one's personality, be it a change in one's perception of the world,
or a change in some particular personality characteristic.

Dream language, as we said earlier, is different from our logical,
daytime cause-and-effect way of expressing reality. Our dream language can frighten us because we have not yet learned its syntax
(the way things get expressed); it frightens us also because the

symbolic forms in dreams are exaggerated and distorted. Think of the exaggeration in political cartoons, or the masks that were used in Greek plays, or the kind of exaggeration found in primitive art and statuary. Seeing such exaggerations, we begin to understand how the dreaming process gets across its message; and we begin to understand that the "frightening" elements of a dream are really simply ways the dream uses to grab our attention. Incidentally, if you do have a dream that frightens you, it is often a good idea to tell the dream to someone else instead of avoiding the fear. In our experience, just relating the dream out loud may be enough to remove some of its strangeness, thereby reducing your own anxiety reactions.

8. Have a notebook to record dreams and keep the notebook in a special place.

Once you begin to record your dreams seriously over weeks and months you will make an interesting discovery: your dreams often have a common theme, a progression of action, which is related to the things going on in your everyday living. For example, a student known to the authors had one dream in which she was studying for a test. In the next dream she awoke in horror because she was found cheating on the test. In a later dream, some four weeks later, she found herself being tried and convicted for some unspecified crime. Some months later she dreamed that she was locking up a tiger. These dreams were accompanied by other dreams, and she might not have seen the continuing theme if she had not kept her dream notebook up to date each day. As she looked back over these dreams later on, she realized they represented a growing awareness of her "hot" temper, plus her conscious attempts to do something about it. She wrote:

> The dreams were reflecting something I have been trying to learn for a long time [studying for a test], which is not to lose my temper. The next dream reflected a moment in which I backslid [cheated]. Then I really determined to do something about my bad temper [the trial]. I think locking up the tiger means I am successfully controlling my temper.

C. G. Jung was so impressed by the necessity for understanding the continuity of dream themes that he eventually chose to work only on a series of dreams rather than on just single dreams.[6] Calvin

Hall confirmed Jung's insight that dreams have a continuity and he discovered another interesting fact: close acquaintances sometimes dream of each other at approximately the same time.[7] Such concurrent dreaming may indicate that the relationship is undergoing dynamic change and may represent mutual attempts to sort out what is happening to the persons involved. If a relationship between two persons is going through a crisis, it is hardly surprising that they may dream of one another. Keeping a record of your dreams over time will help you to confirm or reject Hall's hypothesis.

9. Do not ask just anyone to work on your dreams; choose rather a trained person who knows how to work on dreams.

Only you know the meaning of your dream. Your dream is your painting, your script, your adventure, your poem. You are its author: the artist and the playwright of the dream. And no matter how skilled another person is in dream interpretation, that person cannot possibly know as much about the dream as you do. Of course, that person may have some hunches about certain aspects of your dream, and he may even see quite deeply and clearly into your dream, more than you do at this moment. But, we do insist, only *you* know the real meaning, for *you*, of *your* dream.

If you have never written a line of poetry, or acknowledge that you cannot draw a straight line, at least you are an artist in creating your dreams. By the way, your own dream symbols may seem to be similar, or very much like someone else's symbols, but again, only you will know if a particular interpretation "fits." When it does it will have that particular kind of resonance which says, "Yes, that makes sense!" (Reject everything else!)

One of the ways in which professional dream work (for example, sessions with a psychoanalyst) differs from a "rap session" on dreams is that the professional dream interpreter has been trained in the discipline of dream work. That person has learned that while suggestions are in order, even desirable, each person nonetheless does the dream work for himself or there cannot be the needed insightful breakthrough. More than anywhere else in the area of psychological counseling, work on dreams demands the counselor's noninterference, patience, and willingness to let the person do his own interpreting, his own "working through." Guard your dreams, we say, from persons who suffer too much from curiosity; and never let an amateur "psychologist" practice with you on your dreams.

10. Consider your dreams as potential sources of wisdom, solutions to problems, inspirations, etc.

There are many anecdotes about scientists, artists, and writers who, in their dreams, received creative inspiration and discovered solutions to complex problems, or received guidance on what path to take regarding a life situation.[8] A well-known example is August Kekule's suggestion of the structural formula for benzene in 1858. Kekule had been working to discover the arrangements of the atoms in the benzene molecule for some time, and then, in a dream, he saw the atoms fitted together in a certain pattern, which proved subsequently to be correct. This led to the development of the many compounds containing carbon.

It is not such a strange thing that our dreams are (or seem to be) insightful, perceptive, and even at times prophetic. During the day, the thousands of ordinary details that demand our attention sometimes prevent us from giving conscious consideration to important events and situations which can then resurface in dreams.[9] For example, suppose a mother briefly notices that the swing in the garden looks a little lopsided and thinks, "That might be dangerous for one of the children"; but then before she can even think further about it her attention is instantly diverted—say, by a telephone call. Then suppose she dreams that one of her children has an accident, but she can't seem to pinpoint the nature, cause, or context of the accident. Let's suppose further that a few days later her young son is in fact hurt on the swing when it falls over. In a sense, then, her dream predicted the accident; it was indeed "prophetic." But not supernaturally so: in the dream she went back to the unfinished situation where she noticed the lopsidedness of the swing, and though she had not followed up her intuition regarding the danger explicitly there, the so-called unconscious side of herself filed the information away for further consideration—in this instance, for dreaming about it.

When we dream, daytime stresses and activities usually have diminished, and we are able to relax to the point where we can give attention to the day's unfinished business. Because in our dreaming state we have the time to devote our whole attention to the things we overlooked during the day, they emerge in our nighttime awareness as "dreams."

In the remainder of this chapter we discuss some of the techniques for interpreting dream symbols. But you will need to have records of your own dreams if you are to learn the method correctly and adequately. We suggest you decide now to record your dreams, that you encourage yourself to dream, even to dream certain kinds of dreams you'd like . . . and then see what happens.

GETTING INTO DIALOGUE WITH YOUR DREAM-SELF

Interpreting your own dreams takes a little understanding of symbols, and some examples, and quite a bit of practice. It also takes your absolute willingness and intense desire to understand your dreams. Freud found that his patients often exhibited extreme difficulty in understanding their dream symbols, which he called their *unconscious resistance* to acknowledging their real motivations. No one can guess the meaning of your dream symbols better than you, so you are going to have to work at overcoming *your* resistance processes if you truly want to know and understand your dream-self.

Fritz Perls

Frederick S. ("Fritz") Perls was one of the European psychiatrists and personality theorists who were trained in Freud's psychoanalytic method. He fled Germany and the Nazi regime in 1934 and, after living for a time in the Netherlands and South Africa, emigrated to the United States at the end of World War II. Perls had a fierce energy and a drive to explore ever deeper into the nature of man—partly by exploring his own nature. He crisscrossed our country and eventually became one of the leaders at the Esalen Institute.[10] As a personal acquaintance of the authors, Perls impressed us as a brilliant man who was sometimes dominating and rude (impossible on occasion), often competitive, brave, honest, and at times one of the gentlest of men. In short, he had the kind of energy, intellectual drive, self-awareness, and desire to explore human existence which are so often the mark of genius.

Working with a person's dreams he would ask the dreamer to play every person, animal, and object in the dream scene so that the dreamer could understand what the symbol represented to him. The dreamer was to speak as if he were that individual or object— to describe himself, to talk to the other persons and symbols in the dream. Then, as the next step, he was directed to be his dream-self. Perls advised the person to "ham it up," to "let go" of his mind, and to allow to surface the irrational, emotional, illogical, and sensual parts of himself (i.e., those parts of the person Freud said speak in dream language).

Thus, by acting the part of a dream symbol—standing like the symbol, talking like the symbol, feeling the emotions of the symbol —we come to understand that symbol (be it a person, an object, or even a mood). Whereas Freud had called dreams the "royal road to the unconscious," Perls called dream interpretation the "royal road to the integration of personality."

Sometimes a person says, "But I don't know what that means . . ." or "I don't know who was in my dream with me." According to Perls, that kind of denial indicates that the person is presently disowning some aspect of himself (Jung would say disowning his "Shadow" self). But disowning a part of one's personality or projecting it onto someone else renders one poorer psychically: it becomes a part one does not know and which therefore cannot be called upon for support in everyday living and growing. (You will recall from Chapter 2 that Carl Rogers's clients who had gone through a successful therapeutic experience became more "fully

A significant key to understanding your dreams is to recognize that every person, object, event, color, number, and even mood in your dreams has to do with you.

functioning." Such a person, according to Rogers, came to "own" his feelings rather than deny them; to accept his thoughts and ideas rather than be ashamed of them; and above all, to learn to trust himself.)

"Reality" as a Projection of Personality

Perls's essential thesis is that the "world" is a projection of ourselves. Actually, there is nothing very new in this; it has been one of the traditional philosophic viewpoints since ancient Greek times.

What this really means is that when we see an event (say, a car accident), each of us will interpret the accident differently according to our own perceptions, beliefs, background, and prejudices. In other words, a person does not tell "the truth," but only an interpretation of "the truth" according to his personality patterning.

All "interpretations" of the world, according to Perls, are more simply a "projection" of oneself. Therefore, when one acts out his dream symbols (what Perls called "transforming" onself), he is identifying his own symbols (owning up to them) and his own projections. By "owning" the various parts of one's dream self, the person is integrating those various parts of his personality he has avoided and denied. He thereby not only faces up to his conflicts, but also begins to acknowledge his capacity for growth and change by integrating these split-off potentialities of his self.

Now, how does a person go about transforming himself into those various parts of his dream-self? Perls recorded many sessions of his dream-work seminars on tape and film and in his book *Gestalt Therapy Verbatim*.[11] The reader is referred to these sources if he is serious about interpreting his dreams. In the meantime, the following dialogue illustrates the use (and adaptation) of Perls's "transformation" method. (Notice that this young college student relates her dream—as we asked her to—in the present tense.)

GINNY: In my dream, I am in my car and I am going to my boyfriend's house. Only I can't see anything around me like houses and trees because it is all gray and dark. But anyway, I keep driving along this road and then I come to my boyfriend's house—only it's a garage. And I pull up in my car, and he puts gas in it. Then suddenly I am not there at all, but sitting in a room in a house and it seems as if he has kidnapped me; which I can't understand, because my boyfriend is very nice and wouldn't do such a thing.

O'CONNELL: Go on.

GINNY: Well, anyway, there I am in this room and I have my head down on my arms and I'm crying and crying. And *here's* another strange thing! My father and my brother are also in the room with my boyfriend and me. And the three of them, all of them, are sitting there and laughing at me. And, of course, I keep thinking, "They are laughing at me." And I don't understand why they don't help me or something. And then I wake up.

O'CONNELL: Besides the fact that you have a feeling your boyfriend has "kidnapped" you, is there anything else that seems very strange in your dream?

GINNY: Well, there's the fact that my father and my brother and my boyfriend are all sitting there, just laughing at me. Because I have a good relationship with all three. You see, I'm kind of the baby of the family, so my father and brother kind of pamper me. And my boyfriend is nice, too. Only in this dream, they seem to be laughing at me.

O'CONNELL: All right, let's walk the dream through again. Start from the beginning and try to remember every detail you can and stay in the present tense as you did before.

GINNY: Let's see, I'm in my car and I'm driving on this country road, I think, and it's very dark out so I can't see the cars or houses or anything.

O'CONNELL: OK, let's find out what the car means to you.

GINNY: I don't know.

O'CONNELL: You're the only one who knows. Play-act the car. Talk as if you are the car. Begin: "I am Ginny's car."

GINNY: I am Ginny's car. I am driving her along a country road and I'm running out of gas.

O'CONNELL: Ah, that's interesting. What does "running out of gas" mean to you?

GINNY: I don't know . . . well, maybe getting tired. Yeah, I guess that's it. Getting tired.

O'CONNELL: Do you get tired often?

GINNY: Oh, I see what you mean. Yeah, that's true, I guess I'm going along the road of life. Can that be right, and I'm getting tired . . . ?

O'CONNELL: All right, now what about the grayness. Can you transform yourself into the grayness?

GINNY: You mean play-act the grayness? It was just gray.

O'CONNELL: But we want to find out how you put the grayness in your dream rather than sky or sun.

GINNY: OK. But I don't think it'll do any good. It doesn't mean anything, it was just gray.

O'CONNELL: Nothing is ever "just" in a dream, Ginny.

GINNY: Well, I'm the grayness in my . . . in Ginny's dream. I'm kind of like fog and I cover everything up. I make it hard to see. . . . Hey, does it mean I feel like I'm driving along and don't—can't—see where I'm going? I'm kind of like confused?

O'CONNELL: Sound right to you?

GINNY: Yeah. Can I go on?

O'CONNELL: (*Nods affirmatively.*)

GINNY: So I get to my boyfriend's house, only when I get there he's in a garage, you know, like a filling station. And he comes over and pumps gas in my car. I guess that means something sexual. I guess it means I want to sleep with him.

O'CONNELL: I don't know. Let's find out what it means to you. What's your boyfriend's name?

GINNY: Tim.

O'CONNELL: All right, become Tim in your dreams and let's see what he's doing there.

GINNY: I'm Tim. I'm Ginny's boyfriend. We're going to get married . . . (*stops*). I don't know what else to say.

O'CONNELL: I'm putting gas in Ginny's car.

GINNY: Oh yeah, I'm putting gas in Ginny's car. . . . (*Smiles.*) That's really funny. That's what he does to me. Everytime I begin to feel kind of low and moody, he kind of fills me up . . . you know, charges me up. He's always so enthusiastic about everything. And I'm never really sure about anything, it seems. So I begin to have doubts about something and he comes along and he kind of just straightens out all my problems. And he's always cheerful and good-humored, I forget all my moodiness.

O'CONNELL: Very good. You're really getting "in touch" now. Go on with your dream.

GINNY: Well, suddenly I'm not at the garage anymore but at my boyfriend's house. I don't know how I get there, I'm just there. And I'm at this table with my head down on my arms and I'm crying. And the strange thing is my boyfriend is just sitting there and laughing at me and so is my father and brother. And it seems like I've been taken there against my will. And so I just cry more and when I wake up I'm just sad that nobody cared how I was feeling. There I was crying my heart out and they all just sat there and laughed at me!

O'CONNELL: It seems strange to you that your father is laughing, too.

GINNY: I know it. He was always very nice to me. I have always been kind of the baby of the family. So it sure hurts me in the dream that he just laughed at me.

O'CONNELL: All right, let's find out what that means. Play your father laughing at Ginny.

GINNY: OK, but I don't see what that's going to do.

O'CONNELL: Well, go ahead and try.

GINNY: I'm Ginny's father and I'm laughing at Ginny. And there's Ginny sitting at the table crying because I'm laughing at her. . . . Wait a minute . . . that's not right. I'm not laughing *at* her. Ginny thinks I am, but I'm only laughing *with* her. Only Ginny's not laughing, she's crying. That's strange. I guess I'm not taking her crying seriously.

O'CONNELL: So in some way, your father is not taking you seriously about something. Or your brother and boyfriend either?

GINNY: That's right. (*Silent a moment.*)

O'CONNELL: What is it that you're worried or scared about that your father and brother and boyfriend won't take seriously? In real life. Is there something?

GINNY: Yeah, that's funny. There really is. They think I get worried about foolish things.

O'CONNELL: And what foolish thing are you worried about?

GINNY: Well, whether I should get married or not. I keep trying to tell them that maybe I'm too young to get married, but they all just tell me I'm being silly or something. I really feel as if I haven't lived yet!

O'CONNELL: How old are you Ginny?

GINNY: Eighteen.

O'CONNELL: Do you have a feeling that maybe you're going to be a child-bride?

GINNY: Yeah!

O'CONNELL: In your dream, you are taken to your boyfriend's house against your will.

GINNY: Yeah.

O'CONNELL: In real life, Ginny, do you feel a bit as if you're being kidnapped into marriage?

GINNY: Wow! That's just how I feel! Oh, wow!

After some time elapsed, we asked Ginny to translate her dream symbols into everyday language.

GINNY: I guess I feel lost and confused about getting married and I don't know if I should or not. I am pretty young, I guess. Anyway, everytime I tell my boyfriend I don't know if we should get married—in real life—he just tells me not to worry about it and talks about all the things we're going to do and everything. So I get convinced it's the right thing to do because he makes it sound so exciting. But I guess I'm not really sure it's the right thing to do because I haven't really lived yet, and I feel a little as if I'm being kidnapped.

Ginny was particularly "open" to her dream-self and her dream symbols: she was able to get into a dialogue with the various parts of her dream, and as she did so the "meaning" of her dream symbols became clear to her one by one. If you are just beginning to interpret your own dreams, you may at first experience some difficulty with this method; but if you are willing to work at it, the meanings in your dreams will eventually become clear.

The following are some guidelines to help you a step or two along the path to your own dream-interpretation method:

1. Read over your account of the dream and see if you can associate any specific meanings to the elements of the dream.

The first time you read through the dreams you have been recording, try to recognize the meaning of specific symbols. Some meanings may be very clear. For example, encountering a red traffic light in your dream can be an obvious signal that you ought to stop doing something, or that you should go no farther in a certain direction, or that you ought to pause temporarily and take stock of your situation. Or driving a car over the speed limit may be a clear indication that you ought to slow down. And so on.

The point to realize here is that some symbols become clear if you just ask yourself what they would mean to you if you came across them in everyday life. Often there is no need to search for some deeply hidden meaning. Write down the simple, obvious meanings alongside your dream narrative. And make your comments brief rather than wordy and complex.

2. Transform yourself into any dream symbol that seems puzzling or obscure.

A relative who is usually friendly and kind toward you may act uncharacteristically hostile in your dream. Or, supposing you are generally demure and soft-spoken, you may find yourself in a dream being unnaturally aggressive and loud. Such unusual elements of dreams are often the significant keys to the meaning of the dream. In the latter example, for instance, your dream-self may be telling you that there is one situation in which you'd like to be more ag-

Some dream symbols are very easy to understand. Simply ask yourself what they would mean if you encountered them in real life.

gressive, and it is this situation. In like manner, the dream-hostility of your usually benevolent uncle may symbolize a side of him that you have not been willing to consciously acknowledge.

Get in touch with obscure dream symbols in the same way: "act out" each symbol, talk as if you were that symbol, describe yourself in terms of size, shape, color, weight, etc., and also express how you view the other objects and persons in the dream. In particular, discuss your relationship with the dreamer. And don't ignore "insignificant" details. If, for example, you have a dream about a house, play-act or transform yourself into each feature of the house that you dream of and can remember.

A woman of the authors' acquaintance had a dream about a house that was somewhat in need of repair. She readily understood that she was telling herself that her own person was "in need of repair," that she needed to take more care of her appearance. In the dream she went inside the house, and as she play-acted each piece of furniture she was able to understand the symbolic meanings of her dream—all except a blazing fireplace in the living room.

"I can't imagine what that would mean." We suggested that she "play the fireplace and the fire." She swung easily into that mode of transformation, and before she finished she had come to understand the meaning of the blazing fire in the fireplace:

> I am a blazing fireplace. I contain warm fire. I give out a lot of energy. I am warm and people get warm by standing near me. Even though the rest of my house is dilapidated, I at least give a lot of heat and warmth to people. . . . I see what it means now! The fireplace is my warm personality. I may not look like much on the outside, but there's a lot of love in my heart for people.

3. Be sure to make full contact with the feeling-tone of each dream symbol.

Sometimes a person will say, "I don't seem to be able to say much about this symbol. It's just a . . . [whatever it is]." Here is the resistance process! In such an event, start with your *feelings* about the symbol. Do you like it? Is it pretty? Is it ugly? Is it strong? Find some adjectives to describe the symbol. Compare the object to real ones in waking life.

Suppose the symbol is a bridge. A person may say, "I don't know how to transform myself into a bridge. It's just a bridge." Ask yourself, "How does it differ from bridges in real life?" One person who dreamt of a bridge responded, "Oh . . . it's rickety. Very unstable, not at all like the bridges I am used to. I guess I'm saying that whatever I'm about to cross over on is rather precarious, and not secure."

If you cannot identify the persons in your dream, you can at least get some hunches about what they seem to you to be like—their character, their virtues and faults, their attitudes, and—very important—whether you like or dislike them. (*Decide for yourself.*)

4. Find out what each color means.

Colors in dreams can be very significant. Colors generally stand for emotions or personality traits. And a dream in vivid color may indicate a dream of deep passion, or fear, or anger—any one of the more vigorous emotions.

Certain colors can have very definite meanings in our culture. Red can stand for *danger, "stop!" blood, passion, patriotism, anger,* etc. Which of these meanings apply is up to you, the dreamer, to decide. After all, it is your dream and no one else's. How do you decide. You *try* it out, as it were. You feel out each possible meaning, step inside the feeling-tone of the symbol, and when you find the right answer it will resound inside you—for it will "seem to fit."

Please notice that each color has both positive and negative aspects. *Blue* may indeed mean loyalty, as in "true-blue," but it also may mean feeling "depressed," as in having "the blues."

The "right" meaning or context will *feel* right. "Right" meanings give us moments of insight into something we have been involved and living with. Sometimes the right meaning evokes so deep a response that we feel as if some deep level of ourselves is "vibrating with meaning."

By the way, you will more often find the meaning if you re-relate the dream *with care,* particularly in referring to the background. An example may suffice for now:

A "blue, happy sky" is obviously quite different from a "dark, lowering, threatening sky." And the way we find out what the particular sky *means* is to get into the feeling it portrays or reflects. (Meaning equals relation.)

5. *Make sure you understand the significance of the numbers in your dream.*

Numbers are often significant—particularly since we are a very number-conscious culture. We identify ourselves by our age, our birthdate, and our Social Security number. We live in terms of number of minutes, hours, days, months, and years. We celebrate birthdays, holidays, anniversaries. We deal in money, and even how much mileage we get to a gallon of gasoline. We needn't go on. The essential thing is to get in touch with the significant numbers in your dream . . . and discover the meanings to them. Three rabbits in one lady's dream stood for her three little helpless, sweet, and very un–toilet-trained children. One man dreamt of three doors, representing three possible alternative courses of action he was then trying to choose among.

6. *One or more other people in your dream may represent various aspects of yourself, especially if you are all doing the same thing.*

The first order of business at this point is to find out if you are in contact here with your Shadow-self or some other of your sub-

CHUANGTSE

LAST NIGHT I DREAMT I WAS A BUTTERFLY
AND NOW I DO NOT KNOW
IF I AM A MAN WHO DREAMT I WAS A BUTTERFLY
OR AM I NOW A BUTTERFLY WHO DREAMS I AM A MAN

personalities. A good way of discovering if another person in your dream is the "unknown person" in yourself is to ask, "If I am of two minds or two attitudes concerning such-and-such event, what are my opposing feelings and points of view?" Or you may ask yourself, "What characteristic in myself am I a little ashamed of or guilty about?" In this way you may be able to get in touch with that particular subpersonality. Or maybe the subpersonality is one of the latent "functions" in yourself trying to come through. (Review Chapters 8 and 10 to get some ideas about what your subpersonalities might be.)

7. Listen to what you are saying as you relate your dream!

You will often find a clue to your hard-to-understand symbols if you listen to your precise wording. A man that the authors know had figured out most of one of his dreams except for a certain part. When he came to this part, we had him repeat the sentence over and over, asking him *to listen to what he was saying.* "In my dream," he repeated, "I think I have actually woken up, but the dream continues and then I really wake up." He repeated the sentence again and again until it dawned on him that he was referring to a problem he had thought he had solved. "Actually," he said, "I thought I had woken up to the situation—that I had solved it—but I see that my dream is telling me that I am still asleep and still do not fully understand what is going on."

8. If your dream deals with death, figure out what part of your personality is "dying," or what person is "dying to you."

A young woman dreamt that her brother was in a coffin and stirring around. She understood finally that her brother was, in her eyes, "asleep, even dead" to the world around him; but that maybe he was beginning to show signs of waking up to who he was, and what he was doing with his life.

A word of advice: Don't ever be "spooked out" by taking a death dream literally; there is only a million-to-one chance that death in a dream means literal, physical death! Most of the time what is dying, or ceasing to exist for us, is a *relationship* with another person, or some *aspect of our behavior* we no longer need. Such dreams sometime enable us to see that a relationship with another person is no longer possible; and if we look closely enough, the dream may even tell us why this is so.

In the event of dreaming of your own death, it is usually some aspect of yourself dying—usually a part you no longer need, such as your innocence, or your immaturity, etc. A woman we know has had death dreams regularly all her life, and she is still going strong! "When I have a death dream," she says, "I know I am in for another personality change or stage of growth. Sometimes," she adds wearily, "I wish I wouldn't grow so much."

9. A house, a building, or a vehicle sometimes represents the dreamer and/or a present state of development.

Particularly for women, but also for men, a house in dreams frequently symbolizes the self—particularly one's physical self (the body). If this makes sense for a particular dream, analyze what kind of house you are. Are you tall? or short? Are you strongly built? Do you feel yourself to be a firmly rooted structure? Or do you dream of a house that is dilapidated?

Also analyze each room in your house, what is happening there, and what its atmosphere is. Each room in your dream-house can represent some aspect of your psyche; or it may stand for a relationship or event. Halls and corridors can sometimes represent transitions from one part of your life to another; the outside of the house may symbolize how you appear to others; and so forth.

Particularly for men, the self may be represented in a dream by a car or motorcycle. (At the turn of the century a horse-drawn vehicle might have symbolized the same thing.) In the authors' experience, young boys or students who feel immature and inadequate dream of themselves riding bicycles. The kind of vehicle one dreams about, its age and appearance, how fast it is going, and who is driving it will tell the dreamer a lot about how he feels about himself. One man dreamt of his wife driving his car. As he interpreted it, he realized that he felt that his wife was controlling his life—that she was "in the driver's seat," where he should be!

10. Determine how you experience the world you are in by describing the scenery and landscapes of your dream.

Is your dream world barren and desertlike? Does that mean that there are no nourishing relationships in your life? Or is it overgrown like a rain forest? Can this mean that your emotions are rich but also a bit primitive?

Water in dreams frequently represents emotions. Are you drowning in your emotions? Or are you—as was one of our students in her dreams—learning to water-ski on top of the water? This student interpreted her dream to mean she was learning to stay "on top" of her emotions. (One of the nicest and most "unconscious" compliments we ever received came from this girl—she dreamed that we were the ones who were teaching her to water-ski!)

11. Animals in dreams may represent certain characteristics of ourselves and others.

Animals in your dream may indeed represent the more primitive or childlike aspects of oneself. Young males not infrequently dream of gorillas or other strong jungle animals chasing them or leaping out at them. Generally, these kinds of dreams indicate that the young man is still a mite nervous about his powerful (and quite "normal") sexual and biological urges. On the other hand, one may dream that he is a frightened and timid deer, or even that he would like to escape to a high and private eyrie, like an eagle.

Of course, we may also dream about the "animal" characteristics in someone else's personality—for example, that a friend is really a "snake in the grass" or that a relative is a black widow spider!

Animals have long been used in art and literature to portray human emotions and characteristics. In mythology, gods and goddesses frequently disguised themselves in animal form. Aesop told his all-too-human fables with animal characters. Even today, we avidly read certain comic strips which are no more than human fables disguised in animal form. And in our everyday language we commonly attribute human characteristics to animals—and thus equate the two—when we speak of the "crafty" fox and the "wise" owl, the "sly" snake and the "industrious" beaver. We speak of people having "an elephant's memory," or of being a "lecherous old goat." One young woman dreamt that she was driving a car with a mule in the back seat, which she easily identified as symbolic of her own stubbornness.

12. Investigate the meaning of the geography of your dream.

Are you coming to a fork in the road? Does that mean you have a decision to make? And if so, which will be the "right" path for you to take? One man dreamt that he was driving along in his car and kept watching the scenery in his rear-view mirror (he was look-ing at what was already behind him—at his past life). Are you going *up* a hill or *down?* Is the road smooth, or is it rocky and hard going? If there is a sun, is the sun rising or setting? If there are stairs in your dream, are you climbing *up* (we speak of a "ladder of suc-cess")? Or are you stepping down into a gutter, where you feel helpless? Or are you being surrounded by a fog where there will be confusion and depression? Examine the physical context in which the dream occurs and analyze its characteristics.

13. Finish the dream for yourself.

We can relive a dream and thereby reexperience the emotions involved. Furthermore, we can finish a dream if we want to. We can even change the ending. Many persons already know how to do that. For example, reports from students now indicate that after waking from a dream, they are able to go back and finish the dream for themselves. We can all do this. *We can even finish our dreams while we are wide awake!*

Suppose, for example, that you are having a rather fearful dream that someone is banging menacingly on the door of your house—in fact, ramming it open—and that before you have the chance to find out who it is, you wake up, shaken and terrified! One person had this dream and she was told to go back to her dream, relive it, and find herself a place of safety in the house where she could observe, unharmed, who entered her house. She chose to walk out the back door and peer around the corner. "My heavens," she cried out in astonishment, "it's only my mother-in-law! I know I didn't like her, but I didn't know she bothered me that much!" Having confronted her dream-fear, she could now laugh at it. Her mother-in-law might be the ogre that all mothers-in-law are sup-posed to be, but her nightmare visitor turned out to be much more manageable than she had imagined—once she was in a "safe place."

But you may ask, "Is finishing the dream on the level of con-scious fantasy a valid procedure? Are we not just making it turn out the way we want? The answer to both of these questions is: "Yes."

Creative fantasy in the waking state is as powerful a force as dream fantasy once we learn to discipline it and use it correctly. What you are doing is learning to cope with a threatening situa-tion—it matters little whether the fear is confronted in a sleeping or a waking threat. By actualizing these fears and getting into contact with the balancing forces in ourselves, we learn to cope with our fears and finally to pass beyond them.[12]

RECOMMENDED READINGS

FOULKES, DAVID. *The Psychology of Sleep.* New York: Charles Scribner's Sons, 1966 (paperback).

Of the many books available on dream and sleep research, this one is, in our opinion, the most readable and interesting and informative. Foulkes has the ability to discuss brain-wave research in such a way as to make it understandable even to college freshmen.

HADFIELD, J. A. *Dreams and Nightmares.* Baltimore: Penguin Books, 1954 (paperback).

This is a more comprehensive survey on dream research than Foulkes's book (above), and it discusses the history of dream interpretation as well as modern approaches to dream interpretation.

PERLS, FREDERICK S. *Gestalt Therapy Verbatim.* Edited by John O. Stevens. Lafayette, Cal.: Real People Press, 1967 (hardcover).

This book is a "must" for understanding and fully appreciating Perls's noninterpretive approach to dreams. Actual dream sessions are reproduced in this book, along with commentary by Perls himself. This book can be an eye-opener for those interested in a counterapproach to the traditional method of dream interpretation.

SECHRIST, ELSIE. *Dreams: Your Magic Mirror.* New York: Dell Publishing Co., 1968 (paperback).

An offbeat approach to the interpretation of dreams is presented in this book. The author, who worked with America's most famous psychic, Edgar Cayce, is now well known for her own psychic ability to interpret dreams. Students who have read any Cayce may very well be "turned on" by this book as well.

12

DISCOVERING THE MYTHICAL SELF

During the course of his research into the meaning of dreams, Freud believed he had discovered a basic theme in the deep attachment of sons for their mothers and of daughters for their fathers. As he studied how these attachments developed in the psychosocial development of the child, Freud began to notice that certain themes in the family's interpersonal relations were already discussed in the world's great myths. Freud noticed particularly how the ancient Greek story of Oedipus described what he saw happening in family life in his own time. Oedipus was the Theban king who had (unknowingly) violated the most sacred taboos: killing his father (patricide) and having intercourse with his mother (incest).

THE STORY OF OEDIPUS

The story of Oedipus and his tragic fate was so compelling for the ancient Greeks that the greatest of the Greek playwrights strove to tell this story, just as writers today seek to write the "great American novel." The Oedipus theme has been reworked in literature down through the ages, although different cultures have adapted it to their particular era.

The Oedipus myth begins before the birth of Oedipus, when a certain King Laius of Thebes receives a message from the gods that he will sire a son who will ultimately kill his father (i.e., Laius) and marry his mother (Laius' wife, Jocasta). That possibility was just as horrifying to a king in ancient Greece as it is for us today. So to prevent such an eventuality—as well as save his own life—Laius decides to do away with the child his wife, Jocasta, is carrying in her womb as soon as it is born. When Jocasta gives birth to a male child, Laius gives the infant to a shepherd with orders to leave the child on the mountainside so that it will die from exposure or starvation or be killed by wild beasts.

The shepherd, however, takes pity on the baby and, instead of leaving the child to die, carries him to the neighboring city-state of Corinth, where the child is adopted by King Polybus. Polybus names the child Oedipus ("lame-foot"), since the child's feet were disfigured when Laius had them pierced with a spike.

Oedipus grows to manhood as a prince of Corinth, unaware of his true parentage. One day a companion tells him that he is not the real son of Polybus. Stunned by this news and determined to know the truth, Oedipus journeys to Delphi to seek counsel of the priestess of the god Apollo. The message he receives is cryptic (as oracles tend to be!): Oedipus is told simply not to return to his own land, for if he does, he is fated to kill his own father and to marry his mother. Evidently, Oedipus is satisfied that Polybus is his father, for he decides not to return to Corinth, but to exile himself and travel to another land. He therefore sets out for Thebes—completely unaware that he is doing exactly what the oracle has warned him not to do!

On the road to Thebes, he meets an older man who rudely tells him to give way so that he may pass on the narrow road. Oedipus has been reared as a prince and is not used to putting up with such treatment. In the ensuing fight over the right of way, the older man is killed. But what Oedipus does not know is that the man he has killed is Laius, King of Thebes—his own father!

When Oedipus arrives on the outskirts of Thebes, he learns that the city is being devastated by the Sphinx, a lionness with the head of a woman. The Sphinx has decimated the population of the city by killing anyone who cannot answer her riddle: "What has one voice and yet becomes four-footed, two-footed, and three-footed?" Oedipus solves the riddle when he answers: "Man, for he crawls on all fours as a baby, walks upright on two legs in adulthood, and needs the use of a cane in old age to walk, which makes him three-footed." The Sphinx is thus outwitted and destroyed, and Oedipus enters Thebes as a hero.

In the meantime, news has come to Thebes that the king has been killed by persons unknown. There is grieving for the death of Laius, but the citizens of Thebes are too overjoyed at the death of the Sphinx to mourn for long, or even to determine how the king died. Instead, they turn to Oedipus, their hero, and ask him to become the new king of Thebes by marrying Queen Jocasta. The couple live happily together and produce four children.

All goes well for Thebes until the children of Oedipus and Jocasta approach adulthood, whereupon a great plague descends on the city. The oracle is again consulted and a cryptic message again is delivered: The plague will cease only when the murderer of Laius is discovered and he is driven from the city! Oedipus has all but forgotten the man he killed on the way to Thebes many years ago, and he does not connect that event in any way with the death of King Laius. As he begins to investigate the killing, however, he discovers that he, himself, is the murderer of Laius! He realizes then that he has done exactly what the oracle told him not to do: he has returned to his own land, Thebes, killed his father, and married his mother! In his grief and guilt, Oedipus blinds himself, and, chased by winged furies, goes into exile. Jocasta hangs herself. Their two sons kill each other in the fight for the throne. And their two daughters die in terrible ways. Thus is the tragic story of Oedipus played out to its bitter conclusion.

FREUD AND THE OEDIPAL THEME

The story of Oedipus drew large crowds of Greek citizens every time it was acted out in the great amphitheatres of the Greek city-

states. It has been told and retold down through the ages. For over
three thousand years, the story of King Oedipus has haunted the
souls of men, and the Oedipus theme is still found (in disguised variations) in the folklore and literature of many cultures. Is it simply
a story of ill-luck and the breaking of taboos which has fascinated
men? Or is there in the myth a core of truth concerning human
motivation which suggests there is something of Oedipus in all sons
and something of Jocasta in all mothers?

Freud believed the story of Oedipus does indeed represent aspects of human relationships which are often hidden from conscious
awareness. Furthermore, he surmised that if mythology were studied, other abiding truths about the history of civilization and the
psychosocial development of man would be revealed. With regard
to the Oedipus myth, for example, he said that when a boy-child is
born into a family there develops a natural close attachment between the mother and the child. This attachment or bond is ce-
mented in the love, caring, fondling, nursing, and comforting the
mother gives the child. A child who receives that kind of attention
from his mother in babyhood grows up strong and stable psychically.
(The baby, of course, is aware mostly of the pleasurable sensations
which are associated with his mother. She is not yet even a "person"
for the infant since she is simply the source of security, pleasure,

goodness, and he merely revels in the bliss of having his every want and need taken care of.) If he is well taken care of and loved, he lives in the Garden of Eden. Indeed, he is hardly aware that his mother is a separate being, and he thinks her breast belongs to him in the same way as do his toes and fingers, or his breathing and defecating.

Eventually, however, this small savage, lustful (id-oriented) organism discovers that his mother and her breast (or bottle) are distinct from himself. He finds out she is not always available to him just because he "needs" her. In this moment of frustration the child is introduced to what Freud called the *reality principle.*[1] For the infant, it is the recognition that life is not all pleasure, that there are others in the world beside himself, and that those others also demand his mother's attention. Moreover, included among those "others" who compete for his mother's attention and love is that tall giant whom he learns to call "Father."

Freud believed that the baby would like to get rid of this father, as did Oedipus in the legend, for then he could keep his mother all for himself—*she would be his alone.* Before you dismiss this idea out of hand, we ask you to remember how children very easily play "kill" with their playmates. Remember, also, that children have a somewhat different concept of death than do adults. In their fantasy play, children very often kill each other ("Bang-bang—you're dead."); and they see their playmates fall, and "die," and then everyone gets up to play some more. Death as a finality has little meaning for children until some real death of a friend or relative hits home.

Moreover, anyone who has been around family life long enough has witnessed a little boy saying to his mother (or a girl to her father), "I'm going to marry you when I grow up." But when the little boy begins to show preference for his mother, and makes demands on her time and attention, he soon begins to realize that the tall giant (his father) demands the "first call" on the mother's attention when he is around. Furthermore, if the child intrudes himself at certain times, he can get himself a whack, or a push away, and he learns that he had better keep such power demands to himself when "Father" is around the home.

Incidentally, we do not intend to overlook girl-children here, for the girl-child soon enough begins to show a preference for her father. In turn she's his "pet," his "darling," his love-in-miniature. Freud called this relationship the *Elektra complex,* after another Greek legend. (For a modern retelling of that myth, you might want to read or see the play by the American playwright Eugene O'Neill, *Mourning Becomes Electra.*)

Freud observed that the Oedipus theme is revealed throughout the literature and mythology of Western culture—for example, in Ibsen's *Rosmersholm* and Shakespeare's *Hamlet.* Hamlet, as you will recall, kills his stepfather and he loves (and simultaneously hates) his mother. Freud believed the play reflects Hamlet's own confused Oedipal feelings toward his mother. For example, the fact that Hamlet kills his stepfather (also his uncle) instead of his father is simply a literary device to make the truth of patricide more palatable. We do much the same kind of disguising of these themes in our dreams, and the essence of oracles, myths, and dreams is their elliptical way of speaking the truth.[2] Since the truth is sometimes painful, the story is told in indirect ways. Each one can thus take from it what he needs to know and can stand to acknowledge.

THE OEDIPAL THEME
AS ADOLESCENT REBELLION

Other personality theorists, philologists, mythologists, and writers have looked at mythology and have attempted to uncover the symbolic truths that are to be found in these stories. Many writers say that myths not only reflect real events which took place as mankind emerged from primitive consciousness, but also symbolically reveal profound truths involved in every individual's psychological development.

Consider, for example, the myth where the hero expresses hatred or contempt for the "tyrant" or "evil king." That tyrant or evil king is the symbolic representation of a hated earthly father who interferes radically with the son's rights to grow as a human personality. From this domination and "lack of democracy" in family life comes the subsequent desire to overthrow the authority and domination of the father. It does not take much imagination to read into this hero's mythological rebellion and struggle against the tyrant the age-old adolescent rebellion against the family's authority. Freud believed that such myths symbolically represent the child's psychosocial development in the family as well as restate an essential core of historical truth.

We can accept Freud's thesis or disagree with him (many disagree with Freud and say he has overstated the case, to say the least). But it is interesting to speculate why these myths continued to have such a hold on the imagination of the ancient Greeks, for they were persons who believed in a rational universe. A question: *Is it possible that the Greeks were able to pursue the rational ideal because they provided for the release and catharsis of their irrational desires?* All we know for sure is that they were great storytellers, great masters of the theatre, and that many citizens flocked to watch the dramas of a mythological time that no longer was.

Freud believed that an active and living mythology serves men by enabling society to divert and channel the powerful, instinctual tribal urges on which society rests, just as our individual dreams and fantasies serve to divert and channel the powerful, instinctual urgings of the personal unconscious upon which the personality rests.

FOLKLORE AND FAIRY TALE

Freud believed, then, that at some point primitive man renounced his egoistic and pleasure-centered motives (his heedless sexual and aggressive activities) and chose instead a life that is governed by conscious thought and action. That choice did not eliminate these instinctual urges, however, for they are a basic and essential part of man's makeup. Rather, these feelings and motivations were *repressed,* and they continue to reappear in mythology, folklore, fairy tales, and other forms of literature and art, as well as in dreams.

Fairy tales differ from *myths* and *sagas* in that the fairy tale is not connected with any specific country or locale, nor is it identified with a specific person.[3] Fairy tales happen in an indefinable past ("Once upon a time . . ."), and usually do not involve gods and goddesses. To be sure, in the fairy tale the main characters have names, but fairy tale names always point to some specific characteristic or rank: the *king,* the *queen,* the wicked *stepmother,* the *princess*—rather like stock characters in a Punch-and-Judy show or the medieval *commedia dell'arte.* Once in a while, a character may have a symbolic name, such as *Snow White* (a person of goodness and beauty) or *Sleeping Beauty* (which tells both of her beauty and the spell she is under), or *Prince Charming.*

The essence of the fairy tale, then, is *plot,* and the plot is often stark and primitive, though usually it arrives eventually at a happy ending. But do not be put off by the happy ending—we arrive at *catharsis* (emotional relief) only when the tale has been told in its entirety. And in spinning out the story, the fairy tale deals with murder, suicide, and even taboos such as incest, infanticide, patricide and matricide.

But *it is just because there is no requirement of belief that the fairy tale appeals to our emotions.* Since the events in the story could not have "really" happened, they do not have to be tied to reality or morality, and so we do not have to identify ourselves consciously with the savage themes which happen even as we gain "unconscious" satisfaction.

The fairy tale, like the myth, retells the eternal themes. Evil is punished, the good are rewarded, the poor become rich, the weak and helpless are elevated, the ugly duckling becomes beautiful, our secret heart's longing is fulfilled, and all who deserve it live "happily ever after."

But the tales can also embody our childlike despair, our wishes for revenge, our familial conflicts, our adolescent rebellions, and our hopes and struggles for self-identity. In fairy tales, says Freud, our parents appear as the powerful king and queen, while the prince or princess is the child himself. As children, our parents seem capable of doing no wrong, at least for a time. Then there is the shock of awakening, and the father and mother appear upon a different stage—they are no longer the ones who nurture, but the ones who frustrate, or the ones who punish. And therein is the beginning of *ambivalence.* The mother is then no longer the "good queen," nor is the father the "good king." In the child's eyes they have been transformed into the "wicked" king and the "wicked" queen or "wicked stepmother." But children are told to "love" their parents; that to hate them is wrong. This conflict is solved by the child in a most ingenious way: he separates his "good mother" image from his "bad mother" image and introduces two characters in place of his mother and/or two in place of his father. A typical "fairy tale" thus invented by the child might state that the "good mother" gave birth to him, but died tragically (usually in childbirth), and that the king (his father) then married another woman who turned out to be a "wicked stepmother" who either turned the king away from his child or blinded him to what was going on. One of the authors' colleagues has supplied us with a childhood fantasy–fairy tale of her own making:

When I was about eight or so, and for several years thereafter, I used to resort to a favorite fantasy whenever I was disciplined for some misdemeanor or other. I would throw myself on my bed and, after an outflow of tears, would indulge myself in a delicious and rather melodramatic story.

The basis of my fairy-tale story was that if my mother *really* loved me, she wouldn't be so mean to me. Therefore, she wasn't my *real* mother at all. My *real* mother, who had been kind and loving and gentle and wise, died in childbirth after giving birth to me. My poor father (whom I adored and knew I could twist around my finger) had been sick with grief. He wanted someone to take care of me, so he married *this woman*. Being blind with grief, he didn't see her for what she was. Oh, and she was so sweet and kind to him and also to me when he was around. But when he was gone, she showed her true self. (Because, of course, she was jealous of my father's love for me.)

Then I would go on to imagine that eventually she would get uglier and meaner and eventually she would try to get rid of me. I saw myself, at some future date out in the cold, with no coat, and hungry and penniless, like the "Poor little Match Girl." I would then see myself pale and coughing and unconscious on the ground. Someone would find me and carry me back to my father's house. And there was a lovely death scene in which (amid candles softly lit and people crying) my father would ask my forgiveness for being so blind about his wife (my wicked stepmother).

But fairy tales, like myths, embody deeper psychological realities. One psychoanalyst, for example, sees a meaning in the tale of "'Sleeping Beauty" which may not be readily apparent to the casual reader:

On her thirteenth birthday, Sleeping Beauty makes a forbidden visit to her grandmother in a distant part of her father's castle and inflicts a bleeding wound on herself by pricking her finger with her grandmother's distaff. Right after that, the young princess and the whole castle fall asleep until her prince reaches her by breaking through the hedge of thorny rose-bushes which have grown around the castle, to find her and marry her. To translate: at the age of thirteen Sleeping Beauty begins to menstruate and she is indoctrinated in the facts of life by an older woman, her grandmother. However, she remains an unawakened female until the male partner opens the hedge-(the hymen) which has separated the young virgin from her self-realization as a woman.[4]

A similar theme is perceived in the tale of Red Riding Hood by Erich Fromm.[5] The red cloak Red Riding Hood wears is symbolic of the beginning of menstruation and her approaching womanhood. Once that symbol is understood, Fromm says, the rest of the details of the story fit neatly into place. The mother warns young Red Riding Hood not to stray into the woods, but to stay "on the straight and narrow path," for otherwise she might encounter danger—and besides, there are *wolves* in the woods.

Remembering the fairy tale, or childhood story that once meant much to us is one way of getting in touch with the developmental stages in our lives. When the authors asked their students to remember what childhood story was significant to them and to discover what meaning it had, one young woman wrote:

> I think the story of Snow White and Rose Red meant a lot to me. Although [my sister and I] were very close, I always felt like Rose Red. For some reason, Snow White is the main person in the story, and she gets the prince, and Rose Red only gets to marry the prince's friend. My sister was fair and I was dark, just like Snow White and Rose Red, and I always thought she much prettier than me and had more boyfriends somehow.

A shy young woman wrote:

> The story of the "Three Billy Goat Gruffs" was a very important story to me. I guess because the three goat gruffs were all aspects of me. I am usually very shy and quiet and can usually only make a little noise like the littlest goat gruff, and I am kind of defenseless. The middle-size goat gruff is like me when I have enough courage to assert myself a little more. And the large billy goat gruff is me when I'm angry and really make a loud noise. But I can't do that very often.

The girl went into counseling and worked very hard on a "big billy goat gruff" voice so she could make herself heard when need be.

A young man admitted that a reinterpretation of "Jack and the Beanstalk" hit close to home:

> As a matter of fact, he wrote, I was the youngest of four children and I was a comparatively late-in-life child. My family consisted of my parents who were much older and three grown-up sisters by the time I was three or four. So here I was just a little tot, surrounded by all these grown-ups (and a lot of them were female, to boot), and I was always being told I could not do this and could not do that. I was fascinated by "Jack and the Beanstalk," and I used to get a large charge out of the fact that he outwitted the giant and brought

him down. I can see that I identified with Jack, and the giant was all the grown-ups in my family. And I also have a sneaking suspicion that I get a charge still out of outwitting my boss, or my father, or anyone in authority. I'll have to look into this.

Writer and essayist, Michael Hornyansky insists that "Beauty and the Beast" should be read by every pretty girl who places too high a value on masculine good looks and by every "unfortunate boy who knows he's a prince down deep." [6]

FAIRY TALES PEOPLE PLAY

Eric Berne, author of *Games People Play*, has written of adults who also harbor fairy tales in their hearts. One of the more common, Berne says, is the Santa Claus fable—the belief that if one plays one's cards right, or one is extra-specially good, or is dutiful in one's responsibilities, then "Santa Claus" will surely one day reward one. But, as Berne tells his patients over and over, there ain't no Santa

Claus! Using his *transactional method of psychotherapy* Berne is a "debunker," a slayer of "dragons" and other mythical beasts who prey on the energy and vitality of human personality. If you want something, Berne asserts, you better get up off your haunches and begin to work for it, work to make it happen, work for its reality . . . but also stop complaining! Berne's method aims at what Maslow called actualizing oneself. Better than waiting for Santa Claus! Berne's approach may seem iconoclastic, but people seem to understand it and make good use of it. In *Games People Play*, Berne shows how many of us act out "neurotic scripts"/fairy tales/ plays/games over and over again. The first thing to remember about these neurotic scripts (conditioned behavior patterns), is that they are repetitious—we keep repeating them and therefore fail to learn anything. Second, since they are circular, they are highly predictable. The "neurotic" person is much more predictable than the highly integrated, creative person. Take, for example, the game a wife sometimes acts out called "If it weren't for. . . ." The game she is involved in is to convince herself that her unhappiness and lack of opportunity is because of her husband, or her children, or her "infirmity," or whatever the case may be. A variation of this game is "The reason I'm so fouled up now is that I had an unhappy childhood."

A husband, on the other hand, may be acting out the game called "Alcoholic," which as we all know, consists of falling under the spell of Demon Rum . . . and the spell is so severe that everyone in the family is trying to save him, even to the point of seeking the help of a "psychiatrist"—someone whose business it is to "release the spell" and save the person when everyone else has given up! (In the meantime, of course, the husband's role in the game called Alcoholic is that he is supposed to keep on drinking!)

FROM CHILDHOOD'S FAIRY TALE TO ADULT MYTHOLOGY

As you will remember from Chapter 10, Jung investigated the world of dreams and mythology in a somewhat different manner from Freud. Jung was concerned more with the psychology of the adult years and with those mythological truths that have to do with personal existence as it relates to the quest for the meaning of life. He investigated the meaning of the ancient books of the East, and he strove to understand medieval alchemy as a science by which persons become enlightened. He investigated the nature of man's spiritual quest.

Jung's investigations into myths led him to believe that myths represent the choices and stages of a person's development throughout his life. He says that our task as adults is for each of us to learn what his myth is, to get in touch with it, and to learn from it what we need to know about oneself.[7]

How do we get to know the personal myth we live out? By studying mythology, Jung says, by becoming "religious," and by allowing ourselves to be taught by primitive cultures, by the world's great literature, and by experience. What we each need is to be concerned with the myth that is alive in one's self and to recognize the great archetypes that are a part of our collective unconscious! What kind of myths do we live out? Well, for one thing, each person is working out the life situation he is born into.

For example, if the person is a young man, his particular myth at this stage of his life may be to seek his identity apart from his parents. In that case, he may begin to see himself as a kind of heroic Saint George whose mission is to rescue a maiden, or lovely girl, from a dragon (a future hostile parent-in-law) who is trying to isolate and hang on to her. On the other hand, his myth may be that of Robin Hood and his band of merry outlaws—a theme that is becoming more and more apparent in our present society. As Robin Hood, the young male adult is then outwitting, or "ripping off" the "Establishment." And he derives his psychological support, as with the original Robin Hood, from the "peasants," or common people, who tacitly approve of his exploits because he acts out what they themselves would like to do, but dare not. Robin Hood's enemy is the sheriff of Nottingham—a corrupt, venal, and totally callous "police official" who does exactly what the king wants. Notice that this fable has already gone beyond the world of childhood. Robin doesn't fight directly with the king; he fights mainly with his minister, and other established functionaries of society, who administer the king's laws. He therefore clearly symbolizes a young man, an adult who supports himself and who is no longer beholden to his parents for his survival, though he fights his father's rule.

We find much the same kind of myth acted out in religious literature. Consider, for example, the Bible story of Lucifer's revolt against God's rule. This myth is spoken of first in a book which accounts the beginnings of Western religion. It is, therefore, already a *sacred* myth, having to do with some of the deepest collective experiences in the human personality. So we ask you not to be put off by the "quaintness" of some of these stories. Someone who has experienced the truth of Saint George and the Dragon, or of Robin and the Sheriff of Nottingham, or the Satanic conflict, may be actually fighting the powerful hold of his parent-in-law on his young wife, or asserting his right to live on the basis of sharing and help, or asserting his right to be listened to, no matter what! These remain some of the eternal problems in human personality development. And, as Jung says, we can either admit that these kinds of crises exist and live them out (and through), or we can try to deny that archetypal situations exist—although they will motivate us still, except that we will not be aware of them.

ARCHETYPES IN MYTHOLOGY AND LITERATURE

As you will remember from Chapters 8 and 11, Jung's investigations into dreams and mythology led him to conclude that there are additional "levels" to the unconscious mind other than the *personal unconscious* that Freud postulated in his theory of personality. Jung said there is also a level of personality called the *collective unconscious*, that on that level of personality exists the racial memories of humankind—including memories of the evolution of ego consciousness, that is, the period of time when men began to differentiate themselves from their animal history and became specifically individual human personalities. As you will remember, Jung used the term *archetype* to describe the mythological figures which are representative of these racial memories; and he said that we need to understand how these archetypal forces function in individual personality development if we are to realize ourselves as integrated personalities who direct our destiny as free human beings. We have already discussed several of these Jungian archetypes in Chapter 10, but they bear reexamination here in terms of how they appear in the great myths of civilization.

The Shadow

The Shadow is the negative side of our personality, the aspects of ourselves we try to hide and deny. The Shadow represents all those forces which we hide not only from others but from ourselves.

Yet we cannot get away from this negative aspect of ourselves, for like our real shadow it is always beside us. In mythology and folklore the Shadow appears in many ways. He is usually the dark personality in myth: Lucifer or Mephistopheles, Loki (in Norse literature), or even as an angel who does battle with us in the story of Jacob and the Angel. In the literature of the East he may appear as Vishnu in his demonic aspect. He is the enemy, whatever is most feared in the culture of a time and age, and that is because he represents what is most feared in the consciousness of a society. Yet the Shadow contains wisdom for us if we have the courage to face it. In our society, the black man and the American Indian are powerful shadow archetypes for the white majority—and vice versa!

The Anima and the Animus

Anima means "soul," and Jung explains that woman represents man's soul. This is somehow defeating to man's pride, for he likes to think of himself as superior to woman. He has, in the past, so relegated her to a position of inferiority that she becomes symbolic of the occult.

The Anima can appear as the Mother, or she can appear as the Virgin, or she can appear as the Hag—all simply aspects of woman incarnate. Robert Graves, the English poet, has called these three aspects of woman the threefold aspect of the White Goddess, which symbolizes man's quest from birth to death.[8]

The Virgin, the Great Mother or Madonna, and the Hag or Witch are all three different personifications of the Anima. The Anima is neither good nor evil, hideous nor beautiful, young nor old: she is none of these and yet she is all of these, depending on how she appears to the man and at what stage of his life. What part of womankind has man denied and repressed? Consider modern courtship and marriage and see the Animas that are manifested therein. When a man looks upon his sweetheart as a lovely, innocent nymph or virgin, she is the first aspect of the Anima. When she bears him children, she is seen as the eternal Madonna or Mother stage. When the man feels "henpecked" or "nagged," the woman becomes the Hag, chasing him as a Fury. Yet that woman is one and the same person, always—*it is his perception of her that is changing.*

The nymph or Virgin aspect of the Anima appears in Greek mythology as Kore, the daughter of Demeter. She is also Sleeping Beauty and Cinderella and all of the princesses of every fairy tale.

*Three aspects of the Anima: the Virgin,
the Mother, and the Hag!*

She is, therefore, the prototype of all beauty, as was Freya of Nordic
mythology or the Corn Maiden of the Southwest American Indians.
She is also Shakespeare's Juliet, the maiden whom Saint George
rescues from the Dragon, and the Lily-Maid of Astolat.

As the Great Mother, the Anima is the radiant female the Renaissance painters portrayed with such compelling admiration. She
is seen as Eve, the mother of all men; or as Mary the Queen of

Heaven. She may be the Greek mother-goddess Demeter (known to the Romans as Ceres), and also Hera or Juno. She is the Good Queen of fairy tales, and sometimes the Fairy Godmother. She is portrayed as Molly in the work of Ireland's haunted poet and novelist James Joyce in his novel *Ulysses,* where she appears as universal Woman, larger and deeper than man can understand or fully know.

In her Witch or Hag personification, the Anima is the evil Lilith or the wicked stepmother in fairy tales or the "bad" fairy. She may also be symbolized as a great dragon (as in the early English epic *Beowulf,* or Saint George's Dragon), or she may be the modern mother-in-law of nightclub jokes.

Jung mentions that in the West we still have to polarize reality into good and bad, right and wrong, ugly and beautiful. That is why we perceive the Anima as having two distinct female forms. As we grow up, we love the Great Mother when she is kind to us; and then we see her as a good queen, a fairy godmother, the lovely Madonna; but this female also disciplines us, and then she becomes (in our mind) the Wicked Witch, the cruel stepmother, or a fickle and inhuman goddess. She is neither, says Jung—and again, she is both. She is Woman—always beyond the reach and understanding of every man who does not listen to his "soul." He may conquer the Alps, or land on the moon, but he will never completely understand or conquer woman. She is the mysterious one always, the ultimately unknowable. For some men, she is the sweet one, the good and the kind, his opposite soul; for other men, she is the strange one who irritates or the demon who tortures. In the East, in contrast, Jung says the anima is not split into oppositional tendencies, but is perceived as polar expressions of the same unity. Thus, the Indian Goddess, Kali, has both destructive and creative aspects which complement each other and symbolize the ever recurring relationship of birth and death, existence and non-existence, creation and destruction.

The Animus

As woman represents the opposite aspect of masculine personality, the *Animus* represents the masculine archetype in feminine personality. If a woman identifies herself as a woman only, she denies the male component of herself and therefore will deny the existence and reality of maleness. She will deny all males, then, and be locked in combat with men and with herself and try to conquer them. Her denial may take the form of trying to manipulate the man through dominance or by means of subtler forms of manipulation such as acting "helpless," or by "mothering" him or "fawning" on him. When she recognizes her own male component, she realizes that she is only one-half of the life-form of human beings and on the basis of strength will enter into dialogue with him: neither superior nor inferior; neither dominating, nor submissive, nor engaged in endless struggle with him; competent in her own right but incomplete without him.

The Animus appears symbolically in myths and fairy tales in many guises: as a gypsy, a handsome stranger (Prince Charming), the King of the Dead (who will destroy a young woman's innocence), a robber (he may steal her away and rob her of her independence), a Bluebeard (who will conquer and kill her), a magician who can be both good and evil. Unless the woman is careful, she may see the Animus as the enemy who will destroy her or as the lover who will save her. Actually, both polarities are equally distorted. Man is simply man. He may appear in his "savior" role as Saint George who rescues her, or as a minister or "good" father-king. Or he may be seen as the wicked Faust and Mephistopheles component. But when a woman can connect to the Animus symbol in her own personality, she can grow into a new creative individual, neither passive nor militantly seeking revenge on all men!

The Wise Old Ones

Two archetypes imprinted on our racial memory are the Wise Old Man and the Wise Old Woman. In former times—before the advent of books and writing—there were usually in every tribe or clan certain old people who kept alive the history (the folklore) of the society.

The Wise Old Man.   The Wise Old Man acted as a judge in disputes, officiated at sacred rituals, told the tales of long ago, and acted as a teacher of the tribe. In some societies, the Wise Old Man was (and is still) the priest, the magus, the witch doctor, the medicine man. Sometimes he appears magical (e.g., Merlin); sometimes, he seems the embodiment of divinity itself (e.g., the Greek god Hermes). The Wise Old Man "knows" things unknown to ordinary men; and if he is consulted, he can enable us to find the way out of the tangled web of problems we have woven for ourselves. He seems of the earth, yet he seems also beyond it. His wisdom comes from his many years of experience, from observing men and women from his vantage point of noninterference in the ordinary course of existence. He has true super-vision, even though he may be blind from old age. The Wise Old Man represents our inner wisdom, our higher self that knows what we can do to integrate our lives and personalities.

The Wise Old Woman. The Wise Old Woman archetype is, of course, the female counterpart of the Wise Old Man. She has, however, a special character all of her own. The Wise Old Man seems to be the counselor, the advisor, the judge of rational human decision; but the Wise Old Woman is in touch with the "irrational," with the mysteries of life. She can contact the spirits, produce oracles (as in the Oedipus myth), consult the runes, read the "cards" of one's fortune, and predict the future. She may appear in dreams or tales as a witch, or as a fairy godmother, or as the grandmother in "Sleeping Beauty." She may also appear as a serpent, or as the goddess of wisdom (e.g., Athena), or even as a peasant woman or matchmaker (as in the play *Fiddler on the Roof*). If the Wise Old Man embodies wisdom, the Wise Old Woman embodies intuition, omens, and other irrational aspects of life.

The Wise Old Man and the Wise Old Woman appear in dreams, in folklore, in fairy tales, and in myths. Again and again, these "storytellers" re-present aspects of the Anima-Animus that is within all mankind—even if we are opposite-"sexed."

The Child Archetypes

We come now to an archetype which represents the libidinal, primitive, spontaneous, childlike aspect of personality. In its negative aspect, the child archetype can represent and express the almost savage aspects of survival; but the positive aspect of the child can express the sweetness, purity, and wisdom of that self which Jesus spoke of when he admonished us to "become as little children."

The "Trickster" or Negative Child Archetype. The child in us may come out as the *Trickster*, a mischievous little devil who really does not want to be serious, who is essentially fun-loving—some-times to the point of harm, as in the story of "Till Eulenspiegel's Merry Pranks." He may appear also as Br'er Rabbit, or he may take the form of some other animals, as in American Indian folklore; as a fox or a beaver. Or as in Kipling's story of Kim the Wolf Boy in *The Jungle Stories,* in which the monkeys are seen as essentially babbling, witless creatures who can do harm through their unthinking, pleas-ure-centered life style. The Trickster may appear as a circus clown, or as a jester, or as Charlie Chaplin's lovable tramp who mocks pom-posity and hypocrisy—or even as the Marx brothers, whose antics make the world seem both hilarious and insane.

The Trickster pops up, too, as the leprechaun, the troll, the sprite; or as a juggler, or an acrobat, as in medieval tales. He can also be Jack of "Jack and the Beanstalk" in his more sympathetic form.

The popularity of contemporary comic strips is partly due to the appeal of such figures, who allow the "child" in us to come out. Daily we see how superior to the serious adult world with its dis-honest "niceties" and nastinesses is the more direct world of "Pea-nuts," "Dennis the Menace," and "Pogo."

The Wise Child.   The positive aspect of the Child archetype is the Wise Child or Hero-Child. He is also an aspect of our higher self because of his wisdom. But his wisdom is different from that of the Wise Old Ones. His wisdom comes not from years of experience as with the Wise Old Man, nor is it the wisdom of intuition and of the irrational of the Wise Old Woman. It is rather the wisdom born of goodness and purity, innocence and sweetness—the wisdom per-haps we all possessed when we were young and idealistic, and which is diminished every time we get too entangled in the cruder realities of living.

This archetype is personified in the Christ Child, and also in the cherubim of popular conception. He is a hero in his infancy, strong or supernaturally wise, though his strength does not rely on brute force but is of yielding gentleness and that which comes of love. He is Cupid, or Love; he is also the pure and innocent Sir Galahad (a mature man in body, but with the sweetness of a child). He is the child that the Elf King takes with him into the Land of the Dead. He is also Huckleberry Finn who helps a slave escape from an immoral society. He is Tiny Tim of Dickens's *Christmas Carol* and the other boy-heroes Dickens wrote about: Oliver Twist,

David Copperfield, and Pip. In contemporary literature he is Holden Caulfield of Salinger's *Catcher in the Rye*, whose obscene language hides a heart wounded by the falseness of contemporary society. He is incarnated yet again in Antoine de Saint Exupéry's *The Little Prince* and perhaps now again in the hero of Richard Bach's *Jonathan Livingston Seagull*. The Wise Child is explicitly portrayed in Rudyard Kipling's *Kim*, a young boy who is reared in the jungle by wolves and so lives by the purity of primeval mores.

The child in all of us is wise simply because he represents those ideals and standards which we knew to be true when we were young —the capacity for sweetness and idealism we may have since lost. The Christmas season remains one of the truly holy days even in our culture, perhaps because Christmas celebrates those ideals of loving-kindness, charity, and hope that we perhaps believed in when we were young, but are afraid to acknowledge now except during this season. The Wise Child often appears in our dreams; and when he does, the dreamer is then being asked to look at some new dimension of himself that may be growing within him.

A child dream frequently comes after one has had a death dream. In the authors' experience, the death of something in one's personality sometimes comes just prior to the birth of something new. The death of egotism, the death of pride, or the death of resentment often precedes a dream in which appears a newborn infant or a growing child.

The Wise Child is a powerful archetype.

The Hero as Ego

The Hero in myth and folklore represents the ego, the conscious self realizing and actualizing itself through the experiences which life has to offer. Heroes on this level of myth are the brave and beautiful young men who save the princess from the dragon, or who, like Jason, steal the Golden Fleece. Sir Galahad quested after the Holy Grail, and Robin Hood sought to restore his people to equality. Moses, on the other hand, was a powerful hero-prophet who lived to free—not just a damsel, but an entire nation, the Hebrews—from bondage.

The myth of the Hero summarizes the struggle of a person to emerge into adulthood, the person who wants to take his place as a member of society.[9] The Hero-Child or Hero-Adult usually must perform some great task to prove his worth—overcome some obstacle to gain what is rightfully his. A dragon may have to be slain, a fleece stolen, a Pharoah undone, or a wicked witch destroyed. These obstacles can be viewed, according to those who study the mythology of various cultures, as symbolizing everyone's struggle to overcome the problems of adolescence—and the problems of middle age, or even old age—in order to emerge from past ways of being and realize one's further possibilities as a human being.

The myth of the Hero can thus be seen as a symbolic representation of each individual's struggle toward *personhood* and full human awareness. It is a story of victory over the "lower" aspects of one's nature, wherein the individual struggles to evolve his consciousness until he becomes what Maslow calls a "self-actualized person" or what Rogers has called a "fully functioning person." The *Bhagavad-Gita* tells of the great Hindu mythological hero, Arjuna, a young prince who must fight a battle to regain his rightful throne. He is accompanied by his charioteer Krishna, and the story takes the form of a dialogue between Krishna and Arjuna on the eve of a great battle. Arjuna is overwhelmed and saddened by the realization that his enemies are his own friends and kindred, and Krishna reveals himself to be the Supreme Manifestation of the Lord Himself. Throughout the dialogue, Krishna advises, encourages, and teaches Arjuna regarding the battle.

The story of Arjuna and Krisha has many levels of meanings— as, of course, do all great myths. On one level the story of Arjuna's battle is the story of humankind, in which the battle field is life itself with its rivalries and power struggles. Arjuna's enemies are the forces of the world which he must conquer if he is to attain salvation (his rightful place as a prince).

But according to at least one interpreter, the story of Krishna and Arjuna can be seen from another perspective as individual man's struggle to develop a higher stage of consciousness (what we have been calling personality integration).[10] Arjuna and Krishna are then not two separate beings, but two aspects of man himself, a polarity existing in each person—and the chariot stands for the physical body which the soul inhabits. On that level of meaning, Arjuna may be thought of as the personal soul or consciousness and Krishna as the supreme consciousness which all men share and which is our higher nature. The battlefield is still reality, but the battle is not an external war between good and evil. It has been transformed into a struggle of *inner* reality in which each person attempts to overcome the seductive enemies within himself: slothfulness, anger, pride and the desire to gossip, to slander, to indulge one's passions, etc. Psychologists in the West might describe this struggle as an attempt to overcome our neurotic defending mechanisms and our past conditionings which prevent us from understanding our rightful place in the evolvement of consciousness.

If we accept the myth of the Hero as a symbolic description of the unfolding of individual psychological and spiritual growth, then the many temptations, adventures, and "monsters" in these stories take on a personal meaning also. Myths, fairy tales, and other kinds of folklore then take on a new significance: dragons and demons and other villains symbolize inner conflicts and insufficiencies each person must conquer in order to achieve self-understanding, enlightenment, personality integration, self-actualization—call it what you will. Perhaps this level of meaning explains why these stories continue to have such appeal to one generation after another.

Jason, who steals the Golden Fleece, may seem more "godlike" than Jack the Giant-killer; and Oedipus and Arjuna—who were both princes—may seem to be the kind of overtowering personalities next to which our own, more mundane personalities seem to shrink in size and significance. But one should not be put off by these apparent differences: to every person—you and me and the person down the street—is given the opportunity for the same epic struggle, the same adventures and crises, once we take upon ourselves our personal search for integration of personality. If that search is not fostered in childhood by one's parents and family, then each individual is going to have to "get on with it" on his own, with or without his family's blessing—that's all there is to it.

THE FORCES OF FANTASY

Jung says these mythic elements in our nature are there whether we acknowledge them or not, that they constitute an essential part of each person's psychic reality. These archetypes are woven firmly into our literature, they appear to us in our dreams, and they can even take over our personalities if we do not give them the respect and attention they demand. To enter into dialogue with these powerful forces is not an easy task, and the dialogue may sometimes be frightening, even dangerous, if one does not have a teacher or guide who has already traveled the path before oneself.

Personality theorists have devised methods for getting in touch with these archetypal processes and integrating them into one's ongoing personality. These techniques are varied, but they generally require the person to make himself comfortable, close his eyes, get into a state of relaxed attention. The person is then told to "visualize" or imagine, say, "his" Wise Old Man, or "her" Wise Old Woman.

The authors have done this with students in class, and these journeys of the imagination have never failed to produce interesting results, often including astonishing insights into the person's problem situation and even possible solutions. Often in these "controlled imaginations" the person is able to get in touch with deeper levels of self and to discover the kind of orientation regarding himself and his present problems simply by encountering some of his archetype figures. For example, one young woman saw the Wise Old Man in flowing white robes with a long white beard and using a cane to walk. When she asked him, "How can I find happiness?" he replied: "Be yourself. Learn how to love everything around you. Do not worry about tomorrow but rather think of what you are blessed with today." This girl suffers from an incurable fatal blood disease, and so the words of her Wise Old Man were particularly relevant. These words also bring to mind Maslow's self-actualized persons (Chapter 1) who are able to be the here-and-now of their lives and to see the beauty around them.

In another type of *controlled fantasy*, the person may be encouraged to imagine himself as a plant, and to watch the plant grow. This, too, can provide insights and intuitions regarding the present status of the person's life situation. One young woman saw herself as a beautiful rose bush, which indicated her satisfaction with her present personality. But she also noted that her rose bush had thorns on it, and she concluded that this aspect of her fantasy expressed her sense of vulnerability: she was a bit "thorny" on the outside in order to ward off people who might hurt her, or interfere with her development.

One young man said he couldn't imagine himself as any one thing, but kept "changing form." When asked what he thought was the significance of that fantasy, he replied, "I guess it means that I don't quite know what I want to be or what I want to do. I think I am trying out all kinds of role models, but I can't make up my mind what's good for me and what's not good for me."

Another young woman saw herself as a banana tree. She described the banana tree as being like the one she grew up with in her front yard when she was a child. When the banana tree is plucked, she explained, it just sends a shoot right back up again almost overnight. She thus decided that she was a person of very "bouncy" spirits—she may get hurt by others, but she has a lot of "comeback" and can revive herself to produce further growth.

One final example of insight via controlled fantasy: this one of a young man who imagined himself to be a cactus with a flower on top. The bark of the cactus was very rough and scaled and rather ugly, it seemed to him. He said he didn't know what that meant, whereupon a girl in the group volunteered this response: "You have," she said, "a sense of inferiority about your looks." The young man agreed heartily; and in truth, the young man's outward appearance was not prepossessing, and this seemed to confirm his outward evaluation of himself. "But," continued the girl, "you know there is something beautiful in you because you have that cactus blossom growing on top." The young man agreed that deep down inside he knew he had something special and valuable he could perhaps offer to others.

SUMMARY

Experiencing one's "mythological" self is an extraordinary event. From those levels of personality, Jung says, we can derive much certainty—the sure knowledge of who we are and what we are given to do in this life. Personal archetypes are powerful forces which bring with them possibilities for both good and ill, growth and disaster. And the ways in which we relate ourselves to these deep unconscious forces are characteristic of each life and each personality. If we approach these forces in our selves with forbearance and humility and steadfastness, we will, very likely, survive the encounter and grow to become fuller, more human men and women. If we think we can "play around" with them (as happens sometimes in drug-induced encounters), we can be taken over by these powers and end up in serious difficulties. "Fools rush in where angels fear to tread." (And there are already public testaments to that reality we do not need to mention here.)

In his time, Jung said that archetypal figures begin to appear for the most part in the third or fourth decade of one's life and that they prefigure the onset of the individuation process—his term for the integration of personality. What is remarkable about our own age is that these archetypal motifs are beginning to arise (or seem to be arising) in the dreams of persons in the second decade of life. We do not know yet what these events portend for personality development in our time. Will higher levels of personality awareness be, sometime in the future, an event that happens in the twenties or earlier? Remember that Maslow's self-actualized people were, for the most part, in their later years. If self-realization comes earlier in the lives of present and future men and women, what does that portend for the evolution of personality? We cannot, of course, answer this question—yet.

What does seem clear is the great debt we have to the men and women (many of whom were not mentioned in this chapter) who took upon themselves the search into those mythological truths which are the foundations of personality. We have (to use Freud's metaphor) touched only the surface of the iceberg, and we refer the reader to the Recommended Readings at the end of this chapter for his own further study into the mythical experience and mythical reality. We wish you well for the journey.

RECOMMENDED READINGS

ASSAGIOLI, ROBERT. *A Collection of Basic Writings.* New York: Viking Press, 1965. (An Esalen Book). (paperback).

Assagioli is a Venetian psychiatrist who fell under Freud's influence and then broke away from Freud's group because he (Assagioli) insisted that the integration of personality must include spiritual as well as biological aspects. He developed (long before their present popularity) some of the approaches now used in psychology: encounter, meditation, inner imagery, music therapy, etc. For the serious practitioner, this book is a must.

BACH, RICHARD. *Jonathan Livingston Seagull.* New York: Macmillan, 1970 (hardcover).

This is a story of a bird, unique unto himself, who learns that he is different—he wants to fly higher than the other seagulls . . . and he learns that to be unique is not an easy way of life. This best-seller seems to embody a living truth for our day and age as other tales have personified it for previous ages. It is interesting to note that Bach is and Saint-Exupéry (see below) was a pilot.

BERNE, ERIC. *Games People Play.* New York: Grove Press, 1964 (paperback).

This best-seller is an extraordinarily witty and insightful discussion of the games that people play in their daily lives. The reader is hardly able to go through the book without discovering one or more games he himself indulges in. Berne's approach is extremely relevant to Jung's thesis that we are living out myths we may be largely unaware of.

CAMPBELL, JOSEPH. *The Hero with a Thousand Faces.* New York: Meridian Books, 1956 (paperback).

This book has become a classic in the field of mythology since its first publication in 1949. Campbell traces the hero (that is, you and me) down through the ages and across the continents as he learns to become an adult in his society and to actualize himself as a person. The reader will recognize the influence of Jung and his theory of archetypes on Campbell's interpretations of mythology.

FROMM, ERICH. *You Shall Be As Gods.* Greenwich, Conn.: Fawcett Publications, 1966 (paperback).

In this book Fromm reinterprets the Old Testament as the saga of man's release from the domination of authority to a point of freedom where he knows himself to have the understanding of God so that he can direct his own destiny. Man first saw God as a "jealous" God; then He became a constitutional monarch. But ultimately, the conception of God became that of a nameless spiritual energy which is concordant with and bound by the laws of the physical universe.

JONES, ERNEST. *Hamlet and Oedipus.* Garden City, N.Y.: Doubleday, 1954 (hardcover).

Jones was the English psychiatrist who helped Freud escape from the steel jaws of the Nazi occupation of Austria. In this book, Jones compares the Oedipus myth with Shakespeare's *Hamlet,* and suggests that the story of Hamlet (like the Oedipus myth) captures our fascination because it reveals some of the dark recesses of the human psychobiological complex.

LANDAU, ELLIOTT D., et al., eds. *Child Development Through Literature.* Englewood Cliffs, N.J.: Prentice-Hall, 1972 (paperback).

Landau and his coeditors have taken some of the major writers in contemporary literature and shown how these writers have captured certain crises and other aspects of development in the infant and child. This excellent anthology includes works by Aldous Huxley, B. F. Skinner, Frank O'Connor, Thomas Wolfe, Ernest Hemingway, and Joyce Cary.

METZNER, RALPH. *Maps of Consciousness.* New York: Macmillan, 1971 (hardcover and paperback).

Metzner has followed closely the trail blazed by Jung. A clinical psychologist, Metzner investigates in this book the mythological significance of the *I Ching,* Tantric philosophy and art, the *Tarot,* alchemy, astrology, and actualism. He explores these areas in terms of their correspondences to Western psychology. This is another "turn-on" book for the present student generation interested in the occult.

MULLAHY, PATRICK. *Oedipus: Myth and Complex.* New York: Hermitage Press, 1948 (hardcover).

Mullahy has taken interpretations of the Oedipus myth by Freud and other exponents of the psychoanalytic school and laid them out side-by-side so they could be easily comprehended and compared. Included besides Freud are Adler, Jung, Rank, Horney, Fromm, and Harry Stack Sullivan. In the back of the book is included the story of Oedipus and his children as told by Sophocles in the three Greek plays: *Oedipus Rex, Oedipus at Colonus,* and *Antigone.*

DE SAINT EXUPÉRY, ANTOINE. *The Little Prince.* New York: Harcourt, Brace, 1943 (hardcover).

This tale has become legendary for its magical simplicity. It tells about how a being from another world views our world with its strange sense of values. The Little Prince himself is an excellent embodiment of the Wise Child Archetype.

SINGER, JEROME. *Daydreaming: An Introduction to the Experimental Study of Inner Experience.* New York: Random House, 1966 (hardcover).

Singer has done one of the first thorough investigations of the meaning and frequency of daydreams. His book is remarkably readable since he, like Freud in his study of dreams, begins with his own inner life. He concludes from the study of his own daydreams and those of others that they are not necessarily "neurotic" manifestations of infantile wishes, as Freud supposed. They can function as a means of visualizing one's future goals and aspirations. In other words, they have a positive function when used well.

INCREASING OUR AWARENESS OF THE PHYSICAL SELF

13

LEARNING TO RECOGNIZE SYMPTOMS OF ANXIETY

One of the first steps in the understanding of anxiety is learning how to recognize what anxiety is. But this is not always easy, for anxiety can be expressed in many subtle and specific ways, depending on the situation and the persons involved. One person, for example, may experience anxiety as "tightness" in the stomach, whereas another individual may claim never to experience anxiety —even as we observe that person nervously fidgeting around for still another cigarette.

Learning to identify how you personally experience anxiety is a giant step forward in the management and understanding of anxiety. For once you have learned your particular anxiety pattern or symptoms, you can then learn to monitor just those signals for what they are—signs that an emergency of some kind is in the offing! The box on page 349 lists some symptoms of anxiety. The list is by no means complete, merely a summary of the most common forms that anxiety takes. We suggest that you read over this list and check off any anxiety symptoms you can recognize as your own. (It might help you to ask someone you know and trust to check out your list as well. He or she may see anxiety symptoms you are not aware of.)

Once you have identified your personal set of anxiety symptoms, keep these anxiety behaviors clearly and frequently in mind. Don't *brood* over your symptoms; rather, pay them enough concentrated attention so that the next time you experience one you can say to yourself, "Hey, there it is again—that pain in the belly," or ". . . that choking feeling," or that "feeling of wanting to escape right now," or even sometimes ". . . that desire for another cigarette, or a cookie, etc." Any and all of these experiences can be signals of your particular anxiety pattern.

When you begin consciously recognizing that you are experiencing one or more of your own symptoms of anxiety, what we call your personal anxiety pattern, you can begin to utilize any of the methods described in this chapter to manage or decondition your "early warning system," which tells you there is a situation approaching, or present, that you would like to wish away, but to which you had better pay attention. It says your bodily defense system is beginning to operate to protect your integrity, your present sense of self. Each of us can become so used to our personal anxiety pattern that we accept it as part of the universal human condition. So be on the lookout for that reaction also.*

> When I look back over a period of years, I see how much I've changed. I can hardly recognize myself as I used to be. So much full of worry and fears!
>
> I recall how I dreaded getting up in the morning, and I dreaded

---

* Remember, however, that continuous anxiety attacks (particularly when they are accompanied by physical symptoms that are unusual or painful for you) can be the signals of a *physical* disease process. Whenever these occur, check always first with your physician before you seek out a psychotherapist. Indeed, it is generally wiser to check with a physician and rule out any medical involvement first; then you can say with assurance that you have a psychological difficulty.

going to bed at night. I never wanted to be alone, but I didn't know how to talk to others either—especially about personal feelings.

Life seemed kind of grey when it wasn't black and depressing.

Although I had a perfectly good job and a decent family, I always felt as if something was about to happen—particularly if I was enjoying myself at all. Somehow, there was some kind of monster or demon out there whose job it was to keep an eye on humans (particularly me) to make sure I didn't get too happy.

I suppose that I was destined to be miserable and anxious all my life, and I never dreamed that a person could be free, free of anxiety, or relatively so.

A man with whom we worked in intense encounter-group training workshops wrote the above note to us years later. He came to recognize his own personal anxiety symptoms only after he had disengaged himself from his anxiety pattern.

Common Anxiety Symptoms

Headache
Excessive sneezing
Sighing
Alcoholism
Overeating
Not eating
"Chain smoking"
Insomnia
Nightmares
Stomach cramps
Diarrhea
Constipation
Nausea
Butterfly stomach
Feeling "faint"
Stroking beard or mustache
Hair twirling, pulling, or tossing
Specific phobias
Clenched fists
Fear of falling asleep

Tenseness of body (e.g., gnashing teeth)
Nervous cough
Stuttering
Mouth noises (e.g., tongue-clucking)
Talking too much
Unable to talk
Talking too fast
"Lump" in the throat
Dependence on drugs
Excessive perspiration
Blushing
Fingernail biting
Leg wagging
Rocking back and forth
Overwhelming sadness
Depression
Desire to hit out physically
Desire to "get back" verbally

Desire to "run away"
Tic in eye or elsewhere
Muscle spasms
Fatigue, weariness
Continual boredom
Hypochondria
Irritability
Clammy hands
Biting lip
Easily moved to tears
Feeling "cold" frequently
Hyperactivity
Excessive giggling
Listlessness
Not able to be alone
Sleeping 10–12 hours a day
Vomiting or frequent queasy stomach
Heart palpitations

ANXIETY AS A PROPER, USEFUL AND CREATIVE PHENOMENON

Lest you get the mistaken notion that anxiety *itself* is bad and to be avoided at all costs, we hasten to remind you that anxiety, like pain, is used as an emergency signal by the organism. It is a means whereby we become aware that there is a "danger" somewhere out there which is beginning to evoke the fear and avoidance response. So, please, do not get trapped into the notion that you must eliminate all anxiety experiences from your life.

True, we might be happier and more content if there were less anxiety around and if our overall level of anxiety was less than it is generally. (That kind of living is possible, some say, if we lived less hectic lives and took more time to rest and contemplate where we are and what we want to do.) But eliminating the anxiety that stems more or less directly from societal conditions is not the point —for this is a book on psychology, not sociology. Our point is rather that you can attempt to become aware of *when* your anxiety level starts to rise, that you can discover *what* your personal pattern of anxiety is, and that you can learn *how* to cope with it. In so doing, we believe, you will become better aware of your present life style, the stresses that are presently in your life, and the kinds of changes, if any, you may need to make in your present pattern of adapting to stress.

I. L. Janis has observed that anxiety can be a helpful experience when it enables a person to mobilize his defenses in moments of crisis and threat. As evidence, he interviewed twenty-three patients who were facing major surgery with life-and-death implications (such as the removal of a lung or part of the stomach). Janis subsequently consulted the progress reports of the physicians and nurses who ministered to these patients. He thus obtained a kind of "phenomenological" record of the course of treatment of each patient as he or she went through that crisis point.[1]

Janis categorized his patients into three discrete groups:

1. *Patients with high anticipatory fear.* These patients were very verbal in their anxiety, expressing fears about experiencing pain or dying. They were open in their feelings of vulnerability, were frankly scared of the operation and wanted to put it off, and needed constant reassurance.

2. *Patients with moderate anticipatory fear.* These patients were occasionally openly tense and worried about the operation. But rather than seeking reassurance, they mobilized their anxiety in "useful" ways—e.g., asking questions about specific features of the operation such as the effects of anesthesia. They apparently felt somewhat vulnerable, but they could be engaged in other activities many times during the day (which is to say that they were not inundated by anxiety to the point of incapacity to do anything else).

3. *Patients with low anticipatory fear.* These patients were outwardly surprisingly cheerful and optimistic about the operation they were to undergo. As a matter of fact, they denied feeling worried, and all signs seemed to point to their feelings of invulnerability: they slept well, were able to read, listened to the radio, and even socialized without observable emotional tension.

After the operations, the three groups of patients were again interviewed. Janis found that patients with high anticipatory fear (a lot of preoperation anxiety) were just as highly anxious as previously, and that they reacted anxiously to even routine postoperative treatments. On the other hand, the group with low anticipatory fear seemed in a state of shock over the operation and displayed more anger and resentment toward the staff than the other two groups. (Janis speculates that their lack of realistic concern about the effects of the operation jolted their sense of invulnerability and that they blamed the hospital staff for the mutilation of their body—in much the same way as a child who thinks of himself as invulnerable is rudely awakened by injury or serious sickness.) But the patients that had moderate anticipatory fears were best able to cope with postoperative treatments and showed a better overall emotional adjustment after the operation.

His study and other research convinced Janis that the popular assumption that placid, calm "nonworriers" can stand up better to stress is invalid. Indeed, he concludes that in times of stress, those individuals who appear most confident about their safety will eventually become much more upset than those who experience and acknowledge their anxiety honestly and worry about the crisis beforehand. In other words, Janis says, the person who has *moderate* anticipatory fear is most willing to recognize the reality of the events to be faced, and prepares accordingly.

That is the person who is *worrying creatively: the one making proper use of all danger signals.* He or she is reacting appropriately

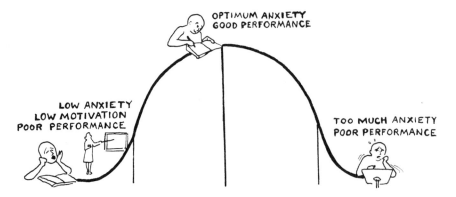

The effects of the inverted-U curve of motivation.

to bodily signs which say there is a serious situation to be confronted. That person is collecting facts about the situation, assessing the chances, and preparing for any number of possibilities. Janis calls this psychological process of preparing oneself the "work of worry." He concludes that much traumatic shock can be avoided if a person allows the work of worrying to happen: that is, if one does not avoid the anxiety by resorting to defense mechanisms, particularly *denial.*

MOTIVATION AND ANXIETY

Janis's findings can be illustrated by what is known in psychology as the U-Curve. (See the diagram above.) Briefly, this diagram shows that there is a common *functional* relationship between anxiety and a person's performance. The polar extremes—*too much* anxiety and *low* anxiety—affect motivation and result in poor performance. At *low* anxiety or motivation, a person is inattentive to his environment and performance is generally poor. At *moderate* levels of anxiety, a person's performance becomes good. But if there is *too much* anxiety or motivation, it interferes with the person's ability to perform and may actually hamper him.

As a student, you may have actually experienced this so-called U-Curve phenomenon for yourself when preparing for and taking an important test. For example, if you have just enough anxiety during the test (backed up, of course, with some studying) you will have enough motivation to do well. But if the anxiety becomes overwhelming you may "freeze" and forget those things you knew before you entered the test situation. Another example is the phe-nomenon of "stage fright," wherein the person is so overwhelmed by anxiety that he cannot perform before an audience. On the other hand, if the person in that situation has just the right amount of anxiety-motivation-drive to do well, he will very likely prepare him-self thoroughly beforehand and do a better-than-average job.

Anxiety, then, is not in and of itself necessarily a negative and undesirable experience. As a matter of fact, it often "starts one's motor going" in a necessary direction—it functions as a motivator that can make us attentive. Just the right degree of tension between our anxiety and our confidence that we can cope may enable us to get to the "creative growing edge" of ourselves. An engineer of our acquaintance once said, "A problem to be solved and the most economical way to solve it is the essence of engineering." What is the most economical way to deal with the stresses of the kind we have just mentioned? Apparently just the right amount of anxiety needs to be present. At that point we are aware of what is happening and what is being demanded of us. If we enter the situation with due preparation and an adequate level of motivation-anxiety, we are "at our best," we perform better, more adequately.

So it is with other products of the personality. Whether a prob-lem in physics, a building to be designed, a blight to be controlled, or a song to be written, the act of creation is the challenge of the situation: one's present level of anxiety, desire, drive, motivation to meet that challenge in a daring, resourceful, and realistic way. With an adequate balance between our anxieties and the demands of the situation, we are motivated (enabled) to go beyond our present limitations and to grow toward new possibilities of reality.

JACOBSON'S PROGRESSIVE RELAXATION

In earlier chapters we discussed the misconception that the mind and the body are separate systems. In fact, we devoted Chapter 3 to a discussion of the effects of prolonged stress and anxiety on bodily health and psychosomatic balance. In Chapter 4, we at-tempted to show how our defense mechanisms eventually desensitize us to pain and the experience of anxiety. In that process, of course, we get cut off also from many of the joys, sensory pleasures, and moments of ecstasy that are part and parcel of the human expe-rience.

In addition, those chapters sought to convey the idea of the body's wholeness—the idea that the human being constitutes a unified organism which is living on many planes of "existence" at the same time. With this in mind we are now ready to appreciate Edmund Jacobson's method for the simultaneous elimination of muscular tension and psychological anxiety.

Jacobson was a physician, not a psychotherapist—but we make that distinction only to indicate that he did not rely only upon "talking" as the primary therapy for tension. Rather, he hypothesized that since anxiety and stress *increase* muscular tensions (and thus make the patient more susceptible to recurring physical problems), then *conscious decrease* of muscular tensions would decrease the incidence of such medical complaints. He called his approach *progressive relaxation,* and he developed a series of exercises that his patients could use to relax their tensions and anxieties.[2]

Jacobson reported that correct application of his method, in which patients were taught to discover their tension patterns and then to exercise what he called self-operations control, produced the following results:

1. Patients began to recognize and understand who they were, and in particular to recognize and locate undue tensions in moments of stress.
2. They learned to relax in moments of stress.
3. They tended to become less worrisome, less hypochondriacal, and less dependent on others (such as physicians) for relief of stress.
4. Patients began not only to diminish their tendency to be hyper-irritable and emotionally overexcited, they also replaced their overcharged life styles with more calm attitudes toward their problems.
5. They slept better, were able to avoid fatigue, were generally healthier in that they had better digestion, better elimination, better sleeping habits, and less hypertension (high blood pressure).
6. They became more objective about themselves and the stimulation from their environment. So they were not so greatly affected by stress and the little things that came up in daily life.

Jacobson's *progressive relaxation* method was a new approach in medicine, and like many new ideas and concepts was not immediately accepted—particularly by his own profession. His popularity, then, is due to other workers in the field of human relations who began to investigate his approach, which relies not on medicines, but on conscious physical relaxation of muscular controls. Jacobson published a manual that the lay person used when practicing tension control by himself (see the Recommended Readings). Since the method is relatively easy to learn, we summarize it here for those who want to try it out for themselves. Incidently, Jacobson advised sessions of no longer than one hour daily. Note also that certain definite steps in relaxation need to be accomplished in a given order for the method to work. The total training period extends from twenty to two hundred hours, depending on the needs of the individual.

The instructions include procedures for gradually relaxing various parts of the body, and we shall come to those presently. But Jacobson also shows the person how to distinguish between a problem he may be facing and his attitude toward it (tension or relaxation). Tension is a real event, and not just an abstraction which exists somewhere out there in space, apart from the person. When we are tense, we are then tensing our muscles and thereby interfering with the natural operations of our muscular and nervous systems. Tense muscles increase not only one's sense of fatigue, but also the wear and tear on one's body (remember Selye's stress syndrome, discussed in Chapter 3). Thus tension decreases our efficiency and our capacity to deal with the present stressful situation as an event. (It also very likely hastens the aging process.) When we begin to relax muscles, the nerves which are embedded in the muscles also begin to "relax," and eventually the entire nervous system and brain relaxes so that we can face the present conflict in a more relaxed manner. That is the basic thesis of Jacobson's theory.

The following is brief description of Jacobson's method:

1. The person is instructed to sit or lie down on a couch—the prone position is preferable—in a private place with the understanding there is to be no interruption for at least one hour. Arms rest at the sides of the body and the legs are uncrossed. Eyes are open for the first three or four minutes, and then the person gradually closes his eyes. He does not open his eyes again even to look at the clock, for with closed eyes the person is better able to monitor his physical reactions.

2. After three or four minutes with eyes closed, the person bends his left arm at the wrist smoothly and steadily. If he feels a "tight-

ness" in the forearm, this is a signal of tension, exactly what it feels like, so he can recognize all such signals in his daily life. The important strain to notice is *not* the one at the wrist. After he identifies the wrist strain, he is instructed to observe the much more delicate strain in his left forearm which is the *result* of his wrist action. This delicate strain in the left forearm Jacobson calls *control sensation*. And it is these control sensations all over the body that Jacobson wants the person to recognize. Once the person gets in touch with the various control sensations in the various parts of his body, he learns how to relax each particular muscle.

3. *Going negative.* After the person has had a chance to identify the control sensation in his left forearm by raising and lowering his left wrist several times (which is called *going positive*), Jacobson instructs the person to *go negative*—that is, to let his wrist lie flat down and to relax his upper arm. But going negative is not just relaxing, it is an act of will to let go of the residual tension in the muscles of the left forearm.

This *going negative* may be a difficult thing for the person to learn because we tend to live so tensed up most of the time. Furthermore, there is residual tension in our muscles even when they are normally relaxed. Therefore, going negative is a much more concerted effort of relaxing than normal relaxing. Doing away with even small amounts of normal residual tension is the whole purpose of progressive relaxation, and for this reason it is a kind of relaxation most people have to *learn* to do.

From the authors' experiences with Jacobson's method, *going negative* (eliminating residual muscle tension) is a process of going so limp that all control over the physical universe is given up, and

Going negative feels somewhat like floating in the air.

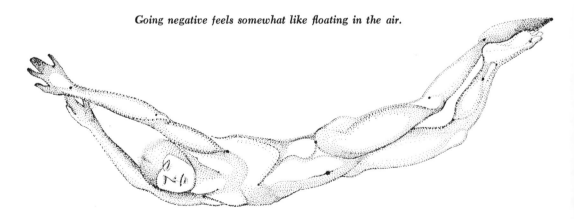

with it our cares and problems. There is even a feeling of floating which is quite unlike normal relaxation in which there is still some muscular tension present. Why do we not learn to relax so completely if it is simply the process of allowing our residual tensions to dissipate from our muscles? Here is Jacobson's reply:

> To relax tension is the easiest thing in the world, for it requires just no work at all.
>
> If so, why does not the nervous person do this easy thing? The answer is clear. The nervous person does things the hard way! He piles up his own nervous difficulties. The tense person has developed the habit of being tense. From habit, he fails to relax.
>
> If you are a nervous person, it is time now for you to face the facts. It is easy to relax. You may be solving problems all day long and may be loath to give this up. Having realized this clearly (step 1), find the tensions (step 2) and go negative (step 3).
>
> At this early stage of your training, you are nervous, anxious or disturbed, see what you are doing with your arms! Look for the tensions there! See what you are trying to do with your arms. Then proceed to go negative.[3]

4. Steps 1, 2, and 3 focus on tensions in the upper left arm. Step 4 is oriented toward finding the tension control sensations in the various parts of the body and eliminating them. The box (p. 358) lists the remaining instructions in outline form.

By following carefully the directions in steps 1, 2, 3, and 4 and the chart in the box, you will find yourself beginning to feel relaxed and more comfortable rather quickly—that is, if you practice the method every day and stick to the instructions as they are given. If you have difficulty with our condensed version of instructions, get Jacobson's book (*Progressive Relaxation*, 2nd ed.) with its much more complete instructions. But discourage yourself from bringing in your own variations of the method in the beginning. Rather, follow the directions without variation until you are completely familiar with the method. Then you may want to experiment with other approaches to relaxation.

The relaxation program we have discussed so far is not the end of the method, but rather the beginning of tension awareness. The next step is to take what you have learned from the couch sessions and to begin studying the tensions which build up as you go through your daily routines. Here is where the payoff, so to say,

Progressive Relaxation Procedure

Part of the Body	Procedure to Identify Control Sensations
Upper forearm	By raising and lowering the left wrist slowly several times
Upper front arm	By bending elbow several times about 35 degrees, which is felt in the biceps
Back of upper arm	By pressing arm down on two books
Front of lower leg	By bending foot up
Calf	By extending foot
Back of thigh	By bending knee back so that shoe is near but not touching the floor
Front thigh	By raising and lowering leg off and on couch
Abdomen toward the back and hip	By raising knee and bending at hip
Buttocks	By lying on two books and pressing lower thigh on them
Front part of abdomen	By pulling in stomach and diaphragm
Back, along spine	By arching back *up*
Chest	By deep breathing
Back, between shoulder blades	By bending shoulder back
Front chest	By lifting each arm one at a time forward and holding it over the chest
Top of shoulders and neck	By elevating the shoulders
Neck	By bending the head back, then down toward the chin, and to the left and right
Eyes	By raising the eyebrows, wrinkling the forehead, frowning, squeezing the eyes tightly shut, then looking in all directions
Speech region	By closing jaws firmly and then opening them, showing teeth as if in a smile and then pouting, protruding the tongue, pulling it back again interspersed with periods of relaxation (going negative)

comes in. For example, when you discover a tension beginning to build up somewhere in your body, give yourself the instruction, *"Go negative* for a few minutes!" With practice, you will eventually be able to do just that—anywhere, anytime. You will then have learned to let go of the situation which is calling forth your bodily tension reaction and be more capable of dealing with what is happening to you in your present environment.

TIGHTENING AS A WAY OF ELIMINATING TENSION

Frederick Perls, whom we discussed in a previous chapter, had his own variation of this relaxation method.[4] It differs somewhat from Jacobson's approach in that when a person felt "uptight" or tense, Perls advised him not to try to relax, but to do just the opposite— *to tense the whole body.* He told the person to tighten every muscle: his facial muscles, his fists, his legs, his abdomen and buttocks—even to crouch, if need be, and get his whole body involved in the tightening-up process. When the tension reached a peak—by then the person is sometimes shaking and trembling as he sustains the tension experience—he was instructed, "Now let go of your tension!" In Perls's approach, the person repeats this procedure several times until he is able to "let go" of his tensing. (If you practice this method for yourself, you will know for certain when the tension is dissolved—your breathing will begin to operate consciously again, and you will know what it is to breathe with pleasure!) The *isometric exercises* which were popular a few years ago work on the same basis as Perls's method. They are said also to supply lost muscle tone to the body and, in that way, to eliminate excess fat and flabbiness.

PHYSICAL YOGA

The yoga approach to personality integration arose in India and other Eastern countries at a time when physical health and bodily ease were considered the basic first step to personal growth and spiritual evolution. Yoga is a complex and elegant system of personality development, and we in the West are now beginning to utilize yoga insights for the undoubted contributions they can make to our own search for personality integration.

There are many forms of yoga—Hatha Yoga, Karma Yoga, Raja Yoga, and so on. But you will not know what yoga is all about if you do not understand that it arose in a time of poverty, poor nutrition, and even inadequate food supplies. The original yogis (practitioners of yoga), who had to contend with these conditions, devised methods for transcending the bodily world of poor food, inadequate sanitation, etc. In other words, they attempt to develop an "impeccable body," one that was free of tension and thus able to grow and evolve despite adverse external circumstances. In our culture most of us do not have to contend with this level of marginal living. Our difficulty seems of another kind: we have become somewhat overfed and overstimulated. Thus, the yoga techniques we now use are primarily oriented toward *physical health* and *bodily awareness*. It's as if we need first to get the "fat" off our frames before we can begin to profit and understand what yoga can teach us.

Those of you who have been involved with any kind of physical yoga may find a striking correspondence between some yoga positions and the tensing of muscles described above. Jacobson's relaxation method, for instance, seems to produce the same kind of results that students of yoga report: greater peace of mind, less anxiety, fewer fears and phobias, better health, better ability to concentrate and solve problems. Indeed, one yoga position calls to mind Jacobson's progressive relaxation technique:

> Among the Hindu postures is one called "corpse posture." It is often prescribed by their old-fashioned physical culturalists to be done after violent exercise, and is described as giving exquisite pleasure. They spread a mat on the ground and lie down flat on the back upon it, with the arms along the sides and without a pillow. Then they relax, beginning with the toes, and proceeding little by little up the legs, trunk and arms, to the neck, face, eyes, ears, forehead and even the scalp. They do this for about fifteen minutes thinking upon something pleasing—a tree, a picture, a person, anything. Then they get up immediately refreshed.[5]

There is still considerable confusion in the West concerning yoga. That confusion has been unfortunately fostered by Western media through their continued emphasis on yoga as a form of self-denial, magic, and even fakery. In actuality, yoga is simply a very practical and systematic method of toning up the muscles of the body so that you can begin to achieve the kind of balance between control and abandon that a dancer feels or that a skier experiences when he skies "perfectly." In other words, it's a method of developing the physical organism to its peak of perfection—to the point where we are perfectly sensing organisms in touch and at peace with our environment.

Yoga involves another belief you will need to understand. Yogis believe that complete control over bodily reactions and processes is a necessary condition for any kind of spiritual evolution (in our terms, personality integration). Jacobson's approach is similarly oriented, including control over worrisome thoughts and anxieties that seem to flow continually through our conscious awareness.

The various positions in yoga are not achieved "violently," as in our Western forms of "exercise," but slowly, gently, and in a contemplative mood. The student of yoga is first taught to put his mind into a restful state of peace and then to concentrate on that restful thought or fantasy as he moves from one yoga position to another. He knows he is involved in attaining a goal, yet he always pays attention to the process of how he is moving toward that goal or the next position. This calming and disciplined form of bodily training enables the person to develop a quiet rhythm in all he does and is, and so he moves through his day as a "dancer"—someone who is fluid and at ease in his bodily self while responding to what is there.

Yet, as Jacobson demonstrates, when we meet a stressful situation in a calmer manner (rather than in defensiveness or confusion), we are better able to cope with the situation. Molehills only become mountains, and teapots only are capable of generating tempests when we meet anger with an angry response, or choose to match aggression with aggression. Yoga and the methods of Jacobson and some other personality therapists are interested primarily in getting across just that simple truth—at least that's what we see in common in these approaches so far.

But what about the exaggerated positions one sees in yoga manuals—such as standing on your head or raising one leg for ten or fifteen minutes—do these exercises help us to be more peaceful? There is a rationale for these positions, and it goes something like this: *reversing* your center of gravity for a few minutes each day allows the internal organs to receive an additional supply of blood which is ordinarily not available to them in the usual eighteen-hour-a-day upright position. Such positions, according to yoga teachers, increase the hormonal activity of certain glands, which in turn help to repair tissues and facilitate bodily functions, and so enable the person to be more aware of his bodily processes, and to become relaxed and peaceful.

Yoga has been reintroduced into the West in the past few decades. Classes are often available in almost every large-sized community; colleges and universities are offering yoga as a form of physical education, and many are beginning to use yoga as a form of physical management of anxiety. We commend the interested reader to investigate yoga, but only if the teacher is competent and well-trained. Ill-prepared practice of yoga positions can have very bad results. A person not trained in yoga may fail to appreciate the power that can be unleashed when the structure of our bodily organization is changed.

There are several good books on yoga now available.[6] Some of these attempt to interpret the classical yoga positions into experi-

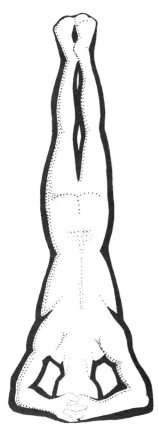

ences and postures that we in the West can more easily understand and use. Some authors wisely suggest postures that are simple to achieve and more manageable for "Western" physiques and minds. One book even promises the reader not to make anyone stand on his head!

WOLPE AND THE CONDITIONING THERAPIES

Joseph Wolpe is a physician who has been able to integrate the teachings of Pavlov, Jacobson, the learning theorists, and medical psychiatry into a modest but significant contribution to personality theory—modest in the sense that Wolpe has chosen to study *one* phenomenon, namely, overt fears and phobias.[7] In fact, he is becoming a master of that domain; and as the authors can attest, he may have already gone beyond into realms where the *meditation* experience of personality begins.* We shall come back to that later on.

To understand Wolpe's work, let us illustrate with a case of extreme fear (or phobia). Let's take a cat first, rather than a person, and assume that we condition the cat to be afraid of a certain cage in a certain room. In other words, we turn a neutral stimulus into a negative stimulus (or learning) which says *FEAR* to the cat everytime the cat sees the cage. It's very easy to condition such a phobic response into a cat. All we need to do is put the cat in the cage a few times and shock him with electricity, and he'll soon develop the pronounced stress response with is called *fear:* he fears the cage because this is where he experienced pain. And if we place him in the cage again without shocking him, he'll still show the same symptoms of stress: he'll "freeze" and exhibit "escape behavior," and he'll do this many times before the symptoms begin to diminish. In fact, they may never diminish!

At this point—i.e., once the cat is conditioned—we do not even have to put the cat in the cage to elicit the phobic reaction: all we have to do is bring him into the same room as the cage—if he's been shocked enough. In other words, the cat has a piece of conditioned behavior over which he has no control: He is more-or-less totally at the mercy of the environment in this one aspect of his behavior repertory.

When a living organism (man or animal) is extremely fearful, it will ordinarily refrain from certain behaviors, such as eating. One has to be in some state of relaxation in order to eat. (Some humans seem to act in contradiction to this rule, but we cannot go into that curious behavior right now.) To return to the conditioned cat who has been shocked in the cage, Wolpe discovered that the cat would not eat, even when he was extremely hungry, if he saw the cage in the same room. He would back away from the cage and arch his back, and his fur and tail would be standing on end. Wolpe decided from this piece of evidence that fear and eating are *antagonistic behaviors.*

If we take this conditioned cat and feed him in the same room,

---

* Wolpe says that the experience of deep relaxation he has been able to engender with his approach is the experience of tingling, numbness, and warmth (personal communication, 1973). He says that these sensations arise when the person is relaxing that particular portion of the body he has so far kept under tension. This correlates with the sensory phenomena reported by persons in the beginning stages of what has been called *meditation,* or in the beginning state in Yoga therapy.

but first take away the cage, the cat will eventually begin to eat. When he is eating once again on a relatively fear-free schedule, we can eventually and quietly bring the cage back into the room and place it in the far corner. The cat may then eat cautiously, periodically stopping to check out his environment ("to make sure he is safe"). From then on its only a matter of time, patience, and being sensitive to the cat's level of fear for the experimenter to decondition the cat's fear of the cage, so that all of the original fear responses are eliminated. While the cat is eating, the cage is brought closer and closer to the cat until he can eat right next to the cage! That is the reconditioning process, and it is this process Wolpe set out to study in detail.

In the case of the cat, in somewhat simplified terms what has happened is that the animal, due to the decrease in fear, has developed a new set of responses—to the point where the sight of the cage no longer equals for him "*Shock—Pain—Emergency!*" The stimulus of the cage no longer controls his behavior; and in that small sense he may be said to be a "freer" organism than he was previously.

There is still another way of describing what happened to the cat. We can say that he has been reconditioned *not to fear* the cage by encouraging behavior which is antagonistic to the fear response —that is, by encouraging him to eat. Wolpe puts it this way: *if a response inhibitory of anxiety can be made to occur in the presence of the anxiety-evoking stimuli, it will weaken the bond between these stimuli and anxiety.*[8] Because of that belief, Wolpe has the patient work on his anxiety *situations* and *symptoms*, rather than spending time talking about the *causes* of his anxiety—as is the more usual approach in the classical "talking therapies."

Working on one anxiety situation and one symptom at a time, Wolpe's patients learn to identify *their specific symptoms of anxiety,* just as Jacobson enabled his patients to learn to identify their control sensations. The box on page 349 lists some of the many symptom-forms that anxiety can take, and we have included that list primarily to give you some kind of reference point in the confused universe that is anxiety. Identifying your own control sensations, (or specific symptoms of anxiety) is not always a simple matter. "Pure anxiety" is an unmistakable phenomenon: it clutches you in such a way that you know something is unmistakeably happening that demands your total attention. But "pure anxiety" is such an exceedingly unpleasant experience for most of us that we begin to physically defend ourselves against the experience almost from the first moments we encounter it (even as infants). And the means we use to protect ourselves from experiencing this raw anxiety, or dread, are our *control sensations,* our muscular tensions, our specific *symptoms* of anxiety. This is why Wolpe believes in identifying that pattern first.

A person therefore needs to "get into" his feelings of anxiety and to acknowledge them head-on; just as one needs to admit to himself (without equivocation or denial) that there is a continuing pain in this or that part of his body. People tend to avoid anxiety just as they wish to avoid pain; and so the difficult first part of Wolpe's method is the identification process—the acknowledgment of symptoms of anxiety over which we appear to have no control.

Once this first step is accomplished by the patient, Wolpe has a three-step method for deconditioning the person's fear *in a particular situation.* Suppose, for example, the person was once in a severe automobile accident in which he was badly shaken up, so much so that he now has a phobia about riding in a car—the kind of "queasy" feeling other persons get when they contemplate flying from New York to Chicago in an airplane. He may even be all right until he gets into a car, and then becomes so "full of fear" he has to get out of the car immediately. That's what a car phobia, or a plane phobia, or any other kind of phobia is: a "gut reaction" that is so unpleasant we have to flee from the situation. Wolpe's *systematic desensitization method* attempts to deal with just these kinds of catastrophic fear reactions. In the case of the car phobia, this three-step method would be approximately as follows:

1. The therapist would first have the person identify all the situations associated with automobiles which call forth his anxiety-fear response—for example, the picture of an automobile, the smell of gasoline, and so on. Wolpe believes the person needs to identify at least twelve to fifteen such situations; these fear responses are then ranked in order, from the response that calls forth the highest level of anxiety to the one which is least fear-evoking.

2. The therapist now gives the person training in progressive relaxation without mentioning the car phobia, and the training continues until the person can relax himself readily and easily on command. That completes step 2.

3. The therapist now has the person examine the list of anxiety-evoking stimuli, and the actual desensitization method begins. Beginning with the least anxiety-provoking stimulus (for example,

a picture of a parked car), the person is instructed to concentrate on visualizing that stimulus until he begins to feel his anxiety level for a few seconds. After a brief rest, the therapist now repeats the relaxation instructions, and then the same car stimulus is reintroduced. This procedure is repeated over and over until the person can visualize the parked car and still remain relaxed and anxiety-free.

Once the person can visualize the parked car and remain emotionally detached from the stimulus, the therapist now introduces the next, more anxiety-evoking, stimulus from the list compiled in step 1. And the same process of relaxation and concentration continues as previously, until this stimulus also becomes anxiety-free. And so on up the scale of the person's fears until he can finally visualize his *most* anxiety-evoking fantasy (riding in the car in which he was hurt) and still remain calm, relaxed, and unattached to the stimulus. At that point, Wolpe says, he is free of his phobic symptom.

Obviously, all the fantasizing in the world would be of little use if there were not some "payoff," some tangible results which the person can use in his daily living. For example, can the car-phobic person who has gone through the visual desensitization procedure actually get into a car again and drive away anxiety-free—that is, without anxiety overwhelming him? Wolpe reports just such successful results with his therapy.[9]

Wolpe's method has been hailed by some who have undergone his systematic desensitization therapy. He has also been criticized on the grounds that his behaviorist approach seems applicable mostly to fear and dread, and that scientific proofs of the method are still not sufficiently established. Deconditioning therapy is nonetheless beginning to take hold in some areas of treating human maladaptive behavior, and it is now recognized as a useful, if limited, clinical procedure. For example, a psychologist of the authors' acquaintance, who was by no means then widely experienced in behavioral therapy, was able to free a patient of a severe airplane phobia in ten one-hour sessions. The patient had been referred to him by an experienced analyst who had been working with the patient for some time on the phobia from the psychoanalytic point of view. Once free of the plane phobia, the patient was able to return to regular psychoanalytic sessions and work through the interpersonal difficulties which invoked the phobia.[10]

ANXIETY AND BREATHING

In Chapter 5 we pointed out that one of the basic human needs is the need for air, specifically, oxygen. Without an adequate supply of oxygen, a person begins to die very quickly. And by the time he begins consciously to notice and experience this lack of oxygen, he may be already at the point of fainting, of becoming "unconscious" due to the depletion of oxygen in his tissues and bloodstream. This statement may seem exaggerated, yet the fact is that many persons in our stressful age often live on the verge of just such an emergency. (What is even more remarkable is that many of us are unaware of this condition.)

A person's breathing pattern is radically affected whenever he becomes anxious, tense, or excited. Instead of breathing deeply and regularly—required behavior for bodily health and mental clarity—his muscles begin to tighten up, and his breathing then becomes shallow, strained, and irregular. There are times (where the input from the environment seems particularly threatening) when he may even stop breathing completely—like the rabbit who in fear of his life freezes, becomes immobilized in the hope that the enemy or threat will pass him by.

Consider for a moment what happens to you when you "brace" yourself in anticipation of pain as when a physician is about to stab you with a hypodermic. Many people, despite themselves (unless they no longer have a fear of needles), will stop breathing and hold themselves stiff, as if to ward off the upcoming feeling of pain. Once the injection has been given one can then begin to relax his diaphragm, his rib cage drops (instead of being held rigid), and he allows himself to breathe once again. This is just one illustration of the *not-breathing syndrome* which many of us go through day after day, year after year, when we confront stress situations.

Not breathing is one way we defend ourselves against the experience of pain and anxiety. In many instances, we begin to stop breathing (or change to a pattern of shallow, irregular breathing) once we perceive a threat. What is particularly serious about this is that *we can become accommodated to it.* Indeed, we seem to have learned somehow in the West to adapt to a chronic pattern of an inadequate oxygen supply and to remain alive. But such short and shallow breathing does not afford us the support and vitality we need to feel fully alive either! To put the matter bluntly: if you want to feel alive again, capable of coping with what is going on in your life, then *learn to breathe all over again.*

In the Gestalt therapy approach of Frederick Perls, a person's breathing pattern is one of the primary considerations. Perls encouraged his patients to become aware of their breathing—not just in a matter-of-fact way, but seriously: by devoting time and attention to what actually happens to them on the breathing level of their awareness. Perls believed it is possible for all of us to learn to develop our breathing in order to live more effective lives just as an opera singer does in order to make optimal use of his or her voice.

> Think of yourself and feel yourself as a breather. . . . At first, it will be simpler for you to notice the breathing of others: the rate, the amplitude, irregularity, stoppages; the yawns, gasps, sighs, coughings, chokings, sniffs, sneezes, wheezings, and so on. Then in your own breathing, see if you can differentiate the parts of this complicated process. Can you feel the air going into your nose, down your throat and neck, into the bronchi? Can you feel your ribs spread apart as you inhale, the stretching of your back, the increase in the amount of space you occupy as you expand your chest? Can you feel the exhalation as simply the effortless, elastic return of the ribs and muscles to the resting condition which preceded inhalation? [11]

The patient in Gestalt therapy is often advised to "keep breathing" during moments of anxiety. He may even be encouraged during a session to give up his continuous explaining and talking about himself and to stretch instead or to yawn—in other words, to adopt any appropriate behavior that will increase his oxygen supply and thus get him back in touch with his body, with what it is like to be alive here and now.

> Make it a habit to yawn and stretch frequently. Take the cat as your model. When you start to yawn let your face drop as if you were going to let it fall right off. Draw in fresh air as if you had not just your lungs to fill but your whole body. Let your arms, bent at the elbows, come up and push your shoulders back as far as they will go. Let go and allow the built-up tensions to collapse.[12]

Learning to breathe freely once again, to stretch and move and yawn, to be a "moving personality," is to get back in touch with those early years when we allowed ourselves the bodily freedom to be who we are. It is, as we all know, the experience of coming

back into contact with our living physical selves, of being consciously aware of how our senses are telling us continually what is happening in our experience right now. When we relearn how to breathe —even in those moments of anxiety and fear when we once clutched and froze—Perls says we are much better able to deal with present crises, no matter what they are or what emergency demands they make on our consciousness. *Living minus oxygen equals anxiety; living plus oxygen equals energy:* that is the Gestalt therapy doctrine with regard to breathing.

A related concept in the Eastern yoga tradition is the form of concentration and special kind of breathing called *pranayama.* Pranayama is considered to be one of the paths to enlightenment, to what we in the West call *full integration of personality* or the *"peak" or mystic experience.* Most books on yoga and most yogis who discuss pranayama stress repeatedly that this particular exercise can be dangerous if attempted casually, and that it is wiser to practice it under the guidance of a trained teacher. Breathing is synonomous with life itself, and breathing patterns, since they express how things really are with us, should not be tampered with frivolously. For example, hyperventilation (exaggerated deep breathing) can actually aggravate anxiety or physical distress!

FROM BODY-MIND CALMNESS TO BODY-MIND EXCITEMENT

So far in this chapter we have been dealing with procedures and methods that relieve psychic distress by *calming the body*, either through relaxation techniques or other forms of physical therapy. The approaches to be discussed now deal with how to get in touch with the "excitement" or "energy" which brings forward full contact with *sensory awareness*. In other words, these approaches concern themselves not so much with stilling and calming the mind-body unity as with stimulating the organism toward a fuller sensory awareness.

WILHELM REICH AND CHARACTER ARMOR

Although Wilhelm Reich's approach to psychotherapy is ignored by much of the therapeutic community, he was nonetheless responsible for a remarkable observation which continues to catch the attention of personality theorists. Reich had been associated for many years with the Psychoanalytic Congress and had practiced for many years the original Freudian methods of free-association therapy with considerable success. He noticed, however, that there are certain patterns of personality which do not profit from classical psychoanalysis, patterns of behavior which seemed to him designed to keep the person from becoming *aware of himself*, and *doing so by deadening his bodily awareness*. Further investigation seemed to Reich to indicate that this deadening of physical awareness is accomplished by habitual *tensing of the muscles*, in much the same way people tense their muscles when they know they are going to get a hypodermic needle—stiffening to ward off the pain!

Reich's theory went something like this: certain persons have experienced so much psychological pain that they have become accustomed to walking, eating, breathing, and working with tensed-up muscles—as if to ward off pain (or any kind of stimuli from their environment). Certain parts of their body become stiff and hard from muscular tension as if to provide some sort of psychic armor. A person with such "character armor" has a "character neurosis," [13] which, said Reich, is much harder to treat than an "anxiety neurosis." Because anxiety neuroses are characterized by uncomfortable symptoms—headaches, butterflies in the stomach, flushes, depression, stuttering, etc.—the person who has these symptoms is glad to get rid of them. The symptoms of a character neurosis, however, are *not painful* to the person—in fact, they *prevent* pain (or any sensation, for that matter) from entering into one's consciousness. Such a person does not want to give up the defending operation; it fits him too well, prevents pain, wards off awareness. But in deadening himself to the experience of anxiety, he also deadens and diminishes his capacity for many other kinds of experience, awareness, free movement, free expression. In other words, his character not only protects him from imagined threat, but it also effectively prevents further growth.

Segmental Arrangement of the Character Armor

Since we inhibit and suppress our emotions by tensing particular muscles, it is relatively easy for the discerning eye to see where a person's blocks are, according to Reich. Whereas the person who is fully integrated expresses himself in well-coordinated, graceful, and flowing movements, a person with a character neurosis exhibits a certain lack of coordination in his movements, a stiffness where his body has become armored.

According to Reich, the body from the top of the skull to the base of the spine may be divided into seven segmental "rings." If one of these rings becomes armored, there results a characteristic stiffness, a certain "deadness" to feelings in that area, and also (and most important) certain organic dysfunctionings. For example, if armoring occurs around the ocular ring, the person will seem to be wearing a mask from which the eyes peer out cold and staring. As well, the person will experience himself as having headaches, or he may have visual problems. To break through that armor ring, Reich would have the person exercise his facial muscles by alternately frowning and raising his eyebrows, or by "rolling" his eyes. For a discussion of the other segmental "rings" and Reich's theory of therapy, see his *Character Analysis*.[13]

Whether or not Reich was a student of Eastern philosophy, his theory of spinal segments from crown to tail have a most unusual correspondence to the yoga tradition of seven chakras or energy centers in approximately (although not exactly) the same locations.[14] According to the Eastern tradition, when a person is truly enlightened there is a free flow of energy from the base of the spine to the topmost chakra or energy center in the head and down again! Reich's energy flow seems to be in reverse order, but both systems insist that there can be blocking in any of the centers (or rings) which diminishes the person's creative activity.

BODILY AWARENESS THROUGH CONTROLLED PHYSICAL MOVEMENT

Other techniques now being developed to enable people to become more physically alive and aware include the approach described by Moshe Feldenkrais in his book *Awareness Through Movement*.[15] Feldenkrais agrees with Reich and others when they say that Westerners suffer manifestly from lack of awareness of many parts of their bodies. Feldenkrais's approach utilizes certain yoga positions and exercises that can be performed by Westerners without the kind of preparation usually required in the study of yoga. The primary aim of these movements and exercises is to establish contact with the muscles in the body we do not ordinarily use in our sedentary way of life. Establishing contact with those muscles we do not normally use has a feedback effect, he says, on the nervous system (including the brain); and with practice, we become more alert, alive, discriminating, even more intelligent, because we are calling back more nerve tissue into action.

Feldenkrais's method belongs to what are now called the *movement therapies*. These therapies have not yet attained the professional recognition and acceptance that the authors believe they will one day receive. Whereas the approaches we have been describing so far are directed toward gross desensitizations of bodily awareness and the alleviation of symptoms which accrue from major repression of emotional experience, the movement therapies seem more fitting to persons who have to some extent broken through into awareness of the body. At that point we are dealing no longer with desensitized awareness, but with people who experience how their bodies feel, respond, and move. The next step, if one wishes, is to study in detail the *subtlety* of bodily movements: what it is like to *really walk* on one's feet, how it is to *open one's arms* in freedom and without fear of reprisal, and so on. *T'ai-Chi*, an Eastern approach to body movement, has developed an elaborate program of movements that are said to free the personality of worry and tensions to the point where genuine peace and contentment is attained.[16]

BODILY AWARENESS THROUGH MASSAGE

One of the less active forms of awakening oneself to bodily consciousness is through massage, an age-old therapeutic method which decreases tension and engenders an experience of well-being and peacefulness. According to biblical tradition, the feet of a traveler were to be washed by the host or hostess, not only to cleanse his feet, but to encourage him to relax after his long and weary journey. In our own time, patients who are bedridden are given massages to increase circulation of the blood and to prevent bedsores and the other symptoms which follow from lack of movement. And persons who have had a debilitating "stroke" or who suffer muscle paralysis or loss of sensation in the limbs are often given special kinds of body massage and exercise. All these techniques have now been gathered together and form a professional discipline called *physical therapy.* Athletes are often given forms of this kind of massage to relax their bodies and to ease cramped muscles. And we have long known that a skillful massage can ease tension headaches even more quickly than aspirin.

Many books now available describe the various theories and approaches to massage. Noteworthy among them is *Sense Relaxation* by Bernard Gunther, who has developed a series of exercises in which the person learns to touch, tap, slap, and stimulate his own or another's head, eyelids, facial muscles, chest, shoulders, limbs, and torso.[17] Some of Gunther's exercises appear to be yoga postures simplified for the Westerner.

STRUCTURAL INTEGRATION

We conclude this chapter with a brief discussion of Ida Rolf's *structural integration method,* which consists of applications of heavy and concentrated pressure with the knuckle, elbow, and fist to various points on the body. The purpose of these sometimes pleasurable, sometimes painful pressures is to realign the bodily segments until the body is once again a structurally whole organism, a technique that has since become known as *rolfing*. What is particularly interesting about Rolf's approach to personality integration is that she apparently believes that we can dispense with "psychological" explanations for bodily ills and psychosomatic conditions and that we can focus on the body itself in psychotherapy.[18]

Dramatic claims for improvement in bodily awareness are claimed for Rolf's method. *Rolfing*, however, is a method of physical therapy that proposes to modify the person's character in radical ways; it is, therefore, an approach which demands trained practitioners—those who know how the body works and who appreciate that character may be modified safely only in a "nonviolent" way. Only a fool rushes in to change an entire organizational pattern of behaviors. Wise men and women wait and see—they learn from what nature and the particular personality has wrought in its endeavor to attain wholeness and integrity; and they are guided always by what the person can now integrate into his ongoing awareness of himself as a personality.

CONCLUSION

The approaches to personality integration by facilitating bodily awareness described in this chapter all emphasize the reality of the body and its place in the ongoing evolution of personality. The so-called physical therapies can be quite sophisticated both in their methods of working on bodily stress and in their overall approach to personality. Moreover, they provide something which has been lacking in the more traditional "talking" therapies: direct and concentrated work on the physical body itself.

Although some of these methods are considered new, many are basically very old, their discoveries regarding health, anxiety, stress, and illness dating back centuries or even, as in yoga, millennia. We believe we shall see more use of these physical therapies in coming years, particularly if we insist on continuing our present breakneck pace of living, disregarding the body's capacities to absorb stress and to remain healthy and growing.

Because in the West these therapies are still in the development stage, we can only guess how they will evolve in, say, the next twenty-five years. One thing seems certain: these therapies will definitely include a highly sophisticated approach to the human personality as a physical event in time and space. Very likely, also, our present emphasis on *psyche* (the *psychological* dimension of personality) will be revaluated and placed in its proper perspective. As far as the authors can see, then, we are moving toward a balanced psychological method in which the emphasis in "psychotherapy" shall be truly psychosomatic—that is, keyed to the total phenomenology of human personality: the psychological, the physical, the spiritual, and the integrative functions which we now haltingly try to delineate.

RECOMMENDED READINGS

DOWNING, GEORGE. *The Massage Book.* New York: Random House, 1972 (paperback).

> Massage has been a therapeutic art since the dawn of time. Recently there has been an upsurge of interest in it as a way to get in touch with bodily awareness. This little book is a lovely work, gently and lovingly illustrated, on methods of massage. It is another "turn-on" book for our present-day student generation.

FAST, JULIUS. *Body Language.* Richmond Hill, Ontario: Simon and Schuster of Canada, 1970 (paperback).

> In easy-to-read language, Fast describes various types of posture, "masks," gestures, facial expressions, etc., and what they indicate about the person. A very easy to read book for the layman.

GUNTHER, BERNARD. *Sense Relaxation Below Your Mind.* New York: Collier Books, 1968 (paperback).

> This is a beautifully illustrated series of exercise instructions for touching and massage. The exercises can be done by yourself or with others.

HUMPHREYS, CHRISTMAS. *Concentration and Meditation: A Manual of Mind Development.* Baltimore: Penguin Books, 1968 (paperback).

> There are many types of meditation and many books on the subject. Even though Humphreys presents only the Buddhist tradition of meditation, we believe this book to be one of the finest treatises on a subject which is difficult to talk or write about. Humphreys has been a leading exponent and explicator of Buddhism for many years.

IYENGAR, B. K. S. *Light on Yoga.* New York: Schocken Books, 1966 (paperback).

> After having surveyed most of the popular books on physical yoga, the authors regard this one as the most comprehensive. It is particularly valuable for the person who wishes detailed and illustrated

step-by-step instructions on yoga positions. For other references, the reader is referred to footnote 6.

JACOBSON, EDMUND. *Anxiety and Tension Control, A Physiologic Approach.* Philadelphia: J. B. Lippincott Co., 1964 (hardcover).

The reader interested in Jacobson's progressive relaxation method should read this book, in which Jacobson gives detailed yet easy-to-understand directions. A paperback by the same author containing much of the same material is *You Must Relax,* 4th ed. (New York: McGraw-Hill, 1957).

LOWEN, ALEXANDER. *The Betrayal of the Body.* London: Collier-Macmillan, 1967 (paperback).

This book covers not only Lowen's own work but also that of Wilhelm Reich in a language that is understandable to the layman. A best-seller among trade publications when it first came out.

ORNSTEIN, ROBERT E. *The Psychology of Consciousness.* San Francisco: W. H. Freeman and Co., 1972 (paperback).

In this book, Ornstein, a research psychologist, attempts to fit Eastern and Western psychologies into some kind of organic correspondence. Some of the topics he discusses are yoga, meditation, breathing exercises, the *I Ching,* and other intuitive modes of consciousness. Of interest also is how he relates the significant differences in the functioning of the two sides of the brain (and therefore the two sides of our physical bodies).

WOLPE, JOSEPH. *Psychotherapy by Reciprocal Inhibition.* Stanford, Cal.: Stanford University Press, 1958 (hardcover).

In this book Wolpe describes how to treat neuroses and their corresponding fears and phobias using the desensitization methods he has developed. For the serious student of therapeutic techniques, this book is a must.

We ask you now to awaken to your choices.

14

BECOMING AWARE OF CHOICE AND CHANGE

Even though we have concentrated on the senses and other dimensions of the physiology of personality, and on the physical-biological methods we rely on and use to integrate our personality, we have never stopped talking about the "psychological" factors in growth. If there is one point we have wanted to stress it is that there is no real distinction or separation between mind and body—and even when (for the sake of brevity and clarity) we have now and then spoken of this unity as two functions, or modalities.

The present chapter focuses more particularly on the psychological aspects of personality, but again we ask you to remember that the body and mind are one totality: it is our dualistic language which splits our unitary functioning into "mind" and "body" and into "inner" or "outer" distinctions.

What we are asking of you in this present chapter is to consider your own psychological awakening in much the same way we asked you to consider your (psychological) dreaming a few chapters back. This psychological awakening consists in recognizing how all of us weave our interpersonal networks of anxiety so as to keep our conflicts alive. We ask you to consider some of the ways in which you can begin to untangle some of the threads of this web of unconsciousness and to become aware (awake to) how you can find newer ways to grow and exist. This chapter deals, then, with your *phenomenology,* or to put it in simpler words, your view of the world, how the world seems to you—your awareness of yourself with others.

You may find this chapter a bit astringent, even hard going at times; for what we will be saying over and over again is that if you want to understand your phenomenology, to make essential changes in your life, in your life style, *it is up to you to change, and no one else.* Lest you be put off right away by the implied threat that this chapter may be on the difficult side, be assured of one thing: all of us begin the precise study of the phenomenology of the self as *amateurs;* however, the joy in your discoveries more than makes up for the hard work and sustained attention involved—of that we can assure you also.

SELF-FULFILLING PROPHECIES, "BLAMING," AND OTHER KINDS OF "NOISE"

The first step in the study of change is, oddly enough, to realize that self-change is possible. So often a person will come to the authors (or to any therapist) and tell us about the difficulties in his life with an undertone of hopelessness.

"I know it's terrible, but I can't do anything about it."

"There's no use trying any more."

"That's just the way it is and nothing is ever going to change it."

These kinds of hopeless statements sometimes come from older persons who have come to accept the suffering and boredom of their daily existence as a fact—or more, as their fate in life! Persons in their thirties and forties and fifties can become a little skeptical of their capacities to change their life style. And sometimes they may have even convinced themselves that there is no way out for them. When that kind of adaptation to a self-fulfilling prophecy occurs, such persons have become reconciled evidently to living a humdrum life—or a frenetic one—even to the point of trying cheerfully to make the best of what seems to be a bad lot. Those persons have conditioned themselves to *avoid change*, if possible, and to assuming the pessimistic attitude that things can never be any better. Any person who believes something like that strongly enough is living out a *self-fulfilling prophecy*.

One of the pleasures of working with younger persons is that their desire to change is often still intact. They recognize and feel the stirrings of hope within themselves still; they know that this may be a propitious time to examine how they are living and what they want to change in the world and themselves so that living can become more of an adventure, more creative. But, young persons can become trapped in the same kind of hopelessness as their fathers and mothers, particularly when they go in for their own kind of *"self-sabotage"* and other kinds of "noise." We discuss examples of that kind of behavior later on. But before that we need to discuss some of the factors associated with change.

Changing Our Environment As Technocracy

There are now essentially two approaches to changing our situation. The first way is to change the world around us. If we don't like the house we live in, we can sell it and get another. If you don't like your job, you can look for another. If our city has too much traffic on one bridge, we can build a second bridge to relieve the congestion. In those ways—the external manifestations of power—we manipulate the physical world (put our hands to it in order to change it) and so effect the changes we want. Western society has developed a high degree of technical skill in changing physical environments, and we now have all kinds of labor-saving devices that have lightened the workloads and continue to change the work habits of men and women today. Indeed, we have today attained such a high level of engineering understanding that we can now move mountains if we wish, or dig tunnels through them, and so on. In other words, we are fast becoming acknowledged masters of changing our physical environment by manipulation and rearrangement.

Changing Others
As Manipulation

We are inclined in the West to carry this technical and manipulative outlook over into our relationships with people. And when we do that, what we are doing is viewing other persons in much the same technical way we perceive our physical environment—as objects which can be changed at will by manipulation, even if we have to move them sometimes like mountains, or dig a (figurative) tunnel through them! Yet we know—as we have learned lately to our cost—that human persons seem to resist and resent being changed when they are not ready, particularly when we attempt to change them through threats, coercion, blackmail, and other power manipulating.

Consider, for example, the stereotypical bride-to-be who says of her fiancee, "I know he is a little irresponsible [*or* immature, *or* cold, *or* bossy, *or whatever*], but I'll change all that after we are married." The authors have listened to stories of the outcomes of such plans, which often begin something like this: "Well, I guess I really knew he was stingy [*or* hot-tempered, *or* jealous, *or whatever*] when I was going with him, but I thought married life would change him." People seem to resent these kinds of plans for themselves, as they also seem to want to continue to be who they are. (How many relationships do you know that have foundered because one or the other of the parties tried to change the other "for his [or her] own good"?) Unlike objects, persons have feelings that are clearly discernible, and, moreover, they eventually begin to resist efforts to control them and change them when they are not ready—and—no matter how often they are told, "It is only for your own good that I'm doing this."

The basic shortcoming of all known forms of manipulation is that they eventually call forth defenses and eventually rebellion against the felt coercion. Wherever there is a dictator, there also we find in time a resistance movement of one kind or another. When we create feelings of unworthiness in other persons, attempt to take away from them their perceived right to be self-determining, we interfere radically with their right to integrate their personality in their own way. As history shows, persons put up with that kind of treatment only so long, and then the "revolution" happens. In sum, manipulation becomes, in time, an essentially uneconomical way of trying to shape, control and change the behavior of other persons and ourselves.

Manipulation as One of
Our Conditioned Behaviors

It is relatively cheap and easy to inveigh against the perceived "badness" of manipulation—for example, to say it is undemocratic and so on. On the other hand, it can be very difficult and time-consuming for us to quit our own manipulating behaviors; for—to put it bluntly—we ourselves have been manipulated for so much of our lives that we have become so accustomed to it that this is mostly what we know. As babies, we were dressed and changed and bottled and bathed. As toddlers, we were told what to do and what not to do. The conditioning process started early and it carried over into the school years, when teachers directed our classroom activities and oftentimes even our play activities. As teenagers, we may have escaped the manipulation of our parents only to conform to the group standards of our friends—and how rigid those standards can be! ("Teenagers," no less than other groups, often have very definite rules about how one should speak—i.e., the latest slang—how one is to dress, how hair is to be worn, etc.) As we move into adulthood, we encounter still more rules and regulations. We are told, for example, when to go to work and what time to come home again. And we learn many other kinds of attitudes and behaviors. For example, "matrons" behave like this, and "men" behave like that. The "establishment" is supposed to behave in certain predictable ways, and "hippies" are supposed to respond in other, different ways.

At the present time perhaps the most devastating kinds of strictures and manipulations of all are those imposed on the elderly in our society. Old people "should" be dignified and content with their lot—no matter how undignified and depersonalizing that lot happens to be. They "should" be willing to step aside and let others have fun; they "should" be happy to be relegated to the security of the old folks' home, or their "special" room set aside in the family house, etc.

Parents, as agents of the society in which we live, make "shoulds" and "should nots" for their children. And young people, in like manner, can practice similar kinds of manipulations on their parents. Though wanting freedom of choice for themselves, young persons can be almost totally resistant to a parent remarrying, for example, or to any new plan that might change the shape and form of family living. For that reason it might be well to discuss some of the known types of manipulation.

Types of Manipulation

Everett Shostrum has developed a theory of manipulation which involves eight basic styles, or types.[1] Although there is a certain amount of overlap, or similarity, among the types, the style of the individual form of manipulation has a distinct and individual character. Shostrum's description of manipulation emphasizes the element of power which is found in each case, what the younger generation calls "putting a power trip on someone."

1. *The Dictator* is the one who dominates others, or tries to, by giving orders, quoting authorities, or by pulling rank and age. He (or she) acts as a "Father Superior" (or "Mother Superior") or a "Junior God." He's always the Authority.

2. *The Weakling* seems to be the victim of the Dictator. But he has also developed great skill in sabotaging the dictator's demands. He "forgets" to do what he is told, does not hear what is said to him, and becomes "mentally retarded" when confronted by the Dictator. Some of the role variations of this type are the Worrier, the Stupid-like-a-Fox, the Giver-Upper, and the Confused One.

3. *The Calculator* is the one who tries to use his wits to gain control over situations and people. He "plays it cool" and will even lie to, seduce, con, and blackmail others to get what he wants.

4. *The Clinging Vine* controls by being dependent on others. This person needs to be taken care of and protected. Actually, he is quite skillful at getting his own way and getting others to do what he wants by being the Parasite, the Crier, the Perpetual Child, the Hypochondriac, the Helpless One, or the Attention Demander.

5. *The Bully* controls and manipulates by aggressing against others with unkindness, cruelty, and sadism. If he is not cruel outright, there is nonetheless always a veiled threat in his mannerisms. Variations of this manipulative style are the Humiliator, the Hater, the Tough Guy, the Threatener, and in the case of women, the Bitch and the Nagger.

6. *The Nice Guy* controls by killing with kindness, caring, and love. Shostrom says that he is one of the most manipulative types of all; and he is the hardest to cope with, since it is so hard to *fight* a Nice Guy. He seems to want to please us, be nonviolent, be vir-

tuous and not to offend us. But he is also the Noninvolved One, the Organization Man, and the Never-Ask-For-What-You-Want One.

7. *The Judge* controls through criticism. He is out to make others feel stupid, guilty, wrong. Variations of this form of manipulation are the Know-It-All, the Blamer, the Deacon, the Resentment Collector, the Vindicator, and the Convictor.

8. *The Protector* controls us by being oversympathetic and overprotective. He prevents others from caring for themselves, taking care of themselves, finding out things for themselves. Variations are the Mother Hen, the Defender, the Embarrassed-for-Others, the Fearful-for-Others, the Sufferer-for-Others, and the Unselfish One.

Offensive Maneuvers Call Forth Defending Mechanisms in Others

Manipulating our physical environment and manipulating other persons in our environment are two vastly different enterprises. Objects in our environment can be manipulated, used, and then discarded as we see fit (though not completely with impunity, as we are finding out). Persons object to being threatened and dismembered in a similar fashion. Situations of control, manipulation and coercion of persons produce alienation rather than sympathy and understanding; and eventually they begin to rebel and resist, as we all know. These are also the kinds of situations which drain everyone's energy; and that is the consideration we would like to discuss now . . . rather than politics.

Control of Others
Is Energy Draining

Laura Archera Huxley, psychiatrist and wife of the late Aldous Huxley, wrote a fine book of "recipes" (techniques) we can use to liberate our energies. She believes, as the authors do also, that human persons are *energy transformers*, "the most prodigious transformers within the known universe." [2] What is germane to our present discussion is that since we are transformers of the energy of the universe, we need to be aware of where we get our energy from and what situations and persons deplete our energy supply system.

Our attemps to control and manipulate other persons is one of the greatest sources of energy drain in present day human relationships. It matters little how subtle are the attempts to coerce, and still less whether we win or lose a particular confrontation—what matters is that all attempts to control other persons by manipulation deplete not only their energy supply but our own as well. The more we insist on controlling the behavior of other persons, the more energy we use on them and the less energy we have available for ourselves and our own growth needs. In short, the basic shortcoming of control through manipulation is that it is *uneconomic;* and it is uneconomic because it is eventually *wasteful of creative human energy.*

BECOMING AWARE OF OUR CHOICES

Once we understand that we do not always have to "please" other persons, or "change" their opinions or way of life—that we do not have to manipulate them to get what we want—we begin, at that point, to get in touch with what we want to do and what we and other persons can perhaps actually do for ourselves. Of course, we then leave the "Blaming Game" behind us—and the "Martyr Game," and the many other kinds of games which use up our energies and leave us so exhausted. We come to the realization that it is up to us to do something for ourselves. And it is exactly at that point that many self-sabotage sentences and games may begin to reappear. (That is because most of our conditioned behaviors "die hard"!)

Being more concerned with your inner feelings, thoughts, and behaviors is, however, not the same as being concerned only with yourself. On the contrary, as you will remember, Rogers's clients who had come to own, accept, and trust their own feelings became also more sensitive and more responsive to the feelings of others than before.[3]

ENDING SELF-SABOTAGE OF OURSELVES

Check It Out

Self-sabotage sentences and other such behaviors operate on the assumption that *thinking* something is so *makes* it so. In other words, we are still involved in confusion—though this time it has mostly to do with not making the differentiation between fantasy and reality. Psychiatrists talk about "magical thinking," and that is what a lot of self-sabotage behaviors involve—the conviction that because we believe or say something to be the case that it is then really the case.

The therapy for most such forms of self-sabotage is to *check it out.* Do not assume anything about another person and his motivations—unless you take upon yourself the responsibility for checking out with him your impressions, thoughts, and fantasies regarding him and your relationship. The point of the "checking-out" process —if we honestly want information rather than confirmation of our prejudices—is that we approach these topics and persons with humility, like a scientist who studies phenomena over which he has no control. What we want to know at such times is, for example: Will my wife move to another city so I can go on and grow in my career? Or: Are my parents willing to support me in a career of my own choosing?

Some of the sentences with which we sabotage our awareness that there are real choices available to us go something like this:

> "I'd really like to take the promotion my company is offering, but my wife just would not let me. It means picking up again and moving, and she would never leave. So I just have not mentioned it to her."

"I'd just like to go into some other kind of work, but I'm just too old to make that kind of change."

"I wish my husband would take me out more, but there is no use trying to mention it to him. I'll just have to sit home night after night and make the best of things."

"I can't get my children to pick up their clothes. No matter how I scream and nag them, they just won't listen."

"No matter what I do, I just can't please my father."

Self-sabotage sentences can be readily identified once we get to know their characteristics. First, they generally assume that something is impossible—in other words, they involve a *no*, a *not*, or a *never* response from us. They express some kind of negative conditioning which we believe we can never change. Second, they often rely on the subtle trap of *either-or* thinking: either *this* or *that*, with no "middle ground" where the personality can operate and decide between several possibilities. True, a person is either male or female, and there are also discrete differences between hot and cold. Yet sometimes, water is neither hot nor cold, but somewhere in the middle; and in that middle hot-*and*-cold where the extremes blend, life becomes more manageable, more livable. (Interpersonal relations and life is a lot like that too.) Third, in self-sabotage behaviors and sentences we "invoke" or project our belief that some other person can make us happy or unhappy, solve or complicate our lives, or in general make our decisions for us. (The man who does not discuss his promotion possibilities because he "knows" his wife won't move is an instance of that kind of thinking.)

Making assumptions about another person's present behavior is risky enough, but when we begin to fantasize how they may feel and think and act in the future, we get started with a particularly insidious form of self-sabotage and noncommunication.

A colleague of the authors once gave us a highly pictorial way of demonstrating the error in making assumptions about other persons. He wrote the following on a piece of paper:

I ASSUME

Then he drew two lines like this:

I ASS/U/ME

"Every time I make an assumption about what you think and feel and are doing," he said, "I make an ASS out of U and ME." *

We make assumptions a priori—that is, without checking out our fantasies to see if they are workable and valid hypotheses. We assume, or believe, how another person is, how she or he will respond to something we say and do. Luckily, most such fantasies are simply that—imaginations—and not reality. Yet the waste in energy is considerable and the interpersonal turmoil can, in like manner, be draining. Do not assume. Find out what you think and feel, and then check yourself out with the reality of other persons. It can be the beginning of the end of self-sabotage (and other-person sabotage).

Learning to Own
Your Own Feelings

Carl Rogers, who has used psychotherapy to enable many persons to find a direction for themselves, says that one of the distinguishing marks of the highly integrated person is that he is able to *own* his or her own feelings. You will remember that Rogers noticed that many of his clients, at the beginning of counseling, were confused about their own feelings. They did not know for sure what they themselves actually felt and thought. They also seemed confused by how they could have several feelings about a situation or a person in their lives. Sometimes, even though they seemed to know how they felt, they were also quite ashamed to admit these feelings to themselves or to anyone else—to "own up" to and own their real selves.

Owning your feelings, thoughts, and responses is a project which demands attention, interest, and effort. It is, therefore, a project which calls forth energy, awareness, consciousness, and not a little dedication and determination—i.e., you decide you want to be that kind of personality. You need to "choose" that kind of path or life style. It can often be a difficult choice in our overbusy society, where we seem to have less and less time for each other and for ourselves. We have seemingly become so frenetic that there is less and less time for the kind of solitude where meditation on our lives can begin, or where we can be alone with another person.

Giving ourselves time to be with someone, to think, to reflect,

* We credit this colleague by name: Dr. Robert Myers.

to meditate, or to fantasize (there's nothing the matter with fantasy so long as we know we are then in a "fantasic world") is required behavior if you want to end self-sabotage.

Avoiding Accusations

Sometimes we are aware we are irritated with someone, that we do not like to be with that other person right now. It is then often difficult to "own" these feelings and then we can fall into the trap of "accusing." An example will illustrate. One young woman resented being called "Baby" by her boyfriend. Instead of owning up to the feeling that she felt diminished by that word, she reacted to her boyfriend in the following manner:

"I hate you when you call me 'Baby'!"

The young man, of course, felt hurt and diminished in return by her explosion, and reacted in turn, by accusing her:

"Well, sometimes you act like a baby!"

Neither person meant either statement, of course, but needless hours were spent before they could unravel that bit of verbal sabotage and manipulation! A simple technique to avoid that kind of trap is simply to own your feelings without the addition of a threat or accusation of the other. She could have said:

"I feel stupid when I am called 'baby.' Would you please not call me that."

This statement reflects her real feelings and yet does not make her boyfriend feel accused of something he did not intend.

Accusing sentences are very frequent. One hears them often:

"You make me mad [*or* angry, *or* irritated, *or* sad]!"

The truth is no one can make us do or feel anything. They can only do things which we can choose to react to in certain ways, like getting hurt or annoyed at! Our feelings are our own. They really are: no one, no one in this world can make you have feelings you do not want to have. When a person makes a statement or does something, we choose to react in a certain way. The young man above could have chosen to understand his girl's feelings. Instead, he chose to become angry (actually, resentful or hurt underneath). We choose to feel hurt, or irritated, or annoyed, or unhappy; just as we choose to feel happy, or glad, or joyful. That may be a little hard to face, but in fact we are choosing all the time. You may know someone, for example, who chooses to get offended by many things which are said in his presence although there was often no offense intended!

Reliance on Ourselves

As we become more aware of our own thoughts and our own feelings and learn to express them, we do not need to rely so completely on other people's thoughts and feelings to tell us what we should or should not do or be. It may not always be possible (at least not immediately) to do what we want to do and be, for there may be many hurdles in the way; but at least we come to appreciate that our salvation and our destiny lies largely in our own hands . . . it's up to us and no one else!

The "martyred" mother who believes she is at the mercy of a demanding husband and spoiled children sometimes waits for "things to change"—for her husband to realize the error of his ways, to recognize how "good" and "patient" she is, and to give up his demanding behavior of his own accord. She hopes, too, that her children will suddenly respond to her "good mothering" and begin to pick up their clothes, or let her know when they will not be home for supper. She is waiting for Santa Claus to come, says Eric Berne, or for Godot, says Samuel Beckett, or for some other fantasy miracle to intercede and change things. It is easy for us to see her illusions as nothing more than fantasy hopes. In the meantime, she is not perceiving the world accurately. If she really wants to stop being the martyred mother (sometimes she gets a secret enjoyment from it), she will need to change her behavior and to modify her own behavior in her family.

How does she do that? We do not want to give further explicit prescriptions other than those mentioned above because each person is a unique individual, each has a unique situation to resolve. These are things each person needs to decide for oneself (or with a friend or therapist or counselor). One woman of our acquaintance decided to exclude her teenage children from her supper plans unless they specifically informed her beforehand that they *would* be home for supper. She didn't nag. She didn't scold. She didn't threaten. She simply changed her own behavior and did not try to exert control over her children's behavior. As a consequence, they began to inform her regularly when they were going to be home for supper—once they discovered that they had not been included in the plans for a steak dinner or two!

Staying Open to Possibilities

One of the most damaging of the self-sabotage routines is the self-fulfilling prophecy, mentioned earlier, that we can't do something, or that something can't be done, or that someone won't like it if we do, or that there will be too many obstacles in the way, etc.—statements that begin with "It's no use trying . . . ," or "He [she] won't listen . . . ," or "There's just no way. . . ." These negations close us off to change before we can even begin to contemplate the possibility of it. We doom ourselves almost before we begin. And these kinds of sentences go on inside our heads more than we realize! They are some of the "static" which prevent us from hearing what people are really saying and from seeing possibilities of change and growth for ourselves.

If we run into an obstacle, we do not have to use this one block to our path as an excuse to confirm what we thought all the time— that it's just no use trying. People who accomplish things do not let one obstacle stop them. There are many ways to get across a river if the bridge is out. We can swim, or ride a horse across, or go down the river till we find another bridge. The Greeks had a saying: There is always a third alternative. (And there's a fourth . . . and a fifth . . . !) We do not have to rely on "either-or" thinking ("Either I do it this way or I don't do it at all"). There are many more possibilities than that in the world, if we have the wit to keep our eyes open and our ears free of static and our minds free of self-sabotage.

The Use of Dialogue
Rather than Gossip

The husband who could not accept the promotion because he believed his wife "would never agree to moving" may actually prefer to moan, complain, and gripe to others about her than discuss the issue with her. Fritz Perls called this "gossiping," by which he

meant *talking about* another person in any way whatsoever—even when the person is present.[4] Perls had a distaste for gossip, and he insisted that each person speak directly to the person concerned, rather than talking about him to someone else. In an encounter session or group therapy session, a person might say, for example, "I don't really understand what she is saying." At this point Perls would reply, "Don't gossip to me about her. Tell her. She is sitting right there!" The person might counter, "But she knows what I'm talking about." Perls would say even more firmly, "You are speaking to me about her. Instead of gossiping about her to me, speak to her!"

When we gossip about someone, we can be doing any number of things: we may be implying that that someone is unwilling to talk over an issue; or we may be misinterpreting their feelings and thoughts; etc. At any rate, we are assuredly not communicating with that person. And communication breakdown is one of the chief problems in any misunderstanding—as any businessman or diplomat can tell you.

When we allow someone to gossip *to* us, we are being parties to sabotage of real communication and may even allow ourselves to be influenced and convinced that something is so when it is not. Consider, for example, the usual kind of gossip about "the boss" or "the administration" or "the front office." Some of those confidences may sound convincingly true and we then begin to act on the gossip as if it were true without checking it out for ourselves! If you hear that John Jones thinks you are stupid, you may stop talking to Jones, and then he may begin to think you really are "stupid." Make it a point to ignore gossip, or else to track it down to the supposed source. If you believe there is no truth to the gossip, you may choose simply to ignore it. If, however, the gossip seems likely to provoke a misunderstanding with someone else, you may then choose to go the third party, discuss the "gossip," and suggest that the two of you straighten out the matter before it gets any worse. In that way, you attempt to replace *gossip* with *dialogue.*

What happens when you attempt to confront another person over a "gossip" situation? The worst that can happen is that the person will refuse to talk to you, or that he will deny the gossip or even get angry. That does happen. But then you are no worse off than you were before. Also, if the person *has* been gossiping, he may just stop it—because you discussed the behavior with him.

In most situations, we have found the person has been more than willing to discuss the gossip situation. Many times he may be genuinely surprised to hear the gossip; for he, too, knows that statements get misinterpreted out of context. Or the gossip may be someone else's paranoia or fantasy.

We are spending considerable time on gossip because of its particular virulence when we get sucked into it. In the situation of the man who "gossiped" that his wife would never move to another city, there may be many things involved. She may have said at an earlier time in their life together that she would never leave. First, we have a tendency to assume that what was once true for someone is true now. And the fact is that the world is changing all the time, and we along with it, whether we will it or not! It is more than possible that her statement of five years ago, or one year ago, or even a month ago, no longer pertains. Second, she might change her mind tomorrow or the day after—if her husband is willing to discuss the advantages of his promotion so that she can consider other things besides the turmoil and shock of moving! He does her and himself a disservice if he does not inform her of his advancement possibilities. He can listen to her anxieties and her objections. Furthermore, in dialogic fashion they can both explore the pros and cons of the moving situation. (And he can give her time to think about them.) We too often want an immediate answer to such questions. Too often we want immediate agreement. But some changes come slowly to a person. We all need time to reflect on an idea, make internal adjustments, solve the problems we foresee by doing what Janis calls the "work of worrying."[5] One thing seems certain: we rarely have to come to such a decision *now*. We need to give it some thought . . . more talk . . . more time . . . more thought . . . and more dialogue and more time. When we are willing to turn a subject around and around with another person, we let him see we are discussing the problem he sees in his own way.

SABOTAGE FROM OTHERS

When you have licked the problem of self-sabotage sentences playing over and over inside your head, you may very well begin to hear them coming from those around you. In fact, the minute you begin to integrate that change into your life, you may hear:

"Oh, come on, you're too old to go for yoga [*or* a new job, *or* going back to school, *or whatever*]. . . ."

Or you may hear:

"You've certainly changed in the last couple of weeks—and I might add, not for the better!" [*From a spouse*]

"What's come over you anyway? You sure aren't like you used to be!" [*From a son or daughter who has not yet realized that his parents exist for reasons other than for his own existence*]

"Everyone's talking about you!" [*From a "good" friend*]

"You don't know anything about life; you're too young [*or* inexperienced, *or* green behind the ears] to go charging off on your own." [*From a parent*]

If you have begun to recognize your own self-sabotage sentences, you will begin to have less difficulty recognizing when others are aiming sabotage sentences in your direction. You will begin to see also that such sentences are designed to make you feel you are doing the wrong thing, behaving in a way which they don't like, or behaving in a way others don't like, etc.

The Confirmation of Change:
Sabotage Sentences and Tyrannical Words!

When you come right down to it, there may be a sudden up-surge of these "observations" from others in your life-space as you become more self-directive. Remember that other persons are also resistant to change. When you begin a course of self-direction and begin to change from depending on others to depending on your-self, when you begin to actively make your own choices, there will also very likely be a change in the personal dynamics of your re-lationships with others. Other persons will sense the change quite easily; and they, in turn, will need to change. And therein lies the paradox. Changing yourself will create a situation in which others will also be required to change. And since people tend to resist change, they may hurl some powerful, emotionally charged accusa-tions at you. An increase in such remarks from others may actually be *proof* that you are beginning to think for yourself and choose for yourself . . . and that they don't like it very much.

Of course, these remarks will only come from those who do not want you to change for one or another reason. If you have been a docile and dutiful son or daughter, your parents may find your quest for independence a baffling and terrifying phenomenon. You may be hit with phrases like "selfish" or "ungrateful" or "know-it-all" and so on. If you are a wife and mother who is finding ways to actualize herself from the domination of husband and teenagers, you may find yourself being labeled with equally loaded words: "silly," "weird," "infantile," etc. If you have been a milquetoast of a father and are beginning to assert yourself in your family, you may also get terms thrown at you like "irresponsible" or "crazy." Or you may hear around-the-corner inferences like, "What's wrong with Dad?" or "Dad must be going through a second childhood"!

Of course, not everyone will react like this. If you consistently anticipate this behavior in others, you might very well be creating a self-fulfilling prophecy. There can always be persons in your en-vironment who will encourage you in your self-growth. These are the loving and enabling persons who are highly evolved and well-integrated themselves. One of the benchmarks of the highly inte-grated persons is not only their striving for their own continued growth, but their sense of commitment to enabling others to grow in personality integration and self-governance. Such persons can be available often to us as soon as we begin to seek them out.

Getting Rid of Tyrannical Words

Sabotaging remarks from others can hurt us, however, even make us stumble a bit, especially if we are feeling a little awkward in our new self-changing behavior. And unfortunately, people tend to make damaging remarks in their attempt to control behavior.

Semantics, a branch of linguistics which deals partly with how language affects our behavior, was founded by the Polish scientist-scholar Alfred Korzybski with the publication of his book *Science and Sanity* in 1933.[6] Korzybski's thesis is that language can be used to distort and confuse us, or it can be used to clarify our concepts and thinking. Similarly, we have been discussing how our remarks can sabotage our efforts to live more satisfying lives. Unfortunately, language is too often used to "tyrannize" us, as another writer, Stuart Chase,[7] has said—just as an overlong list of "shoulds" and "should nots" can tyrannize us! People throw tyrannical words at one another all the time, with the result that we begin to feel ashamed, guilty, diminished, anxious, etc. In Chapter 8 we told the story of Michael who was tyrannized by words that referred to his short stature.

For most of us there are words or phrases or sentences that when applied to us seem to have catastrophic effects. For one, it may be the word "selfish," which is another person's way of saying you are doing what *you* want to do instead of what *he* or *she* wants you to do. For another, it may be the word "stupid"—if we are unsure of our capacity to think for ourselves! Generally, these tyrannical words are ones that were thrown at us when we were young and defenseless and so caused us to feel miserably. We still react to these words, Berne would say, in our Child-Ego State—with our childhood emotions.

We have already mentioned in Chapter 4 another tyrannical phrase—"You are being defensive," which became quite popular for a time among people who were "hip" regarding "psychological" jargon. We discussed then the uselessness of that remark. But there is another term in use now which is threatening to become equally vicious—namely, "manipulative." In this chapter we have discussed various forms of manipulation as forms of controlling other persons'

behavior. And the word itself can be tyrannical when used by academically sophisticated persons as a way of controlling another's behavior. So be careful in accepting any person's statement that you are becoming "manipulative"—that person may be trying hard to manipulate you with that very word!

What can be done about the words that seem to tyrannize you, i.e., that affect you in such a way that you feel immobilized by guilt or hurt or confusion? The first step is always to cultivate awareness. And awareness is achieved by making a list (mental or actual) of the words which people have thrown at you and which seem to *stab* you, *annihilate* you, or get you *off balance!*

The next thing to do is to use the Jacobson-Wolpe desensitization technique and practice saying these words to yourself in a state of relaxation until they cause you no more moments of anguish and fear. Or better still, you can have one or more of your friends hurl these words at you in rapid succession (as you remain relaxed and in an anxiety-free state) until they contain no more dynamite for you. When these words are thrown at you over and over again (when you are in a state of relaxation), they will soon begin to sound like what they are: sounds, noise, static, words, and no more. In fact, the whole process of *verbal manipulation* will then become so absurd to you that you will find yourself laughing at those words which formerly caused you distress. Those words will no longer be anxiety-provoking stimuli; they will no longer be able to control your behavior, for now they will no longer arouse negative emotions in you.

DISCOVERING OTHER MODES OF RELATING

We have been dealing in this chapter essentially with two concerns: how to avoid manipulating others (and yourself) and how to avoid letting others manipulate you. But we ask now is there a way of relating to persons that is not based on power needs and manipulation? Is there a way of communication in which persons do not "put power trips" on each other but, instead, talk to each other, be with each other, and learn how to appreciate and understand one another? This way of being with another person was called *dialogue* by Martin Buber. To understand Buber's theory of human communication more fully, we refer you to two of his books, *I and Thou* and *Between Man and Man.*[8] Martin Buber became a legend in his own lifetime, largely as a result of *I and Thou*, which was published when he was still a young man. What Buber was saying was that there are three forms of address in relating oneself to the world: *I-Thou, I-It,* and *I-You.*

I-Thou

The primary mode of address or communication for Buber was the *I-Thou* relation. This is the form of address which occurs in loving understanding, where persons prize their differences and similarities and where their relation and dialogue with each other is free of attempts to control the other by any means. The *I-Thou* form of dialogue is to be seen in the loving caring of a mother for her infant child, where the mother appreciates what the infant needs and supplies that need. Friends who know and accept each other as separate (but related) individuals can often reach the depth of the *I-Thou* relation; and this is what friendship is essentially all about—the sharing of uniqueness in the presence of understanding. Buber says that men can also have an *I-Thou* relation with God, and in that they come to know reverence and awe. For the word *God,* some of you may wish to use a phrase like Universal Consciousness or Mind or Energy or Spirit . . . any word that has essential meaning for you.

I-It

We cannot relate to the world all the time in the *I-Thou* mode of address, for that would require simply too much time, energy, and attention. There is, therefore, a second level of address. And, then, we come to the objective relation where we relate to the objective facts of our world. This is the *I-It* mode. It is the objective form of address in which one perceives objects in one's environment. We do what we want with them, and when these objects are no longer useful we discard them. If there is an appropriate piece of wood, we may cut it, saw it, and hammer it until we have (by our manipulations) turned it into a chair. We may then use it to our satisfaction until we no longer find it useful and then we may chop it up for firewood. Such manipulation is part of our approach to objects. But we are beginning to discover also that there are limits to this approach, particularly when we abuse our planet and fail to appreciate that we are its caretakers. Think of the shortages that are beginning to appear—the energy crisis, etc.

I-You

We have many transactions during the day—hundreds, even thousands as we interact with our family, our friends, our coworkers, the strangers we pass on the street, the grocery clerk who takes our money. It is obvious we cannot invest the time, energy, and attention of the *I-Thou* mode of address to all these persons without feeling drained and diminished ourselves. Yet we do not want to *use* them, pass by them, speak to them as objects. Nor do *we* wish to be treated and used as objects by them. What, then, is left? Buber says there is a third mode which is not as manipulative as *I-It* nor as intense as *I-Thou:* the *I-You* mode of relating.

The *I-You* mode is social, polite, cooperative, and generally the expression of a shared goodwill which may stop short of real intimacy. It is not a masquerade of good will, however: It is always a genuine concern for oneself as well as for the other. The mother who needs to devote energy to herself for a while can treat her child in the *I-You* mode in spite of his insistence that he be treated otherwise. The husband who needs to retire to his workshop or his den and get away from the events in the rest of the house for an evening is not treating his family as objects so much as he is treating himself well for a change.

Allowing a person his full humanness—his "personhood," as some are fond of saying—means that we allow that person to control his own life, to make his own choices, to have freedom of decision, and to participate freely in the events that make up everyday living. Just as we learn to become aware of our own choices, we also enable others to become aware of their own choices. It means that a wife does not "run" her husband's life (or a husband his wife's life), and even that parents don't "run" the lives of their children. It means that an employer doesn't "manage" his office personnel without allowing them to participate in decisions that have to do with them. We each acknowledge not only our own freedoms, but also the freedom of others to make their choices and to change their lives in directions that have meaning for them.

CONTROL VERSUS "LETTING GO" AND "LETTING BE"

We come now to a concept which, it seems to us, is paramount in any address to others in the human way—the concept of "letting go" or "letting be."

You have already encountered the concept of "letting go" in Chapter 13, although it was not specifically described as such. As we discussed the desensitization methods of Wolpe and of yoga, and the various other methods of personality integration through physical awareness, there was a common theme in all: each enables a person to "let go" of the anxieties, fears, and embarrassments which are manifested as tight muscles and "dead" areas in the body. In those approaches we learn how to let go of our physical control and "be" ourselves and our bodies.

Now we approach "letting go" and "letting be" in terms of psychological control.

"Letting go" is hard. We are so used to controlling, so long conditioned to it as a life style, that it is far easier to talk or write about letting go than to do it. "Letting go" is simply letting go of our anxieties, fears, and nagging doubts, on the one hand, but it is also "letting go" of our control and nagging of others, and our anxieties regarding them, on the other. It means letting go of how *we* think others should be and allowing them to be themselves.

Letting go means also taking responsibility for our lives and our choices. It means no longer saying to ourselves that the reason that we do this or that is because our parents (or child or spouse or whatever) is preventing us or holding us back. We simply remember that as others are free to make their choices, we are free to make ours. This means letting go of needing the approval of others when we make our choices.

Letting the other person "be" means recognizing that each person needs to learn how to get along in the world even if it means he may "make a mistake" or 'fall on his face." We frequently learn better from our mistakes than we do from our successes. We can be at another's side when he makes choices, and he can counsel with us (if he wants to), but we do not interfere with him on the basis of punishment, threat, approval, or disapproval. We do not accuse, but we can say honestly how we feel about his choice and still allow him to make it even if we don't think that choice is a good one.

Letting Go of Children

At this point, parents of children may say, "But I have to guide and control my children's life. They are too young to make decisions for themselves." And we agree that small children do need the guidance of parents.

But in this day and age of anxiety, we have a tendency to hold on to our children far too long, to continue to make their choices for them until they rebel in adolescence. We have managed to produce a society in which human beings are virtual dependents until well in their upper twenties. Again, we don't have to go in for the "blaming game" at this point. We want so many things for our children—to give them the benefit of things, perhaps, that we never had. So we tend to push off onto them our own unfulfilled desires and objects hoped for but never gotten. In this way, however, we rob them of finding out for themselves what they want and where they wish to go. Small wonder the present younger generation has revolted from their parents' hopes and dreams for them.

But the parent may say at this point, "Should I just let my

child make mistakes without helping him? Doesn't a child need guidance?"

Of course he does, particularly when he is small. But when he approaches the middle teens he is simply resentful of all the guidance he is getting from everywhere: his parents, his teachers, his older brothers and sisters, etc., etc. He needs at this point to begin to learn for himself—to be his own guide. He needs our willingness to let go of controlling his behavior and letting him be the way he wants, even if it means "making mistakes."

The important learning is to learn how to learn (to pick oneself up and dust oneself off and go on from there):

> "But my sixteen-year-old son wants to drop out of school? Are you saying that I should let him?"

How can you stop him?

> "I know once he's sixteen, he's allowed to sign out of school on his own signature. But I can talk to him."

Yes, you can. But will you stop there or will you go on to nag him?

> "Well, I'll try to make him see the error of his ways!"

By making him feel angry, guilty, resentful, rebellious? You can shame him into staying in school, but will that do him any good? Or you? He'll simply become resentful of you. And if he stays, he may simply be a "dead body."

> "But at least he'll have gotten his high school diploma!"

He may, indeed. And then again he may sabotage your control of him by failing or by joining a crowd of teenagers you don't like.

> "But at least he can go to college if he wants then."

Does he want to go to college?

> "We've never discussed it, but I'm sure he would like it once he got there. And we are willing to sacrifice ourselves to give him the benefits we never got."

You may sacrifice yourself if you want to, but why sacrifice your husband too?

"Why, because we want to be good parents. He'll thank us later."

He may only resent you later for your nagging, for imposing your control, and for refusing to let him choose what he wanted to do. And if he goes to college to satisfy you, he won't get out of it what he would if he went of his own desire!

"But I've only been trying to do what's right!"

Of course, you have been. It is also right to let him learn from his own experiences, his own decisions, his own choices.

"Wouldn't it be better, though, for him to stay on in high school so at least he has a chance to go to college?"

Why not let him make his choices? If he chooses to drop out at sixteen to go to work, he may very well be doing just the thing to fulfill his need to be independent and self-sustaining.

"But he has a good mind. It's such a pity to see it go to waste."

His mind may not be going to waste at all. On the contrary, he may be doing just the thing he needs to do to realize he has a "good mind" and will not want to be a laborer or a shop clerk or a salesman the rest of his life. He may really be putting his mind to *good* use.

"But then it would be too late!"

How so?

"He's dropped out of high school, he didn't complete his education."

He can always drop back in—many young men and women are doing it. They go back to night school or they sign up for high school correspondence courses. From their own choice—and from choice comes change.

Other examples of "letting go" of children includes letting go of who they go around with (otherwise, they'll only stop telling you who their friends are), letting go of telling them how to wear their hair, what clothes they should or should not wear, when to do their homework, etc.

"But somebody's got to run this house. If they had their way, they'd never clean their rooms."

Let it stay dirty. You can let go of nagging that way.

"But what if they don't come in all night?"

If they want to sleep in their own beds, they better be in by whatever time you set or you lock the door.

"I can't even get them to wash the dishes, as big as they are."

If they want to eat well-cooked food it seems reasonable that they could help with the dishes once or twice a week.

"But you said not to nag. Aren't you being inconsistent?"

We said let go of nagging them—simply make a choice of your own. If they want to eat your meals, you would like them to help wash dishes once in a while. Now let them make a choice.

"But what if they say they don't want to do the dishes."

That is for you to decide. In our house we allow them to make a choice. If they wish to eat the meals that are cooked, then they do their fair share of dishes. If they don't want to take part in this, they don't eat with us.

"But they'll starve!"

Hardly! They are welcome to anything in the house that isn't cooked: sandwiches, cookies, apples, cold cereal, etc. But sandwiches do get tiresome after a while. We are also giving them a choice: variety and dishes—or sandwiches and cookies and no dishes. It's up to them!

THE CONCEPT OF KARMA

Karma has several meanings as it is used in the East. One of these meanings is that *we create what happens to us.* If we have been unkind to friends, they may treat us unkindly. If we live violently, we may die violently. If we lie as a matter of course, others will not trust us to tell the truth. Karma is not to be confused with punishment. It is simply the existential reality that our behavior has consequences. Given such-and-such, then this-or-that follows! If we eat too many calories, we get fat. No one is punishing us: we are doing it to ourselves! No use to look outside ourselves for what is happening to us. No profit in finding others to blame.

Other examples are:

> If a student doesn't study, he may fail his course.
>
> If a white community continues to discriminate against blacks, they may find themselves in the middle of a race riot.
>
> If a mother insists on managing her daughter's life, she may find that her daughter is incapable of managing her own life and is dependent on her even when in her thirties or forties or fifties.
>
> A middle-aged man who divorces his wife for a pretty young thing may find out that when *she* is middle-aged, she may find him unsatisfactory for her sexual needs.
>
> If we live by hating others, we will hardly find them loving us in return.
>
> If we refuse to listen to the problems of our employees, we may suffer the consequences of poor employee morale: rapid turnover, lateness, frequent absenteeism, sabotage, and "shortages" (that peculiar industrial word that means thievery).

We could go on and on. But the essential thing to remember is that we are always experiencing the end result of something that we have begun before. At the same time, we are now deciding our fate of the morrow.

Karma has the dark or negative side which says when we harm or injure someone else the harm comes home to roost eventually. But there is an equally positive karma possible. When we become genuinely loving persons, we find that we receive more love from others; when we allow others their freedom, we discover our own freedoms; and so on.

In this manner, we need to appreciate that letting go of control of others does not necessarily produce bad results. When we let others have more choices, they learn more, grow more, have more insight into their behaviors. We do not get trapped into thinking that we can save someone else. We do not get trapped into thinking we have to make a good place for them to live. Each person must find his own good place to live and discover his own sources of happiness. No one else can do it for him, and no one generation can save the next generation from pain. Pain and learning how to handle pain is still part of the process of living.

When others see that we are letting go of controlling them, letting them make their own choices and willing to allow them to suffer the consequences, they can become more responsible for their own actions and decisions. In other words, they become available for response-ability—the ability to respond.

"PROCESSING"

The psychotherapist, counselor, and parent attempt to teach two basic understandings: (1) behavior has consequences; (2) part of the joy in life is becoming a center of responsibility and decision. We have spoken many times of the highly integrated person's determination to take responsibility upon himself and to enable others to take responsibility upon themselves. But they balance this determination to be themselves with good will and an unflagging respect for the worthiness of others who touch their lives. They do not judge others as "better" or "worse" than themselves, although they may experience themselves as "more aware" "more alive" or "more awake" than others, just as parents themselves are "more experienced" than their children—but not "better than" their children. Being more alive or more aware or more awake than one's fellows fills one with compassion. Awakening requires *"processing,"* and that is never without a little pain. The highly integrated person remembers his own awakening and the pain and joy involved. But that pain and that joy enable him to apprehend fully and to carry out the Golden Rule: Do as you would be done by. When we know that someone is going to have a rude awakening, then we can do for them what we would like them to do for us should the time come when we need support from others. But we cannot save them from *processing,* which is another concept we would like to introduce to you before we end this chapter.

Processing means learning through experiences, and most of us perhaps learn primarily through our own experiences. Unfortunately, much of our processing can be negative. We don't fear fire until we get burned. But we may then leave matches alone. If we drop out of school, we may find out that we can't get as good a job as we could with further education. But then we will really understand what adults were saying that we didn't really believe. If one drinks himself into oblivion until his wife, children, boss, and friends are no longer willing to put up with his behavior, he may finally have the motivation and understanding to do something about his drinking behavior.

> "My sister is about to make a terrible mistake. She's shacking up with a real bad guy. Are you telling me I shouldn't try to prevent her? She and I have been close since we were kids."

How can you prevent her?

> "Well, I can't really prevent her . . . she's eighteen. But I can talk to her and tell her what this dude is really like."

You mean she doesn't know how you feel about him now?

> "Oh, she knows, all right! I told her just what I thought about him the first night she went out with him."

Well, if she knows how you feel already, how will talking to her change her mind?

> "Probably it won't, but I'd feel better! Truth is I'd like to smash that guy right in the kisser."

Will that improve the situation?

> "No! I'm not that stupid! That would only make her feel sorry for him. But he isn't any good. Eventually he'll give her a bad time and walk out on her."

What will happen then?

> "At least she'll know what kind of dude he really is."

Exactly so.

"But she'll get hurt. And I can't stand to see her hurt."

Is it she or your own self you want to save from being hurt?

- "Her! I've been hurt a lot of times! I've learned a lot from the school of hard knocks."

But you want to prevent her from having the same kind of experience.

"I guess so, when you put it that way. That's what you mean by processing, eh?"

That's what I mean by processing: we learn by our own experiences.

"It sure seems a shame to always have to learn the 'hard way.'"

We don't always learn that way, but much of our learning does come by our own experience rather than through the experience of others.

"Is there anything I can do to help the kid?"

Well, I don't want to make your choices for you. My own choice would be to go to her and tell her what I think without judgment or with the idea she must not go into this liason. But I'd also add that everyone has to make his own choices in the world. No one can do that for us. If she finds out that the arrangement is hurtful, I'll be there to talk to and we've got an extra bed for her for a while if she decides she wants out. And, I might add, in spite of negative feelings about him, he may even turn out to be a better person than given credit for.

"Then she can turn to me later if she needs to without the feeling that 'I told her so.'"

Of course. Furthermore, you've given her some room to move—given her at least one more available choice—not the either-or judgment: "Either you live with him, you're stupid, and I won't have anything to do with you—or be a good little girl, come back, and do what I say, and I'll still love you and be proud of you."

The idea of letting persons make mistakes, of allowing them to be processed, may seem callous, but it may be more unfeeling not to allow them to grow, not to allow them to stand on their own two feet, not to allow them to make mistakes, not to allow them to handle their own situations, not to allow them to suffer things through until they wake up and understand what they want to do with their own lives.

RECOMMENDED READINGS

BUBER, MARTIN. *I and Thou.* 2nd ed. New York: Charles Scribner's Sons, 1958 (paperback).

This book became a classic in the lifetime of its author, so powerful was its message regarding man's relation to his world and all that relates to it. It is philosophy, it is theology, it is poetry . . . above all, it is a book to be treasured.

The student may want to read other books by this same poet-philosopher-theologian: *Between Man and Man, The Eclipse of God,* etc. Buber is recommended only for the person with philosophic background who is willing to engage in depth study.

GINOTT, HAIM G. *Between Parent and Child.* New York: Hearst Corporation (an Avon book), 1965 (paperback).

This book was a best-seller for sixty weeks. Evidently, it provided some need for parents to learn new ways of interacting with their children without manipulating them and also without being manipulated. Another best-seller by the same author was *Between Parent and Teenager.*

HAYAKAWA, S. I., ed. *The Use and Misuse of Language.* Greenwich, Conn.: Fawcett (paperback).

Recommended for any student who wishes to know more about how people tyrannize each other through language. Hayakawa has for years been one of the leading exponents of a sane use of language. This book is a selection of outstanding articles from *Etc.,* the journal of the discipline of general semantics.

MAY, ROLLO. *Man's Search for Himself.* New York: New American Library, 1953 (hardcover).

One of the advantages of this age of insecurity, says Rollo May, is that we are being forced back upon ourselves for judgments and answers—we are no longer able to take it for granted from some outside authority. It is not an easy task. In this book he suggests ways by which a person can find a center of strength within himself so that he can act from within himself, for himself.

PRABHAVANANDA, SWAMI, and CHRISTOPHER ISHERWOOD. *How to Know God: The Yoga Aphorisms of Patanjali.* New York: Harper and Bros., 1953 (hardcover).

This is an interpretation of the ancient Indian sage Patanjali by an Indian and an English poet. We recommend it chiefly for its excellent treatment of the concept of karma.

SHOSTROM, EVERETT L. *Man, the Manipulator.* Nashville, Tenn.: Abingdon Press (Bantam Books), 1967 (paperback).

For a more complete account of Shostrom's work as presented in this chapter, the reader may find this book quite engaging and easy to read. In addition to the manipulative patterns described in this chapter, Shostrum presents some ways for people to actualize themselves instead of manipulating each other.

In one sense, one's world view is simply a projection of one's personality.

15

CENTERING OURSELVES IN THE PHENOMENAL WORLD

We have spoken much of the highly integrated persons, how they seem better able to withstand the crises and the blows of fate that come to us all. Calamities and misfortunes visit those persons just as they visit all of us. They, too, are visited by sickness, and they, too, experience the death of those close to them. Those persons can be made also the object of slander or gossip, petty revenge and jealousies, and the other disappointments which are part of human living.

But highly integrated persons seem better able to survive these crises, to take up their lives again and walk on. They are not so bowed down by disaster, or so discouraged that they lose sight of their path—what they want to do with their lives. Misfortune doesn't so cripple them that they are unable to seek out their own destiny. Wailing and woe-is-me is not for them, as it can be for many of us on occasion. In fact, as Maslow says, these "loving" personalities seem able to integrate even these experiences into their quest for self-actualization. "Negative" experiences, therefore, do not so much close them off from what life has to offer, since even misfortune can become a catalyst (or "fiery furnace") in which their characters become even more finely tempered. They are not crippled by "negative" experiences, they are made more sensitive, more finely tempered, more supple, more adaptable. They are not embittered by negative experiences, they are made wiser—these are Maslow's findings.

We do not know a great deal yet about how such persons come upon those qualities of personality which enable them to recycle the "raw data" of their lives into insights and understandings so they can become teachers of all of us. All we know is there have been, and are, such teachers: Jesus, Buddha, Ghandi, Mohammed, Lao-tse, and others. We do know that those persons have managed to reach a level of integrative functioning in which they "center" themselves; and that because of that stability they are less likely to be swept away by the storms and emotions of events. Those teachers and Maslow's creative personalities had a way of centering themselves in their phenomenal world: they were able to maintain a sense of balance in the *center* of themselves—and despite those experiences which drive the rest of us from one extreme to the other. They are personalities, in our words, who have become *"impersonal."*

PERSONALITY AND IMPERSONALITY

Impersonality (as we are using the term here) can be a difficult concept to understand without some explanation. We are not referring here to the "schizoid" reaction of noninvolvement with others in which we are disengaged from our own emotions. Nor is impersonality to be confused with the "psychopathic" disregard for human life. Impersonality is rather the level of functioning that permits us to remain rooted in the here-and-now, able to perceive that events painful to us are not the result of some malicious god or evil demon, that these events happen to all of us—regardless of our lot or station in life. The impersonal attitude does not necessarily prevent us from experiencing sadness or shock; nor does it diminish the beauty of our emotional life. But it does enable us to let go of needless suffering and pain—at least, that is what Maslow's research data seems to confirm. The "impersonal attitude" thus seems to provide us with a vehicle with which to "catharsize" our hurts or resentments (to "travel through" them) so that we do not waste as much creative energy on things and situations we cannot change. "Impersonality" involves an insight and an outlook which recognizes and understands that some of the misfortunes which cross our path are of our own making—in which case, it is fruitless to look for someone else, or someplace else, on which to displace our angers or our hurts! In the event catastrophes happen in our lives which are not of our own making, the impersonal attitude enables us to recognize that such events occur to all of us and that it is not a personal affront, or the finger of fate "doing a job" on us. The impersonal attitude takes into account that there has been no one who has not suffered pain, heartache, and injury in the course of living one's life . . . it's how we seem to learn. The Angel of Death, as it is said in Hebrew, visits all of us ultimately. So we all face trials, and there are tribulations for all of us in like measure. No one's life has ever been so smooth that he has not suffered occasional setbacks. We can do nothing about our "fate," in the sense of our inheritance. We can do something about our attitude toward our fate. That can be our choice. We can, for example, choose to "personalize" our suffering, to get "sucked in" to the interpersonal games so we begin to focus in on our sufferings and magnify them ("Why, oh, why did this happen to me?"). We can choose also to work on achieving an impersonal attitude to the point where we can confront just these circumstances and then "go through" the crisis. ("I can't do anything about that event in the past since it is over and done with. But I can learn from it. I can always ask myself the question: 'Well, what did you learn about yourself there?' ")

The highly integrated person suffers when painful events happen to him. He feels pain, he is hurt by slander, he experiences disappointment when someone does him an injustice. When death strikes close to him, he, too, mourns. When someone close to him takes a destructive path, he, too, feels sadness. Such a person is not heartless or unfeeling just because he is "impersonal"—he simply suffers what is necessary and moves on.

Nor is the highly integrated person immune to those darker emotions which all of us suffer—resentment, "feeling sorry for oneself," etc. But she does *not* stay fixated in sadness and suffering.

She suffers her miseries, yes, but she *suffers them through.* She finishes her suffering as best she can and moves on as soon as she can. In a sense, you could say she knows she has work to do in her life, and she knows for she has already too little time to complete it.

There is a level of existence of personality which allows us to rise above the negative experiences of life. It is a level of personality that we can rise to and so transcend the turbulence of our most painful emotions. *How do we get through to that level of functioning?* This is the question we address ourselves to in this, our last chapter.

DISCOVERING THAT YOU ARE NOT THE TARGET

Psychiatrist Laura Huxley, the widow of Aldous Huxley, has written a lovely little book of exercises with which a person can foster more awareness of the here-and-now.[1] A particularly insightful chapter for the authors is "You Are Not the Target" (this happens also to be the title of the book). This chapter describes in detail one way to develop the impersonal attitude, and although we shall only summarize Huxley's message here, we hope that our summary will whet your appetite for the book itself.

Throughout the day, the author explains, as we go through the normal course of events, we act and react with many, many others. All of these interactions have a "valence" of some kind. If the interaction has left us feeling bright and "high," we have had a charge of our positive emotions. But we may also receive a charge of negative emotions: A husband may have complained about the cooking, or a wife may have nagged about the washing machine, or the boss may have been irritable with you. One's boyfriend may have forgotten to call when he said he would, or one's parents may have snapped at him; or one's children may have been particularly obnoxious. Any or all of these latter kinds of negatively charged events may leave us with a feeling that somehow we don't deserve what we get. We will tend then to feel mistreated, misunderstood, wronged, or insulted. And when we do, of course, there is a consequent physical reaction in us. If we take a personal attitude then, we may react with anger. Our adrenals become stirred up, sending hormones into our bloodstream; our heart pounds a little, and despite ourselves we may want to get back at the other verbally and

Some days we may experience one negative bolt of energy after another.

"have it out," or we may harbor a secret desire for revenge—the counterpart of the pain-attack response.

Of course, one may equally feel wounded and hurt, with tears welling up despite oneself. And one may actually burst into tears or withdraw into a shell to nurse his "hurt feelings." These reactions are all examples of *"taking things personally"* (although Laura Huxley does not use that term).

Huxley points out that many of the negatively charged "messages" that get hurled at us come from those who are nearest and dearest to us. But it does happen occasionally that as we interact with others who are strangers, we may experience negative bolts of energy from them also—for example, from a truck driver in the frenzy of traffic, or from a salesclerk as she snaps a reply to our inquiry, or from a teacher who has had a harrowing hour of problems in the classroom.

The point to remember is that many times, even though you appear to be the person the anger and hostility is aimed at, in all probability *you are not the* (actual) *target:* you are simply the nearest, most convenient target! Now sometimes it is true that persons are really trying to hurt you; but in most situations, Huxley explains, you are not the target—you just happen to be there when the person steams off, unloads his anger, lets go all of a sudden and "defuses" himself!

Is that really the case? you might ask. Consider: all people go about their daily lives encountering positive and negative charges of emotion. That truck driver, for example, may just have had a flat tire, or he may have just been given a ticket by some policeman.

Any of these events can appear to him as "fate" ruining his day—and then he has a deadline to make, and he's behind schedule and he may be fined for each hour he is behind time. Then let's suppose your car stalls in the middle of the street and blocks his way—and at that point he *explodes!* He either shouts or gestures an obscenity at you. Yet you are *not* the real target! You just happened to be there when his pressure valve finally blew.

In like manner, let's suppose the salesclerk was just jumped on by her boss, and since no such person can very well snap back at her boss she holds her tongue but her body is bristling (where before she was calm). And then you happened into the store and up to her counter. She snapped at *you;* but *you* are not the target—*you* just happened to be there.

The teacher who barked at you has just taken two aspirin for a headache that resulted from the irritations she felt (and did not express) at a particularly undisciplined and rowdy bunch of students in her last class. *You* are not the object of her snapping; *you* just happened to be there before the aspirin had a chance to work.

But you may say, "I didn't do anything!" No, not this time. But if you will allow yourself to think back over your own days, you will recall times when you also yelled at your children when you were exhausted, or at your employees when a particularly nerve-wracking foul-up occurred higher up that you had to straighten out. Or (and we have all had these experiences) you may have taken your irritation out on a member of the family because the girl or boy you are interested in did not seem to be interested in you.

As soon as we begin to understand that another person's day is sometimes filled with those same kinds of events which frustrate, hurt, and irritate us, we begin to understand that the more irritable and hurting a person appears to be to us, the more likely he or she is to be simply suffering. Once we come to that realization—and live it—we begin then to adopt the impersonal and compassionate attitude.

Everyone has "off-days." Momentary snaps, angry retorts, and sarcastic replies are then possible, even likely. But they lose their sting and fail to arouse in us the flight-or-fight response or the pain-attack response *if we do not "personalize" them*—if we remain aware of the other person's frustration and conflict. These behaviors have less to do with us personally than they are an expression of where the other person is right then. That understanding and kind of acceptance is the basis of an impersonal attitude. At that point we do not have to suffer hurt, annoyance, or anger nearly as much. We can choose to react impersonally rather than personally, as a personality—with compassion rather than irritation to that person out there. The impersonal attitude thus allows us to stay centered "within" ourselves so that *we are aware* that *we are not to blame* for this person's present suffering—nor are we the real target. We do not have to feel sorry for that person nor be apologetic either. We simply withdraw into our own "center" and become aware of what is happening. In so rising above the bolt of "negative energy" that is being directed toward us we enable the other person—if that is the wish—to come closer to us and to himself and herself. But—more specifically—we prevent our energy from being drained. And in that moment *we are growing*. We have made a choice, and are changing right then. Why? Because we have "died" to our resentment, to our "power needs," to revenge and being "one up" on another person who is right now sending out "negative vibrations." In avoiding responding "personally," we can see what is happening and so do not get caught up in the other's negative "karma." Impersonality, therefore, as we shall indicate later on, always involves "dying" in some measure to one's unnecessary defensive self or ego.

SEPARATION, SUFFERING, AND DEATH

There are events in our lives which are not so easily dealt with as in those hypothetical situations just discussed. To any of us can come those moments of darkness when we are separated from those we love. A divorce in the family may have rent us from a father or sister or brother. Or an intimate friendship or love affair may be terminated rudely when one of the partners decides suddenly to end it. Or actual death may take a close friend, or a child, or a spouse from us.

Separation and dying are not impersonal events. On the contrary, these are among the most intensely personal moments in human existence. No one else can share the extent of the pain and suffering that happens to us then, although they may want to. Happiness is more easily shared; grief, sadness, and pain are more often solitary in nature. Pain is also almost irrevocably personal. Also, in those experiences of intense pain such as death and mourning, a person can experience such an intense sense of loss that the world appears "weary, stale, flat, and unprofitable."

The Separation Syndrome in Children

When the experience of separation occurs in a child's life—as, for example, when the child undergoes a stay in the hospital—research suggests that there are three definite stages in his reaction to his sense of loss and separation.[2]

1. The stage of protest. First, there is rage and anger and screaming and crying. This state of protest is active and aggressive with much emotional energy displayed.

2. The stage of despair. After several days, however, the child's emotions take another turn. He seems now to show characteristic reactions of grief: flaccid facial expressions, moaning, quiet weeping. To observers, he appears to be considerably depressed and seems "defeated."

3. The stage of withdrawal. A third stage can follow in which the weeping ceases and the child seems to begin to make adjustment to his situation. He may appear indifferent, for example, when his mother visits him; and there can be a blandness of emotion—what psychologists call a *lack of affect.* He seems to have withdrawn his attention from the world of emotional interaction. He has become increasingly more apathetic and unemotional. He is detached much in the same way Lowen describes as characteristic of the "schizoid" personality.[3] * In brief, separation from one's mother when one is placed in a hospital at an early age results in a kind of reaction almost as if the mother had actually died.

The Separation Syndrome in Adults

Research on the effects of family death reveal that adults also go through three stages in the mourning process.[4]

1. The stage of disbelief. In the "normal" or usual grief pattern, an adult may react to death first with disbelief, numbness, and shock. In following days his feelings may be "hazed over" by the shock reaction, and he may not experience the full sense of loss of

---

* A "schizoid" personality is a person who has "split off" his thoughts from his emotions and feelings.

the person who has died. He may also respond by feeling angry or irritable. Or he may appear to be making an excellent adjustment to the loss—that is, to be accepting of it.

2. The stage of mourning.   The stage of disbelief sometimes ends dramatically at the funeral, which is where the person is made aware of the reality of the loss of the loved one being lowered into the grave before his very eyes. He may weep copiously then, shedding all the tears he withheld before; or he may "withdraw from the external world" into the realm of his own private suffering. He may experience at that moment regrets that he was not more considerate and kind while the person lived, and that he did not really say and do all the things he always meant to. He can also feel guilt or remorse, or begin to believe that he could have done something to prevent the death. He may even spend some time in a kind of communion with the dead person, and withdraw from outgoing social relationships. He may suffer loss of appetite and sleep and be irritable. He may also begin to idealize the dead person. What is important to understand, however, is that the pattern of response is as individual in mourning as it is in other behavior patterns.

3. The stage of return.   After some days or weeks, the mourner will usually begin to withdraw his attention from the dead person and to give more attention to himself and the outside world once again. Although he may occasionally experience sadness or even attacks of acute and painful loss in the ensuing weeks and months, the person will eventually come through the mourning with a sense of his own integrity (although he may not want to return to certain areas of social interaction he shared with the dead person). Eventually, however, once the mourning is completed, he will return to the world of the living and bring his attention back from the grave to himself and his own life in the world. In other words, he has buried the person, said goodbye, and allowed the deceased person to "die" to his own existence.

Pathological Grief

"Pathological" grief and bereavement show some significantly different reactions to the pattern of mourning described above. Here, the person may continue to exhibit numbness and be seemingly emotionless regarding the death of the person—similar to the

child's *stage of withdrawal* or to those reactions that are characteristic of the adult *stage of disbelief*. But whether the person seems
to show indifference or shock, he can also experience a sense of
depression, worthlessness, bewilderment, and even detachment. He
may contemplate suicide and even attempt it. He may react with
sexual promiscuity, or in other ways which are opposed to his "normal" behavior pattern when the dead person was alive.

The Work of Mourning

Sigmund Freud noted that the process of mourning is a significant and necessary step in our understanding of the event of
death[5]. All primitive cultures have evolved ritualistic mourning rites
which variously involve weeping, moaning, marching behind the
corpse, blackening parts of the body with ashes or paint, wearing
of mourning colors, withdrawal from society for a period of time,
etc. These rites enable the mourner to act out (actualize) his sense
of grief and loss, and they facilitate identification with the dead
person until such time as the emotions have been "worked through."
The mourner may reminisce about the dead and even engage in
fantasy conversations with him. In contrast, someone who reacts
pathologically to the death does not do the "work of mourning";
rather, he seems to want to deny the finality of his loss.

The significant understanding, however, is to know what it is
to suffer *through* the mourning and to emerge on the other side a
reintegrated person. The loss we experience is for the person who
is gone, yes, but it is also an experience of loss of part of oneself—of
part of one's being, as it were. In that respect, it is similar to the
sense of loss that can be experienced by persons who have had a
limb amputated [6]—there is a loss or damage to the integrity of the
self. The work of mourning helps us to focus on this sense of being
diminished, and we mourn for our lost self until at length we begin
to realize we will survive, go on, and even grow beyond the experience.

Living in the Here-and-Now

To go on living means giving our attention to the here-and-
now; so there must come a time when the loss is experienced less
personally, less intensely—that is, when we no longer constantly
reminisce of times spent with the dead person or fantasize what

could have happened *if the person had not died.* These two adaptations to the experience of death represent modes of living in the past or in an imaginary present. The here-and-now experience, by contrast, is the centering of ourselves in the reality of the present.

Yet, in the authors' experience, some persons do not seem able to make that final step of return. Lest they exhibit disloyalty, perhaps, or because of feelings of guilt that there was something that they could have done to save the person, or even of anger toward the person who has left them, they remain fixated in the past and so carry a ghost of the lost one around with them. They are the persons who have not completed the work of mourning, who have not be able to say the *goodbye* with finality.

Incompleted mourning is more common in our society than we may realize; and since the death of a loved one is then the occasion for developing protective behaviors which insulate us from experiencing further loss, incompleted mourning is one great source of energy drain.

One's sense of loss is not restricted to persons who have died; we can feel it regarding animals, objects—indeed, anything in which we invest ourselves. An interrupted grief reaction that the authors enabled someone to work through many years ago had to do with a loved dog. In another instance, a woman had been forced to give up her house and home in Cuba and had not yet completely mourned for it and that loss now interfered with her ability to *say hello* to a new home—and to a new stage of her life. Yet another example was the sense of loss suffered by a girl who had an abortion. Her healing did not come until she was able to say goodbye to the fetus that was torn from her.

Never underestimate how much you can care about things and persons. We "hallow" objects and persons, make them important to us by investing our energies in them. And when we lose them through death, or loss, or by moving to another place, there is always some form of mourning necessary. And the mourning always involves in some measure saying goodbye personally in the here-and-now. In the event we go through the grief of mourning the loss but fail to say goodbye, we are then, as Freud said, involved not in *mourning* but in *melancholia* or *depression.* That is, we are still fixated in the past rather than being in the here-and-now.

The *depressive* aspect in loss and death is often very difficult to manage and to admit into our ongoing sense of self at the time of such loss. We are diminished by the loss, damaged by the fates

The refusal to mourn or bury a loved one saps one's energy to survive and live in the here-and-now.

which have decreed, seemingly, that this event must happen to us. Very often we *fend off* the suffering which that loss entails. And we do that kind of protective defending primarily by tightening up our muscles so that we do not *feel* the full import of what is happening to us. It was Jesus who said, "Let the dead bury the dead," and there is therapeutic wisdom in that saying. Yet each one of us can only manage his grief according to the ability to enter one's suffering, and that is why there are delayed responses to "saying goodbye."

Each of us manages to say goodbye to his sense of loss when it is time, when we are ready and able, and not before that. Thus, we must never *demand* that another person enter into mourning until he says he is ready. When that person is willing to reopen the ritual of mourning, he tells us clearly that he is at last ready to suffer his loss through and to lay the ghosts of the past to rest.

The process of saying goodbye sometimes involves anger. More frequently, it involves the necessary tears that were at first held back, the final words that were not then spoken. When the person allows himself to live these events through, there comes the finality of understanding that the lost one (or lost treasure) no longer has to be mourned—that all that was said or unsaid, finished and unfinished have now been said, at last . . . completed and done. And with this understanding the person knows relief: the slow filling up of expressive energy which revitalizes the organism and his present life forces. The following dialogue illustrates (in condensed form) an actual instance of one such completed mourning work.

During the course of working in counseling on another difficulty, a young man becomes very quiet—in distinct contrast to his previously spontaneous and energetic discussions. At that moment, he began to twirl a ring on his left hand. I asked what was happening to him at that moment.

STUDENT: Oh, I was just thinking about my father, for a minute.

O'CONNELL: What about your father?

STUDENT: Nothing much. He died when I was young. I didn't know him very well. It seems strange to be thinking of him right now. I hardly ever do.

O'CONNELL: Are you aware of what you are doing with your hands?

STUDENT: (*Looking at his hands*) Oh, this? This is just a habit I have.

O'CONNELL: Your hands are speaking.

STUDENT: You know, now that I come to think of it, my father used to do that. It's one of the memories that I have of him. He was away a lot of the time on business so I didn't get to know him very well. But I remember sometimes sitting next to him when he was home and watching him turn this ring around. . . . Hmmmm!

O'CONNELL: What's going on now?

STUDENT: It just occurred to me that I wear this ring on the same hand he did. I used to wish that ring was mine and now I've got one like it. Not exactly like it, but close enough. (*Silence*)

O'CONNELL: What's going on now?

STUDENT: I just feel sad all of a sudden. I'd forgotten this, but I used to play a game about my father after he died. I used to pretend he was still alive, that he was just off somewhere on business. And he would come back some day. I guess I missed him. Or I missed the fact I never had a father like other kids. There would be these father-and-son things, you know, like Cub Scout dinners and things, and I would either show up with my mother or not go at all. I used to hate going with my mother. It was embarrassing. But she didn't know. I just used to tell her they were dumb things I'd rather not go to at all. (*Silence*)

O'CONNELL: What's going on now?

STUDENT: I was thinking about my mother. How dumb she always was. She used to think I didn't care whether my father died or not. She used to tell me that all the time.

O'CONNELL: Do you know how come she thought that?

STUDENT: Sure I do! You see, my father didn't just die—he killed himself. It was pretty awful. I was just a kid, nine years old, but I was the oldest. When it happened, there were a lot of people. I mean afterward. I had just come home from school, and there was my mother crying and the neighbors and the police and even some photographers shooting pictures. I don't remember exactly, but anyway my uncle called me over and told me what had happened. I couldn't believe it, I just couldn't believe it and then I started to cry. But he said I shouldn't cry because that would upset Mom. What a goddamn bastard! Anyway, he said I was to be a big man and all that, and I'd have to be the man in the family now and not to let my Mom see me crying because that would upset her even more. So I didn't cry. Not once. Not then. Not at the funeral. Not ever. So Mom came to the conclusion that I didn't have any feelings about my father.

O'CONNELL: But you did have feelings.

STUDENT: You bet I did. (*He is suddenly holding his head and the tears are coming down very quietly.*) I feel pretty stupid crying after all these years.

O'CONNELL: You have a right to cry. Everyone has the right to cry.

STUDENT: Yeah. You know I really did miss my Dad. I guess I never realized how much. (*He cries now more quietly*) Why does a person commit suicide? How does he do it, I mean? I can't imagine it. I can't even imagine it. (*He cries some more*) I feel a little better now.

O'CONNELL: You look a little better. But what are your hands saying now?

STUDENT: Oh, I'm twisting the ring again.

O'CONNELL: Something is still unfinished, evidently.

STUDENT: Isn't it just a habit?

O'CONNELL: Nothing is ever "just." Would you be willing to take another step?

STUDENT: What?

O'CONNELL: You've finally cried for your father. Are you willing to bury him now?

STUDENT: I have to get used to that idea. . . . Yeah, I guess so. What do I have to do?

O'CONNELL: Put your father over there. Do you want him alive or dead?

STUDENT: Alive. OK. He's on the chair.*

O'CONNELL: All right, what do you want to say to him now?

STUDENT: I guess I gotta say goodbye to you, Dad. I never really knew you to begin with. You never got to know me either. (*Turns to therapist*) Is that all?

O'CONNELL: Are you ready to say goodbye? Have you said everything you've wanted to say?

STUDENT: I guess I want to tell him it wasn't right to do what he did.

O'CONNELL: Tell him, now.

STUDENT: You know, it wasn't right to do that, Dad. It was just not right. Mom needed you. I needed you. And Tina and Betta needed you. God, I needed you so much. (*Breaks down now into real weeping and sobbing*) Every kid needs a dad. (*Weeps some more*) I guess I've said it all.

O'CONNELL: Can you still see your father in the chair?

STUDENT: Yeah.

O'CONNELL: How does he seem to you?

STUDENT: Kind of sad.

O'CONNELL: Does he say anything to you?

STUDENT: I guess he says he's sorry.

O'CONNELL: Do you want to say anything back?

STUDENT: Yeah, I'd like to tell him it's all right. I made out all right.

O'CONNELL: Go ahead.

STUDENT: It's OK. I've made out all right. I'm going to keep making it. I guess that's it.

O'CONNELL: How does he seem to you now?

STUDENT: He's not there anymore. He's really gone.

---

* It should be noted that this young man was used to the visualizing methods of Gestalt therapy.

O'Connell: Can you say farewell?

Student: Sure I can. Goodbye, Dad. I don't have to keep you alive anymore.*

Saying goodbye and saying hello are "opposite sides" of the
same event which is your life. To be able to "say hello" to a new
personal involvement is, in some measure, directly related to our
willingness to say the goodbye when a death or separation happens
to us. When we fail to say goodbye to what is past, gone, completed,
and finished, we interrupt and interfere with our expressiveness, our
ongoing energies. Rather than being expressive then, we become
depressive—turned in on ourselves and the past—and so we are less
available to these next persons who cross our paths and can fill up
our heart yet again.

The highly evolved persons we have held up as models seem
able to traverse this very painful barrier. There is no reason you
cannot do as much. It is your choice, and you can be the better
for the mourning. Frederick Perls said once, "If you want to be
happy, learn to weep!" And by being happy he did not mean "having
fun," he meant just what he said.[7] And so we take up next one of
the abiding barriers to happiness—our resentments.

RESENTMENT AND GROWTH

We might be overstating the case if we were to call resentment one
of the more serious contemporary difficulties. Obviously, things like
pollution, the continuing drug problem, and the many other difficulties we now face would take precedence if we were to make up
a list of the difficulties in our time. Resentment is a less obvious
difficulty, but it, too, is on the increase because of the pressures and
demands of contemporary living. And, as we shall see in a moment,
it is no less serious a problem just because so many of us have become accommodated to living with it.

---

* There is a difficulty in protocols such as the one you have just read through.
They can often seem all too "neat," too contrived, too simple, even mechanical.
What is missing is the feeling atmosphere that was present and that was shared by
the participants: the nuances of tone and tempo, those shared moments where no
words were spoken, and the intuitive moments of sympathy where one person simply
appreciates where both of them are in the here-and-now and responds accordingly.
Film and tape capture that atmosphere more successfully, making it possible for us
to be moved by what is happening when someone "says goodbye."

Resentment as an Obstacle
to Growth

To understand your own resentment, to appreciate how this emotion functions in your own living and how it impedes your growth, you will need to understand how resentment is related to feelings of frustration and guilt—and then how this emotion seems irrevocably tied to the use of the word "should."

Take, for example, the case of a woman who refuses to divorce her husband—not because she loves him or because of religious scruples, but just because she does not want to "give him the satisfaction." She has a score to settle with him and she'll be damned if she will allow another woman to have him if she can't! As any marriage counselor can attest, that kind of deadlock situation is quite common, and the resentment which accompanies the deadlock is an expression of the couple's long-standing incompatibility and frustration with each other. Closer examination of their relationship will also very likely reveal that there is a long list of "shoulds" by means of which each partner has attempted to control the other's behavior over the years. ("You *should* do this," "You *shouldn't* do that"!) It will not be until much later on in their counseling that their feelings of failure, worthlessness, and guilt will come into view. What we see first is the resentment, the interpersonal "war" with the perceived enemy, and the bitterness with which the frustration is expressed. And every failure and frustration each partner experiences is taken as a *personal* affront. That is what resentment is and what resentment does; and when couples reach that level of estrangement from one another, more often than not they go looking for an attorney rather than a psychotherapist.

One of the difficulties in resolving our resentments is the sense of *self-justification* that can accompany them. We feel justified in being angry with another; we say, "It wasn't *fair* of him . . . ," or "He shouldn't have . . . ," and so on. In those ways we avoid facing up to our own contribution to the misunderstanding, and so the other person can be perceived as the one "to blame." Resentment and self-justification are thus part and parcel of the "blaming game." And we can indulge ourselves by blaming others in our past for what we are now, or for what we lack in our present life, just as the couple mentioned above.

Many persons can be enabled to become aware of their "blaming game," to see that this behavior is not doing them any good—that, in fact, their feelings of hatred and resentment present a serious obsatcle to their growth. For example, resentment of a mother may interfere with a young man's ability to have a satisfying relationship with another woman. Or resentment of a father may generalize to any authority figure, so that one is unable to see *any* adult person other than as his own father. When we carry around the feeling that life has mistreated us, we carry the proverbial chip on the shoulder into many of our relationships, and then feel justified in excusing ourselves for the "lousy breaks" we continue to encounter, etc.—for self-justification grows like a weed, and resentment is the soil in which it flourishes.

Since harboring resentment is by and large an unpleasant experience for most of us, we often try to get rid of the resentments of the day by talking about them. This is where friends come in, and husbands and wives and psychotherapists. Sometimes persons use hours in psychotherapy just pouring out their list of resentments and long-harbored angers. If the therapy is successful—in the sense of meeting the person's needs—the client will be able to finish his bill of complaints and to work then on *letting go* of his anger and resentment. When we let go of our personal resentment and our unresolved hatreds, we release the energy that is bound down in ourselves, and this energy now is available for our continuing growth.

Resentment Collectors

Some persons seem unable to make that step. They are the *resentment collectors,* and despite the hours spent reciting the ills and misfortunes they had to suffer as a child or adolescent, they seem unable to take the step of letting go of the past. In calling such persons "resentment collectors," we acknowledge simply that there seem to be some persons for whom resentment can be a way of life. They are, or can be, the despair of a psychotherapist's professional work, since no matter what he does, or how skillful his approach (or unlimited his patience), the person refuses to acknowledge that *forgiveness* is a necessary element in the equation of human living. Sometimes such persons are apparently aware that much of their creative energy is now bound down in the resentments of the past; yet they choose to remain fixated in those past sufferings, and so are not able to make the step into the here-and-now,

where all real change of self takes place. To explain how such para-doxical behavior is possible, we need to go back for a moment and refresh your memory about the physiological component in human behaviors.

You will recall that we discussed in Chapter 3 the physiological effects in stepped-up muscular tensions and the increase in hormonal secretions that occur in moments of prolonged stress. As Hans Selye puts it, there is probably no emotion that does not have a corre-sponding physiological reaction.[8] The so-called "positive" emotions (joy, love, etc.) have "gentle" physiological reactions; and "nega-tive" emotions (fear, resentment, anger, hatred, etc.) have corre-sponding "harsh" physiological reactions that can wear down the body tissues. You will remember also, as Selye has pointed out, that a person can get used to living in the state of overcharged emotional and physiological activity characteristic of the negative emotions and then not know that there is any other way to live. In other words, the difficulty with these patterns of emotional and physiological response is that they can become self-sustaining: in time they can become nearly autonomous behaviors over which we no longer have control. Anger, fear, and resentment produce more anger, more fear, and more resentment. The resentment collector, as far as we understand him, is trapped in just that pattern of response. He gets "high" on his resentment and then refuses to give up the pattern of resentful behavior despite the toll on his bodily health and his growth as a personality.

When we carry around with us a belief, say, that the world has done us wrong, we enter and react to new situations with suspicion—with the sense that if we are not careful, more misfortune and wrong will befall us. Suspicion and distrust can then become a part of our character, our abiding pattern of responding to the world of other persons—what Reich called a character neurosis.[9] We will act this belief out, talk as if it were unalterable truth; and even our facial features will come to reflect in time our abiding attitude: I have been wronged, and if I am not careful, it's likely to happen to me again! Other persons will of course sense our distrust, or our resentment, and they will in turn hold back their trust and their spontaneity, which will only confirm—as do all self-fulfilling prophecies—our present understanding that other persons are hard to deal with. And so the cycle continues, and we will hang on (for dear life) to our defending mechanisms.

When we carry our past around with us, we cannot attend to the here-and-now newness of the moment that reverses our self-fulfilling prophecies. Our fears and our conditioned responses cast their shadow before us so that we are looking at the world through our prejudices.

Resolving Resentments

But how, then, you may be asking, do I "let go" of my hurts, my past suffering and my present resentments? In the authors' experience, the answer is simple enough, really so simple and obvious that to know it you will need to *experience* the solution for yourself. The answer is not original with us; indeed, sages and teachers have been saying the same thing for centuries. Our only contribution may be to put the answer into "Gestalt therapy" language—so that you can easily understand it in terms of a step-by-step procedure wherein you practice and learn for yourself the principles of the phenomenology of here-and-now.

The "answer" is *forgiveness:* if you want to get over your resentments and let go of your suffering of the past, then *learn to forgive. Work on forgiving* each person for the imagined hurt and anxiety you believe he or she has "caused" you to suffer in the long ago or recent past or present. You will need "to forgive" every wrong you believe has been done to you, imagined or otherwise. And you may need to *repeat the process of forgiving* over and over again until nothing is left of your resentment, your guilt, or the fears that may still cripple your present abilities to grow according to your own measure. What you will be doing, then, is deconditioning as many of those past and present miseries as you can. In that process, you will be getting in touch with the energy which is still bound up in those past memories of suffering and resentment. And the more you *practice* forgiving, the more adept you will become in the *psychotherapy of resentment.*

Forgiveness as the psychotherapy of resentment and fixation on the past can be described as a three-step procedure: the *act of accusation,* the *act of dialogue, a*nd the *act of forgiveness.*

Step I. The Act of Accusation. In this first step you are to visualize the person or persons with whom you have scores to settle. (When you are first learning this procedure it is easier to concentrate your attention on one person at the time; later on, as you become proficient at visualization, you may be able to deal with several persons at once.) Sit in a comfortable chair, and then pay attention to your breathing. Generally, in the beginning of this procedure, the visualized person is placed at some distance—say, at the farther end of your room. For like the cat we spoke of in an earlier chapter who had a conditioned response to the feared cage, you may also have approach-avoidance behaviors going that can interfere with your capacity to make contact with the person intended. Later on, you will be able to allow the visualized person to come up close.

As soon as your breathing is adequate and you feel ready, "conjure up" the person (imagine he or she is there) and begin to speak to him or her—aloud, in a normal speaking voice. Call that person by name, and whenever you address the person continue to use his and her given name. In that way you will not lose touch and drift off into the "memories" that can interfere with your ability to focus your attention on what is happening to you in the here-and-now.

As you call the person by name, begin to let out your resentments and irritations and frustrations, regarding him or her, that you have bottled up. At that point you begin to send out those "negative" bolts of energy you have held back for so long. And the wonderful thing is that no one is being hurt or damaged any longer by your present resentment since the person that you are whipping with your words is not there. Go down the list of injuries you think that person did to you. This is the time to let yourself "hang out"! You may need to shout, or to pound on a pillow as you express the full measure of what you feel and have not yet said. (Don't use a wall, or a hard object, for you'll only end up by hurting yourself.) But the main thing in this first step is to let yourself feel and express in the fantasy conversation your need to *accuse* the other person. (We recommend, by the way, that you practice this technique in a private place where you will not disturb, or be disturbed by, other persons. Growing always involves in some measure the matter of appropriateness; and we do not get over our resentments by making the lives of others untenable and miserable as we go through our growing!)

If you practice this first step with concentration and attention to the here-and-now, you may already relieve yourself of some of your fears and angers. On the other hand, you may get even further charged up by your resentment. Or you may break down into a kind of weeping you have not experienced for a long time. But whatever happens to you at that time, the rule here is to *break off the fantasy conversation at the exact moment you feel you can do no more today*—that is, when you feel you have "had enough." (We did not grow when we were pushed beyond the point we could manage earlier on, and this same reality applies now. Growing takes time—that's the point of this rule!)

Step II. The Act of Dialogue.   When you have allowed yourself to sound out to the other person about every upsetting act or deed of ommission that you believe that person has been "guilty of," you may be ready to take the second step in resolving your resentments. In step I, you are engaged in a fantasy monologue: the one-way kind of conversation where you listen primarily to yourself and have less regard for the other person's existence. This is the "one-way" thoroughfare where we accuse the other person and try to get him to *feel guilty* by using the word "should." So the first step has to do with getting in touch with our resentment and really telling the other person how *we* feel.

In the fantasy dialogue of step II, we provide the opportunity for the imagined person to reply to what has been said to him so far. Thus, this step is where you begin to imagine how the other person replies, where you imagine and fantasize what he says back to you. Here also is where your attention and energy are directed into listening to what is being said by the other person. At that point, so to say, you become engaged with him. You speak to each other back and forth until there are no longer any words left to say between you.

This act of fantasy dialogue may demand a lot of your energy in the beginning, for you will be learning how to listen to a person you resent. Our resentments, in a sense, invoke the situation of not-listening. So if you find yourself unable to imagine how the other person replies, you may still be involved primarily with yourself and your own resentments, and thus not yet ready for a dialogue. If that happens, we would advise you to break off the conversation for now. You can begin another time, another day, to take that particular conversation up again.

There may be another time when you will be able to take step II and engage the other person in imagined dialogue—that is, if you genuinely want to take the step. All you will need, at this point, is to keep the dialogue going back and forth until it is completed and finished. You address him or her with how you feel, as in step I; and then you listen to the reply. It is the kind of creative work which can be demanding of your energies, so remember: you are in the process of deconditioning yourself to past resentments. And when a sense of exhaustion comes upon you, or you begin to feel "spent," or there comes a point when the dialogue lapses into silence, that is the point at which you need to stop. For all that needs to be said has then been said. Whatever you decide to do then, be assured you are on the threshold of the third step of the deconditioning process, which is the act of forgiveness.

Step III. The Act of Forgiveness. The act of forgiveness is one of the sublime expressions of growth in the human personality. This is where we come to understand and acknowledge that other persons in our lives are themselves sometimes crippled by their past conditioning; yet despite their inherited difficulties, they are still and always doing the best they can. In the act of forgiving another person for his misdeeds and his real and imagined limitations, we come to understand the meaning of impersonality and compassion. We begin to realize that each one of us has a "karma" he is working on, and that each one of us is gifted and diminished in ways which none of us so far really or fully understands. We come, that is to say, to face and to accept that now-too-familiar concept, the human condition.

We are still today, most of us, imperfect, incomplete, and that is perhaps how it is that we have need of each other. To get in touch with that kind of realization, you may need to invest a goodly amount of your creative energy. This step can also demand "acting" on your part: that is where you try new behaviors out for size, and learn thereby how forgiveness actually works. Since this is the place where your efforts to decondition your resentments can founder, and your energies can begin to wane, we speak yet again of the self-sabotage that comes up when you genuinely want to change yourself.

The Bible says rightly that we do not grow and change by taking thought. What that saying means in terms of your personal situation is that you do not learn how to forgive by *thinking about* the action—you learn what forgiveness is in the *act of forgiving*. But just as soon as you attempt to decondition your resentment pattern which is rooted in the past, those present behaviors of yours can fight—sometimes even unto the death—to maintain their sovereignty and control. In other words, the closer you get to the moment where you are now capable of saying "I forgive you," the more likely the resistance against change mounts, and the more distractions you may encounter to actually becoming a forgiving person.

Do not be put off by these distractions. They are merely the "noise" we spoke of earlier which prevents us from staying in touch with the business at hand—which is letting go of past resentment and stepping "into" the moment of the here-and-now.

A friend of the authors, Herman Rednick, said once that we can deal with that kind of sabotage and distraction of our will to change by *starving our resentments out of existence,* and that we can do that by *not putting our energies* into resenting. We agree with Rednick's approach, and we know that it works when there is a sincere desire to let go of past suffering. We do not come upon that kind of understanding and impersonality all at once; for learning is a step-by-step process in which we integrate all that has gone by before into the moment that is here-and-now. And this is how "acting" can apply to changes in our behavior.

Young persons in our time have a professed distaste for what is phoney, the so-called "as if" kinds of relationships where no one seems to be real and everyone seems to be acting out some kind of role or game. The "acting" we are speaking of has nothing to do with phoney games: we speak rather of the *trial act* in which we try out new behavior patterns. The act of forgiveness can be one such trial action.

Go back now over your list of angers, resentments, fears, and hurts you "spewed out" in step I. You can take them up one by one and specify each one in detail, and simply begin to forgive the person for all those real or imaginary insults to your personhood. Be sure to call that person by name with each statement of forgiveness. In the case of a father, you would say, "Father, I forgive you for . . . ," and complete the sentence by specifying one of the resentments, hurts, or angers you have already delineated. Then you go on to the next statement, beginning again with "Father, I forgive you for . . . ," etc. In those moments of speaking the forgiveness sentences where you really do forgive, you get in contact with the impersonal sympathy and compassion we described earlier, so that can really also experience *the other person.* You begin then to see the other person as he is and was: inadequate as are we all, incomplete as are we all, suffering as are we all, striving for his growth as are we all. In that moment, you are no longer isolated, living unto yourself, but capable of being touched and changed by the suffering the other person has also experienced, and by his attempts to survive as well.

The feelings you experience at that point will assuredly tell you that the process of forgiving is done. You may get a sense of elation and even exhilaration then: that sudden burst of energy where you feel "high," the sense of being released from something you no longer need. Many times also we experience in that moment another kind of understanding: that there was actually nothing to forgive after all. Confucianism has two concepts that describe this experience very well. The first is the concept of "no blame"—that no one is actually to blame for whatever has happened to anyone. The second is that "it furthers one to cross the great water"—that is, to continue the tasks of our lives and not look back.[10] When you begin to understand that no one is to blame for your misfortune, not even yourself, you have begun to reach into the realm of impersonal sympathy and compassionate understanding where you are no longer so liable to be trapped in the past. In other words, you are not so likely to "look back," for you are living in the here-and-now.

Another concept we inherit from Chinese philosophy is the Zen

concept of the "gateless gate." [11] What that concept means is that before you get to an achievement, you perceive before you a gate, or a barrier: a doorway that you feel you need to enter upon and cross. Many times traversing that pathway seems an impossible task, and so we often hold back from the act of stepping forward into the doorway because our present pattern of conditioning says it is impossible. (See self-fulfilling prophesies, p. 380.) Yet, when you have passed through the doorway and look around, you see that there was actually no barrier there, after all. It was a gateless gate—a barrier to our growth only before we passed through it, the realization that the barrier existed only in our own perception. Once we acknowledge its existence and dared to encounter it the barrier to growth disappeared.

We have described the process of resolving resentments. It may appear to be an impossible gate still. Therefore, we have provided the reader with an actual example of how one person passed through his gateless gate to come out on the other side.

We return now to the young man who suffered the loss of his father, a suicide. You have already seen how he began to work through the grief reaction and resentments he felt for his father. In the following dialogue he begins to deal with some of the unresolved resentments toward his mother.

STUDENT: She was always talking about how she had it so bad, all the time. Always saying what it would have been like if Dad was alive. And how hard it was to be a mother and a father to three children, and how we should be more considerate and on and on. It was a record that got played everytime something happened and one of us acted up. And especially when she got tipsy! It was no use going to her with a problem! She'd just play this record. Actually, it was like it was the other way. Everytime Tina or Betta got in trouble, she'd ask me what she should do about it. How the hell would I know?

O'CONNELL: That's kind of a burden to put on a young boy.

STUDENT: You said it. What the hell could I do? Just let me hop on their backs, and she was down on me again.

O'CONNELL: Nothing you could do was right, evidently.

STUDENT: Except get good grades. That was a *right* thing to do. You could really show me off then. Prance me around to the relatives. I don't think she ever really knew me. I don't think she knows me now. I'm just somebody to be proud of, or to run errands or to make her feel good.

O'CONNELL: Sort of an object?

STUDENT: Yeah! Just like an object! I don't think she's ever really seen me as a person who has feelings or thoughts or upsets. I'm good old Robert. I never cause her upsets! She doesn't see me as a person! I'm a robot!

O'CONNELL: Can you see her as a person?

STUDENT: I don't know. I guess not.

O'CONNELL: Are you ready to?

STUDENT: More work?

O'CONNELL: Only if you want to. It means letting go of some of your resentments.

STUDENT: (*With a sigh*) I guess so.

O'CONNELL: (*Laughs*) It's so nice to hang on to our resentments, isn't it? We can hug them! So comforting!

STUDENT: I guess I'm ready. Put my mother over there, right?

O'CONNELL: Tell me when you can see her.

STUDENT: OK. I can see her.

O'CONNELL: How does she seem to you?

STUDENT: Oh, just her usual stupid self! She's got a glass in her hand. She's drinking as usual. Slightly foggy.

O'CONNELL: (*Laughs*) I guess that'll have to do. Now tell her exactly what you've been telling me.

STUDENT: You mean about how she never let me be a person?

O'CONNELL: OK. Start from there. But start each sentence with the words "Mom, I resent . . . ," and go on from there.

STUDENT: Mom, I resent you never seeing me as a person. I resent I always had to be a little man. I could never come to you with a problem.

O'CONNELL: (*Prompting*) "Mom, I resent . . ."

STUDENT: Mom, I resent I could never come to you with a problem. I resent I could never be a child. I resent how insensitive you were. Always thinking about yourself. . . . I guess that's all.

O'CONNELL: Does she say anything back to you?

STUDENT: No, she never listened to anything I said anyway.

O'CONNELL: You mean she was psychologically deaf.

STUDENT: Yeah, deaf! And dumb! Deaf! Dumb! And blind!

O'CONNELL: Tell her you resent her for being deaf, dumb, and blind.

STUDENT: Mom, I resent you because you are deaf and dumb and blind. You're stupid! You're really stupid!

O'CONNELL: Anything else?

STUDENT: And what I resent the most is that you were always saying I didn't care about my father just because I didn't cry. You were so stupid you didn't realize I was trying not to hurt your feelings, you stupid ass!

O'CONNELL: That hurt the most?

STUDENT: It sure did!

O'CONNELL: Tell her that.

STUDENT: That really hurt, Mom.

O'CONNELL: Does she say anything back?

STUDENT: She just says, "What did you say, Sonny?" *

O'CONNELL: Ready for the next step?

STUDENT: I guess so.

O'CONNELL: Now go back over all the things you said you resent her for and forgive her for each one. Literally! Start with the first one, and say, "Mom, I forgive you for. . . ." Can you?

STUDENT: I guess so. Mom, I forgive you for being dumb. (*To therapist*) Is that right?

O'CONNELL: Yes, say it again until you feel it, and then go on to the next item . . .

STUDENT: I forgive you for not letting me be a child. I forgive you for being a child yourself! . . . That's something I never realized before. She is a child.

O'CONNELL: Can you forgive her for not being a mother? For being a child?

STUDENT: I forgive you for not being a mother. I forgive you for being a child. (*To therapist*) I guess it isn't her fault if she never grew up any.

---

* In the actual counseling, this dialogue continued until the student had made an explicit statement of all his resentments toward his mother. Then came Step III.

O'CONNELL: Whose fault is it?

STUDENT: Her parents, I guess. They were pretty strict with her. But that's not their fault either. They came from the old country, Holland. They were very poor, and they all had to work hard. It was the Depression, too.

O'CONNELL: So whose fault is it?

STUDENT: No one's, I guess. It just keeps going back and back, doesn't it?

O'CONNELL: Sure.

STUDENT: Kind of puts the whole thing on us.

O'CONNELL: Sure. Have you forgiven her for everything now?

STUDENT: Except for thinking I didn't care about my father. I really did. And she was just too stupid to know it.

O'CONNELL: But I thought you forgave her for being stupid.

STUDENT: I do, but not for that.

O'CONNELL: OK, how about trying it out and see what happens.

STUDENT: But it'll be a lie!

O'CONNELL: Let it be a lie. But say it, try it out.

STUDENT: OK. I'll try it. Mom, I forgive you for always saying I didn't love my father. (*To therapist*) I don't feel any different!

O'CONNELL: Say it again.

STUDENT: I forgive you for thinking I didn't care about my father. I really did. You were just too stupid to know it.

O'CONNELL: See if you can forgive her for being too stupid to know you really loved your father.

STUDENT: I don't know. . . . Yeah, I guess so. I forgive you, Mom, for being too stupid to know that I really loved my father. Mom, I forgive you for being stupid. I forgive you for being stupid. (*To therapist*) I really do.

O'CONNELL: What do you experience now?

STUDENT: There really isn't anything to forgive. It wasn't her fault. It wasn't anybody's fault. (*Silence*) I really understand now. That's really good to know.

O'CONNELL: How do you feel?

STUDENT: Kind of peaceful. That's really nice.

As we said previously, few written protocols can convey the living experience of those moments where a person resolves a past conflict for himself and becomes available to himself there in the here-and-now. At the end of the earlier interview this young man was asked, "Can you say farewell?" and he replied, "Sure I can.

Goodbye, Dad. I don't have to keep you alive anymore." In this interview he was able to let go of some of his resentments toward his mother, and when asked how he feels he says, "Kind of peaceful. That's really nice." And so it is: it is really "nice," and it is peaceful when we do let go of our past suffering, let go of the resentments which are bound up in the suffering of long ago. We cannot say anything further on his therapy here, yet we do hope that, despite the inevitable limitations of the present discussion you will get the point. Perhaps you may want to read over what we have said in this chapter so far. In that way you will be ready for the section where we speak of meditation, that is, where you not only learn to speak but also begin to learn to listen.

PSYCHOTHERAPY AND MEDITATION

Our present psychotherapies in the West are an ongoing process of theories and techniques that are constantly changing and evolving. Freud in his time dealt with the repression of sexuality, infantile wishes, and the function of aggression in personality development. His psychoanalytic method was, and still is, a remarkable achievement, for he provided us with valid explanations for some neurotic difficulties and a method for alleviating the crippling symptoms that those neuroses can call forth. Freud was a scientist of the late nineteenth century and his thinking was shaped by the "reductionist" approach, that is, where psychological factors in personality are grounded in physiological and biological explanations. His pansexual explanations of neurosis flowed out of the approach but were manifestly limited, since they did not explain all neurotic forms of adaptation even in his own time.

C. G. Jung was one of the first of the neo-Freudians, who attempted to modify and extend Freud's classical psychoanalytic thinking beyond the exclusively sexual emphasis of the original approach. Other psychoanalytic theorists—particularly Erich Fromm, Harry Stack Sullivan, Otto Rank, and Alfred Adler—followed this neo-Freudian impetus to free personality research of Freud's dogma; and they enabled us to see that we are not just instinctive organisms governed by overweening sexual impulses but also *social* beings, who, they said, require respect and consideration if we are to be enabled to grow and mature beyond purely sexual and instinctive levels of development. These personality theorists began to focus on the new factor of anxiety: how the fact of anxiety itself can interfere with a person's ability to deal with what is happening in the here-and-now—an aspect of personality that Freud avoided. The neo-Freudian approaches were, in a word, additions to the original Freudian theory, a step forward into the psychology of twentieth-century attitudes.

The insights derived from psychoanalytic theory and practice have had a profound effect on child rearing in the past 75 years, and on education, even on how we perceive ourselves today. We have discussed some of those theorists in earlier chapters, particularly the ones we believe have reference to your present search. But the essential thing now is that these men and women dared to investigate the reality of personality functioning in their own time, and that we are richer and more aware for their courage and determination. They enabled us to be free of many superstitions and misconceptions which had hitherto been ignored or "pushed under the rug," or else blithely accepted. Our debt to them is enormous, we say.

Psychoanalysis and psychoanalytic thinking is only one stream of thought in the psychology of personality. Particularly in the United States there has been a continuing emphasis on *behavior:* the actual and visible operations which each person engages in as he goes about his daily life and attempts to grow and mature. The behaviorists in professional psychology are the "hard heads" who ask us to stop all this apparently useless and introspective philosophizing about the nature of man and the human condition. They want us to acknowledge that the body is a reality we can no longer ignore, that each person *learns* how to behave—how to be the person he is—primarily because of the environment to which he is exposed. We have chosen, for the sake of brevity, to discuss only selected theorists in this behaviorist or Learning Theory approach to personality; we have passed over, for example, the work of B. F. Skinner and others whose research has now made possible such things as teaching machines (which are already beginning to change the shape of education in our own time).

The behavior therapists are one branch of the Learning Theory school who have begun to come out of the psychological laboratory in the past ten years and to apply their research findings in the human situation of conflict. A well-known exponent of that approach is Joseph Wolpe, whom we discussed in Chapter 13. Wolpe's approach is now becoming an alternate to the "psychotherapy" of personality functioning, and there are already many practitioners trained in his method. This approach says, in brief, that what is called "neurosis" is primarily conditioned behavior in the presence of stress and fear, the person now apparently having little choice and control. And their therapeutic method, called behavior modification, is oriented toward eliminating those symptoms of past fear and anxiety that interfere with the person's ability to deal with his ongoing living here-and-now.

There has been a concurrent growth in the last 30 years in the research findings concerning personality from the side of medicine and physiology, as in the research studies on the higher brain processes by Wilder Penfield.[12] Indeed, research on higher brain processes has now come so far forward that Russian scientists, for example, are now seriously studying extrasensory perception (ESP).[13] We could describe all of these research findings and many other breakthroughs in personality research, but the result would be a far too long and ponderous book. What we have done instead is discuss representative studies that we believe will have direct application to your own personal situation: for example, Selye's practical studies of stress and Jacobson's progressive relaxation method. We have included, also, brief sketches of such techniques as massage and yoga, where the physical body is taken as a phenomenon that requires interpersonal contact if personality is to evolve and mature. There are many excellent books describing the physical aspect of personality integration; some are mentioned in the following Recommended Readings.

We wish to say something further of meditation and another approach to personality integration, however, since each offers valid, incisive techniques which can contribute to your growth.

MEDITATION

Meditation is a technique by means of which you begin to understand, and learn to avoid, the excessive drain on your energy which resentment and the other negative emotions are calling forth. To be sure, meditation at the present time all too frequently suggests some kind of Eastern, occult, ritualistic procedure in which you are supposed to take to a foreign religion and give up your Western sense of self. Do not be put off by these prejudices. They are merely the "noise" of our Western defense mechanisms. For indeed, if you look further into the literature of meditation, you will find that there has been always a strong and viable current toward meditation in the Judaeo-Christian tradition as well.[14]

Meditation is in some respects equivalent to Jacobson's progressive relaxation method.[15] That is, it is an approach where you learn progressively to let go of those disturbing thoughts, those nagging demands, doubts, fears, and anxieties which keep you out of touch with yourself and the here-and-now moment of living. If you want to practice meditation, we would advise you (as a beginner) to spend no more than fifteen minutes each day in learning these techniques. Indeed, you may discover that those fifteen minutes are all too long for you to manage. And as we said earlier when we spoke of resolving resentments, the rule is to break off and give up your learning when you are no longer able to encompass its boundaries in safety.

The practice of meditation is not easily learned by many of us in the West because of the "noise" we seem to carry around in our heads for so much of the time. We have all those frantic thoughts and worries to which we have become conditioned; and we come actually to believe in some instances that our "mental" uproar is the natural and normal state of human existence as personality.

You cannot ignore these factors in your own present behavior pattern, however. And so it is essential that you pay attention to "noise"—whether you like to or not. *There* is the signal that tells you how much you can now bear and how much further energy and information you can now integrate into yourself and grow. The process of meditation, of letting go of your worries and fears, can provide you with a respite, a "holding pattern," where you can move beyond the barrage of self-nagging, self-sabotage, and other self-destructive behaviors you are presently accustomed to meeting each day and living with. But remember: it's the *"noise"* you are getting away from now, just as in an earlier section you were working to get away from *resentment*.

A frequent question that is asked by a person of Western religious bent is: What is the difference between prayer and meditation? The traditional answer is that prayer is where you talk to God and meditation is where you listen. Devout persons of the authors' acquaintance have been able frequently to combine both of these aspects.

If you are the kind of person who cannot now integrate into yourself the possibility of God, you may prefer to consider some area of your own growth you want by reading some passage in a book that makes sense to you; in which case you may then meditate on the meaning of the words. Do not worry about your progress. Each one of us can be in transit to a "higher" form of consciousness and personality integration. And you can trust that wisdom which is in yourself if you choose this path.

Among the kinds of writings that you may want to read before attempting meditation, our own Western Bible is a powerful source of meditative energy; and there are also numerous poets and philosophers who continue to express the abiding values involving personality. Kahlil Gibran has provided inspiration for many persons, and you can perhaps discover in his books, such as *Thoughts and Meditations*, the kinds of impulses you will need to meditate on in finding out who you are and who you want to become.

Many students are now turning to the literature and poetry of the Eastern tradition. And if you are one of these persons we can recommend the *Aphorisms of Patanjali* [16] and the *Upanishads* [17] of India, or Zen literature as interpreted by D. T. Suzuki,[18] or the eloquent *Tao Te Ching*.[19] There is a vast collection of literature which can be your arena once you begin the practice of the arts of meditation. And the books that are now becoming available are already so many that we can only mention a few of them.

The *actual practice* of meditation is very similar to Jacobson's progressive relaxation method discussed in Chapter 13. What you need to do when you meditate is find a private place where you will not be disturbed. Then get to work on the process of getting yourself relaxed and comfortable in that place.

If you are an ardent devotee of the Eastern approach to personality integration, you may want to experiment with yoga positions at that point (although yoga is not necessary for your growth).

What is necessary is that you pay attention to your bodily awareness, for therein, so to say, is the factor which can distract you from meditating. So it is necessary that you sit in a comfortable chair—or lie down, if you prefer. We recommend that you keep your back straight (vertically or horizontally) just as soon as you can manage that posture. Then just relax into where you are right now. Just relax, begin to study how you relax, and work on those thoughts and feelings which prevent you from relaxing—from becoming the impersonal and sympathetic being who no longer "has any work to do."

If you are unable to get away from your nagging thoughts and the other kinds of negative involvements from the past, try meditating then on the experience of floating on a calm sea or lake. Or you can let yourself relax in imagination in a favorite forest, or on a beach where you know you have nothing further to do. But get in touch with yourself and the forces of the world around you. Those kinds of fantasy experiences can be an excellent way of learning the process of meditation.

By the way, it matters little what your choice is of place to fantasize: what matters and is necessary is that you select a place where you know you can be relaxed, where you can be free of "shoulds" and of the "noise" that interferes with your present ability to be simply yourself.

Once you have become accustomed to giving yourself those fifteen private minutes which are apart from the demands of yourself and other persons, you will then begin to enter gradually fifteen minutes of *peace*. These are the fifteen minutes that are set aside solely for your own growth: where you learn to let go of the noise in your head, where you learn to relax and simply to be, without plans or obstructions, even without cares or memories. We cannot go further into meditation techniques here. We refer you, therefore, to a number of books if your interest stretches into these dimensions of personality.[20]

The results of meditation are varied. Generally, persons report that they have become more calm, better able to concentrate and pay attention to what is happening in the here-and-now. They say also that they seem less caught up in other persons' difficulties, and that the difficulties that they once thought were large and overwhelming seem now to be less dominating, less significant. The classic literature in the field of meditation seems to indicate that meditation leads eventually to what Maslow has called the "peak experience." Other writers have called that moment by different names—the "mystic experience," "cosmic consciousness," "self-realization," and so on.

THE ARICA APPROACH
TO THE INTEGRATION OF PERSONALITY

We have attempted to describe some of the biological and psychological considerations which underlie personality as a phenomenon and your own growth as a person. We hope you understand that our description has been selective: determined by our personal experiences and our present understanding of what we can ourselves become as persons. We are assuredly persons in change, it seems to us, persons open to the possibilities of our future, even as we appreciate our past heritage and do justice and give honor to those creative persons who have gone before us—those who can still teach us something essential about the integration of our personal humanness.

Approaches to personality integration that attempt to combine into a new synthesis the many factors in personality we have been discussing in our separate chapters are now beginning to develop. One is Arica, which sees itself as a *school* rather than a specific form of therapy. Arica's stated objective is reduction of the person along physical, mental, and spiritual avenues so that in place of a split in the personality there is a total psychobiological awareness. Arica believes that we are now coming to a crisis in personality, even to a crisis in the evolution of the consciousness of our planet. Arica says that there is no longer time to fool around with time-wasting ego procedures that delay full consciousness and realization of the self, for the vital need of our revolutionary times is the full realization of conscious awareness of mankind.[21]

Arica offers its students many opportunities for training in self-realization, including weekend seminars, nine-day workshops in its methods, and forty-day intensive training programs that are said to convey essential understanding of its theory and approach. Since late 1973, Arica has chosen some persons for advanced training beyond the forty-day training period. We know little of this graduate training; we understand that it studies and attempts to pass on to graduate students the Zen "satori" experience: what we referred to earlier as the experience of the gateless gate!

Arica utilizes many of the physical techniques described in Chapter 13: yoga methods of breath control, meditation, Tantric chanting techniques we have not discussed, and a continuing emphasis on bodily awareness. The Arica approach to personality has so far proven successful with some hard drug abusers and with other alienated persons. It is also being studied increasingly by persons in the mental health professions. We cannot say now how much influence Arica and other schools will have on the shape of the "new" psychotherapy of the twenty-first century.

AND NOW . . . AT LAST

Our twentieth century is a remarkable time, even as it has been a time of turbulence, stress, and change. To borrow from Charles Dickens: we live in the best of times and the worst of times. And that we know, assuredly, from the demands that are being placed upon each of us, seemingly with ever-increasing frequency. But whatever else it is, life in our late twentieth century is an adventure, and a great part of this adventure is the great change taking place in the consciousness of man. We are beginning to understand ourselves as perhaps no other time has ever done. And though we struggle and stumble with our new awareness, there seems to be a viable strength and hope under all our confusion, our excesses, and our searching for what can be possible. We are taking heed of the ancient Greek dictum to "know thyself."

We are also taking upon ourselves the knowledge (and the responsibility) that we ourselves are the creators and the destroyers of our own persons and, to an even greater extent, of our species and our total (planetary) environment. We are beginning to rid ourselves of the fallacies and dangers of looking to "higher" authorities for our salvation; and we are beginning to give up also the beliefs that "outer" authorities can tell us what to do and how to live our lives. We are beginning to get in touch with what it means to be free, to become aware of our choices, and to think of making changes in our society and ourselves that we want to make. Most important of all, we are beginning to acknowledge and understand that change in the world, our shared world, begins with change in ourselves: that, for example, violence in oneself breeds, in turn, violence in the world at large. In the extended world of plants, trees, air, and water, that kind of consciousness is now called *ecological* thinking. In the realm of psychology and individual personality development, which is what we have been discussing, it is beginning to be called becoming a *psychonaut*.

What is a psychonaut? He and she is the person who realizes that we are all together in this world of ours, that we are mankind: persons with the remarkable ability not only to act but also to think about how we act and to change how we are.

Becoming an *original*, a psychonaut, an aware person, the integrated personality who works for the individual good and the

common good of mankind, is not an "easy trip." For it requires dedication and resolve: and the kind of cussed stick-to-it-ness which has been the mark of those *originals* we discussed in Chapter 2. As we said in that chapter, we do not expect you to become a Socrates, or a Shakespeare, or a Michelangelo, or to copy any of the other remarkable women and men who have left their mark on history. But you can become yourself, if you want to, and if you want to work for that exciting and remarkable event.

All we can say at this point, at the last, is that it seems worth the effort. And that we wish you well for your personal journey into self, . . . where you discover the roots and history of who you are: how you came to be who you are right now and how you can go on from there. It is the journey into the "gateless gate." What you encounter and live through in your own journey toward the gateless gate will be your personal discoveries. And if you are determined to make it, these discoveries can happen to you all through your life.

We wish you well for that journey.

RECOMMENDED READINGS

ALLPORT, GORDON W. *Becoming: Basic Considerations for a Psychology of Personality.* New Haven: Yale University Press, 1955 (paperback).

In this very small monograph Allport discusses the personality as a steadily growing evolution. While early man needed taboos and structures of early civilization, Allport asserts, we are evolving toward self-governance and inner authority.

DE ROPP, ROBERT S. *The Master Game.* New York: Dell Publishing Co., 1968 (paperback).

This remarkable book was written by a noted biochemist who believes that man can transcend his manipulative and aggressive nature through exploring higher levels of consciousness. This book has great appeal for our present student generation and (we must confess) for your authors as well.

FINGARETTE, HERBERT. *The Self in Transformation.* New York: Basic Books, 1963 (hardcover).

Finagrette's book is for the serious student who wishes to confront directly the differences between *blame, karma, guilt,* and *responsibility.* He rejects the psychoanalytic reduction of *spiritual* goals to neurosis, and draws on Eastern literature as well as psychoanalytic literature to extend our understanding of existence and the nature of man.

HUXLEY, LAURA ARCHERA. *You Are Not the Target.* New York: Farrar, Strauss and Giroux, 1963 (paperback).

We cannot recommend this book highly enough for some of the simple and effective "recipes" she offers for learning what we have called the "impersonal" attitude. Students to whom we have recommended this book have come back singing its praises and vow they will not part with it ever.

LORENZ, KONRAD. *On Aggression.* New York: Bantam Books, 1966 (paperback).

This is an interesting book on the nature of man by a Nobel prize-winning scientist who believes that man has a natural "killer instinct."

This book provides a good counterpoint to Chapter 15, which emphasizes the ability to forgive as a way to overcome our desire to aggress and revenge ourselves on others.

MASLOW, A. H. *The Farther Reaches of Human Nature.* New York: Viking Press, 1971 (paperback).

Published posthumously, this book represents Maslow's conceptualizations of where human personality could go. He discusses the peak experience and what he called the transcending experience. He focuses on the creative person, blocks to creativity, and the need for creative people.

PAYNE, BURYL. *Getting There Without Drugs.* New York: Viking Press, 1973 (hardcover).

This book provides an interesting contrast to the Weil book (see below). Payne presents some meditational exercises to help the person get in touch with the spiritual aspect of his personality without drugs. She insists that there is no shortcut to higher consciousness as the drug users would like to believe.

WATTS, ALAN W. *The Book: On the Taboo Against Knowing Who You Are.* New York: Collier Books, 1966 (paperback).

Watts is one of the chief interpreters of Eastern thought to English-speaking peoples. In this book, he discusses what Vedanta calls the "real nature of man," which, when known, helps the person to discard many of his fears and phobias and center himself as a person.

WEIL, ANDREW. *The Natural Mind: A New Way of Looking at Drugs and the Higher Consciousness.* Boston: Houghton Mifflin, 1972 (hardcover).

Weil has done an interesting job in this book by demonstrating that drug consciousness is a way of altering one's stereotypical thinking. While admitting that there has been little unemotional and factual material on drug consciousness, he relates this consciousness to other kinds of altered states of consciousness which when used well can produce creative thinking (or nonthinking).

NOTES

CHAPTER 1

1. A typical book with this point of view was authored by James W. Bridges, *Psychology, Normal and Abnormal* (New York: D. Appleton and Co., 1930).

2. Some of the early protests against the "adjustment" concept can be found in Theodore B. Hyslop, *The Great Abnormals* (London: Philips Allan and Co., 1925).

3. There are many such studies. Three of the classic studies in the field are:
Cora A. Dubois, *The People of Alor* (Cambridge, Mass.: Harvard University Press, 1960).
R. F. Fortune, *Sorcerers of Dobu* (London: Routledge, 1937).
Margaret Mead, *Coming of Age in Samoa* (New York: William Morrow, 1929).

4. Edward Joseph Shoben, Jr., "Toward a Concept of the Normal Personality," *Amer. Psychologist* 12 (1957): 183–89.

5. Abraham H. Maslow, *Motivation and Personality*, 2nd ed. (New York: Harper and Row, 1954), pp. 171–74.

6. Alan F. Westin et al., *Views of America* (New York: Harcourt, Brace and World, 1966).

7. Although it is one of Charles Dickens's lesser works, *Martin Chuzzlewit* is well worth reading to get a look at nineteenth-century America through the eyes of a famous English novelist.

8. Philip Wylie, *A Generation of Vipers*, ann. ed. (New York: Holt, Rinehart and Winston, 1955). Wylie has written a sequel to this first shocker, which might be of more interest to today's generation: *Sons and Daughters of Mom* (Garden City, N.Y.: Doubleday, 1971).

9. Erich Fromm, *Escape from Freedom* (New York: Rinehart and Winston, 1941).

10. David Riesman, *A Lonely Crowd: A Study of the Changing American Character*, rev. ed. (New Haven: Yale University Press, 1969).

11. There are many excellent studies on this subject including:

Allison Davis et al., *Deep South: A Social Anthropological Study of Caste and Class* (Chicago: U. of Chicago Press, 1941);

John Dollard, *Caste and Class in a Southern Town* (New Haven: Yale University Press, 1937; and

W. Lloyd Warner et al., *Social Class in America* (Chicago: Science Research Institutes, 1949).

12. Michael Harrington, *The Other America: Poverty in the United States* (New York: The Macmillan Co., 1963).

13. The settling of the West has a different perspective when seen from the point-of-view of the American Indian:

Virginia I. Armstrong, ed., *I Have Spoken*. American History through the voices of the Indian (Chicago: Swallow Press, 1971, and

John G. Neihardt, *Black Elk Speaks* (Lincoln, Nebr.: University of Nebraska Press, 1961).

14. Theodore Roszak, *The Making of a Counter-Culture* (Garden City, N.Y.: Doubleday, 1968).

15. Lawrence K. Frank, "Society as the Patient" in *Dimensions of Social Psychology*, eds., W. Edgar Vinacke *et al.* (Glenview, Ill.: Scott, Foresman, 1964), pp. 50–53.

Ronald D. Laing, *The Politics of Experience* (New York: Pantheon Books, 1967).

16. Karl Menninger, *The Crime of Punishment* (New York: Viking Press, Inc., 1968).

17. Sullivan, *The Interpersonal Theory of Psychiatry* (New York: W. W. Norton and Co., 1953).

18. Szasz, *"Moral Conflict and Psychiatry,"* *Yale Review* 49 (June 1960): 555–66.

19. Carl R. Rogers, "Toward a Modern Approach to Values: the Valuing Process in the Mature Person," in *Person to Person: The Problem of Being Human*, eds. Carl Rogers and Barry Stevens (New York: Pocket Books, 1971), pp. 19–20. (Orig. published by Real People Press, 1967.)

20. See Menninger, *The Crime of Punishment*.

21. Erik H. Erikson, *Childhood and Society*, 2nd ed. (New York: W. W. Norton and Co., 1950).

Phillippe Muller, *The Tasks of Childhood* (New York: McGraw-Hill, 1969).

Walter Neff, *Work and Human Behavior* (New York: Atherton Press, 1968).

"A Healthy Personality for Every Child: A Digest of the Fact-Finding Report to the Mid-Century White House Conference on Children and Youth, 1951," in *The Causes of Behavior II*, eds. Judy F. Rosenblith and Wesley Allensmith (Boston: Allyn and Bacon, 1966), pp. 289–99.

22. There have been many studies on the effects of long-term institutionalism on babies and children. Some of the classic studies are listed below:

Sally Provence and Rose C. Lipton, *Infants in Institutions* (New York: International University Press, 1963);

John Bowlby, "Observations of Older Children Who Were Deprived in Infancy," in *Outside Readings in Psychology*, eds. Eugene L. Hartley and Ruth E. Hartley (New York: Thomas Y. Crowell Co., 1957), pp. 378–91; and

W. Goldfarb, "The Effects of Early Institutional Care on Adolescent Personality," *J. of Exper. Ed.* 12 (1943): 106–29.

23. For two extraordinary books written in old age and commemorating that time of life, see:

Florida Scott-Maxwell, *The Measure of My Days* (New York: Knopf, 1968), and

Carl G. Jung, *Memories, Dreams and Reflections* (New York: Pantheon Books, 1961).

CHAPTER 2

1. See, for example, Freud, *The Interpretation of Dreams*, trans. James Strachey (1900; reprint ed., New York: Avon Books, 1967).

2. See T. W. Adorno et al., *The Authoritarian Personality* (New York: Harper and Row, 1950), and

Milton Rokeach, *The Open and Closed Mind* (New York: Basic Books, 1960).

3. On creative scientists, see Calvin W. Taylor and Frank Barron, eds., *Scientific Creativity: Its Recognition and Development* (New York: Wiley, 1963).

On artists and engineers, see J. P. Guilford, "The Psychology of Creativity," *Creative Crafts* 1 (1960): 5–8;

D. W. MacKinnon, "The Nature and Nurture of Creative Talent," *Amer. Psychol.* 17 (1962): 484–95;

Anne Roe, "The Personality of Artists," *Educ. Psych. Measmt.* 6 (1964): 401–8, and

Calvin W. Taylor, ed., *Creativity: Progress and Potential* (New York: McGraw-Hill, 1964).

On businessmen, see D. C. McClelland et al., *The Achievement Motive* (New York: Appleton-Century-Crofts, 1953), and

Eugene K. VonFange, *Professional Creativity* (Englewood Cliffs, N.J.: Prentice-Hall, 1959).

On the "gifted," see S. L. Pressey, "Concerning the Nature and Nurture of Genius," *Scientific Monthly* 81, no. 3 (1955): 123–29, and

L. M. Terman, "The Discovery and Encouragement of Exceptional Talent," *Amer. Psychol.* 9 (1954): 221–30.

4. See Maslow, *Motivation and Personality* (New York: Harper and Row, 1954).

5. See Rogers, *On Becoming a Person* (Boston: Houghton Mifflin, 1961).

6. See Jung, *Modern Man in Search of a Soul* (New York: Harcourt Brace).

7. See "Effects of Group Pressure Upon the Modification and Distortion of Judgments," in *Basic Studies in Social Psychology*, eds. H. Proshansky and B. Seidenberg (New York: Holt, Rinehart and Winston, 1965), pp. 393–401.

8. For those interested in investigating Zen philosophy and some of its insights, the following books are recommended:

Christmas Humphreys, *Zen: A Way of Life* (Boston: Little, Brown, 1970);

D. T. Suzuki, *Introduction to Zen Buddhism* (New York: Grove Press, 1968); and

Alan W. Watts, *Psychotherapy East and West* (New York: Ballantine Books, 1961).

9. D. W. MacKinnon, "The Nature and Nurture of Creative Talent," *Amer. Psychol.* 17 (1962): 484–95.

10. *Motivation and Personality* and "The Nature and Nurture of Creative Talent."

11. *Ibid.,* p. 164.

12. Adorno et al., *The Authoritarian Personality.*

13. *Ibid.,* pp. 163–64.

14. MacKinnon, "The Nature and Nurture of Creative Talent."

15. Karen Horney, *The Collected Works of Karen Horney* (New York: W. W. Norton, 1942) 2:65.

CHAPTER 3

1. F. S. Perls, *Ego, Hunger, and Aggression* (New York: Random House, 1969), p. 266.

2. "Angst," *Time,* March 31, 1961, p. 46.

3. There have been many treatises written on this subject (i.e., the inhumanness of the organization); some of the most widely publicized are
Chester Burger, *Survival in the Executive Jungle* (New York: Macmillan, 1966);
Crawford H. Greenewalt, *Uncommon Man: The Individual in the Organization* (New York: Harper and Row, 1970);
Harry Levinson, *Executive Stress* (New York: Harper and Row, 1970);
Vance Packard, *The Pyramid Climbers* (New York: Fawcett World Library, 1964);
A. N. Schoonmaker, *Anxiety and the Executive* (New York: Macmillan, 1969), and
William H. Whyte, Jr., *The Organization Man* (New York: Simon and Schuster, 1956).

4. C. P. Snow, *Two Cultures: A Second Look* (Cambridge: Cambridge University Press, 1964).

5. Daniel Boorstin, *The Image: A Guide to Pseudo-Events in America* (New York: Harper and Row, 1964).

6. Now available in paperback edition (Greenwich, Conn.: Fawcett Publications, 1970).

7. *Silent Spring,* pp. 16–17.

8. George S. Counts, "The Impact of Technological Change," in *The Planning of Social Change: Readings in the Applied Behavioral Sciences,* ed. Warren G. Bennes et al. (New York: Holt, Rinehart and Winston, 1961), pp. 20–28.

9. See Gordon W. Allport and Leo Postman, *The Psychology of Rumor* (New York: Holt, Rinehart and Winston, 1947), and
F. J. Roethlisberger, *Management and Morale* (Cambridge: Harvard University Press, 1941).

10. "Has the Church Lost Its Soul?" *Newsweek,* Oct. 4, 1971, p. 84.

11. *Life,* Dec. 31, 1971, p. 75.

12. *Future Shock* (New York: Random House, 1970).

13. *Future Shock,* pp. 10–12.

14. Edgar H. Schein, "Reaction Patterns to Severe, Chronic Stress in American Prisoners of War of the Chinese," in *Dimensions of Social Psychology,* ed. W. Edgar Vinacke et al. (Glenview, Ill.: Scott, Foresman, 1964), pp. 224–29. See also Roy R. Grinker and John P. Spiegel, *Men Under Stress* (New York: McGraw-Hill, 1945).

15. German philosopher Martin Heidegger, in his treatise *Discourse on Thinking* (New York: Harper and Row, 1966), has said that part of organized rational thought is "knowing who you are and where you belong."

16. Edgar H. Schein et al., *Coercive Persuasions* (New York: W. W. Norton, 1961).

17. H. G. Wolff, "A Concept of Disease in Man," *Psychosomatic Medicine* 24 (1962): 25–30.

18. R. Spitz, *The First Year of Life* (New York: International Press, 1965).

19. Franz Alexander, *Psychosomatic Medicine* (New York: W. W. Norton, 1950).

20. W. L. Sawrey et al., "An Experimental Investigation of the Role of Psychological Factors in the Production of Gastric Ulcers in Rats," *J. Comp. Physiol. Psychol.* 49 (1956): 457–61.

21. E. Farmer and E. G. Chambers, "A Psychological Study of Individual Differences in Accident Rates," Report No. 38 of the Industrial Fatigue Research Board (London: H. M. Stationary Office, 1926).

22. Karl Menninger, *Man Against Himself* (New York: Harcourt, Brace and World, 1938, 1966). This quotation can be found also in *General Psychology: Selected Readings,* eds. Joseph F. Perez et al. (New York: Van Nostrand, 1967), p. 335.

23. Selye relates his personal and scientific lives very charmingly and very intimately in his autobiography *The Stress of Life* (New York: McGraw-Hill, 1956). But if the student wishes to read an abridged account of the general adaptation syndrome, he can obtain the *Scientific American* Offprint by P. F. Constantinides and Niall Carey, no. 4 (San Francisco: W. H. Freeman).

24. Walter B. Cannon, *Bodily Changes in Pain, Hunger, Fear, and Rage,* rev. ed. (New York: Appleton-Century-Crofts, 1929).

25. See T. Holmes and R. H. Rahe, "The Social Readjustment Scale," *J. Psychosom. Res.* 11 (1967): 213–17.

26. R. H. Rahe and T. H. Holmes, "Life Crises and Disease Onset: II. Qualitative and Quantitative Definition of the Life Crises and its Association with Health Change." *J. Psychosom. Med.*

27. Richard H. Rahe, Jack L. Mahan, Jr., and Ransom J. Arthur, "Prediction of Near-Future Health Change from Subjects Preceding Life Changes." *J. Psychosom. Res.* 14 (1970): 401–5.

28. Sol Levine and Norman A. Scotch, *Social Stress* (Chicago: Aldine, 1970).

29. A. B. Hollingshead and F. C. Redlick, *Social Class and Mental Illness* (New York: Wiley, 1958).

CHAPTER 4

1. John Dollard and Neal E. Miller, "What Is a Neurosis?" in *Basic Contributions to Psychology: Readings,* ed. Robert L. Wrenn (Belmont, Cal.: Wadsworth Publishing Co., 1966), pp. 206–11.

2. "Pain and Aggression," in *Readings in Psychology Today* (Del Mar, Cal.: CRM Books, 1967), pp. 114–21.

3. For a more complete glossary of name-calling see H. L. Mencken, *The American Language,* 4th ed. (New York: Alfred A. Knopf, 1936), pp. 294–300.

4. P. S. Sears, "Levels of Aspiration in Academically Successful and Unsuccessful Children," *J. Abnorm. Soc. Psychol.* 35 (1940): 498–536.

5. Sigmund Freud, *A General Introduction to Psycho-Analysis,* trans. Joan Riviere (New York: Liverwright, 1935), pp. 253–62.

6. Sigmund Freud, *The Psychopathology of Everyday Life,* trans. Alan Tyson, in *Standard Edition of the Complete Psychological Works of Sigmund Freud,* ed. James Strachey (London: Hogarth, 1952), 6: pp. 1–310.

7. John M. Darley and Bibb Latane, "When Will People Help in a Crisis?" in *Readings in Psychology Today* (Del Mar, Cal.: CRM Books, 1967), pp. 428–33.

8. Anna Freud, *The Ego and the Mechanisms of Defense* (New York: International Universities Press, 1946).

CHAPTER 5

1. See C. S. Sherrington, *Man on His Nature* (New York: Macmillan, 1941).

2. Abraham Maslow, *Motivation and Personality* (New York: Harper & Row, 1954).

3. R. L. Gregory, *Eye and Brain: The Psychology of Seeing* (New York: McGraw-Hill, 1966).

4. E. G. Wever and C. W. Bray, "Present Possibilities for Auditory Theory," *Psychol. Rev.* 37 (1930): 365–80.

5. Ralph G. Nichols and Leonard A. Stevens, *Are You Listening?* (New York: McGraw-Hill, 1957).

6. Carl R. Rogers, *Client-Centered Therapy* (Boston: Houghton Mifflin, 1951).

7. Ashley Montagu, *Touching: The Human Significance of the Skin* (New York: Columbia University Press, 1971).

8. Maslow, *Toward a Psychology of Being,* 2nd ed. (New York: Van Nostrand–Reinhold, 1968).

9. Alexander Lowen, *The Betrayal of the Body* (New York: Macmillan, 1966).

10. F. S. Perls et al., *Gestalt Therapy: Excitement and Growth in the Human Personality* (New York: Dell, 1951).

11. Y. C. Tsang, "Hunger Motivation in Gastrectomized Rats," *J. Comp. Psychol.* 26 (1938): 1–17.

12. Harmon Bro, *High Play: Turning on Without Drugs* (New York: Coward, 1971).

13. N. Cameron, *Personality Development and Psychopathology* (Boston: Houghton Mifflin, 1963).

CHAPTER 6

1. I. P. Pavlov, *Conditioned Reflexes,* trans. G. V. Anrep (New York: Dover Publications, 1960), p. 26.

2. C. I. Hovland, "The Generalization of Conditioned Responses: I. The Sensory Generalization of Conditioned Responses with Varying Frequencies of Tone," *J. Gen. Psychol.* 17: 125–48.

3. J. B. Watson and R. Rayner, "Conditioned Emotional Reactions," *J. of Exp. Psychol.* 3: 1–14.

4. B. F. Skinner, *The Behavior of Organisms* (New York: Appleton-Century-Crofts, 1938).

5. Colin Wilson, "Existential Psychology: A Novelist's Approach," in *Challenges of Humanistic Psychology,* ed. James F. T. Bugental (New York: McGraw-Hill, 1967), pp. 69–79.

6. Wilson, "Existential Psychology."

7. K. Breland and H. Breland, "A Field of Applied Animal Psychology," *Amer. Psychologist* 6 (1951): 202–4.

8. F. R. Harris et al., "Effects of Adult Social Reinforcement on Child Behavior," in *The Causes of Behavior II. Readings in Child Development and Educational Psychology*, 2nd ed., eds. Judy F. Rosenblith and Wesley Allensmith (Boston: Allyn and Bacon, 1966), pp. 99–106.

9. If the reader would like to pursue some of the astonishing results reported by psychologists using operant conditioning, we suggest the following references:

T. Ayllon and E. Haughton, "Modification of Symptomatic Verbal Behavior of Mental Patients," *Behavior Research and Therapy* 2 (1964): 87–97;

G. L. Martin, et al., "Operant Conditioning in Dressing Behavior of Severely Retarded Girls," *Mental Retardation* 9 (1971): 27–31;

S. R. Smolev, "Use of Operant Techniques for the Modification of Self-Injurious Behavior," *American Journal of Mental Deficiency* 76 (1971): 295–305, and

A. W. Staats and W. H. Butterfield, "Treatment of Nonreading in a Culturally Deprived Juvenile Delinquent: An Application of Reinforcement Schedules," *Child Development* 36 (1965): 925–42.

CHAPTER 7

1. K. M. B. Bridges, "Emotional Development in Early Infancy," *Child Development*, 3 (1932): 324–91.

2. Abraham Maslow, *Motivation and Being* (New York: Harper & Row, 1954).

3. Carl Rogers, "The Process of the Basic Encounter Group," in *Challenges of Humanistic Psychology*, ed. James F. T. Bugental (New York: McGraw-Hill, 1967), pp. 261–76.

4. Desmond Morris, *The Naked Ape* (New York: McGraw-Hill, 1967), and *The Human Zoo* (New York: McGraw-Hill, 1969).

5. K. Buhler, "Displeasure and Pleasure in Relation to Activity," in *Feelings and Emotions*, ed. M. L. Reynart (Worcester, Mass.: Clark University Press, 1928).

6. H. W. Nissen, "A Study of Exploratory Behavior in the White Rat by Means of the Obstruction Method," *J. Genet. Psychol.* 37 (1930): 361–76.

7. Maslow, *Motivation and Being*.

8. Sigmund Freud, *An Outline of Psychoanalysis*, trans. James Strachey (New York: W. W. Norton, 1949).

9. N. R. F. Maier, "Frustration: A Study of Behavior Without a Goal" (New York: McGraw-Hill, 1949).

10. Two representative reviews in this area are:

R. Spitz, *The First Year of Life* (New York: International Press, 1955), and

R. G. Patton and L. J. Gardner, *Growth Failure in Maternal Deprivation* (Springfield, Ill.: Charles C. Thomas, 1963).

11. Eric Berne, *Transactional Analysis in Psychotherapy* (New York: Grove Press, 1961).

12. Thomas Harris, *"I'm OK—You're OK: A Practical Guide to Transactional Analysis* (New York: Harper & Row, 1969).

13. Ibid., p. 18.

14. Sigmund Freud, *The Ego and the Id* (London: Hogarth Press, 1935).

15. Brian Sutton-Smith and B. C. Rosenberg, *The Sibling* (New York: McGraw-Hill, 1967).

16. Donald W. MacKinnon, "What Makes a Person Creative?" in *Contemporary*

Readings in General Psychology, 2nd ed., ed. Robert S. Daniel (Boston: Houghton Mifflin, 1965), pp. 153–57.

17. Irving D. Harris, *The Promised Seed* (New York: Macmillan, 1964).

18. Alfred Adler, *Understanding Human Nature* (New York: Fawcett Publications, 1959), pp. 125–28.

19. G. S. Lesser et al., "Mental Abilities of Children from Different Social Class and Cultural Groups," *Manag. Society for Res. in Child Development,* Vol. 30, No. 4 (1968);

H. E. Jones, "The Environment and Mental Development," in *Manual of Child Psychology,* 2nd ed., ed. L. Carmichael (New York: Wiley, 1954);

L. R. Wheeler, "A Comparative Study of the Intelligence of East Tennessee Mountain Children," *J. Educ. Psych.,* 33: 321–34.

20. R. M. Cooper and J. P. Zubek, "Effects of Enriched and Restricted Early Environments on the Learning Ability of Bright and Dull Rats," *Canadian J. Psychol.* 12 (1958): 159–64.

21. G. W. Allport, "The Functional Autonomy of Motives," *Amer. J. Psychol.,* 50: 141–45;

M. E. Fries and P. J. Woolf, "Some Hypotheses on the Role of the Congenital Activity Type in Personality Development," in *Psychoanalytic Study of the Child,* Vol. 8 (1951): 48–62.

22. Erving Goffman, *Stigma: Notes on the Management of Spoiled Identity* (Englewood Cliffs, N.J.: Prentice-Hall, 1963).

23. M. M. Shirley, *The First Two Years: Personality Manifestations* (Minneapolis: University of Minnesota Press, 1933).

CHAPTER 8

1. Frederick S. (Fritz) Perls, *In and Out of the Garbage Pail* (Lafayette, Cal.: Real People Press, 1969).

2. C. G. Jung, *The Basic Writings of C. G. Jung* (New York: Modern Library, 1959), pp. 286–326.

3. C. H. Thigpen and H. Cleckley, *The Three Faces of Eve* (New York: McGraw-Hill, 1957).

4. Flora Rheta Schreiber, *Sybil* (Chicago: Henry Regnery, 1973).

5. Alexander Lowen, *The Betrayal of the Body* (London: Collier-Macmillan, 1967).

6. Floyd L. Ruch, *Psychology and Life,* 7th ed. (Glenview, Ill.: Scott, Foresman, 1967), p. 416.

7. Sigmund Freud, *Beyond the Pleasure Principle,* rev. ed., trans. James Strachey (New York: Liveright, 1970).

8. Sigmund Freud, *Civilization and Its Discontents,* ed. James Strachey (New York: W. W. Norton, 1962).

9. Carl Jung, "Approaching the Unconscious," in *Man and His Symbols,* ed. Carl G. Jung et al. (Garden City, N.Y.: Doubleday, 1964), pp. 18–103.

10. Aldous Huxley, *The Devils of Loudon: Demonic Possession and Witchcraft in a Seventeenth-Century Convent* (New York: Harper & Row, 1970).

11. For two reports on the relationship of economic recession and lynching, see C. I. Hovland, and R. R. Sears, "Minor Studies of Aggression: VI. Correlation of Lynchings with Economic Indices," *J. Psychol.* 9 (1940): 301–10, and A. Mintz, "A

Re-examination of Correlations Between Lynchings and Economic Indices," *J. Abnorm. Soc. Psychol.* 41 (1946): 154–60.

CHAPTER 9

1. Edwin G. Boring, *A History of Experimental Psychology*, 2nd ed. (New York: Appleton-Century-Crofts, 1950).

2. G. Zilboorg and G. W. Henry, *A History of Medical Psychology* (New York: W. W. Norton, 1941).

3. J. Breuer and S. Freud, *Studies on Hysteria* (New York: Basic Books, 1957).

4. H. S. Sullivan, *The Interpersonal Theory of Psychiatry*, ed. S. Perry and M. L. Gowel (New York: W. W. Norton, 1953).

5. Carl R. Rogers, *Client-Centered Therapy* (Boston: Houghton Mifflin, 1951).

6. Leland P. Bradford et al., eds., *T-Group Theory and Laboratory Method: Innovation in Re-Education* (New York: John Wiley, 1964).

7. Morton A. Liberman et al., "Encounter: the Leader Makes the Difference," *Psychology Today* 8, no. 10 (March 1973): 69–76.

8. Abraham Maslow, *Motivation and Being*, 2nd ed. (New York: Harper & Row, 1970).

9. Everett Shostrum, "Let the Buyer Beware," *Psychology Today* 2, no. 12 (May 1969): 38–40.

CHAPTER 10

1. *The Interpretation of Dreams*, trans. J. Strachey (New York: Avon Books, 1965), p. xxv.

2. Genesis 40, 41. All quotations from the Bible are from *The Jerusalem Bible* (Garden City, New York: Doubleday, 1966).

3. Genesis 37.

4. I Kings 3.

5. Matthew 1:20.

6. Matthew 2:12.

7. Matthew 2:13.

8. Matthew 2:19, 20.

9. Matthew 27:6.

10. Norman Mackenzie, *Dreams and Dreaming* (New York: Vanguard Press, 1965). p. 31.

11. "The Babylonian Talmud," trans. Rev. A. Cohen, in *The World of Dreams*, ed. R. Woods (New York: Random House, 1947), p. 123.

12. Nathaniel Bland, "Muhammedan Tabir on Dream Interpretation," in Woods, *The World of Dreams*, pp. 71–76.

13. *Oneirocritica*, trans. H. G. McAudy, in MacKenzie, *Dreams and Dreaming*, pp. 55–56.

14. C. G. Jung, *Memories, Dreams, and Reflections*, ed. Aniela Jaffe, trans. Richard and Clara Winston (New York: Pantheon Books, Random House, 1963), pp. 168–69.

15. Carl G. Jung, *Memories, Dreams, Reflections,* ed. Aniela Jaffé (New York: Random House, Pantheon Books, 1961).

16. Carl G. Jung, *Collected Papers on Analytical Psychology,* 2nd ed. (London: Balliere, Tindall and Cox), pp. xiii–xiv.

17. Carl G. Jung et al., *Man and His Symbols* (Garden City, N.Y.: Doubleday, 1964).

18. *Man and his Symbols* (Garden City, N.Y., 1964), p. 85.

19. Carl G. Jung, *Two Essays on Analytical Psychology* (New York: Meridian, 1956), pp. 63–73.

20. *Modern Man in Search of a Soul,* pp. 92–93.

CHAPTER 11

1. David Foulkes, *The Psychology of Sleep* (New York: Charles Scribners' Sons, 1966).

2. E. Aserinsky and N. Kleitman, "Regularly Occurring Periods of Eye Motility, and Concomitant Phenomena, During Sleep," *Science* 118 (1953): 273–74.

3. E. A. Wolpert and H. Trosman, "Studies in Psychophysiology of Dreams: I. Experimental Evocation of Sequential Dream Episodes," *Arch. of Neur. and Psychiatry* 79 (1958): 603–6.

4. In addition to books and articles cited in other footnotes in this chapter, the following references comprise a good introduction to dream research: H. W. Agnew et al., "The Effects of Stage Four Sleep Deprivation," *Electroencephalography and Clin. Neurophys.* 17 (1964): 68–70; CIBA Foundation, *The Nature of Sleep* (Boston: Little, Brown, 1961); W. Dement, "The Effect of Dream Deprivation," *Science* 131 (1960): 1705–7; D. R. Goodenough et al., "Dream Reporting Following Abrupt and Gradual Awakenings from Different Types of Sleep," *J. Personality and Soc. Psych.* 2 (1965): 170–79; C. S. Hall, *The Meaning of Dreams* (New York: Dell, 1959); N. Kleitman, *Sleep and Wakefulness,* 2nd ed. (Chicago: University of Chicago Press, 1963); A. Rechtschoffen et al., "Patterns of Sleep Talking," *Arch. of Gen. Psychiatry* 7 (1962): 418–26; R. A. Schonbar, "Some Manifest Characteristics of Recallers and Nonrecallers of Dreams," *J. Consult. Psych.* 23 (1959): 414–18; and A. Shapers et al., "Dream Recall and the Physiology of Sleep," *J. Appl. Phys.* 19 (1964): 778–83.

5. W. Dement and N. Kleitman, "The Relation of Eye Movements During Sleep to Dream Activity: An Objective Method for the Study of Dreaming," *J. Exp. Psych.* 53 (1957): 339–46.

6. Carl G. Jung, "On the Nature of Dreams," in *The Basic Writings of C. G. Jung,* ed. Violet S. DeLaszlo (New York: Modern Library, 1959), pp. 363–79.

7. Calvin S. Hall, *The Meaning of Dreams* (New York: McGraw-Hill, 1966).

8. R. L. Woods, ed., *The World of Dreams* (New York: Random House, 1947).

9. Jung, "On the Nature of Dreams."

10. Frederick S. Perls, *In and Out of the Garbage Pail* (Lafayette, Cal.: Real People Press, 1969).

11. Frederick S. Perls, *Gestalt Therapy Verbatim,* ed. John O. Stevens (Lafayette, Cal.: Real People Press, 1967).

12. On the value of creative fantasy, see Jerome Singer, *Daydreaming: An Introduction to the Experimental Study of Inner Experience* (New York: Random House, 1966), and Roberto Assagioli, *Psychosynthesis: A Manual of Principles and Techniques* (Big Sur, Cal.: Esalen Institute Press, 1971).

CHAPTER 12

1. Sigmund Freud, *The Ego and the Id* (London: Hogarth Press and the Institute of Psycho-Analysis, 1935).

2. Sigmund Freud, *Totem and Taboo,* trans. A. A. Brill (New York: Dodd, Mead, 1918).

3. Edwin S. Hartland, *The Science of Fairy Tales: An Inquiry into Fairy Mythology* (London: Walter Scott, 1891; reissued by Singing Tree Press, Detroit, 1968), pp. 1–22.

4. Frieda Fromm-Reichman, *Principles of Intensive Psychotherapy* (Chicago: University of Chicago Press, 1950), pp. 167–68.

5. Erich Fromm, *The Forgotten Language* (New York: Grove Press, 1957).

6. Michael Hornyansky, "The Truth of Fables," in *Only Connect: Readings on Children's Literature,* ed. Sheila Egoff et al. (Toronto: Oxford University Press, 1969), pp. 121–32.

7. Carl G. Jung, *Archetypes and the Collective Unconscious,* Vol. 9, Part I, 2nd ed.: Bollingen Series XX, eds. G. Adler et al., trans. R. F. C. Hull (New York: Pantheon Books, 1969).

8. Robert Graves, *The White Goddess: A Historical Grammar of Poetic Myth,* rev. ed. (New York: Farrar, Straus and Giroux, 1966).

9. Clyde Kluckhohn, "Recurrent Themes in Myths and Mythmaking," in *Myths and Mythmaking,* ed. Henry A. Murray (Boston: Beacon Press, 1969), pp. 46–80.

10. Swami Nikhilananda, introduction to *The Bhagavad-Gita* (New York: Ramakrishna-Vivekananda Center, 1952), pp. 1–49.

CHAPTER 13

1. I. L. Janis, *Psychological Stress* (New York: John Wiley and Sons, 1958).

2. Edmund Jacobson, *Progressive Relaxation,* 2nd ed. (Chicago: University of Chicago Press, 1938).

3. Edmund Jacobson, *Anxiety and Tension Control: a Physiological Approach* (Philadelphia: J. B. Lippincott, 1964), p. 72.

4. Frederick Perls, personal communication.

5. Ernest E. Wood, *Practical Yoga* (North Hollywood, Cal.: Wilshire Book Company, 1972), p. 116.

6. The following books on yoga are recommended to the beginner: Harvey Day, *Practical Yoga for the Businessman* (New York: Diahe Publishers, 1971); J. M. Dechanet, *Christian Yoga* (New York: Harper & Row, 1960); Indra Devi, *Yoga for Americans* (Englewood Cliffs, N.J.: Prentice-Hall, 1959); Desmond Dunne, *Yoga Made Easy* (Englewood Cliffs, N.J.: Prentice-Hall, 1961); Richard L. Hittleman, *Be Young with Yoga* (New York: Paperback Library, 1971); B. K. Iyengar, *Light on Yoga* (New York: Schocken Books, 1970); Dodi Schultz, *Slimming with Yoga* (New York: Dell, 1969); Clare Spring, and Madeleine Gross, *Yoga for Today: The Way to Health, Youth, and Beauty* (New York: Holt, Rinehart and Winston, 1959).

7. Joseph Wolpe, *Psychotherapy by Reciprocal Inhibition* (Stanford, Cal.: Stanford University Press, 1958).

8. Joseph Wolpe et al., *The Conditioning Therapies* (New York: Holt, Rinehart and Winston, 1964), p. 10.

9. Joseph Wolpe, "The Systematic Desensitization Treatment of Neuroses," *J. Nerv. Mental Disorder* 132 (1961): 189–203.

10. Angus MacDonald, personal communication.

11. Frederick Perls et al., *Gestalt Therapy* (New York: Dell, 1951).

12. Perls, *Gestalt Therapy Verbatim* (Lafayette, Cal.: Real People Press, 1969).

13. Wilhelm Reich, *Character Analysis* (New York: Farrar, Straus and Giroux, 1949).

14. For an interpretation of the Chakras, see Devi, *Yoga for Americans.*

15. Moshe Feldenkrais, *Awareness Through Movement: Health Exercises for Personal Growth* (New York: Harper & Row, 1972).

16. Gia-Fu Feng, and Jerome Kirk, *Tai Chi: A Way of Centering; and the I Ching* (London: Collier-Macmillan, 1970).

17. Bernard Gunther, *Sense Relaxation Below Your Mind* (New York: Collier Books, 1968).

18. J. Calvin Leonard, personal communication, 1971.

CHAPTER 14

1. Everett L. Shostrum, *Man the Manipulator: The Journey from Manipulation to Actualization* (New York: Bantam Books, 1967).

2. Laura Archera Huxley, *You Are Not the Target* (New York: Farrar, Straus and Giroux, 1963).

3. Carl Rogers, *Counseling and Psychotherapy* (Boston: Houghton Mifflin, 1942).

4. Frederick Perls, personal communication.

5. I. L. Janis, *Psychological Stress* (New York: Wiley, 1958).

6. Alfred Korzybski, *Science and Sanity,* 4th ed. (Lakeville, Conn.: Institute of General Semantics, 1958).

7. Stuart Chase, *Tyranny of Words* (New York: Harcourt Brace Jovanovich, 1966), paperback.

8. Martin Buber, *I and Thou,* 2nd ed. (New York: Charles Scribner's Sons, 1958); and Buber, *Between Man and Man* (New York: MacMillan, 1965).

CHAPTER 15

1. Laura Huxley, *You Are Not the Target* (New York: Farrar, Straus and Giroux, 1963).

2. J. Bowlby, "Grief and Mourning in Infancy and Early Childhood," *Psychoan. Study of the Child* 15 (1960): 9–52; J. Robertson, *Young Children in Hospitals* (London: Tavistock Publications, 1958).

3. Alexander Lowen, *Betrayal of the Body* (New York: Macmillan, 1966).

4. Edith Jacobson, "On Normal and Pathological Moods," in *The Psychoanalytic Study of the Child,* ed. R. S. Eissler et al. (New York: International Universities Press, 1957), 12:73–113.

5. Sigmund Freud, "Mourning and Melancholia," in *Standard Edition* (London: Hogarth Press, 1957), 14:237–58.

6. M. L. Simmel, "Development Aspects of the Body Schema," *Child Development* 37 (1963), 83–95.

7. Frederick Perls, personal communication.

8. Hans Selye, *The Stress of Life* (New York: McGraw-Hill, 1956).

9. Wilhelm Reich, *Character Analysis*, 3rd ed. (New York: Orgone Institute Press, 1949).

10. We take both the concepts of "no blame" and "it furthers one to cross the great water" from the *I Ching* as translated by Richard Wilhelm: *The I Ching or Book of Changes* (New York: Pantheon Books, 1950).

11. James Legge, *The Four Books* (New York: Paragon Book Reprint Corp., 1966).

12. Wilder Penfield and T. Rasmussen, *The Cerebral Cortex of Man* (New York: Macmillan, 1950).

13. Sheila Ostander and Lynn Schroeder, *Psychic Discoveries Behind the Iron Curtain* (New York: Bantam Books, 1970).

14. Carl G. Jung, *Modern Man in Search of a Soul* (New York: Harcourt Brace, 1957).

15. Joseph Wolpe, personal communication.

16. Swami Prabhavananda and Christopher Isherwood, *How to Know God: The Yoga Aphorisms of Patanjali* (New York: Harper & Bros., 1953).

17. Sri Aurobindo, *Guide to the Upanishads*, ed. M. P. Pandit (Mystic, Conn.: Verry, Lawrence, 1967).

18. D. T. Suzuki, *Essays in Zen Buddhism* (New York: Grove Press, 1961).

19. J. Legge, *Texts of Taoism: The Sacred Books of China*, 2 vols. (New York: Dover, 1899, 2nd ed.)

20. Here is a highly selective list on meditation selected for the beginning student: J. M. Dechanet, *Christian Yoga* (New York: Harper & Row, 1963); Adelaide Gardner, *Meditation: A Practical Study* (Wheaton, Ill.: Theosophical Publishing House, 1968); Christian Humphreys, *Concentration and Meditation* (Baltimore: Penguin Books, 1970); Thomas Merton, *Contemplative Prayer* (New York: Herder and Herder, 1969); Paul Reps, *Ten Ways to Meditate: No Need to Kill* (New York: Weatherhill, 1969); Elsie Sechrist, *Meditation, Gateway to Light* (Virginia Beach, Va.: ARE Press, 1964); Jim Wilson, *First Steps in Meditation for Young People* (Greenwood, S.C.: Attic Press, 1958); and Ernest Wood, *Concentration: An Approach to Meditation* (Wheaton, Ill.: Theosophical Publishing House).

21. Sam Keen, "A Conversation About Ego Destruction with Oscar Ichazo," *Psychology Today* 7, no. 2 (July 1973), 66–72.

INDEX